Werner Kluge (Ed.)

Implementation of Functional Languages

8th International Workshop, IFL'96
Bad Godesberg, Germany
September 16-18, 1996
Selected Papers

Springer

Series Editors

Gerhard Goos, Karlsruhe University, Germany

Juris Hartmanis, Cornell University, NY, USA

Jan van Leeuwen, Utrecht University, The Netherlands

Volume Editor

Werner Kluge
CAU Kiel, Institut für Informatik II
Preusserstr. 1-9, D-24105 Kiel, Germany
E-mail: wk@informatik.uni-kiel.de

Cataloging-in-Publication data applied for

Die Deutsche Bibliothek - CIP-Einheitsaufnahme

Implementation of functional languages : 8th international
workshop, Bad Godesberg, Germany, September 1996 ; selected
papers / Werner Kluge (ed.). - Berlin ; Heidelberg ; New York ;
Barcelona ; Budapest ; Hong Kong ; London ; Milan ; Paris ; Santa
Clara ; Singapore ; Tokyo : Springer, 1997
    (Lecture notes in computer science ; Vol. 1268)
    ISBN 3-540-63237-9

CR Subject Classification (1991): D.3, D.1.1,F.3

ISSN 0302-9743
ISBN 3-540-63237-9 Springer-Verlag Berlin Heidelberg New York

© Springer-Verlag Berlin Heidelberg 1997
Printed in Germany

Typesetting: Camera-ready by author
SPIN 10548872   06/3142 – 5 4 3 2 1 0   Printed on acid-free paper

Lecture Notes in Computer Science   1268

Edited by G. Goos, J. Hartmanis and J. van Leeuwen

Advisory Board: W. Brauer   D. Gries   J. Stoer

Springer
Berlin
Heidelberg
New York
Barcelona
Budapest
Hong Kong
London
Milan
Paris
Santa Clara
Singapore
Tokyo

Preface and Overview of Papers

This LNCS volume contains a selection of papers presented at the 1996 International Workshop on the Implementation of Functional Languages which took place in Bonn-Bad-Godesberg, Germany, Sept. 16-18, 1996. It was the 8th in a series of workshops of which the others were held in Nijmegen (The Netherlands) in 1989 and 1990, in Southampton (UK) in 1991, in Aachen (Germany) in 1992, again in Nijmegen in 1993, in Norwich (UK) in 1994, and in Bastad (Sweden) in 1995.

The idea of organizing the first of these workshops came up during the 1989 PARLE (Parallel Architectures and Languages Europe) conference, when a group of people from various European countries who were involved in research on implementation issues of functional languages felt that it was desirable to create a forum for a quick and informal exchange of new ideas and concepts, of experience gathered from ongoing research activities, and of emerging results. The workshop was met with interest and enthusiasm from the start so that, after the second meeting, it was decided to establish it as an annual event. The workshop initially focused on parallel implementation issues, but over the years its scope has been widened to include language concepts and design, type systems, interpretation and compilation techniques, automatic program generation, concurrent processing, machine architectures, runtime profiling, application programming, and theoretical work.

As implementation techniques are improving, functional and function-based languages are becoming increasingly popular both in education and in serious application programming. Languages like SCHEME, ML, MIRANDA, HASKELL, or GOFER are successfully replacing traditional imperative languages in undergraduate programming courses, and several large software systems have already been programmed in some of these languages, e.g., tools for the design and simulation of higher-order Petri nets, hardware design tools, or a natural language processing system, each consisting of some ten thousand lines of source code. Functional programming concepts are also beginning to influence other language designs (a more recent development being JAVA) and are making some inroads into large-scale industrial software engineering (e.g., the function-based language ERLANG used by Ericsson to implement telephone switching systems).

Nevertheless, much work remains to be done to overcome the acceptance problems which functional languages, to some extent, are still facing with respect to style of programming, and also to close the performance gap that still exists relative to imperative languages. Areas of primary concern are language and tool support for 'real world' application programming as well as more sophisticated implementation techniques. There is demand for abstraction mechanisms which, beyond those that are already available, consequently liberate programming from low-level details, e.g., relating to operations on large data structures. Pragmatic considerations also suggest that functional languages be enriched by logic or object-oriented features, or that they be combined with process coordination (or actor) languages in order to enhance concurrent processing capabilities. Modularization, interfacing with other languages, and the integration of input / output operations or, more generally, of interactions with state-based environments (e.g., file systems), though conceptually solved, still remain practical (programming and implementation) problems. Compilation techniques for sequentially as well as non-sequentially executable code, specifically code optimization, must be further improved, and designing complex application programs also requires support by programming environments, including debugging and profiling tools, which are as comfortable as those that are available for imperative languages.

Since these issues are addressed in most of the workshop contributions, we thought it was time to publish selected papers on research that has reached some degree of maturity in widely available proceedings, rather than just as hand-outs to the workshop participants. As the LNCS series is dedicated to an early dissemination of current research work, it appeared to be the perfect choice for this purpose. We therefore gratefully appreciate that Springer, and especially the series editor, Prof. Jan van Leeuwen, went along with our project.

The papers included in this volume represent a good mix of conceptual and implementation work dealing with language concepts and design, support for numerical applications, compilation techniques, concurrent processing concepts and their implementation, and runtime profiling. Two papers of a more theoretical nature relate to control flow analysis and to the systematic transformation of formal specifications into executable programs.

Clack and Braine introduce an object-oriented functional language called CLOVER which combines functional features such as referential transparency, type safety, higher-order functions and lazy evaluation with object-oriented features such as class hierarchies, inheritance, dynamic typing and overloading. They give an overview of the ensuing compatibility problems, e.g., type safety in the presence of dynamic message dispatching, the meaning of partial applications and of lazy evaluation in an object-oriented context, the meaning of subtyping in a functional context, and a notion of object identity that lends itself more naturally to the functional paradigm (behaviors rather than states of objects). The paper should be an interesting reading to language designers, implementors and application programmers both in the functional and in the object-oriented community.

Two papers deal with novel approaches to pattern matching which simplify the specification of searches for specific substructures in large structural contexts. The active patterns proposed by Erwig traverse argument structures until matches specified as simple base cases can succeed. These base cases serve as interfaces to (recursive) functions which define the details of the traversals somewhere else. The paper specifies the rules by which programs containing active patterns may be transformed into semantically equivalent ordinary ML programs. The context patterns introduced by Mohnen are to search for and match against substructures occurring at variable depths in arguments, and to bind the contexts in which these structures occur to variables as well, if so desired. The paper defines context patterns as an extension to HASKELL, and their semantics by translation into equivalent Haskell code. The benefit of both approaches is a more concise and elegant program design, as demonstrated by several examples.

Boquist and Johnsson introduce a novel monad-based intermediate level of code generation for the compilation of lazy functional languages. It combines the advantages of a functional representation (which facilitates code-optimizing transformations) with the sequencing of elementary operations and the use of temporary variables, as required for compilation to conventional target machine code. In conjunction with compiler backend techniques that focus on interprocedural register allocation and procedure inlining, the paper makes an important contribution to compiler technology which, beyond lazy functional languages, is generally applicable to all function- and logic-based languages.

Three papers are on support for efficient array operations in functional languages. Scholz introduces a strict language SAC which is primarily designed for numerical applications. It integrates into a functional kernel of C an array calculus in which array operations can be specified in a very concise, shape-independent form. The programming style supported by SAC is illustrated by means of a multigrid benchmark program. Runtimes and memory consumption for this program are only about 30% higher than for equivalent FORTRAN implementations. The other two papers deal with arrays in the lazy language CLEAN 1.1. Van Groningen describes the integration of lazy, strict and unboxed arrays, and specifically the type constructors classes that allow primitive array functions to be uniformly applied to all three array types. It also addresses the problems of destructive array updates based on uniqueness typing, and of memory consumption and uncertainties about the evaluation status of array elements in lazy arrays. Serrarens compares elegance of program design and runtime performance of the conjugate gradient algorithm implemented in CLEAN 1.1 (using lazy and strict lists, lazy, strict and unboxed arrays), in HASKELL, and in C. As expected, the lazy versions turn out to be by far the slowest and most wasteful in terms of memory consumption, whereas unboxed arrays yield runtimes that, again, are only about 30% higher than the respective imperative implementations (this time in C), with memory demand only marginally exceeding the space needed for the data representation. The fastest CLEAN version outperforms the fastest HASKELL implementation by a factor of about 15 with respect to execution time and by a factor of about 5 in terms of memory consumption.

Concurrent processing concepts and their implementations are the subject of two papers. Breitinger, Klusik and Loogen discuss implementation aspects of EDEN, an extension of HASKELL by constructs for the specification and creation of dynamically evolving systems of communicating processes. The authors specify the compilation of EDEN into CONCURRENT HASKELL, and in doing so, give some insight into the relationship between both languages, thereby exposing limitations of the latter. The implementation itself is a considerable piece of application programming in CONCURRENT HASKELL. Aßmann proposes a process coordination language K2 on top of a functional language which cleanly separates the specification of process systems and their communication structures from the computations to be performed by the individual processes. This approach, which also supports a notion of recursively expandable process systems, facilitates both program design and independent formal reasoning about safety and liveness properties and about program correctness. The paper also outlines a PVM-based implementation which is currently in progress.

Performance-related issues of concurrent processing are the subject of a paper by Loidl and Hammond who investigate the effects of various message-packing and latency-hiding schemes on program runtimes in lazy distributed graph reduction systems with varying packet transmission latencies. These investigations, which were performed on several HASKELL programs of the divide-and-conquer variety, basically compare two variants of bulk transfers (bounded packet sizes, limited number of 'thunks') with incremental transfers of single thunks on the one hand, and the effects of four re-scheduling strategies of varying aggressiveness on the other hand. They nicely identify, with respect to latencies, the break-even points among these strategies.

Other performance aspects are addressed in the papers by Jarvis and Morgan on cost profiling large functional programs and by Runciman and Röjemo on heap profiling. Both report on sophisticated runtime profiling tools which enable programmers to analyze heap space and processing time consumption, and to relate profiles to specific data or program components. As functional programs completely abstract from execution details, these tools are absolutely essential, probably even more so than in the imperative domain, for large-scale program development in order to be able to identify and re-code potential performance trouble spots. Both papers primarily describe the properties of the tools, how they can be used to profile programs, and what typical profiles look like.

The paper by Pil on first class file I/O introduces an extension by dynamic types of the static type system used in CLEAN. They are to treat the contents of files, including in particular functions, as properly typed objects of the language rather than just as strings of characters. Typed files can be included in a consistent way into the entire type-checking process. The file part has to be done at runtime though, since programs that exchange data with their environments cannot generally be typed statically. The paper outlines how this extended type system is going to be implemented in CLEAN, and specifically the problems of integrating the dynamic parts into an existing static type system.

Typing in another context plays a key role in the paper by Debabbi, Faour and Tawbi on analyzing the flow of control in concurrent functional programs. It reports on an efficient algorithm which approximates, for code optimization purposes, control flow graphs of programs with higher-order functions and communication primitives. In constructing such graphs, the algorithm propagates types, communication effects, and control information that comes with function calls.

Finally, Dosch and Möller demonstrate, by means of binary search trees, how efficiently executable functional programs can be systematically derived from formal specifications by purely algebraic calculations (inductions over tree structures). Each of these transformation steps involves design decisions which in a controllable form bring the formal specifications closer to implementations. Functional languages are a perfect platform for such transformation processes as their construction and execution follows algebraic laws.

These papers were selected, through a fairly rigorous a posteriori reviewing process, out of 26 papers presented at the workshop. The reviewing was mainly shared among the programme committee members

Makoto Amamiya	Kyushu University, Japan
Marko van Eekelen	University of Nijmegen, The Netherlands
John Glauert	University of East Anglia, UK
Kevin Hammond	University of St. Andrews, UK
Thomas Johnsson	Chalmers University of Technology, Sweden
Werner Kluge	University of Kiel, Germany
Pieter Koopman	University of Leiden, The Netherlands
Herbert Kuchen	University of Münster, Germany
Rita Loogen	University of Marburg, Germany
Rinus Plasmeijer	University of Nijmegen, The Netherlands
Colin Runciman	University of York, UK

The overall balance of the papers is fairly representative, both in scope and technical substance, of the contributions made to the Bonn workshop as well as to those that preceded it. Publication in the LNCS series is not only intended to make these contributions more widely known in the computer science community but also to encourage researchers in the field to participate in future workshops, of which the next one will be held in St. Andrews, Scotland, Sept. 10-12, 1997 (for more information see http://www.dcs.st-and.ac.uk/~ifl97/).

April 1997   Werner Kluge

Table of Contents

Introducing CLOVER: An Object-Oriented Functional Language............ 1
Lee Braine and Chris Clack

Active Patterns... 21
Martin Erwig

Context Patterns in Haskell... 41
Markus Mohnen

The GRIN Project: A Highly Optimising Back End for
Lazy Functional Languages 58
Urban Boquist and Thomas Johnsson

On Programming Scientific Applications in SAC - A Functional Language
Extended by a Subsystem for High-Level Array Operations 85
Sven-Bodo Scholz

The Implementation and Efficiency of Arrays in Clean 1.1 105
John H.G. van Groningen

Implementing the Conjugate Gradient Algorithm in a Functional Language 125
Pascal R. Serrarens

An Implementation of Eden on Top of Concurrent Haskell 141
Silvia Breitinger, Ulrike Klusik and Rita Loogen

Coordinating Functional Processes Using Petri Nets 162
Claus Aßmann

Making a Packet: Cost-Effective Communication for a
Parallel Graph Reducer... 184
Hans-Wolfgang Loidl and Kevin Hammond

The Results of: Profiling Large-Scale Lazy Functional Programs........... 200
Stephen A. Jarvis and Richard G. Morgan

Two-Pass Heap Profiling: A Matter of Life and Death.................... 222
Colin Runciman and Niklas Röjemo

First Class File I/O 233
Marco Pil

A Type-Based Algorithm for the Control-Flow Analysis of
Higher-Order Concurrent Programs...................................... 247
Mourad Debbabi, Ali Faour, and Nadia Tawbi

Calculating a Functional Module for Binary Search Trees 267
Walter Dosch and Bernhard Möller

Introducing CLOVER: An Object-Oriented Functional Language

Lee Braine* and Chris Clack

Department of Computer Science, University College London,
Gower Street, London WC1E 6BT, UK

L.Braine@cs.ucl.ac.uk   C.Clack@cs.ucl.ac.uk

Abstract. The search for a language which combines both functional and object-oriented features has a long and distinguished history [Can82, Car84, BK86, BD88, BGW91, MHH91, AP93, CL91, MMH91, Sar93, CL96]. The aim is to integrate the formal methods benefits of functional programming with the software engineering benefits of both paradigms. However, to date we know of no language which can claim to be both purely functional and purely object-oriented (and retains complete type safety). We present CLOVER, a new language which is 100% functional and 99% object-oriented. It is also completely type safe. We explain the design issues and how CLOVER achieves its aim. We also explain the "missing" 1%, discuss its relevance, and illustrate how its loss can be extenuated through the use of a new visual programming notation.

1 Introduction

The object-oriented (OO) paradigm, together with an appropriate methodology, has successfully delivered many large projects. OO design (OOD) is used extensively in industry since it provides good control and componentisation characteristics for structuring the design of large applications. However, OO programming (OOP) has been rather disappointing: in particular, the expected level of code reuse has not been observed. Furthermore, OOP languages have done little to reduce testing and debugging times: current OOP languages are not *completely* type safe and require extensive run-time testing and debugging.

By contrast, functional programming (FP) is not used extensively in industry, mainly due to perceived low performance, restricted programmer skill base, and poor support for large-scale applications programming (there is typically no methodology supporting analysis and design). However, FP languages can bring major benefits to program development. Complete type safety ensures that a very high percentage of all errors are detected at compile time, thereby significantly reducing the time required for run-time debugging. Furthermore, functional languages have simple syntax and semantics and the key property of referential transparency ensures that encapsulation cannot be breached and programmers can work securely at an appropriate level of abstraction.

---

* During the course of this work, Lee Braine was supported by an EPSRC research studentship and a CASE award from Andersen Consulting.

Our goal is to provide a specification language which is both purely functional and purely object-oriented. Since the definition of these two terms is open
to interpretation (and indeed there is no universally agreed definition of OO),
we choose to define the first in terms of features that are common to most
lazy functional languages and to define the second in terms of a minimal subset
that is common to most object-oriented languages and, we believe, captures the
essence of object-oriented programming. We define the former as "referentially
transparent with no side-effects and completely type safe, with lazy evaluation,
parametric polymorphism, higher-order functions and partial applications" and
the latter as "purely object-oriented (where everything is an object), using a class
hierarchy with inheritance and pure encapsulation, subsumption through subtyping, method overloading, method overriding and dynamic despatch". Object-
oriented purists may argue that something is missing: this is "the 1%" which we
discuss at the end of the paper.

The paper is structured as follows: after a brief overview of relevant OOP
terms, we establish the problem by discussing related work and the difficult
design issues; we then present the new language CLOVER, its design features,
abstract syntax, type system and an overview of its abstract semantics; we also
explain the "missing" 1%, discuss its relevance, and illustrate how its loss can
be extenuated through the use of a new visual programming notation; finally, we
report the current status of the CLOVER project, suggest directions for further
work, and conclude.

2   Overview of Object-Oriented Terms

We assume the reader has a knowledge of FP terms, but not necessarily of OOP
terms. This section therefore briefly summarises relevant OO terms as often used
in the OO community.

Basic Concepts: A *class* comprises both *attributes* (private data items) and
methods (interface functions). Each class has a special *constructor* function which
is used to define (*instantiate*) an instance of that class with specific values for its
attributes. An *object* is the instantiation of a class. An object may be manipulated by sending it a *message*, which is the name of one of the object's methods
together with the actual parameters for that method.

Further Terms:

- *Binary methods* take a parameter (in addition to the distinguished object)
  which has the same type as the distinguished object.
- *Delegation* is the act of one object forwarding an operation to another object,
  to be performed on behalf of the first object [Boo94].
- A *distinguished object* (DO) is used at run-time to resolve method overriding
  and determine which implementation should be used for a given method
  application (*vide* overloading and overriding).

- *Dynamic binding* associates a name with a value at run-time (and often a type, if this is not known statically — *vide* dynamic typing).
- *Dynamic despatch* is a run-time feature which invokes the implementation associated with a method name according to the actual type of the distinguished object.
- *Dynamic typing* associates a name with a type at run-time.
- *Inheritance* is a relationship among classes, wherein a class shares the attributes or methods defined in one (single inheritance) or more (multiple inheritance) other classes (see also [Boo94]).
- *Multi-methods* is a run-time feature which allows dynamic despatch to be based on more than one parameter.
- *Overloading* provides multiple implementations for a method, each with a distinct type.
- *Overriding* provides a replacement implementation for an inherited method or attribute.
- `self` is an identifier, defined in every method, that is bound dynamically to the distinguished object.
- *Subsumption* allows a function of type $\sigma_1 \to \sigma_2$ to be provided with an argument of type σ_3 iff σ_3 is a subtype of σ_1.
- *Subtyping* has been defined in many ways (see, for example, [CW85]). In general, it can be viewed as a type system with a pairwise relation on types which provides a partial ordering.

3 Related Work

Since at least the early 1980s there has been considerable interest in the formalisation of OOP, most notable being attempts to integrate OOP and FP.

3.1 1980-1989

Early work such as Flavors [Can82] and CommonLOOPS [BK86] involved the extension of LISP with object-oriented features. This work culminated in CLOS [BD88], a set of tools for developing object-oriented programs in Common LISP [Ste84]. Significant claims have been made [BGW91] that CLOS combines both OOP and FP yet, because it is based on LISP (like Flavors and Common-LOOPS), it is not referentially transparent and therefore fails to satisfy our primary criterion.

3.2 1990-1992

In the early 1990s interest in OOP/FP integration increased, with several newly developed languages. However, four of these languages (Leda [Bud95], Quest [CL91], Rapide [MMH91] and UFO [Sar93]) are not referentially transparent, FOOPS [Soc93] has no higher-order programming facilities, LIFE [AP93] only supports a simulation of FP, and HOP [DV96] does not support full OOP. Kea [MHH91], Rapide and HOP are briefly outlined below:

- Kea is a higher-order, polymorphic, lazy functional language supporting multi-methods and a type inference system. Unlike Smalltalk [GR83], Kea does not enforce certain aspects of OO encapsulation. In particular, Kea functions do not have to be associated with classes according to a distinguished object. Furthermore, Kea's notion of polymorphism only admits the single type variable Any, and [MHH91] mentions that Kea "is currently being extended to include higher-order and (implicitly) polymorphic functions", which implies that it does not have these features.

- Rapide extends Standard ML (SML) [MTH90] with subtyping and inheritance. Objects are modelled as structures, and SML is extended so that structures may be passed to and from functions. Unfortunately, Rapide retains SML's lack of referential transparency and, indeed, relies on it.

- HOP is a functional language with object-oriented features incorporating dynamic binding and subtyping; it is also referentially transparent and lazy. Based on an extension of the λ-calculus called *label-selective λ-calculus* (also known as the λN-calculus), HOP is an experimental language for testing the provision of OO features within FP. However, there is as yet no clear notion of "object" and no explanation of how dynamic despatch, inheritance, subsumption, overloading and overriding would be implemented.

3.3   1993–1995

In this period there were a number of notable attempts at integration, plus extensions of previous systems. OBJ [GWM93] is a functional language that supports multiple inheritance, exception handling and overloading but has no higher-order programming facilities. ST&T [DY94] is an extension of Smalltalk's type system bringing it closer to ML, though the result is first-order, strict, and still not referentially transparent. Uflow [SKA94] is an extension to UFO using a data-flow model for visualising execution, but is still not referentially transparent. Finally, Caml Special Light [Ler95] (later re-named Objective Caml) laid the foundations for Objective ML (see next subsection), but unfortunately these foundations are not referentially transparent.

3.4   1996

This year has witnessed an intensifying of interest in the field with several new languages being established, including our language CLOVER. Objective ML [RV96] is implemented on top of Caml Special Light and is an extension of ML with objects, top-level classes, multiple inheritance, methods returning self, binary methods and parametric classes. Object ML [RR96] extends ML with objects, subtyping and heterogeneous collections. CLAIRE [CL96] is a high-level functional and object-oriented language with advanced rule processing capabilities. Bla [Oor96] claims to unite functional and object-oriented programming through *first class environments* [GJL87]. However, none of these languages except CLOVER is referentially transparent.

3.5 Summary of Related Work

It seems that, despite considerable attention from the research community, it has been impossible to combine object-oriented features such as inheritance, subsumption and dynamic method despatch with functional features such as referential transparency, higher-order functions, currying, partial applications and lazy evaluation, into a single, completely type-safe, language. The closest attempts so far are Kea, Rapide, HOP, LIFE, Objective ML and Object ML.

4   Design Issues

The most stringent criterion that we can devise for an object-oriented functional language is that it must be purely functional — that is, it must be referentially transparent with no side effects — for without this property most of the formal-methods advantages of the functional paradigm are lost (e.g. most static analysis techniques for FP languages assume referential transparency).

Thus, our view is one of extending FP towards OOP rather than the other way around. Note that this requires us immediately to discard imperative notions of multiple assignment (see the later section: "The Missing 1%").

We make two more design decisions at the outset:

1. We discard any notion of multiple inheritance because it complicates the semantics of OOP considerably (e.g. resolving attribute and method naming conflicts and upwards type coercion). If necessary, similar behaviour can be achieved using explicit object delegation.
2. We choose dynamic despatch based on a single distinguished object to avoid the complexities of the multi-methods approach and increase encapsulation.

In the remainder of this section we present five design issues which illustrate why the integration of OOP and FP is such a difficult task.

4.1   Type Safety versus Dynamic Despatch

A key feature of OO languages is dynamic typing (resolving the type of an object at run-time). In particular, data arriving from an external source may be of heterogeneous type (whereas FP languages statically define the actual type of input data). Furthermore, subtyping permits conditional statements to return different subtypes of the declared return type. Thus, in general, it is not possible to resolve method despatch statically for dynamically-typed objects.

With dynamic method despatch, a run-time check is made on the actual type of the object receiving a message; the ambiguities arising from inheritance and method overriding are then resolved and the appropriate code is executed.

Many OO languages assume and accept that this implies type errors may occur at run-time. Having realised that this is undesirable, some OO language designers have created what they claim to be "type safe" OO languages: Eiffel [Mey91], for example, makes this claim. However, Eiffel actually provides an *assignment attempt operator* which handles run-time type errors in a controlled manner by assigning a `void` value; it is assumed that the programmer will always check for the possibility of a `void` value and take appropriate action. This is not what functional programmers think of as "type safe"! The FP world requires *complete* type safety, where the type system guarantees that it is impossible for a type error to occur at run-time.

Dynamic types thus appear to compromise type safety, though recent work [AW94, AF95, AM90] partially extenuates the problem.

4.2 Type Safety versus Overloading and Partial Applications

Overloading is a common feature of OO languages, allowing different definitions for the same method name. These overloadings can be distinguished by the types of the message arguments and return value: each overloading must have a unique type signature. Overloading is certainly a desirable feature that we would wish to incorporate since it allows, for example, multiple ways to set a date:

```
date (7,"August",1996)
date (7,8,1996)
```

In the above example, the two overloaded versions of `date` take the same number of arguments. However, it is also important to support overloading with different numbers of arguments. For example:

```
time (12,0,0)
time ("noon")
```

We wish to support *full overloading*: that is, overloaded methods able to vary both in the type and number of arguments declared.

Unfortunately, *it would appear to be impossible to combine dynamic despatch with curried partial applications and full overloading.* With full overloading, the number of arguments in different overloadings may vary. With partial applications, a method may be applied to only some of its arguments. If the partial application uses the curried style (rather than, for example, a tuple with dummy values for the missing arguments), then there are ambiguities which are impossible to resolve at run-time. For example, given the following overloaded definitions (using the 24-hour and the 12-hour clock):

```
time (a:int) (b:int) (c:int)
time (a:int) (b:int) (c:int) (d:string)
```

then is the application `time 6 0 0` a full application of the first overloading (meaning 6 am) or a partial application of the second overloading (which could eventually be 6 am or 6 pm)?

If this cannot be resolved at run-time, then we must require all types to be known at compile-time so that overloaded functions can be resolved statically and complete type safety can be guaranteed. However, we have already established that dynamic typing implies we cannot know all actual types at compile-time.

4.3 Curried and Partially-Applied Methods

Currying, higher-order functions and partial applications are key features of the functional programming style, yet are absent from OOP. This is not unreasonable, since OO programmers normally perceive messages to be indivisible and it is not clear what a partially applied message would mean. For example, if the method f takes distinguished object o and normally takes three arguments a, b and c, then what does the message f a b denote? Can it be given a name? What does it mean operationally? Can it be sent as it is to the object o or must it be delayed until the final argument is ready? If it is sent to the object, what does the object do with it? Must it store it and wait for the final argument to arrive? The denotational and operational semantics of partial applications have not been fully addressed in the OO world.

Furthermore, as we have already seen, it is difficult to reconcile curried partial applications with dynamic despatch and full overloading.

4.4 Subtyping

Subtyping is central to OOP but absent from current "production" FP languages. Haskell [HPW91] has at various times been the subject of claims that its type classes mechanism [WB89] facilitates OO programming [Ber92]; this has promulgated the mistaken assumption that Haskell's type classes provide subtyping. Unfortunately type classes do not provide the subtype relationship that we require; rather, they support a structured form of overloading.

If we are to support dynamic despatch, then the run-time method despatcher must accept an argument of many different types (the method's distinguished object); this requires either subtyping or flattening the entire type system into what is essentially a monotyped language. Similarly, subsumption requires subtyping to be applied to method arguments.

FP languages rely on advanced polymorphic type inference to ensure type correctness. The type systems of most FP languages are based on the Hindley/Milner algorithm [DM82] which does not admit subtypes. A notable exception is Mitchell's extension to the SML type system to admit inclusion polymorphism through subtyping [MMH91]. Subtyping in HOP [DV96] claims to be based largely on Mitchell's work (using recursive type constraints).

Whereas polymorphic type inference used to be considered undecidable for inclusion types, recent work [BM96] has demonstrated that decidable systems can be implemented.

4.5   Lazy Evaluation versus Discrete Messages and State Update

We wish to retain the powerful FP feature of lazy evaluation, yet this does not seem to have a natural meaning within the message-passing view of OOP. For example:

1. Multiple assignment semantics require strict state update;
2. State update is driven by the arrival of a message (data-driven);
3. Messages are discrete, finite and pre-evaluated;
4. Sending a message is an atomic action.

The above views seem to preclude the incorporation of any notion of lazy evaluation into OOP.

5   CLOVER

CLOVER is a higher-order, lazy, object-oriented, functional language that is completely type safe. CLOVER provides:

1. a new design for completely type safe dynamic method despatch and over-loading; [2]
2. a new object-oriented semantics for partially applied messages and higher-order functions;
3. a new design for full overloading of methods in the presence of curried partial applications and dynamic despatch;
4. a new programming notation and semantics for object state, object identity and object-oriented lazy evaluation.

CLOVER is intended to be used for application development, not low-level systems programming. We support programming at the specification level, much as functional languages can be used to write executable specifications [Tur85].

CLOVER supports the traditional OOP features of a class hierarchy, subtyping, subsumption, inheritance, method overloading, method overriding and dynamic despatch. It also incorporates the FP features of referential transparency, single-assignment attributes, polymorphism, curried partial applications, higher-order functions and lazy evaluation. Methods are defined as expressions — they are pure functions with no side effects.

The language is completely type safe, there are no pointers and memory allocation is automatic; thus, CLOVER is a secure language which could be used, for example, to produce totally secure applets for the World Wide Web. However, a secure CLOVER run-time system as a Netscape plug-in is left for future work!

In our prototype, a lazy functional programming language is used as an intermediate language: CLOVER code is first type-checked using a bespoke type-checker and then is translated into a standard functional language. This allows the use of a standard compiler for code generation.

---

[2] Eiffel claims type-safe dynamic despatch but at the cost of losing overloading, whereas Haskell has overloading but not dynamic despatch.

5.1   Design Features

The key to CLOVER's successful support of both OOP and FP is in the careful integration of a number of different design criteria. Since there are so many design parameters (subtyping, subsumption, inheritance, overloading, overriding, genericity, partial applications, currying, laziness, etc.), the design space is extremely large and our goal has proven to be remarkably elusive. However, as is so often the case, the solution appears quite natural in retrospect.

The key design criteria are all related to type safety, including bounded universal quantification, monotonic inheritance, and shallow subtyping. Furthermore, in order to deal with curried partial applications, we enforce an unusual ordering constraint on the implementation of message application. Finally, we support an object-oriented view of lazy evaluation through the use of a new visual notation (see "The Missing 1%"); thus, CLOVER is a visual object-oriented functional language.

Bounded universal quantification: It is clear that dynamic typing is incompatible with knowledge of actual types at compile time, yet we require a language which has dynamic typing and is also completely type safe.

The first step to solving this apparent conflict is to ensure that upperbounds on types are always known statically. This allows dynamic typing (in that the actual type of an expression can be any subtype of the known upperbound), whilst ensuring that all type errors can be detected at compile time. We currently require the programmer to give explicit upperbound types in all method type signatures and for all method arguments, though in future we hope to implement a subtype inference system. Inclusion polymorphism is thus implemented as bounded universal quantification [CW85].

Monotonic inheritance: For completely safe method despatch, statically resolvable upperbounds are only part of the solution. When a message is passed to an object, the required method must also actually be defined for that object. The static knowledge of the upperbound type of the object must therefore be coupled with the restriction that inheritance be monotonic; that is, if a method or attribute exists for a given class then it will also exist (with identical type signature) for all of its subclasses.

Shallow subtyping: In order to achieve complete type safety, it is essential that full method overloading can be resolved statically. Since only upperbound types are available at compile-time, we must therefore restrict CLOVER to shallow subtyping — that is, an inherited or reimplemented method must have the same type as its ancestor. We provide full method overloading (with different types and numbers of arguments) but insist that all overloadings are declared in the class where the method name is first defined. Thus, if an overloaded method application is valid for a given type then it will be valid for all subtypes.

Implementation of message application: A message application to an object is often written as o.f(a,b,c). The traditional way to implement this is as the function call f(o,a,b,c).

For CLOVER, we wish to support curried partial applications and so it would seem that the above application could naturally be implemented as f o a b c. However, this causes problems for partial applications of messages. As previously discussed, there is a problem with the semantics of partial applications in an object-oriented context. Considering the above implementation technique, what would f o a mean, both denotationally and operationally?

We define a *partially-applied message* as a method that has not yet been applied to all its arguments and that has not yet been applied to its distinguished object. We allow a partial application to be named, to be passed as an argument to a method, and to be returned as a result from a method. However, only a fully-applied message can be sent to a distinguished object.

To implement these semantics precisely, we adopt the unusual procedure of placing the distinguished object as the *last* in the sequence of curried arguments: f a b c o.

Laziness: The key to the incorporation of laziness in CLOVER is our new concept of object identity, as explained in the later section "The Missing 1%".

5.2 Language Overview

A CLOVER program consists of three components:

1. an invocation (an expression);
2. a class hierarchy (a tree with at least one class);
3. for each class, an unordered set of attribute declarations and method definitions.

The class hierarchy is single-rooted with single monotonic inheritance for the definition of new classes as extensions of existing classes; thus, there is no sharing in the class hierarchy, and inherited attributes and methods cannot be discarded. As in the Smalltalk tradition, everything is either an object or a message — thus, the class hierarchy contains class definitions for even the most primitive types such as integer and character. A fully-applied message is a method applied to all of its arguments except the distinguished object; the distinguished object is always the last argument. Messages may be specialised through partial application. Arguments to methods and results from methods may be objects or messages (including partial messages). Thus, CLOVER is higher-order, treating messages as first-class citizens.

The class hierarchy represents the subtype structure (see later). Subclasses may inherit methods and attributes through shallow subtyping only - that is, an inherited or reimplemented method must have the same type as its ancestor. Overloaded method declaration is allowed, but only in the greatest superclass where the method is first defined; thereafter, the separate overloaded instances may be inherited and reimplemented through shallow subtyping as described above. Thus, CLOVER supports both overloading and overriding.

Each class is a subtype of its parent and subsumption allows a formal method parameter of type σ to be bound to an actual parameter of type τ as long as τ is a subtype of σ (and using the contravariant rule to establish subtypes of higher-order arguments). Method overloading is resolved at compile-time, whereas method overriding is resolved at run-time by dynamic despatch on the type of the distinguished object (if the distinguished object's class does not define or override the method, the despatcher searches up the inheritance hierarchy to find the least superclass which has a definition for the method — note that this cannot fail at run-time).

CLOVER provides completely type-safe subsumption and dynamic despatch using bounded universal quantification of type names. There is consequently no need for type variables in order to support genericity.

5.3   CLOVER Abstract Expression Syntax

The following abstract syntax for an expression is based on the typed λ-calculus (extended with *let* and *case* constructs) and with objects as constants:

$$value :: C^\sigma\, x_1^{\sigma_1} \ldots x_n^{\sigma_n} \qquad n \geq 0 \;\; (object\; constructor)$$
$$\mid\; \lambda x^{\sigma_x}\!.\,e^{\sigma_e} \qquad\qquad\qquad (curried\; method\; definition)$$
$$\mid\; \Phi_i^\sigma \qquad\qquad\qquad\qquad\quad (built\!-\!in\; method)$$
$$\mid\; literal \qquad\qquad\qquad\qquad (immediate\; data)$$

$$expr :: value \qquad\qquad\qquad\qquad (value)$$
$$\mid\; e^{\sigma_1 \to \sigma_2}\, x^{\sigma_x} \qquad\qquad\quad \sigma_x \preceq \sigma_1 \;\; (curried\; application)$$
$$\mid\; x^\sigma \qquad\qquad\qquad\qquad\quad (name)$$
$$\mid\; let\, (x_1 = e_1^{\sigma_1}) \ldots (x_n = e_n^{\sigma_n})\; in\; e^{\sigma_e} \quad n > 0$$
$$\mid\; case\; e^\sigma\; of\; (C_j^\sigma\, x_{j1}^{\sigma_{j1}} \ldots x_{jn_j}^{\sigma_{jn_j}} \to e_j^{\sigma_j}) \quad j = 1 \ldots m,\; m > 0,\; n_j \geq 0 \;\; \forall j$$

In the above syntax, σ denotes a type. Methods, bound variables and object attributes are referenced through identifiers ("x") and key primitive methods are built-in to facilitate the implementation. λ-abstractions are only used at the top level of a method binding.

Support is provided for bindings with local scope using *let*. However, these bindings may only be constant applicative forms (CAFs). That is, they may not be parameterised λ-abstractions but they may be any other expression which returns either an object or a (partial) message. The restriction which outlaws the λ-abstraction in *let* bindings outlaws the undesirable creation of new methods as local definitions, since all methods should formally be specified as part of a class interface.

The typechecker's (static) overloading resolution and the implementation of (dynamic) method despatch are illustrated in the abstract expression semantics (see later).

6 The CLOVER Type System

In the following subsections we briefly sketch the design of the CLOVER type system. Our prototype currently supports simple type matching rather than full type inference (which is left for further work).

6.1 Type Syntax

A type is either an object, a message (which has function type), or a bracketed message. The explicit bracketing is necessary to denote a function type being returned from a method — this facilitates identification of the distinguished object (the last argument to a method). Each class has a distinct type constructor name κ (we define a one-to-one correspondence between the class name and the type constructor name). Thus, the syntax for types in CLOVER is given by:

$$\sigma :: \kappa \mid \sigma_1 \to \sigma_2 \mid (\sigma_1 \to \sigma_2)$$

6.2 Overview of Type Semantics

We define an object's type as the set of the names and types of all its attributes and methods:

$$\mathcal{T}[[\kappa]] = \{x_i\} \cup \{m_i\}, x_i \in Attributes(\kappa), m_i \in Methods(\kappa)$$
$$\mathcal{T}[[\sigma_1 \to \sigma_2]] = \mathcal{T}[[\sigma_1]] \to \mathcal{T}[[\sigma_2]]$$
$$\mathcal{T}[[(\sigma_1 \to \sigma_2)]] = (\mathcal{T}[[\sigma_1]] \to \mathcal{T}[[\sigma_2]])$$

6.3 Subtyping

Although we would rather have the intermediate FP compiler do the type checking, our preferred language (Haskell) does not yet provide subtyping and is therefore unable to check inclusion polymorphism. We therefore currently implement a simple subtype matching algorithm.

We take a traditional set-theoretic view of the class system [Car84]: class types are sets of attributes and methods, with subclassing equivalent to subtyping. Subtypes are ordered inversely by set-inclusion over the above semantic domain.

We define the subtype relation operator $\preceq$ as follows:

$$\kappa_1 \preceq \kappa_2 \quad iff \ \mathcal{T}[[\kappa_2]] \subseteq \mathcal{T}[[\kappa_1]]$$
$$\sigma_1 \to \sigma_2 \preceq \tau_1 \to \tau_2 \quad iff \ (\tau_1 \preceq \sigma_1) \wedge (\sigma_2 \preceq \tau_2)$$
$$(\sigma_1 \to \sigma_2) \preceq (\tau_1 \to \tau_2) \quad iff \ (\tau_1 \preceq \sigma_1) \wedge (\sigma_2 \preceq \tau_2)$$
$$\kappa_i \npreceq \tau_1 \to \tau_2$$
$$\kappa_i \npreceq (\tau_1 \to \tau_2)$$
$$\sigma_1 \to \sigma_2 \npreceq \kappa_i$$
$$(\sigma_1 \to \sigma_2) \npreceq \kappa_i$$
$$(\sigma_1 \to \sigma_2) \npreceq \tau_1 \to \tau_2$$
$$\sigma_1 \to \sigma_2 \npreceq (\tau_1 \to \tau_2)$$

6.4 Overloading

A method may be defined at many different types, where the types are completely unrelated. However, we require each overloaded definition to have a unique type signature that is statically-resolvable from the other overloaded definitions. Thus, given two overloaded method definitions of type $\sigma_1 \to \sigma_{dist} \to \sigma_2$ and $\tau_1 \to \sigma_{dist} \to \tau_2$ (where σ_{dist} is the type of the distinguished object), we require that either $(\sigma_1 \not\preceq \tau_1) \wedge (\tau_1 \not\preceq \sigma_1)$ or $(\sigma_2 \not\preceq \tau_2) \wedge (\tau_2 \not\preceq \sigma_2)$. This generalises to multiple arguments and overloadings with different numbers of arguments. Note that this style of overloading permits some covariant specialisation.

6.5 Polymorphism

Polymorphism is supported in CLOVER through bounded universal quantification [CW85] which provides both inclusion and parametric polymorphism without the need for type variables (which are replaced by subtype constraints).

Our prototype does not yet support recursive types, though they are an essential element of CLOVER. We plan to implement F-Bounded quantification [CC89].

Our type matcher checks declared return types against declared argument types, for every application, to ensure that the subset relationship holds. We do not attempt type inference; type inference for inclusion polymorphism has long been considered problematic, yet we are encouraged by recent work [AW93, BM96]. We also intend to investigate the provision of incremental type inference, but this is left for future work.

7   Abstract Expression Semantics

Space does not permit a full exposition of CLOVER's abstract expression semantics. However, the following partial definition illustrates the key issues of subsumption, (static) overloading resolution and (dynamic) method despatch:

$$\mathcal{E}[[e^{\sigma_1 \to \kappa} \, x^{\sigma_x}]] = \mathcal{E}[[select \, x^{\sigma_x} \, \Psi(e^{\sigma_1 \to \kappa})]] \, \mathcal{E}[[x^{\sigma_x}]], \quad \sigma_x \preceq \sigma_1$$

$$\mathcal{E}[[e^{\sigma_1 \to (\sigma_2 \to \sigma_3)} \, x^{\sigma_x}]] = \mathcal{E}[[select \, x^{\sigma_x} \, \Psi(e^{\sigma_1 \to (\sigma_2 \to \sigma_3)})]] \, \mathcal{E}[[x^{\sigma_x}]], \quad \sigma_x \preceq \sigma_1$$

$$\mathcal{E}[[e^{\sigma_1 \to \sigma_2} \, x^{\sigma_x}]] = \mathcal{E}[[e^{\sigma_1 \to \sigma_2}]] \, \mathcal{E}[[x^{\sigma_x}]], \quad \sigma_x \preceq \sigma_1$$

In the above equations, *select* $x^{\sigma_x} \, \Psi(e^{\sigma_e})$ dynamically despatches method e from class σ_x at overloaded type σ_e, using $\Psi(e)$ to obtain statically the overloading-resolved name of the method in the head position of expression e. In essence, the first two equations above illustrate how the last argument of a method application is given special status as the distinguished object. Note that the special bracketing syntax for types is required so that we may detect the distinguished object for a method which returns a message.

8 The Missing 1%

In this section, we discuss the inappropriateness of the traditional OO notion of
object identity for object-oriented functional programming (OOFP) and propose
an alternative notion of object identity that could be adopted for OOFP.

8.1 Inappropriateness of Traditional Object Identity

Whilst encapsulation is an extremely important concept for software engineering,
it is not clear that mutable internal state is as important. Indeed, it is not clear
that object identity should be enforced in OOFP in the same manner as in OOP.

We propose that a finer level of identity should be assumed in OOFP, based
on the concept of object behaviour. For example, a digital watch has entirely
different behaviour according to whether it has or does not have a new battery
installed. These two behaviours can be viewed as different "incarnations" of the
watch, and given different names. A watch may go through several phases of
having or not having a fully charged battery, with each incarnation having a
separate identity.

In this way, we provide a history of identities which provide immediate
"hooks" back into the past. For example, a student might have different option choices in different years: by providing different identities to the different
stages of each student, it is possible to ask questions about (send messages to)
the different stages of the student's academic study. This also provides obvious
benefits for searching algorithms which use backtracking; previous incarnations
of an object are immediately accessible. The idea is not new: CLAIRE [CL96]
provides versioning for the entire object database, however we provide versioning
on a per-object basis.

As a final example of the inappropriateness of the traditional notion of object identity in OOFP, we note that the message-passing view of OOP requires
discrete messages to be passed as an atomic action to an object: not only is there
no explicit declaration of the behaviour that is expected from that object, but
there is also no way in which lazy evaluation could be given meaning in such
a system. By contrast, if we view objects as having identities which explicitly
change as their behaviour changes, then expected behaviour is made explicit
and sequencing of behaviour change is made explicit; this latter change opens
the way to the incorporation of lazy evaluation (as shown below).

From the foregoing discussion it can be seen that we align ourselves with the
Actor model [AH87] used for distributed OOP based on sequences of behaviours
rather than state changes. This is also similar to the continuation-passing style
often used by FP programmers.

This notion of separating identities by behaviour requires a new object identifier to be created for each change in the internal state of an object, and has
two main consequences. Firstly, it affects the utility of the resulting language
and, in particular, the patterns of programming that are supported most naturally. Typical functional patterns, such as mathematical algorithms exploiting
laziness, are captured well (and also benefit from the addition of OO features).

OO patterns exploiting mutable state, such as network simulations, are captured less naturally and require additional "plumbing". Secondly, it affects the execution efficiency by requiring what is essentially copy semantics: to update the state of an object, the old object is copied and given a new state and identity. Fortunately, it is possible to implement this procedure with low overhead and without name proliferation, as illustrated below.

8.2 Object-Flow: a New Visual Notation

CLOVER provides a visual programming interface. Methods are defined using nodes and arcs to build up a representation of a CLOVER expression.

The choice of a visual notation should be straightforward, yet it is not. This choice is of paramount importance and yet there is no existing suitable notation. Control-flow diagrams are clearly inappropriate for a single-assignment, expression-based language, and data-flow diagrams provide no semantics for OO notions of object identity (with or without behaviours), subsumption, dynamic despatch, etc. A common OO notation is the object diagram [Boo94], otherwise known as message-passing or message-flow notation; unfortunately, this notation relies on multiple assignment and does not support the concept of laziness.

Our solution is to use a notation that is almost the dual of message-flow notation, and is similar to Uflow notation [SKA94]. Instead of nodes representing objects and messages flowing along arcs, in our notation the nodes represent the application of methods to their arguments and objects flow along the arcs. When we include higher-order methods, we allow both objects and messages (which may be partial) to flow along the arcs. We call this notation *object-flow.*

With object-flow notation, objects actively flow from node to node along the arcs. Each arc can carry either an object or, being higher-order, a partially-applied message to an application node. This notation makes the changing state of an object explicit; an object flowing along an arc has a particular state and is accessible either by name or (if we wish to avoid a plethora of names) by joining a new arc to the existing arc (making a junction shares access to that incarnation of that object).

Figure 1 illustrates an **Account** object flowing into a node which represents the application of the **deposit** method to the argument **100.00**. A node comprises a sequence of boxes — the top box represents the result, the box under that represents the message to be applied, all lower boxes represent parameters and the last box represents the distinguished object. The distinguished object flows into a node from the bottom right and flows out as the result from the top left; this is a new incarnation of the object, which may have a different state. Thus, state changes are explicit and the object-flow notation provides a timeline for the life of an object. Each stage of an object's life is accessible, providing a versioning feature which supports easy exploration of search spaces through backtracking.

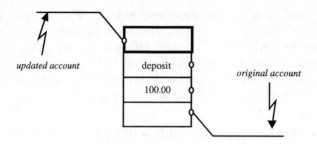

Fig. 1. Using the method `deposit`

Figure 2 illustrates the definition of the method **deposit**. The arguments (the credit amount and the account) flow in from the right and are given names (the account is called **self** because it is the distinguished object). The method updates[3] **self** with a new balance, which is calculated by adding the credit amount to the existing balance. The result of a node can either be transmitted via an arc or it can be given a name and referenced elsewhere (see **newBalance**).

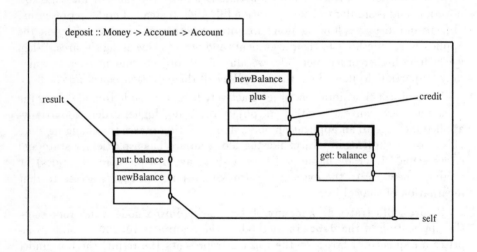

Fig. 2. Method definition for `deposit`

Our final examples illustrate method overriding, dynamic despatch and higher-order functions. We assume that the method **charge** is defined in class **Account** and inherited in the two subclasses **CorpAccount** and **PersAccount**. This method calculates the bank charges (of type **Money**) if an account balance is too low. It is overridden in both of the two subclasses to reflect different charging thresholds

---

[3] In the implementation, of course, the result is a modified copy of `self`.

and charging rates. Figure 3 demonstrates how the `charge` method might be used on a list of `Accounts`. The method is passed as a higher-order parameter to `map` (a method of the `List` class), which applies it to every `Account` in the list. This produces a list of `Money`, which is then summed by the `sum` method (also a method of the `List` class). The original list of accounts can include both `CorpAccounts` and `PersAccounts` — the appropriate `charge` method for each is selected using dynamic despatch.

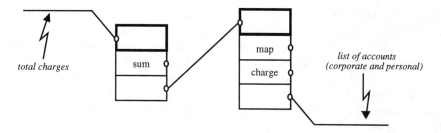

Fig. 3. Using the method `charge`

The two overridden definitions of `charge` are illustrated in Figure 4. Note that corporate accounts are charged as soon as their balance is negative, whereas personal accounts are allowed to be 100 units overdrawn before incurring charges.

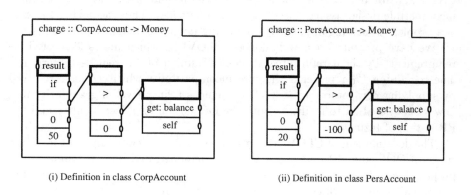

(i) Definition in class CorpAccount   (ii) Definition in class PersAccount

Fig. 4. Method definitions for `charge`

The semantics of object-flow method application are lazy: object-flow is demand driven and an object or message is only "pulled" along an arc (evaluated) if and when it is required. Hence, there are no flow arrows on the arcs — each method definition is demand driven by `result`. Shared demand for any object will be evaluated by whichever method issues the first demand. All incarnations of an object are preserved for as long as the run-time system can determine that they may be required: as soon as there are no remaining links to an incarnation, it is automatically garbage-collected.

9 Further Work

The abstract syntax and semantics are complete, though we expect them to change as we experiment with additional features. We have a draft concrete syntax for the visual notation and have implemented a prototype visual front-end, type-checker, and translator to Haskell.

Further work includes the implementation of subtype inference incorporating F-bounded polymorphism, the design of an incremental type checker [PM93], the design of CLOVER's real-world interface (including file input/output and user interaction), support for event-driven programming and the construction of a GUI builder. Run-time analyses can be assisted by the addition of algorithm animation and the extension of lexical profiling [CCP95] to visual profiling.

A revised object-oriented analysis and design notation will be required because existing notations assume stateful objects. Alternatively, we might define a translation from a standard implicit-state notation into explicit-state object-flow notation.

10 Summary and Conclusion

There have been many attempts at integrating OOP and FP, starting from at least the early 1980s. We have shown why achieving this goal is difficult by identifying key differences between the two paradigms and discussing the seemingly incompatible design issues raised by these differences. Thus, achieving the goal is a problem of solving apparently-conflicting language design requirements.

We have presented a new language, CLOVER, which meets 99% of these requirements by the careful integration of a number of different design criteria. The remaining 1% represents the core incompatibility which we have resolved by supplying new interpretations. This includes a finer level of granularity in a new visual notation to facilitate both the OO notion of object identity and the FP notion of laziness.

The development of CLOVER contributes to the understanding of the design space of OOP and FP languages. We have demonstrated how, through an appropriate set of design decisions, it is possible to implement an object-oriented functional language which integrates both paradigms.

Acknowledgements

We are grateful to Andersen Consulting for their encouragement and sponsorship in relation to this work.

References

[AF95]   Aiken, A., Fahndrich, M.: Dynamic Typing and Subtype Inference. Technical Report, Computer Science Division, University of California, Berkeley, (1995)

[AH87]   Agha, G., Hewitt, C.: Actors: A Conceptual Foundation for Concurrent Object-Oriented Programming. In Shriver & Wegner (Eds), Research Directions in Object-Oriented Programming, MIT Press, (1987) 47–74

[AM90]   Aiken, A., Murphy, B.: Static Type Inference in a Dynamically Typed Language. Technical Report, IBM Almaden Research Centre, (1990)

[AP93]   Ait-Kaci, H., Podelski, A.: Towards a Meaning of LIFE. Journal of Logic Programming, 16(3–4), (1993) 195–234

[AW93]   Aiken, A., Wimmer, E.: Type Inclusion Constraints and Type Inference. Technical Report, IBM Almaden Research Center, (1993)

[AW94]   Aiken, A., Wimmers, E.: Soft Typing with Conditional Types. In Proc. 21st POPL, (1994)

[BD88]   Bobrow, D., DeMichiel, L., et al.: Common Lisp Object System Specification. SIGPLAN Notices v23, (1988)

[Ber92]   Berger, E.: FP + OOP = Haskell. Technical Report, Department of Computer Science, University of Texas at Austin, (1992)

[BGW91]   Bobrow, D., Gabriel, R., White, J.: CLOS: Integrating Object-Oriented and Functional Programming. CACM 34(9), (1991) 28–38

[BK86]   Bobrow, D., Kahn, K., et al.: CommonLOOPS: Merging Lisp and Object-Oriented Programming. In Proc. ACM OOPSLA, (1986)

[BM96]   Bourdoncle, F., Merz, S.: Primitive subtyping $\wedge$ implicit polymorphism $\models$ object-orientation. In Proc. 3rd FOOL, (1996)

[Boo94]   Booch, G.: Object-Oriented Analysis and Design with Applications, Second Edition. Benjamin-Cummings, (1994)

[Bud95]   Budd, T.: Multiparadigm Programming in Leda. Addison-Wesley, (1995)

[Can82]   Cannon, H.: Flavors: A non-hierarchical approach to object-oriented programming. Symbolics Inc., (1982)

[Car84]   Cardelli, L.: A Semantics of Multiple Inheritance. In Proc. Intl. Symposium on Semantics of Data Types, (1984) 51–67

[Cas95]   Castagna, G.: Covariance and Contravariance: Conflict without a Cause. ACM TOPLAS, 17(3), (1995) 431–447

[CC89]   Canning, P., Cook, W., et al.: F-Bounded Polymorphism for Object-Oriented Programming. In Proc. FPCLA, (1989) 273–280

[CCP95]   Clack, C., Clayman, S., Parrott, D.: Lexical Profiling — Theory and Practice. Journal of Functional Programming, 5(2), (1995) 225-277

[CL91]   Cardelli, L., Longo, G.: A Semantic Basis for Quest. Journal of Functional Programming, 1(4), (1991) 417–458

[CL96]   Caseau, Y., Laburthe, F.: Introduction to the CLAIRE Programming Language. Technical Report, LIENS, (1996)

[CW85]   Cardelli, L., Wegner, P.: On understanding types, data abstraction, and polymorphism. Computing Surveys, 17(4), (1985) 471–522

[DM82]   Damas, L., Milner, R.: Principal type schemes for functional programs. In Proc. 9th POPL, (1982) 207–212

[DV96]   Dami, L., Vitek, J.: Introduction to HOP, a Functional and Object-Oriented Language. Submitted for publication, (1996)

[DY94]   Drossopoulou, S., Yang, D.: ST&T: Smalltalk with Types. Technical Report DOC 94/11, Imperial College, (1994)

[DY96]   Drossopoulou, S., Yang, D.: Permissive Types. Proc. 3rd FOOL, (1996)

[GJL87]   Gelernter, D., Jagannathan, S., London, T.: Environments as First Class Objects. In Proc. 14th POPL, (1987) 98–100

[GR83]   Goldberg, A., Robson, D.: Smalltalk-80: The Language and its Implementation. Addison-Wesley, (1983)

[GWM93]   Goguen, J., Winkler, T., Meseguer, J., Futatsugi, K., Jouannaud, J.: Introducing OBJ. Tutorial and Manual, Computing Laboratory, Oxford University, (1993)

[HPW91]   Hudak, P., Peyton Jones, S., Wadler, P. (Eds): Report on the Programming Language Haskell. Department of Computing Science, University of Glasgow, (1991)

[Ler95]   Leroy, X.: Le systeme Caml Special Light: modules et compilation efficace en Caml. Research Report 2721, Institut National de Recherche en Informatique et Automatique (INRIA), (1995)

[Mey91]   Meyer, B.: Eiffel: The Language. Prentice Hall, (1991)

[MHH91]   Mugridge, W., Hosking, J., Hammer, J.: Multi-methods in a Statically-Typed Programming Language. In Proc. ECOOP'91, (1991)

[MMH91]   Mitchell, J., Meldal, S., Hadhav, N.: An Extension of Standard ML Modules with Subtyping and Inheritance. In Proc. 18th POPL, (1991)

[MTH90]   Milner, R., Tofte, M., Harper, R.: The Definition of Standard ML. MIT Press, (1990)

[Oor96]   Oortmerssen, W.: The Bla Language: Extending Functional Programming with First Class Environments. Masters thesis, Department of Computational Linguistics, University of Amsterdam, (1996)

[PM93]   Poswig, J., Moraga, C.: Incremental type systems and implicit parametric overloading in visual languages. IEEE Symposium on Visual Languages, (1993) 126–133

[RR96]   Reppy, J., Riecke, J.: Simple objects for Standard ML. In Proc. PLDI'97, (1997) 171–180

[RV96]   Remy, D., Vouillon, J.: Objective ML: A simple object-oriented extension of ML. In Proc. 3rd FOOL, (1996)

[Sar93]   Sargeant, J.: Uniting Functional and Object-Oriented Programming. In Proc. ISOTAS'93, LNCS 742, Springer-Verlag, (1993) 1–26

[SKA94]   Sargeant, J., Kirkham, C., Anderson, S.: The Uflow Computational Model and Intermediate Format. Technical Report UMCS-94-5-1, Department of Computer Science, University of Manchester, (1994)

[Soc93]   Socorro, A.: Design, implementation and evaluation of a declarative object-oriented programming language. DPhil thesis, Computing Laboratory, University of Oxford, (1993)

[Ste84]   Steele Jr, G.: Common LISP: The Language. Digital Press, (1984)

[Tur85]   Turner, D.: Functional Programs as Executable Specifications. In Hoare & Shepherdson (Eds), Mathematical Logic and Programming Languages, Prentice Hall, (1985)

[WB89]   Wadler, P., Blott, S.: How to make ad-hoc polymorphism less ad-hoc. In Proc. 16th POPL, (1989) 60–76

Active Patterns

Martin Erwig

FernUniversität Hagen, Praktische Informatik IV
58084 Hagen, Germany
erwig@fernuni-hagen.de

Abstract. Active patterns apply preprocessing functions to data type values before they are matched. This is of use for unfree data types where more than one representation exists for an abstract value: in many cases there is a specific representation for which function definitions become very simple, and active patterns just allow to assume this specific representation in function definitions. We define the semantics of active patterns and describe their implementation.

1 Introduction

Pattern matching is a well-appreciated concept of (functional) programming. It contributes to concise function definitions by implicitly decomposing data type values. In many cases, a large part of a function's definition is only needed to prepare for recursive application and to finally lead to a base case for which the definition itself is rather simple. Such function definitions could be simplified considerably if these preparatory computations could be factorized and given in a separate place. Recognizing that the same normalization is often used in more than one function definition this seems even more reasonable since avoiding code means reducing the risk of introducing programming errors.

We propose to hide these computations in the definition of a special kind of patterns that allow the programmer to assume the "simple base case" in a function definition. Consider, for example, the implementation of sets based on lists. Function definitions for membership test, insertion and deletion typically check whether the first list element equals the argument element to be searched, inserted, or deleted, and, depending on the result, a value is returned or the function being defined is recursively called. Given the following data type definition:[1]

```
datatype 'a set = Empty | Add of 'a * 'a set
```

the function definition, for example, for membership test is:

```
fun member x (Add (y,s)) = if x=y then true else member x s
  | member x Empty       = false
```

---

[1] Throughout this paper we will use ML syntax.

If we can use a pattern that, when it matches, guarantees that the required element is in the first position of the list, the function definition becomes remarkably simple. Assume for a moment we have already defined such a pattern, say Add' (x,s), which transforms any set value v matched against into a set-term Add (x,t) (if possible, that is, if x is contained in v). Then the definition of member is:

```
fun member x (Add' (x,s)) = true
  | member x s            = false
```

Informally, member now works as follows: when called with an element x and a set value v, the computational part of Add' is applied to v to move the item x to the first position. If this can be performed successfully, we know that x is contained in v, and thus we can simply return true. Moreover, the rest of v is bound to the variable s. Otherwise, that is, if v cannot be rearranged as demanded, the match fails and the second line of member applies. Under the assumption that lists representing sets do not contain duplicates (this has to be ensured by the insertion function) a function definition for deletion is simply given by:

```
fun delete x (Add' (x,s)) = s
  | delete x s            = s
```

Finally, insertion leaves a term already containing the element to be inserted unchanged or otherwise simply performs insertion by applying the Add-constructor.

```
fun insert x (Add' (x,s)) = Add (x,s)
  | insert x s            = Add (x,s)
```

The given function definitions come up to equational specifications of abstract data types, yet they are efficiently executable function definitions. Of course, the correctness of the above definitions critically depends on the proper definition for Add': on the one hand, the process of rearranging must preserve the represented set value, and on the other hand, rearrangement has to fail exactly if x is not contained in v.

Due to their computational content we call patterns like Add' *active patterns*. A definition of an active pattern actually consists of two parts: a *function* that performs the described rearrangement and an *interface* to the function that serves two purposes:

1. The interface defines the *syntax* of the pattern, that is, the actual appearance when used in the left hand side of a function definition. The appearance is derived from the constructor term produced by its function and differs only in the constructor name to distinguish it from an ordinary constructor term.[2]

---

[2] In this paper we use the convention that the pattern name is the constructor name followed by an apostrophe. This helps identifying the constructor which is actually to be expected at the position of an active pattern.

2. The interface introduces the *free variables* of the pattern's function, if there are any. Recall that the function transforms a term into a specific form which is often guided by an external value. (In the example above this was the element x.) This value might be a constant or a variable, which then appears free in the pattern function. We call these variable positions in an active pattern *free positions*.

The definition of an active pattern is introduced by the keyword pat. For example, the definition of Add' is:

```
pat Add' (x,_) =
    Add (y,s) => if x=y then Add (y,s)
                  else let val Add' (x,t)=s
                       in Add (x,Add (y,t)) end
```

Informally, the above code reads as follows: Add' is an active pattern, and the associated pattern function might use the free variable x. The function itself expects a term Add (y,s), and if x equals y, that term is already the result and the unbound variables of the pattern (the positions of which are indicated in the interface by an underscore) are bound to the corresponding parts of the term. If $x \neq y$, the pattern function searches for x in s, that is, s is rearranged by recursively matching the active pattern Add'. If this succeeds, x is swapped with y, yielding the desired result. Thus if x is contained in the argument term, it will "bubble up" by recursively being exchanged with preceding elements in the term. Note that the function expects a term Add (y,s), that is, it fails for Empty which means that if x is not found in the term, the function would usually (that is, according to the semantics of Standard ML) raise a Match exception. But this is handled by the semantics to move to the next case (following the current active pattern) in the function definition.

It might seem the described effects could also be achieved by a language extension allowing just repeated variables in patterns, but this is not the case, since plain non-linear patterns miss the computational part of active patterns, that is, they match only if the argument is already in the desired shape. For example, member 2 (Add (1,Add (2,Empty))) correctly yields true for the definition with active patterns, but it gives false with just repeated variables in patterns which are merely checked for equality.

As in the above example, the work of active patterns is often guided by an external value which results in repeated variables in patterns, but active patterns do not always require non-linear patterns. Consider, for example, the implementation of queues by two lists [Bur82]. The first list contains the front part of the queue, and the second list contains the rear part of the queue in reverse order. This makes it possible to append new elements by simply consing to the second list while dequeuing can still be performed by simply removing the first element of the first list. Now when the first list is empty, it is exchanged with the reverse of the second list. We use the following data type.

```
datatype 'a queue = Q of 'a list * 'a list
```

Appending to the queue needs no active pattern at all, the definition is:

```
fun append x (Q (f,r)) = Q (f,x::r)
```

Using a pattern that asserts the first list is not empty:

```
pat Q' (_,_) = (Q ([],r)) => Q (rev r,[])
           | q              => q
```

inspection and deletion of the front element is now very simple:

```
fun front   (Q' (x::_,_)) = x
fun dequeue (Q' (x::f,r)) = Q (f,r)
```

Here the rearrangement of the data type value just depends on the value itself, no external value is needed, and patterns stay linear. Another example is the implementation of priority queues based on lists. There an active pattern has to move the list's minimum to the front which does not require an external value either.

In the next section we consider more applications of active patterns, and in Section 3 we define static and dynamic semantics of a core language containing active patterns. In Section 4 we show a straightforward implementation of active patterns using a rather simple source code transformation. We also sketch a fusion algorithm that is able to optimize some function definitions very well. We comment on related work in Section 5, and some conclusions are drawn in Section 6.

2 More Examples

Active patterns can be used to write highly concise function definitions. We illustrate this with an implementation of binary search trees.

Trees are represented by the following data type.

```
datatype tree = Nil | Node of int * tree * tree
```

Now we can define an active pattern Node' that realizes a generalized form of rotation for moving a specific node to the root:

```
pat Node' (x,_,_) = (t as Node (y,l,r)) =>
    if x=y then t else
    if x<y then let val Node' (x,l',r') = l
                in Node (x,l',Node (y,r',r)) end
           else let val Node' (x,l',r') = r
                in Node (x,Node (y,l,l'),r') end
```

Using this active pattern the code for testing membership in a tree looks very similar to the definition given for member:

```
fun isin x (Node' (x,_,_)) = true
  | isin x _                = false
```

More interesting is the function for deletion. The definition employs a function delmin that deletes the minimum from a binary tree and returns the minimum itself and the remaining tree:

```
fun delmin (Node (x,Nil,r)) = (x,r)
  | delmin (Node (x,l,r))   = let val (m,s) = delmin l
                              in (m,Node (x,s,r)) end
```

Now the function remove can be defined by:

```
fun remove x (Node' (x,Nil,r)) = r
  | remove x (Node' (x,l,Nil)) = l
  | remove x (Node' (x,l,r))   = let val (m,s) = delmin r
                                 in Node (m,l,s) end
  | remove x t                 = t
```

This is already a quite compact definition. However, we can go even further by extending the data type by a new variant serving as an interface between remove and delmin.

```
datatype tree =
    Nil
  | Node   of int * tree * tree
  | DelMin of int * tree
```

This extension is not very problematic since it is only used locally within the definition of remove; isin (and also a possible function for insertion) are not affected. Now we can define an active pattern DelMin' for extracting the minimum of a tree by returning a term DelMin (i,t).

```
pat DelMin' (x,_) =
       Node (x,Nil,r) => DelMin (x,r)
     | Node (x,l,r)   => let val DelMin' (m,s) = l
                         in DelMin (m,Node (x,s,r)) end
```

This could also be specified by using the active pattern recursively in the LHS:

```
pat DelMin' (_,_) =
       Node (x,Nil,r)             => DelMin (x,r)
     | Node (x,DelMin' (m,s),r) => DelMin (m,Node (x,s,r))
```

Now, remove can be defined even more succinctly:

```
fun remove x (Node' (x,Nil,r)) = r
  | remove x (Node' (x,l,Nil)) = l
  | remove x (Node' (x,l,DelMin' (m,s))) = Node (m,l,s)
  | remove x t = t
```

Another interesting application area for active patterns are graphs: in order to realize graph algorithms in functional languages it is convenient to view a graph inductively as a term Graph (v,p,s,g) adding a node v with predecessors p and successors s to another graph g. Now many graph algorithms traverse graphs in a particular node order. This means to access a graph repeatedly at specific nodes, which is possible by an active pattern Graph' having v as a free variable. This is explained in more detail in [Erw97].

3 Syntax and Semantics

In the following we consider the language defined in Figure 1.[3] As usual we have constants, variables, abstraction, and application. Tuples are needed to build data type terms. In addition to value declarations, local definitions for active patterns are also possible. Both kinds of let-expressions allow for recursive definitions.

exp	$::=$	con		pat	$::=$	$atpat$
	$\mid$	var			$\mid$	$cpat$
	$\mid$	$(exp_1,\ldots,exp_n)$		$cpat$	$::=$	$con\ atpat$
	$\mid$	$exp\ exp$		$atpat$	$::=$	$\_$
	$\mid$	fn $match$			$\mid$	con
	$\mid$	let val $pat=exp$ in exp end			$\mid$	var
	$\mid$	let pat $cpat=match$ in exp end			$\mid$	$(pat_1,\ldots,pat_n)$
$match$	$::=$	$rule\ \langle\mid match\rangle$				
$rule$	$::=$	pat => exp				

Fig. 1. Syntax of Expressions and Patterns.

Note that a function does not simply abstract over a variable, but is given by a collection of rules where a rule associates an expression with a pattern. This is the place where active patterns come into play. A pattern is either atomic, or it is a constructor pattern which is an application of a constructor to an atomic pattern. An atomic pattern is a wildcard, a variable, or a tuple of patterns.

The use of repeated variables in patterns is restricted to the following case: in the preorder traversal of a pattern, the first occurence of each variable must be in non-free position (that is, not matching a parameter of a pattern function), and each further occurrence must be in free position. This guarantees that repeated

---

[3] Phrases enclosed in angle bracket are optional.

variables are just used to supply parameters for active patterns.

For example, the function definition for member using this austere syntax is:[4]

```
let pat Add' (x,_) =
    Add (y,s) => if x=y then Add (y,s)
                        else let val Add' (x,t)=s
                             in Add (x,Add (y,t)) end
  in
let val member = fn x =>
         fn (Add' (x,s)) => true
          | s            => false
  in
      exp
end end
```

3.1 Static semantics

The static semantics include, of course, type inference rules, but especially for active patterns there is a more fine-grained analysis possible which we call "constructor checking". We begin with the description of the type system. The language of types is given in Figure 2.

$$
\begin{array}{llll}
\tau & ::= & \alpha & \text{type variable} \\
& | & \tau \to \tau & \text{function type} \\
& | & (\tau_1, \ldots, \tau_n) & \text{tuple type } (n > 1) \\
& | & \langle \tau \rangle \ con & \text{data type} \\
\sigma & ::= & \forall \alpha_1, \ldots, \alpha_n.\tau & \text{type scheme}
\end{array}
$$

Fig. 2. Types.

The typing rules for constants, variables, application and local value definition are standard. Type checking for abstractions over patterns might not be so well-known, and this is explained best by dealing with two kinds of sentences in the type inference system: (1) $A \vdash exp : \tau$ says that expression exp has type τ under the set of assumptions A. Usually, A is a finite map from variables and constructors to types, but for a constructor of an active pattern we store its type together with its interface in A. (2) For a pattern we derive, in addition to its type, also a set of assumptions (for the variables occurring within the pattern). We write such assertions as $A \vdash pat \hookrightarrow (A', \tau)$.

Since we have to treat repeated variables in patterns we must be careful about the definition of the union of two assumptions. Defining $A + A'$ as usual by "overwriting" the definitions in A by those in A' leaves some type errors

---

[4] Note that we still keep conditionals. To be precise, if c then e_1 else e_2 translates to (fn true => e_1 | false => e_2) c.

undetected. We thus require identity on common subdomains, that is:

$$(A + A')(x) = \begin{cases} A(x) & \text{if } x \in dom(A) \wedge (x \in dom(A') \Rightarrow A(x) = A'(x)) \\ A'(x) & \text{if } x \in (dom(A') - dom(A)) \\ \bot & \text{otherwise} \end{cases}$$

The type system is given in Figure 3, and the derivation of assertions from patterns is shown in Figure 4.

$$
\text{CON}\vdash \frac{A(con) \succ \tau}{A \vdash con : \tau}
\qquad\qquad
\text{VAR}\vdash \frac{A(var) \succ \tau}{A \vdash var : \tau}
$$

$$
\text{TUP}\vdash \frac{A \vdash exp_1 : \tau_1 \quad \cdots \quad A \vdash exp_n : \tau_n}{A \vdash (exp_1, \ldots, exp_n) : (\tau_1, \ldots, \tau_n)}
$$

$$
\text{APP}\vdash \frac{A \vdash exp : \tau' \rightarrow \tau \quad A \vdash exp' : \tau'}{A \vdash exp\ exp' : \tau}
$$

$$
\text{ABS}\vdash \frac{A \vdash match : \tau}{A \vdash \mathbf{fn}\ match : \tau}
\qquad
\text{MATCH}\vdash \frac{A \vdash rule : \tau \quad A \vdash match : \tau}{A \vdash rule \mid match : \tau}
$$

$$
\text{RULE}\vdash \frac{A \vdash pat \hookrightarrow (A', \tau') \quad A + A' \vdash exp : \tau}{A \vdash pat \Rightarrow exp : \tau' \rightarrow \tau}
$$

$$
\text{LET}\vdash \frac{A \vdash pat \hookrightarrow (A', \tau') \quad A + A' \vdash exp' : \tau' \quad A + gen(A, A') \vdash exp : \tau}{A \vdash \mathbf{let\ val}\ pat{=}exp'\ \mathbf{in}\ exp\ \mathbf{end} : \tau}
$$

$$
\text{LETP}\vdash \frac{A(con') = \tau'' \rightarrow \tau' \quad A \vdash atpat \hookrightarrow (A', \tau'') \quad A + A' \vdash match : \tau' \rightarrow \tau' \quad A + \{con' \mapsto (gen(A, \tau'' \rightarrow \tau'), atpat)\} \vdash exp : \tau}{A \vdash \mathbf{let\ pat}\ con'\ atpat{=}match\ \mathbf{in}\ exp\ \mathbf{end} : \tau}
$$

Fig. 3. Type System.

The operation *gen* in rules LET$\vdash$ and LETP$\vdash$ is for the generalization of types to type schemes so that different occurrences of variables and patterns can be instantiated to different types. Let $\alpha_1, \ldots, \alpha_k$ be the type variables that are contained in type τ, but not in the assumption A. Then $gen(A, \tau) = \forall \alpha_1, \ldots, \alpha_k.\tau$. Now *gen* is extended in a natural way to assumptions. For

$$A' = \{var_1 \mapsto \tau_1, \ldots, var_n \mapsto \tau_n\}$$

we have

$$gen(A, A') = \{var_1 \mapsto gen(A, \tau_1), \ldots, var_n \mapsto gen(A, \tau_n)\}$$

Note also in rules LET$\vdash$ and LETP$\vdash$ that using assumptions $A + A'$ in the inference of *exp'*, respectively *match*, accounts for recursive value and pattern definitions. Apart from this, A' is needed in the inference of *match* to provide types for its free variables. However, A' is not used in the inference of *exp* in rule LETP$\vdash$, to ensure that free variables of *match* are defined within *exp*; only the generalized type of the active pattern's constructor might be used. In addition to this type the interface (*atpat*) is also put into the assumption to enable the identification of variables in free positions within the rule ACTIVE$'_\vdash$. This is done as follows: variables in the actual pattern *atpat* that are in free position with respect to the interface *atpat'* are determined by a function F defined by:

$$
\begin{array}{rcl}
F(var', var) & = & \{var\} \\
F(con\ atpat', con\ atpat) & = & F(atpat', atpat) \\
F((pat'_1, \ldots, pat'_n), (pat_1, \ldots, pat_n)) & = & \cup_{i=1}^n F(pat_i, pat'_i)
\end{array}
$$

In all other cases, $F(pat, pat') = \emptyset$. The assumption A' is then restricted to those variables not contained in this set. This is needed to reject definitions, such as fun foo (Add' (x,_)) = x, which would lead to a runtime error because x is undefined.

$$
\text{WILD}'_\vdash \quad \frac{}{A \vdash \_ \hookrightarrow (\{\}, \tau)} \qquad\qquad \text{VAR}'_\vdash \quad \frac{}{A \vdash var \hookrightarrow (\{var \mapsto \tau\}, \tau)}
$$

$$
\text{CON}'_\vdash \quad \frac{A(con) \succ \tau}{A \vdash con \hookrightarrow (\{\}, \tau)}
$$

$$
\text{TUP}'_\vdash \quad \frac{A \vdash pat_1 \hookrightarrow (A_1, \tau_1) \quad \ldots \quad A \vdash pat_n \hookrightarrow (A_n, \tau_n)}{A \vdash (pat_1, \ldots, pat_n) \hookrightarrow (A_1 + \ldots + A_n, (\tau_1, \ldots, \tau_n))}
$$

$$
\text{ACTIVE}'_\vdash \quad \frac{A(con) = (\tau', atpat') \quad \tau' \succ \tau'' \to \tau \quad A \vdash atpat \hookrightarrow (A', \tau'')}{A \vdash con\ atpat \hookrightarrow (A'|_{dom(A')-F(atpat', atpat)}, \tau)}
$$

$$
\text{CPAT}'_\vdash \quad \frac{A(con) \succ \tau' \to \tau \quad A \vdash atpat \hookrightarrow (A', \tau')}{A \vdash con\ atpat \hookrightarrow (A', \tau)}
$$

Fig. 4. Derivation of Assumptions.

As already mentioned, within static elaboration we can actually do a bit more for active patterns than just type checking: we know that all rules of a pattern's match have to build a term of exactly the same shape (which additionally has to match the pattern's interface). For example, each case in the function of Add' – actually, there is just one case – has to return a term with an outermost Add-constructor; an Empty-constructor, which would be legal according to the type system, makes no sense here and should be prevented.

We can formalize this *constructor checking* by re-using the above type system in a slightly modified way: we simply assume for each constructor *con* the "type" *con* instead of the associated data type (resolving name clashes between constructor and type names appropriately), that is, rule CON$_\vdash$ changes to

$$
\frac{A(con) = con}{A \vdash con :: con}
$$

For example, whereas in the type system true and false would be both mapped to the type `bool`, the modified "constructor system" infers for `true` the constructor `true` and for `false` the constructor `false`. Now, within this modified rule system the sentence $exp :: con$ states that the outermost constructor of expression exp is con.

Constructor checking actually has two applications: first, we can strengthen the type checking of active patterns by enforcing equal constructors in all rules of the pattern function. This is reflected by the adding the following precondition to rule LETP$\vdash$:

$$\{\,\} \vdash match :: \tau' \to con$$

This means that in addition to proving a function type for $match$ we must also be able to infer a corresponding constructor. (The name con is chosen to distinguish the constructor from con', which is the name of the active pattern.)

The second application of constructor checking is found in the transformation of active patterns: there we have to refer to a pattern's associated constructor (for example, `Add` is the associated constructor of `Add'`). This can be expressed as follows. If con' is defined by the expression `let pat` con' `atpat`=$match$ `in` exp `end`, the associated constructor of con' is con if $\{\,\} \vdash match :: \tau' \to con$.

Though described here as a separate phase, in practice constructor checking should be integrated with type checking.

3.2 Operational semantics

An expression is evaluated call-by-value relative to an environment E and reduces to a value which is either a constant, a tuple of values, or a closure. A closure is a triple $clos = (match, E, E')$ where E captures the environment at the time of the definition of $match$ and E' contains definitions for variables that are bound to recursive functions. Terms (values of data types) are represented by pairs (constructor, argument).

Moreover, we need a value representation for evaluated active patterns since in addition to the pattern function (which reduces to a closure) we need the interface in the evaluation, too. This is used when in an application of an active pattern an expression exp appears at the position of a free variable var. Then we must use the additional binding $\{var \mapsto v\}$ (v being the value of exp) in the evaluation of the active pattern. In order to identify the free variable positions we thus need the interface when applying active patterns.

A pattern is evaluated against a value and yields an environment giving bindings for its variables. However, this is only true if the pattern really matches the value, otherwise the special object FAIL is returned. FAIL is not a value, it is a semantic object that controls the order of pattern matching. FAIL propagates to rule MATCH$_\Rightarrow$ expressing that when a rule successfully matches, then the obtained result is the result of the whole match and if a rule does not match, that is, when it yields FAIL, the remaining match is evaluated. If FAIL is not caught eventually by rule MATCH$_\Rightarrow$, this is left an undefined situation by our semantics and can be considered a runtime error. (In the semantics of Standard ML [MTH90], a match exception is generated.) In the semantic rules we make use of what we will call the "FAIL-assumption": if any precondition of a rule yields FAIL, then the conclusion also yields FAIL. Places where FAIL might occur are indicated by appending "/FAIL" to the usually expected object. The semantics is given in Figure 5.

$$
\text{CON}_\Rightarrow \quad \frac{}{E \vdash con \Rightarrow con} \qquad \text{TUP}_\Rightarrow \quad \frac{E \vdash exp_1 \Rightarrow v_1 \quad \dots \quad E \vdash exp_n \Rightarrow v_n}{E \vdash (exp_1, \dots, exp_n) \Rightarrow (v_1, \dots, v_n)}
$$

$$
\text{VAR}_\Rightarrow \quad \frac{E(var) = v}{E \vdash var \Rightarrow v} \qquad \text{ABS}_\Rightarrow \quad \frac{}{E \vdash \mathbf{fn}\ match \Rightarrow (match, E, \{\})}
$$

$$
\text{APP}_\Rightarrow \quad \frac{E \vdash exp \Rightarrow (match, E', E'') \qquad E \vdash exp' \Rightarrow v' \qquad E' + \mathbf{rec}\ E'', v' \vdash match \Rightarrow v}{E \vdash exp\ exp' \Rightarrow v}
$$

$$
\frac{E \vdash exp \Rightarrow con \qquad E \vdash exp' \Rightarrow v}{E \vdash exp\ exp' \Rightarrow (con, v)}
$$

$$
\text{LET}_\Rightarrow \quad \frac{E \vdash exp' \Rightarrow v' \qquad E, v' \vdash pat \Rightarrow E' \qquad E + \mathbf{rec}\ E' \vdash exp \Rightarrow v}{E \vdash \mathbf{let\ val}\ pat{=}exp'\ \mathbf{in}\ exp\ \mathbf{end} \Rightarrow v}
$$

$$
\text{LETP}_\Rightarrow \quad \frac{E + \mathbf{rec}\ \{con' \mapsto (atpat, (match, E, \{\}))\} \vdash exp \Rightarrow v}{E \vdash \mathbf{let\ pat}\ con'\ atpat{=}match\ \mathbf{in}\ exp\ \mathbf{end} \Rightarrow v}
$$

$$
\text{MATCH}_\Rightarrow \quad \frac{E, v \vdash rule \Rightarrow v'}{E, v \vdash rule\ |\ match \Rightarrow v'} \qquad \frac{E, v \vdash rule \Rightarrow \text{FAIL} \qquad E, v \vdash match \Rightarrow v'}{E, v \vdash rule\ |\ match \Rightarrow v'}
$$

$$
\text{RULE}_\Rightarrow \quad \frac{E, v \vdash pat \Rightarrow E'/\text{FAIL} \qquad E + E' \vdash exp \Rightarrow v'}{E, v \vdash pat\ \texttt{=>}\ exp \Rightarrow v'/\text{FAIL}}
$$

Fig. 5. Operational Semantics.

The operator rec employed in rules APP$_\Rightarrow$ and LET$_\Rightarrow$ performs a one-step unfolding of recursive function definitions, that is, with

$$
\text{rec}(E, v) = \begin{cases} (match, E', E) & \text{if } v = (match, E', E'') \\ (pat, (match, E', E)) & \text{if } v = (pat, (match, E', E'')) \\ v & \text{otherwise} \end{cases}
$$

we obtain for an environment $E = \{var_1 \mapsto v_1, \dots, var_n \mapsto v_n\}$ the collection of unrolled definitions $\text{rec}\ E = \{var_1 \mapsto \text{rec}(E, v_1), \dots, var_n \mapsto \text{rec}(E, v_n)\}$.

In rule LETP$_\Rightarrow$ the interface and function definition of the active pattern are pushed into the environment in which expression exp is to be evaluated. This definition is used in rule ACTIVE$'_\Rightarrow$ (see below).

The pattern matching semantics are given separately in Figure 6. The last three rules describe the matching of patterns against constructor terms (data type values). Rule ACTIVE$'_\Rightarrow$ describes the essence of active pattern matching: to match an active pattern $con'\ atpat$ against a value v the pattern function $match$ obtained from the environment E (1st precondition) is used to transform v into a term (con, v') (3rd precondition). However, before *match* can be applied, we must ensure that bindings exist for all free variables of *match*. This is done by matching the actual "pattern call" *atpat* against the interface of con' (2nd precondition). To describe this we need another rule system defining the matching of patterns against patterns, see Figure 7. Note that matching the constructor of v, which happens to be *con*, is done during the matching of *match*. Thus v' denotes just the argument of the rearranged term. Finally, the variables of *atpat* are bound by matching *atpat* against v' (last precondition). Rule CPAT$'_\Rightarrow$ applies whenever *con* is not defined in the environment E. In that case the constructor of the term to be matched must be the same as in the pattern, otherwise matching fails.

$$\text{WILD}'_\Rightarrow \quad \frac{}{E, v \vdash \_ \Rightarrow \{\}} \qquad\qquad \text{VAR}'_\Rightarrow \quad \frac{}{E, v \vdash var \Rightarrow \{var \mapsto v\}}$$

$$\text{CON}'_\Rightarrow \quad \frac{}{E, con \vdash con \Rightarrow \{\}} \qquad \frac{con' \neq con}{E, con' \vdash con \Rightarrow \text{FAIL}}$$

$$\text{TUP}'_\Rightarrow \quad \frac{E, v_1 \vdash pat_1 \Rightarrow E_1/\text{FAIL} \quad\cdots\quad E, v_n \vdash pat_n \Rightarrow E_n/\text{FAIL}}{E, (v_1, \ldots, v_n) \vdash (pat_1, \ldots, pat_n) \Rightarrow E_1 + \ldots + E_n/\text{FAIL}}$$

$$\text{ACTIVE}'_\Rightarrow \quad \frac{\begin{array}{c} E(con') = (atpat', (match, E_1, E_2)) \qquad E, atpat \vdash atpat' \Rightarrow E_P \\ E + E_1 + \text{rec } E_2 + E_P, v \vdash match \Rightarrow (con, v')/\text{FAIL} \\ E, v' \vdash atpat \Rightarrow E'/\text{FAIL} \end{array}}{E, v \vdash con' \; atpat \Rightarrow E'/\text{FAIL}}$$

$$\text{CPAT}'_\Rightarrow \quad \frac{con \notin dom(E) \qquad E, v \vdash atpat \Rightarrow E'/\text{FAIL}}{E, (con, v) \vdash con \; atpat \Rightarrow E'/\text{FAIL}}$$

$$\frac{con \notin dom(E) \qquad con \neq con'}{E, (con', v) \vdash con \; atpat \Rightarrow \text{FAIL}}$$

Fig. 6. Pattern Matching Semantics.

When matching patterns against patterns the main case is matching a variable *var* (of the interface) against another pattern *pat*: rule VAR$''_\Rightarrow$ expresses that this results in a binding $\{var \mapsto v\}$ whenever *pat* reduces to value v. This is well-defined since, disregarding the wildcard, patterns make up a subset of expressions. (Formally, we need yet another rule system defining evaluation of such patterns, but actually this is perfectly done by the semantics of Figure 5.) The meaning of the remaining rules are: matching a wildcard does not give any binding (WILD$''_\Rightarrow$), and recursive application for tuples (TUP$''_\Rightarrow$) and terms (CPAT$''_\Rightarrow$).

4 Implementation

In the following we define a function $\mathcal{T}$ that transforms an expression possibly containing active patterns into a semantically equivalent expression without active patterns.

$$\text{WILD}''_{\Rightarrow} \quad \frac{}{E, pat \vdash \_ \Rightarrow \{\,\}} \qquad\qquad \text{VAR}''_{\Rightarrow} \quad \frac{pat \neq \_ \qquad E \vdash pat \Rightarrow v}{E, pat \vdash var \Rightarrow \{var \mapsto v\}}$$

$$\text{TUP}''_{\Rightarrow} \quad \frac{E, pat_1 \vdash pat'_1 \Rightarrow E_1 \quad \ldots \quad E, pat_n \vdash pat'_n \Rightarrow E_n}{E, (pat_1, \ldots, pat_n) \vdash (pat'_1, \ldots, pat'_n) \Rightarrow E_1 + \ldots + E_n}$$

$$\text{CPAT}''_{\Rightarrow} \quad \frac{E, atpat \vdash atpat' \Rightarrow E'}{E, con\ atpat \vdash con\ atpat' \Rightarrow E'}$$

Fig. 7. Matching Pattern Calls Against Interfaces.

The idea is to replace active patterns by functions that perform the desired rearrangement for matching values and leave other values unchanged. Uses of active patterns are then replaced by applications of these functions. Consider the following pattern definition

```
let pat con' atpat=match
```

where $var_1, \ldots, var_n$ is the sequence of free variables of $atpat$ (obtained by a preorder traversal). Then

$$\mathcal{P}(atpat) = \texttt{fn}\ var_1\ \texttt{=>}\ \ldots\ \texttt{=>}\ \texttt{fn}\ var_n\ \texttt{=>}$$

denotes the additional parameters of the pattern function that are needed in the definition of the corresponding function. The definition is:

```
let val con'=P(atpat) fn match | x => x
```

Since *match* is only defined for one constructor of a data type we append a rule realizing an identity mapping to allow non-matching values to pass con' unchanged. The need for this can be seen as follows: whereas a non-matching active pattern simply moves evaluation to the next case of the function definition, an application of the corresponding function would be undefined.

Active patterns can be used in two ways: (i) on the LHS of a rule, and (ii) in value definitions. When used in a rule

```
con' atpat => exp
```

the LHS is replaced by a fresh variable $\overline{var}$ that does not yet occur anywhere in the currently transformed expression. This variable matches any value, say v. The transformation of the value and the pattern matching both happens on the RHS: first, the newly defined function con' is applied to $\overline{var}$ (which is bound to v) and possibly additional arguments. If v matches the data type case of con', it is transformed into the representation v', otherwise v stays unchanged. After that the actual pattern matching takes place. In the first case, v' must be matched against the (non-active) pattern $con\ atpat$, and exp is returned.

Otherwise, no rearrangement did happen, and the match following the current rule must be applied to v. We can achieve this behavior by a function consisting of a rule for pattern *con atpat* and the rest of the current match. Thus, as a first approximation, the transformation of the rule gives something like:

$$\overline{var} \Rightarrow (\texttt{fn}\ con\ atpat \Rightarrow \langle 1 \rangle\ \langle 2 \rangle)\ (con'\ \langle 3 \rangle\ var)$$

$con = \mathcal{C}(con')$ denotes the constructor associated with the active pattern. We assume that the function $\mathcal{C}$ has been determined by the type/constructor checking phase as described in Section 3.1.

In the transformed expression, $\langle 1 \rangle$ denotes the transformation of *exp*, and $\langle 2 \rangle$ stands for the transformation of the remaining match, which itself is an abstraction applied to *var*. Finally, $\langle 3 \rangle$ denotes the additional arguments for the free variables of con''s pattern interface. These values are given by sub-expressions of the currently transformed rule's LHS. More precisely, each parameter var_i gets its argument from the expression exp_i that occurs (in the rule's LHS) in the same position as var_i in the pattern interface. We can compute all arguments in the correct order by performing a parallel preorder traversal of the pattern interface and *atpat*: whenever we encounter a free variable in the interface, we have found in *atpat* the corresponding expression. Let $\mathcal{I}(con')$ denote the interface of the active pattern constructor con' (like $\mathcal{C}$, $\mathcal{I}$ is also given by static elaboration). Then the function $\mathcal{A}$ computes the sequence of argument expressions with respect to a pattern interface as follows (ε denotes the empty word).

$$
\begin{aligned}
\mathcal{A}(\_, exp) &= \varepsilon \\
\mathcal{A}(var, exp) &= exp \\
\mathcal{A}((pat_1, \ldots, pat_n), (exp_1, \ldots, exp_n)) &= \mathcal{A}(pat_1, exp_1) \ldots \mathcal{A}(pat_n, exp_n) \\
\mathcal{A}(con\ atpat, con\ exp) &= \mathcal{A}(atpat, exp)
\end{aligned}
$$

Thus, the missing arguments are given by the expression $\mathcal{A}(\mathcal{I}(con'), atpat)$.

Finally, consider the transformation of a value declaration containing an active pattern, such as

```
let val con' atpat=exp' in exp end
```

The rearrangement of the active pattern happens by applying con' to $\mathcal{A}(\mathcal{I}(con'), atpat)$ (giving the arguments for the additional parameters) and to the translation of exp'. Again, exp' might not match *con*, in which case it should pass unchanged. So we again transform the value declaration into a function application with two cases: one for the pattern *con atpat* and one for other values.

The complete translation algorithm is shown in Figure 8. The angle brackets in the translation of rules say that the enclosed code is only produced if *match* is not empty, that is, consists of one or more rules.

A possible optimization is to group a sequence of function equations with the same active pattern con' together to avoid possibly repeated calls to the function con'. To illustrate the algorithm, we transform the definition of **member**. We apply

$$\mathcal{T}\,[\![con]\!] \quad\qquad = \quad con$$

$$\mathcal{T}\,[\![var]\!] \quad\qquad = \quad var$$

$$\mathcal{T}\,[\![(exp_1,\ldots,exp_n)]\!] \ = \ (\mathcal{T}\,[\![exp_1]\!],\ldots,\mathcal{T}\,[\![exp_n]\!])$$

$$\mathcal{T}\,[\![exp\ exp']\!] \quad\quad = \quad \mathcal{T}\,[\![exp]\!]\ \mathcal{T}\,[\![exp']\!]$$

$$\mathcal{T}\,[\![\mathtt{fn}\ match]\!] \quad\quad = \quad \mathtt{fn}\ \mathcal{T}\,[\![match]\!]$$

$\mathcal{T}\,[\![pat \Rightarrow exp\ \langle\mid match\rangle]\!]\ =$

$$\begin{cases}
\overline{var}\ \Rightarrow\ \mathcal{T}\,[\![(\mathtt{fn}\ con\ atpat \Rightarrow exp & \text{if } pat = con'\ atpat\\
\qquad\qquad \langle\mid\ \_\ \Rightarrow\ (\mathtt{fn}\ match)\ var\,)] & \quad \wedge\,\mathcal{C}(con') = con\\
\qquad (con'\ \mathcal{A}(\mathcal{I}(con'),atpat)\ var) & \\[4pt]
pat\ \Rightarrow\ \mathcal{T}\,[\![exp]\!]\ \langle\mid\ \mathcal{T}\,[\![match]\!]\rangle & \text{otherwise}
\end{cases}$$

$\mathcal{T}\,[\![\mathtt{let\ val}\ pat{=}exp'\ \mathtt{in}\ exp\ \mathtt{end}]\!]\ =$

$$\begin{cases}
\mathtt{let\ val}\ con\ atpat{=}con'\ \mathcal{A}(\mathcal{I}(con'),atpat)\ \mathcal{T}\,[\![exp']\!] & \text{if } pat = con'\ atpat\\
\quad \mathtt{in}\ \mathcal{T}\,[\![exp]\!]\ \mathtt{end} & \quad \wedge\,\mathcal{C}(con') = con\\[4pt]
\mathtt{let\ val}\ pat{=}\mathcal{T}\,[\![exp']\!]\ \mathtt{in}\ \mathcal{T}\,[\![exp]\!]\ \mathtt{end} & \text{otherwise}
\end{cases}$$

$\mathcal{T}\,[\![\mathtt{let\ pat}\ con'\ atpat{=}match\ \mathtt{in}\ exp\ \mathtt{end}]\!]\ =$
$\quad \mathtt{let\ val}\ con'{=}\mathcal{P}(atpat)\ \mathtt{fn}\ \mathcal{T}\,[\![match]\!]\ \mid\ \mathtt{x}\ \Rightarrow\ \mathtt{x}\ \mathtt{in}\ \mathcal{T}\,[\![exp]\!]\ \mathtt{end}$

Fig. 8. Transformation of Active Patterns.

$\mathcal{T}$ to the following expression.

```
let pat Add' (x,_)=add in
let val member=memb
 in exp end end
```

where *add* and *memb* represent the parts of the corresponding expression from the beginning of Section 3.

In the first step we obtain the expression:

```
let val Add'=𝒫((x,_)) fn 𝒯 [add] | x => x
 in 𝒯 [let val member=memb in exp end] end
```

which immediately transforms to:

```
let val Add'=fn x => fn 𝒯 [add] | x => x
 in let val member=𝒯 [memb]
 in 𝒯 [exp] end end
```

Next we consider the translation of *add* and *memb* separately. Since the LHS of match *add* is not an active pattern $\mathcal{T}\,[\![add]\!]$ gives:

```
      Add (y,s) => T [ if x=y then Add (y,s)
                            else let val Add' (x,t)=s
                                 in Add (x,Add (y,t)) end ]
```

which is

```
      Add (y,s) => if x=y then Add (y,s)
                        else T [ let val Add' (x,t)=s
                                 in Add (x,Add (y,t)) end ]
```

With $\mathcal{C}(\text{Add'}) = \text{Add}$, $\mathcal{I}(\text{Add'}) = (\text{x},\_)$, and $\mathcal{A}((\text{x},\_),(\text{x},\text{t})) = \text{x}$ we obtain:

```
      let val Add (x,t) = Add' x s in Add (x,Add (y,t)) end
```

In the translation of *memb* the first abstraction over x is passed unchanged by $\mathcal{T}$. We get the expression:

```
      fn x => fn T [(Add' (x,s)) => true | s => false]
```

Now we let z be a fresh variable, and with $\mathcal{A}((\text{x},\_),(\text{x},\text{s})) = \text{x}$ we obtain:

```
      fn x => fn z =>
        (fn Add (x,s) => true | _ => (fn s => false) z) (Add' x z)
```

Summarizing, the complete translation is:

```
      let val Add'=fn x =>
            fn Add (y,s) => if x=y then Add (y,s) else
                                 let val Add (x,t) = Add' x s
                                 in Add (x,Add (y,t)) end
              | x            => x
        in
      let val member=fn x => fn z =>
            (fn Add (x,s) => true
              | _            => (fn s=>false) z) (Add' x z)
        in T [exp] end end
```

We recognize that the resulting function for member is not very efficient because of the terms that are unnecessarily built by Add': in the worst case (when x is the last element), the set representing list is duplicated. This is not surprising since we use a rather general rearrangement function (Add') which has to build a reorganized value in the computation of a specific task where that value itself is never needed. Is there a way to improve the function definitions so to avoid unnecessary computations? Immediately, the *deforestation* fusion technique of Wadler [Wad90] comes to mind. However, deforestation cannot be applied since the definition of Add' is not "treeless" (due to the term-producing Add'-call being an argument of another function call). The method of Chin [Chi92] is applicable, but it seems to ignore `Add'` during optimization since the definition of `Add'` produces function terms.

Still in search of the appropriate technique to apply we shortly sketch another fusion scheme that is tailored for the optimization of active patterns. (What follows is still under development, and some restrictions are expected to be dropped in future.) Consider the definition of a function f containing one rule with an active pattern con' $atpat$ => exp. The translation resulting from $\mathcal{T}$ gives something like

$$(\texttt{fn}\ con\ atpat\ \texttt{=>}\ exp\ |\ \ldots)\ (con'\ \ldots)$$

The goal is to fuse the definition of f for this case with the definition of the function con' to eliminate any computations for variables in the definition of con' that are not used in exp. This can be achieved by the following three fusion rules (in all other cases fusion is recursively applied to sub-expressions). A general precondition for the method is that there is at most one variable shared by $atpat$ and exp, that is, only one part of the term computed by con' is actually used within exp. This prevents the introduction of repeated computations.

(F1) Replace "global" terms[5] $con\ exp'$ in con' by a properly instantiated version of exp[6]

(F2) Replace recursive applications of con' by f.

(F3) Replace patterns $con\ pat$ in anonymous functions (resulting from the translation of `let val`-expressions) by patterns matching the results of exp.

The last rule deserves some comments: The need for replacing function patterns can be seen as follows: a con-pattern catches the result of a con'-call. Since con'-applications are replaced by f the cases in function patterns have to be adapted. In particular, since the pattern occurs in that case of f's definition where the active pattern was used, the corresponding result expression exp is relevant here. Now, if exp is a constant, say c, this is obviously the pattern to be substituted. More general, if we can determine that exp will return any constant of $c_1, \ldots, c_n$, we can replace the rule by a set of rules, each for one constant c_i. If exp is a variable var, the pattern is replaced by var. All other cases are not completely clear at the moment (except a straightforward extension to tuples), and we abort the fusion process in those cases.

Let us illustrate the fusion rules in the optimization of `member`. $\mathcal{F}[\![exp]\!]$ denotes the application of the fusion algorithm to expression exp. An implicit argument is the function definition being actually fused; this should be clear from the context. Recall the $\mathcal{T}$-translation of `Add'` from above. Fusion moves over abstraction and conditional, so we get the expression:

---

[5] These are terms that can be returned as a result of con'.

[6] Each (local) variable in exp is substituted by the matching sub-expression of exp', in the sense of matching $con\ exp'$ against $con\ atpat$ as defined in Figure 6.

```
fn x => fn Add (y,s) =>
         if x=y then F[[Add (y,s)]] else
           (fn F[[Add (x,t)]] => F[[Add (x,Add (y,t))]]
             | x              => x) F[[Add' x s]]
    | x            => x
```

For member we obtain the following fused sub-expressions/patterns:

$$
\begin{array}{llll}
\mathcal{F}[\![\text{Add } (y,s)]\!] & = & \text{true} & (F1)\\
\mathcal{F}[\![\text{Add } (x,t)]\!] & = & \text{true} & (F3)\\
\mathcal{F}[\![\text{Add } (x,\text{Add } (y,t))]\!] & = & \text{true} & (F1)\\
\mathcal{F}[\![\text{Add' } x\ s]\!] & = & \text{member } x\ s & (F2)
\end{array}
$$

This results in the function:

```
fn x => fn Add (y,s) => if x=y then true else
                         (fn true => true
                           | x      => x) member x s
     | x           => x
```

We see that no intermediate Add-terms are constructed. With some algebraic postprocessing we can arrive at the original member-definition without active patterns.

Currently, the presented fusion method is rather crude and somewhat limited. Algebraic transformations are needed to get concise definitions, and functions like insert cannot be optimized at all.

5   Related Work

Pattern matching with unfree data types has been addressed by Miranda *laws* [Tur85, Tho90], Wadler's *views* [Wad87], or the recent work of Burton and Cameron [BC93]. Common to all approaches is the mapping of equal terms to a canonical representation.

The demand for a canonical representation is a rather strong requirement which often entails a certain overspecification of the data type. For example, implementing sets by lists requires keeping lists in sorted order. This approach has the following two drawbacks:

1. *Overspecification restricts applicability.* Keeping elements sorted requires a comparison function on set elements. In contrast, working with unsorted lists only needs equality on list elements.
2. *Overspecification might need more computation than necessary.* All three set operations need linear time when implemented on base of sorted lists. With unsorted lists, member and delete are again linear, but insert takes just constant time if we allow duplicates.[7]

---

[7] However, if the number of duplicates is large compared to the size of the represented sets, then member and delete are no longer linear in the size of the represented set.

In contrast, active patterns do not require a canonical representation and thus offer more freedom in the implementation.

Views and Miranda laws both cause some trouble with equational reasoning because constructors of non-free data types can be used to construct values. This is overcome by the proposal of [BC93] where these constructors may be only used within patterns. We expect the same for active patterns since they too can only be used in patterns.

Context Patterns [Moh96] are intended to give direct access to arbitrary deeply nested sub-parts of terms, but they only work for free data types.

The *abstract value constructors* of [AR92] provide a kind of macro facility to denote terms in a more convenient (and abstract) way. However, no computations in the sense of changing the representation of the matched values are performed. We could cover abstract value constructors by active patterns if we dropped the restriction that the argument type must be the same as the result type. (We would have to adapt the semantics and the implementation.) The intent of active patterns is, however, different: they are meant as a device for abstracting data type laws and not as a macro language.

Finally, the *active destructors* introduced in [PGPN96] are essentially functions that can be used within patterns to produce bindings. Active destructors can perform computations much like active patterns, and they are even more general since they (like abstract value constructors) have no type restriction imposed. In [PGPN96] it is also sketched how active destructors can use external values, but active destructors only work with linear patterns. However, in many cases it is just the combination of external values and non-linear patterns that is needed, namely pushing one function parameter into an active pattern defining another parameter. Thus the set, tree, and graph examples cannot be expressed by active destructors.

6 Conclusions

Active patterns might be considered problematic since some applications require non-linear patterns which are not part of most functional languages. One implication is that the evaluation order of arguments is restricted: before an active pattern can be evaluated, its free variables must be bound. (In ML this is not a problem since the evaluation order is fixed left-to-right.) A related aspect is that parallel pattern matching is generally not possible in languages with imperative features (such as references and exceptions in ML) since the computations of active patterns make the order of pattern matching significant.

On the other hand, active patterns offer a *powerful abstraction* concept: reorganizations of data type values are removed from function definitions and are given in separate pattern definitions. There are two benefits gained from this: first, function definitions become remarkably simple, and second, by "factorizing" the data type laws, the risk of introducing errors in function definitions is reduced since reorganizational expressions do not have to be repeated for each new function definition. The effort needed to integrate active patterns into a functional language depends on the destination language. As far as ML is concerned, this presents no great difficulties: only the parser (and maybe the type checker) need to be extended; thanks to the presented source code transformation, the rest of a language implementation can be left unchanged. Finally, the sketched fusion technique is a first step to obtaining *efficient implementations* of functions defined with active patterns.

Acknowledgements

Thanks to Pedro Palao Gonstanza and John Boyland for their helpful comments on a previous version of this paper.

References

[AR92]   W. E. Aitken and J. H. Reppy. Abstract Value Constructors. In *ACM Workshop on ML and its Applications*, pages 1–11, 1992.

[BC93]   F. W. Burton and R. D. Cameron. Pattern Matching with Abstract Data Types. *Journal of Functional Programming*, 3(2):171–190, 1993.

[Bur82] F. W. Burton. An Efficient Functional Implementation of FIFO queues. *Information Processing Letters*, 14:205–206, 1982.

[Chi92] W. N. Chin. Safe Fusion of Functional Expressions. In *ACM Conf. on Lisp and Functional Programming*, pages 11–20, 1992.

[Erw97] M. Erwig. Functional Programming with Graphs. In *2nd ACM SIGPLAN Int. Conf. on Functional Programming*, 1997. To appear.

[Moh96] M. Mohnen. Context Patterns in Haskell. In *8th Int. Workshop on Implementation of Functional Languages*, LNCS (this volume), 1996.

[MTH90] R. Milner, M. Tofte, and R. Harper. *The Definition of Standard ML*. MIT Press, Cambridge, MA, 1990.

[PGPN96] P. Palao Gonstanza, R. Peña, and M. Núñez. A New Look at Pattern Matching in Abstract Data Types. In *1st ACM SIGPLAN Int. Conf. on Functional Programming*, pages 110–121, 1996.

[Tho90] S. Thompson. Lawful Functions and Program Verification in Miranda. *Science of Computer Programming*, 13:181–218, 1990.

[Tur85] D. A. Turner. Miranda: A Non-strict Functional Language with Polymorphic Types. In *Conf. on Functional Programming and Computer Architecture*, LNCS 201, pages 1–16, 1985.

[Wad87] P. Wadler. Views: A Way for Pattern Matching to Cohabit with Data Abstraction. In *ACM Symp. on Principles of Programming Languages*, pages 307–313, 1987.

[Wad90] P. Wadler. Deforestation: Transforming Programs to Eliminate Trees. *Theoretical Computer Science*, 73:231–284, 1990.

Context Patterns in Haskell

Markus Mohnen

Lehrstuhl für Informatik II, RWTH Aachen, Germany
mohnen@informatik.rwth-aachen.de

Abstract. In modern functional languages, pattern matching is used to define functions or expressions by performing an analysis of the *structure of values*. We extend `Haskell` with a new non–local form of patterns called *context patterns*, which allow the matching of subterms without fixed distance from the root of the whole term. The semantics of context patterns is defined by transforming them to standard `Haskell` programs. Typical applications of context patterns are functions which *search* a data structure and possibly *transform* it.

This concept can easily be adopted for other languages using pattern matching like `ML` or `Clean`.

1 Introduction

Pattern matching in functional languages like `Haskell` [HF92, HPW92] is a powerful and elegant tool for the definition of functions. When a pattern matches a structure, the resulting bindings of the pattern variables yield access to sub-structures. Typically, definitions with patterns are used for structurally recursive function definitions.

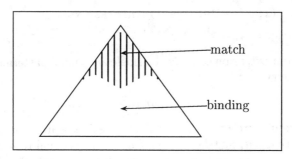

Fig. 1.: Match with standard pattern

However, the patterns allow only the matching of a fixed region near the root of the structure. Consequently, the resulting bindings are substructures adjacent to the region (see Fig. 1). It is neither possible to specify patterns at a non–fixed distance (possibly far) from the root, nor to bind the context of such a pattern to a variable (see Fig. 2).

Consider a toy example of a function

```
initlast :: [a] -> ([a],a)
```

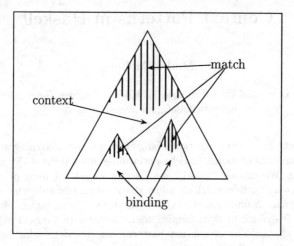

Fig. 2.: Match with context pattern

which splits a list into its initial part and its last element. Informally, we can describe an implementation as a single match:

> Take everything up to but not including a one–element list as initial part and the element of the list as last element.

However, using the standard patterns, we are not able to express this. Instead, the recursive search must be programmed explicitly:

```
initlast []     = error "Empty list"
initlast [x]    = ([],x)
initlast (x:xs) = let (ys,l)=initlast xs
                  in (x:ys,l)
```

Essentially, our extension consists of a single additional pattern called *context pattern*, with the syntax:

$$cpat \quad \rightarrow \quad var\ pat_1\ \ldots\ pat_k$$

A context pattern matches a value v if there exists a function f and values $v_1, \ldots, v_k$ such that pat_i matches v_i and $f\ v_1\ \ldots\ v_k$ is equal to v. Furthermore, this function f is a representation of a *constructor context* [Bar85], i.e. a constructor term with "holes" in it. The representation consists of modelling the "hole" by the function arguments, i.e. in general, f has the following form:

$$f = \lambda h_1. \ldots .\lambda h_k.C[h_1, \ldots, h_k]$$

where C is a constructor context with k "holes", which imitates the shape of the value v. If the pattern matches the value, the function f is bound to the variable *var*.

In our example, we can reformulate `initlast` using context patterns in the following way:

```
initlast []      = error "Empty list"
initlast (c [x]) = ((c []), x)
```

Applying `initlast` to a list $[a_1, \ldots, a_{n-1}, a_n]$ gives us the following bindings:

$$[x/a_n, c/\backslash 1\text{->}(a_1:\ldots(a_{n-1}:1)\ldots)]$$

Hence, evaluation of the application (`c []`) on the right hand side. yields the initial part $[a_1, \ldots, a_{n-1}]$.

Apart from the greater expressive power of context patterns, they provide a means to reduce the impact of any change of data structures. If a function is defined recursively for an algebraic data type, the patterns must handle all constructors. If the data type is changed during development of the program, all these functions must be changed, too. With context patterns, however, functions only need to know those constructors which are of interest for them. Therefore, not all functions must be reconsidered.

The paper is organised as follows. In Section 2 we review some of the previous work in pattern matching and topics related to our approach. Section 3 gives a formal definition of context patterns as an extension of `Haskell`'s patterns. Some examples of context pattern programs are given in Section 4. In Section 5 we define the semantics of context patterns by translating them into `Haskell` code. Section 6 concludes.

2 Related Work

Patterns beyond the scope of the `Haskell` pattern have been studied in [Hec88, Fer90, Wil90] in the context of `TrafoLa`, a functional languages for program transformations. Their *insertion patterns* allow an effect similar to our context patterns, but instead of modelling a context as a function they introduce special *hole constructors* @n to denote the position where a match was cut from the context. Additionally, they introduce several other special purpose patterns for lists, and allow non–linear patterns, which may interfere with lazy evaluation [Pey87, p. 65]. Pattern matching usually results in a list of solutions (see 3.1).

An even more general approach was taken in [HL78] where *second–order schemas* are used to describe transformation rules. These allow the specification and selection of arbitrary subtrees but are not integrated in a functional language.

In [Que90] patterns with *segment assignments* and their compilation are studied in the context of Lisp. The segments allow the access to parts of a matched list, e.g. the pattern (`?x ??y ?x`) matches all lists which start and end with x. The inner part of the list can be accessed via y.

Another root of our work can be seen in *higher–order unification* [Hue75, SG89, DJ95]. The general approach is to synthesise λ–terms in order to find bindings for free function variable in applications, such that equations β–reduce to equal terms. In general, this problem is undecidable [Gol81]. However, for certain subclasses of generated λ–terms and equations, this problem becomes decidable [Pre94]. Especially in our case, where only the pattern can contain unbound variables, i.e. unification becomes matching, the problem is decidable [Hue75].

The representation of context by functions are related to [Hug86], where lists of type `[a]` are represented by a function of type `[a]->[a]`. Given a list `l`, the representation is obtained by `append l`. In our setting such functions can occur as a special case, where the "hole" is the rest of the list (see `initlast`).

3 Context Patterns

The syntax of `Haskell`'s patterns is shown in Fig. 3(a) (taken from [HPW92, pp. 17–18]). For simplicity, we omit infix patterns and $n + k$ patterns. Our extension is in Fig. 3(b). In addition to the basic syntax given in the introduction, there a three extras features:

- *context wildcards* (_), which can be used to match contexts which are not used on the right hand side
- *guards* at the sub patterns, which allow the test of additional conditions during the recursive search
- *explicit types* at the sub patterns, which allow the restriction of possible matches

Later we discuss these facilities in more detail, and give examples for their use.

There is one small conflict which arises with this extension: the definition

$$\text{let x (y:ys)} = e_1 \text{ in } e_2$$

can be either a function definition for x using the pattern y:ys, or a context pattern. In these cases, function definitions are preferred.

The context–sensitive conditions for `Haskell`'s patterns are

1. All patterns must be linear, i.e. no repeated variable
2. The arity of a constructor must match the number of sub–patterns associated with it, i.e. no partially applied constructors

In addition, we require that

3. If a context variable *var* has the functional type $t_1 \rightarrow \ldots \rightarrow t_k \rightarrow t$, then there must exist a value v of type t and values v_i of type t_i such that all v_i are independent subexpressions of v and occur in the sequence $v_1, \ldots, v_n$ in a top–down, left–to–right traversal of v.

This condition ensures that the pattern is not superfluous in the sense that it can match at least one value. If there is a t_i which can not be the type of a subexpression then no value v of type t has a subvalue v_i of type t_i and hence the context pattern can never match. The same is true if there are two t_i and

$$pat \rightarrow apat$$
$$| \ con \ apat_1 \ ... \ apat_k$$
$$apat \rightarrow var[@apat]$$
$$| \ con$$
$$| \ literal$$
$$| \ \_$$
$$| \ ()$$
$$| \ (\ pat\ )$$
$$| \ (\ pat_1, ..., pat_k\ )$$
$$| \ [\ pat_1, ..., pat_k\ ]$$
$$| \ \tilde{}\ apat$$

(a) `Haskell`'s patterns (simplified)

$$pat \rightarrow cpat$$
$$cpat \rightarrow (var \ | \ \_) \ mat_1 \ ... \ mat_k$$
$$mat \rightarrow apat \ [\ \text{if} \ guard] \ [:: \ type]$$

(b) context pattern extension

Fig. 3.: Extended `Haskell` patterns

t_j which are not independent. During matching, a subvalue v_j matching mat_j is not matched further. Therefore a possible match of mat_i is not checked within v_j.

To further motivate this condition, it is worthwhile to look at a few examples. Consider the following (malformed) function definition

```
foo :: [a] -> [a]
foo (c (x:xs) (y:ys)) = exp
```

This context is not admissible, because a list cannot contain two non–overlapping sublists.

The left–to–right part of condition 3 ensures that matching can be performed by traversing the value once top–down and left–to–right. For example,

```
bar :: [a] -> [a]
bar (c x (y:ys)) = exp
```

is allowed. Matching with a list $[a_1, a_2, \ldots, a_n]$ with at least two elements results in the bindings[1]

$$x/a_1,\ y/a_2,\ ys/[a_3, \ldots, a_n] \text{ and } c/\backslash z\ zs\text{->}(z\text{:}zs)$$

On the other hand, switching the arguments in the pattern is not allowed:

```
bar' :: [a] -> [a]
bar' (c (x:xs) y) = exp
```

After finding a match for (x:xs) with a value v, there is nothing left in v to match y.

3.1 Uniqueness of The Solution

In general there are several possibilities to find a match for a context pattern. Consider the following function definition

```
foo :: [a] -> a
foo (c (x:xs)) = x
```

When applying foo to a non–empty list we must choose deterministically which entry of the list should be bound to x. However, Haskell is a language with lazy evaluation, and therefore the match of context patterns should also be as lazy as possible. The match we choose is hence the *shortest possible*. In the above example, x is bound to the head of the list, xs to the tail, and the context c is bound to the identity function \1->1.

More precisely, the matching process traverses the value once *top–down, left–to–right*, similar to the pattern matching semantics of Haskell [HPW92, p. 19]. There is no PROLOG–like backtracking if the match fails. Hence the matching can be done in linear time in the size of the value.

An alternative possibility would be to consider *all possible* matchings, by binding variables of a context pattern to non–empty *lists* of all possible matches, if the context pattern matches at all. The advantage of this is the satisfaction of a need for *completeness of the solution*. Furthermore, in a lazy language like Haskell this list would also be computed lazily. If we assume that the top–down, left–to–right solution is the first element of the list, then only this element needs to be evaluated in order to check whether the context pattern matches. All other solutions can then be evaluated lazily. However, we have *not* chosen this approach for several reasons:

– *It is unclear what to do with all the solutions.* For transformational tasks, we will typically replace or modify a position and return the transformed value.

---

[1] Please note that the binding for c is a function taking *two* arguments, one for each of the *patterns* in the context pattern. A common error is to assume that c is a function taking *three* arguments, one argument for each *variable* in the context pattern.

Of course, we can do that for all solutions, but then we have the problem that we must recombine all these transformed values into a single result. Since the solutions need not be independent, this would be a hard task. The latter could be avoided by choosing the list of all non–overlapping solutions as the result of a context pattern match, but then we would loose the completeness again.

— *The incompleteness is already there.* Even the standard patterns of `Haskell` do not generate complete sets of solutions, due to the fact that equations are used in the order they occur in the program and are matched in a top–down, left–to–right manner.

— *The types of variables would change.* If a variable has type t in the pattern then it would have type $[t]$ in the right hand side of the equation. This would be very confusing.

This non–deterministic approach would fit better in a integrated functional–logic language like `Curry` [HKMN95] or `Babel` [KLMNRA96], than in a purely functional one.

3.2 Additional Features

Sometimes it is necessary to restrict the possible matches of a context pattern. Suppose we use the following data structure to represent trees with a list of attributes at each node:

```
data Tree a = TNode [a] [Tree a]
```

Now consider the following context pattern:

```
fooatt (c [s]) = exp₁
```

Which list in the definition of `Tree` is going to be matched here? By default, we choose the first possibility to match a list type in `Tree`, i.e. the list of attributes. Therefore the context c has the type `[a]->Tree a`. But suppose we want to match the last element of a non–empty successor list. Of course, we can increase the pattern accordingly:

```
foosuc (c1 (Tnode atts (c2 [s]))) = exp₂
```

This definition, however, has lost the clarity of the previous one. Therefore, we allow the type of a context pattern to be restricted. Changing the above definition to

```
foosuc' (c [s]::[Tree a] ) = exp₂
```

restricts the pattern `[s]` to match the tail of a list of successors.

A further extension is the possibility to move Boolean guards into the pattern. Without context patterns it is sufficient to have guards *at the end* of patterns. In the presence of context patterns, however, this is no longer satisfactory:

```
member' y (c (x:xs)) | x==y = True
member' _ _                 = False
```

At first sight, `member'` seems to be equivalent to the function `elem` from the standard prelude, i.e. it seems to implement checking for membership of an element in a list. However, this is not true. Given a list $[a_1, \ldots, a_n]$, the pattern (c (x:xs)) matches with x/a_1, $xs/[a_2, \ldots, a_n]$, and $c/\lambda x.x$. After that, the guard x==y is checked, i.e. a_1 is compared with y. If it is not equal, this rule fails and the second rule is selected, yielding `False` as result.

The problem is that the guard is checked *after* the pattern was matched. If the check fails, there is no search for the *next* possible match of the pattern. In order to overcome this restriction, we allow guards inside context patterns[2]:

```
member y (_ (x:xs) if x==y) = True
member _ _                  = False
```

Now the list is searched until the pattern (x:xs) matches *and* the guard x==y becomes true.

3.3   Type Inference

During type inference, each subpattern is assigned a type, constraints between this types are recorded, and this set of constraints is solved yielding a principal type for each subpattern. In addition, the context–sensitive condition for context patterns may introduce additional constraints. Recall the introductory example `initlast`. If we omit the first line

```
initlast []    = error "Empty list"
```

then the following (preliminary) types are derived for the subpatterns of the context pattern c [x]:

- a for the context pattern c [x]
- [b]->a for the context function c
- b for the variable x

In order to fulfil condition 3, we then unify [b] and a and therefore obtain the following types:

- [b] for the context pattern c [x]

---

[2] In a preliminary version we used the guard symbol | instead of the keyword if to separate pattern and guard. But the resulting similarity between guards inside and outside context patterns was prone to cause errors.

- `[b]->[b]` for the context function `c`
- `b` for the variable `x`

3.4 Abstraction Boundaries

Assume that we have a module M which encapsulates an *abstract type* Z, and that we have another type X which is build by using Z in some way: $X = Y * Z$. Applying context patterns to values of type X *cannot violate the abstraction boundary*. If the functions outside M cannot see inside X then neither can context patterns. So if both Y and Z contain some type which is matched by a context pattern, then only Y is searched.

Of course, the same principle holds for polymorphic components: context patterns can not search inside those components.

4 Examples of Context Pattern Programs

In order to demonstrate some possible applications of context patterns, we give some example programs.

4.1 Lists As Sets

Consider the implementation of sets based on lists. A function using this representation for membership test was given at the end of Section 3. In addition, we give functions for insertion and deletion using context patterns:

```
insert x l@(_ y if y==x) = l
insert x l               = x:l
```

Here he have a context pattern inside an at–pattern, which allows the access to the whole list. Because we do not use the context function on the right hand side, we use an anonymous context of type `Eq a => a->[a]`.

```
delete x (c (y:l) if y==x) = c l
delete x l                 = l
```

The context must have type `[a]->[a]` because we must be able to *remove* an element. If x is the last element of the list, l will be bound to the empty list.

4.2 Sorting

Nested context patterns are allowed, and we can use them to implement a sort function as follows:

```
sort :: Ord a => [a] -> [a]
sort (outer (x:inner (y:zs) if y<x)) =
          sort (outer (y:inner (x:zs)))
sort zs = zs
```

If the context pattern matches x and y are of type a such that x occurs before y and y<x is true. The context outer :: Ord a => [a]->[a] contains everthing before x, the context inner :: Ord a => [a]->[a] everthing between x and y and the list zs the tail after y.

However, we can observe that the constructors : are only needed to ensure that x and y are elements. We can simplify this function in the following way:

```
sort :: Ord a => [a] -> [a]
sort (outer x (inner y if y<x)) =
          sort (outer y (inner x))
sort zs = zs
```

The context outer now has the type Ord a => a -> [a] -> [a] and still contains everthing before y. The tail of the list and everthing between x and y is now in the inner context inner of type Ord a => a -> [a].

But now we have two contexts meeting directly, i.e. without a separating standard pattern and we can fuse them in the following way:

```
sort :: Ord a => [a] -> [a]
sort (c x y if y<x) = sort (c y x)
sort zs = zs
```

In this version the context c :: Ord a => a -> a-> [a] contains everthing but x and y. This sort of fusion is always possible when two contexts meet directly.

4.3 A Desugarer

The Glasgow Haskell Compiler ghc compiles Haskell programs by translation into an intermediate language Core [PS94, Pey96]. The part which performs this translation is called *desugarer*, because it removes the syntactic sugar like pattern–matching, list comprehensions, etc. One small subtask is the translation of conditionals into case.

Assume we represent (a subset of) Haskell expressions with the following data structures:

```
data Expr = EVar String    | ECon String
          | EAp Expr [Expr] | ELam [String] Expr
          | EIf Expr Expr Expr | ECas Expr [(Pattern,Expr)]
```

```
data Pattern = PCon String [String] | PVar String
```

An expression is either a variable, a constructor, an application, a λ-abstraction, an if, or a case. Patterns are used in case expressions and are *flat*. Removing all conditionals can simply be done in the following way:

```
uncond :: Expr -> Expr
uncond (c (EIf ec et ef)) =
    uncond (c (ECas ec [pt,pf]))
    where pt = (PCon "True" [],et)
          pf = (PCon "False" [],ef)
uncond e = e
```

4.4 A Transformer

Another part of the ghc is the Simplifier, which transforms Core programs for better efficiency. One of these transformations is called *case of known constructor*. Its idea is that when the argument of a case is a constructor, the whole case can be removed (since all patterns are flat):

```
cokc :: Expr -> Expr
cokc (ce (ECas (EAp (ECon k1) as)
                 (_ (PCon k2 vs,e) if k1==k2)))
    = cokc (ce (rplc vs as e))
cokc e = e
```

Here, we use two contexts in one pattern: the outer context ce is the context of the case expression in the whole expression, and the inner (anonymous) context _ is the context within the list of alternatives in the case. The function rplc which replaces the constructor arguments for the pattern variables in the expression can also be defined with context patterns:

```
rplc :: [String] -> [Expr] -> Expr -> Expr
rplc [] [] e' = e'
rplc (v:vs) (e:es) e'
    = rplc vs es (rplc' v e e')

rplc' :: String -> Expr -> Expr -> Expr
rplc' v1 e (c (EVar v2) if v1==v2)
    = rplc' v1 e (c e)
rplc' v1 e e'
    = e'
```

The above examples all have the property that all occurrences of a pattern are transformed, which leads to tail–recursive functions. In these cases it is not

(a) `case` e_0 `of` $\{p_1\ mat_1;\ \ldots;\ p_n\ mat_n\}$
$= $ `case` e_0 `of` $\{p_1\ mat_1;$
$\qquad\qquad\qquad$ `_ ->` ... `case` e_0 `of` $\{p_n\ mat_n;$
$\qquad\qquad\qquad\qquad\qquad$ `_ -> error "No match"}` ...$\}$

     where each mat_i has the form:

     `|` $g_{i,1}$ `->` $e_{i,1}$ `;` $\ldots$ `;` `|` g_{i,m_i} `->` e_{i,m_i} `where` $\{decls\}$

(b) `case` e_0 `of` $\{\ p\ |\ g_1$ `->`e_1 `;` $\ldots$`|` g_n `->` e_n `where` $\{decls\}$
$\qquad\qquad\qquad$ `_ ->` $e'\}$
$= $ `let` $\{y\ =\ e'\}$
     `in case` e_0 `of` $\{p$ `-> let {` $decls$ `}`
$\qquad\qquad\qquad\qquad$ `in if` g_1 `then` e_1 $\ldots$
$\qquad\qquad\qquad\qquad\qquad$ `else if` g_n `then` e_n `else` y
$\qquad\qquad$ `_ ->` $y\}$

     where y is a new variable

(c) `case` e_0 `of` $\{\tilde{\ }p$ `->` e `;` `_ ->` $e'\}$
$= $ `let` $\{y\ =\ e_0\}$
     `in let` $\{x'_1\ =$ `case` y `of` $\{p$ `->` $x_1\}\}$
        `in` $\ldots$ `let` $\{x'_n\ =$ `case` y `of` $\{p$ `->` $x_n\}\}$
           `in` $e[x'_1/x_1,\ldots,x'_n/x_n]$

     where $x_1,\ldots,x_n$ are the variables in p and $y,x'_1,\ldots,x'_n$ are new variables

(d) `case` e_0 `of` $\{x@p$ `->` e `;` `_ ->` $e'\}$
$= $ `let` $\{y\ =\ e_0\}$ `in case` y `of` $\{p$ `-> (\x->e)` y `;` `_ ->` $e'\}$

     where y is a new variable

(e) `case` e_0 `of` $\{\_$ `->` e `;` `_ ->` $e'\}\ =\ e$

(f) `case` e_0 `of` $\{K\ p_1\ \ldots\ p_n$ `->` e `;` `_ ->` $e'\}$
$= $ `let` $\{y\ =\ e'\}$
     `in case` e_0 `of` $\{K\ x_1\ \ldots\ x_n$ `-> case` x_1 `of {`
$\qquad\qquad\qquad\qquad\qquad$ p_1 `->` $\ldots$ `case` x_n `of` $\{p_n$ `->` $e;$
$\qquad\qquad\qquad\qquad\qquad\qquad\qquad$ `_ ->` $y\}$
$\qquad\qquad\qquad\qquad$ `_ ->` $y\}$
$\qquad\qquad$ `_ ->` $y\}$

     at least one p_i is not a variable; $y,x_1,\ldots,x_n$ are new variables

(g) `case` e_0 $\{x$ `->` e `;` `_->` $e'\}\ =\ $ `case` e_0 $\{x$ `->` $e\}$

(h) `case` e_0 $\{x$ `->` $e\}\ =\ ($ `\x -> e` $)\ e_0$

Fig. 4.: Semantics of `case` Expressions

necessary to check the complete structure again. Using this idea for an optimised implementation of context patterns leads to functions which transform the input by traversing it only once.

5   Translating Context Patterns into Haskell

All pattern matching constructs may appear in several places, i.e. lambda abstractions, function definitions, pattern bindings, list comprehensions, and `case` expressions. However, the first four of these can be translated into `case` expressions, so we only consider patterns in `case` expressions.

In [HPW92], the semantics of `case` expressions is defined by a translation into *simple case expressions*:

$$\texttt{case } e_0 \texttt{ \{} K \; x_1 \; \ldots \; x_n \texttt{ -> } e_1 \texttt{ ; } \_ \texttt{ -> } e_2\texttt{\}}$$

where K is constructor (including tuple constructor) and x_i are variables. Using the rules given in Fig. 4 (taken from the semantics of `case` expressions [HPW92, p. 22]) in a left–to–right manner defines the translation. The rule (a) sequentialises `case` expressions, rule (b) removes additional guards, rules (c)–(e) remove irrefutable patterns and as–patterns, rule (f) flattens nested patterns, and rules (g) and (h) remove trivial patterns. For brevity, we omitted $n + k$ patterns.

We extend this semantics by the additional rule (cp) in Fig. 5 which remove context patterns. The computation of the context function can be omitted if it is the anonymous context. A more detailed description of the translation process can be found in an accompanying paper [MT97].

The idea is to perform a top–down left–to–right traversal of e_0. Therefore we define a function

$$chk_{t_j} :: (\texttt{Int}, t_{xs}) \texttt{ -> } t_j \texttt{ -> } (\texttt{Int}, t_1 \texttt{->} \ldots \texttt{->} t_n \texttt{->} t_j, t_{xs})$$

for each type t_j which may occur as sub–type of e_0. Each chk_{t_j} traverses a value of type t_j. By definition t_1 is the type of e_0 and hence chk_{t_1} is used to check all of e_0. The first component of the argument tuple of chk_{t_j} is the number i of the pattern p_i which is to be searched for next. The remaining arguments are bindings for all variables in the pattern found until the call to chk_{t_j}. The result tuple contains the same information after traversing the second argument and, in addition, the context created during traversal. Obviously, if the number of the next pattern is $n + 1$ all patterns were found and the match is successful.

Each chk_{t_j} is defined as a `case` on which pattern is to be matched next. If there is no more to match, all bindings and a trivial context containing the complete sub–structure are returned *without further evaluation*. Hereby, we keep the matching process as lazy as possible. For case i, we check the value for pattern p_i and guard g_i (which we assume to be `True`, if there is no guard), if this is possible with the current type t_j. If the match succeeds, we return $i + 1$ as next pattern number, an empty context, and updated bindings.

If the match is not successful or not possible at all, the value has to be examined recursively. All constructors of type t_j are matched and their arguments are traversed from left to right. At the end of the traversal, a new context is built by inserting the resulting contexts in the constructor.

Applying the transformation rule to our introductory example `initlast`

```
initlast (c [x]) = ((c []), x)
```

yields the following program:

```
case e₀ of { c p₁ if g₁ ... pₙ if gₙ -> e ; _ -> e'}
= let {chk_{t₁}-decl ; ... ; chk_{t_m}-decl}
   in case ( chk_{t₁} (1,⊥,...,⊥) e₀ ) of {
        (n+1,c,x_{1,1},...,x_{n,kₙ}) -> e ;
        _ -> e' }
```

where $\bar{x}_{i,1},\ldots,\bar{x}_{i,k_i}$ are the variables in p_i, $t_0,\ldots,t_m$ are the types of all sub-patterns of $c\ p_1$ if $g_1\ \ldots\ p_n$ if g_n such that t_0 is the type of the complete pattern (and e_0), t_i is the type of pattern p_i $(1 \leq i \leq n)$, chk_{t_i} are new identifiers, and $\perp$ is an abbreviation for **undefined**.
We abbreviate $\bar{y}^i := y^i_{1,1},\ldots,y^i_{n,k_n}$, $\bar{z} := z_1,\ldots,z_n$ (new variables) and define each chk_{t_j}-decl:

```
chk_{t_j} (n⁰,ȳ⁰) x = case n⁰ of {
                    1 -> chk_{t_j,1} ; ... ; n -> chk_{t_j,n} ;
                    n+1 -> (n+1,(\z̄->x),ȳ⁰)}
```

If t_i is subtype of t_j then we have to search for pattern p_i in x^0 and we define $chk_{t_j,i} = $ **case** x^0 **of** $\{ p_i\text{-}chk_{t_j}\ r_{t_j}\text{-}decl\}$. Otherwise, pattern p_i cannot occur and hence we define $chk_{t_j,i} = (i,(\backslash\bar{z}\text{->}x^0),\bar{y}^0)$.
If t_j is the type of p_i, then we have to check for pattern p_i and consequently $p_i\text{-}chk_{t_j}$ is defined as

$$p_i\ |\ g_i\ \text{->}\ (i+1,(\backslash\bar{z}\ \text{->}\ z_i),y^0_{1,1},\ldots,y^0_{i-1,k_{i-1}},$$
$$x_{i,1},\ldots,x_{i,k_i},\perp,\ldots,\perp);$$

Otherwise, $p_i\text{-}chk_{t_j}$ is empty. Each $r_{t_j}\text{-}decl$ performs the recursive search and has the form (w_i new variables):

$$K_{t_j,1}\ w_1\ \ldots\ w_{a_{j,1}}\ \text{->}\ chkrek_{t_j,1}\ ;$$
$$\ldots\ ;$$
$$K_{t_j,n_j}\ w_1\ \ldots\ w_{a_{j,n_j}}\ \text{->}\ chkrek_{t_j,n_j}$$

where $K_{t_j,1},\ldots,K_{t_j,n_j}$ are all constructors of type t_j and $a_{j,i}$ is the arity of constructor $K_{t_j,i}$. For each j,k we abbreviate $K := K_{t_j,k}$ and $a := a_{j,k}$. If $a = 0$, we define $chkrek_{t_j,k} = (n^0,(\backslash\bar{z}\text{->}x^0),\bar{y}^0)$. If $a > 0$ we define:

```
chkrek_{t_j,k} = let { (n¹,c¹,ȳ¹) = chk_{l₁} (n⁰,ȳ⁰) w₁ } in {
                 ...
                 let { (nᵃ,cᵃ,ȳᵃ) = chk_{lₐ} (nᵃ⁻¹,ȳᵃ⁻¹) wₐ }
                 in { (nᵃ,(\z̄ -> K (c¹ z̄) ... (cᵃ z̄)),ȳᵃ) } ...}
```

where $t_{l_1},\ldots,t_{l_a}$ are the argument types of constructor K, and c^i,n^i,x are new variables.

Fig. 5.: Semantics of Context–Patterns: Rule (cp)

```
initlast = \l -> let
chk1 (n0,xb0) x0 = case n0 of
   1 -> case x0 of
         [x] -> (n0+1,(\z->z),x) ;
         []  -> (n0,(\z->x0),xb0);
         (w1:w2) ->
               let (n1,c1,xb1)=chk2 (n0,xb0) w1
                   (n2,c2,xb2)=chk1 (n1,xb1) w2
               in (n2,(\z->((c1 z):(c2 z))),xb2)
      ;
   2 -> (2,(\z->z),xb0); ;
chk2 (n0,xb0) x0 = case n0 of
   1 -> (n0,(\z->x0),xb0);
   2 -> (n0,(\z->x0),xb0); ;
 in case (chk1 (1,undefined) 1) of
      (2,c,x) -> (c [],x);
         _         -> undefined
```

Of course, the resulting programs can be optimised. We can distinguish three classes of possible optimisations:

1. simple well–known program transformations like *inlining* (e.g. chk2) and β–*reduction* (e.g. application of chk2) as for instance used in ghc [PS94, Pey96]
2. more efficient pattern matching strategies like those in [Pey87, Chapter 7] or [Thi93] can be adopted
3. completely new optimisations can be performed. If the function using a context pattern is recursive, it may be unnecessary to check the complete structure again. Using this idea on the programs given in Section 4 yields implementations which traverse each input only once.

6   Conclusion

The context patterns we have presented are a flexible and elegant extension of traditional patterns, which allow the matching of regions not adjacent to the root and their corresponding contexts as functional bindings. Typical examples of functions using this increased expressive power are functions which search and/or transform data structures. Moreover, context patterns allow the definition of functions which are less affected by representation changes than usual definitions. We have presented the semantics of context patterns in terms of a translation into Haskell, which also gives us a first possibility for an implementation. Our next aim is to implement this translation in the Glasgow Haskell Compiler and to investigate possible optimisations. The translation and the integration is described in greater detail in an accompanying paper [MT97].

Although we have presented context patterns in the language Haskell, this concept can easily be adopted for other (functional) languages using pattern matching like ML [Mil84], Clean [BvELP87], or PIZZA [OW97].

References

[Bar85]   H. P. Barendregt. *The Lambda Calculus: Its Syntax and Semantics*, volume 103 of *Studies in Logic and The Foundations of Mathematics*. North–Holland, 1985.

[BvELP87]   T. Brus, M. van Ecklen, M. Van Leer, and M. Plasmeijer. Clean – A Language for Functional Graph Rewriting. In G. Kahn, editor, *Proccedings of the 3rd Conference on Functional Programming Languages and Computer Architecture (FPCA)*, number 274 in Lecture Notes in Computer Science, pages 364–384. Springer–Verlag, September 1987.

[DJ95]   D. J. Dougherty and P. Johann. A Combinatory Approach to Higher-Order *E*-Unification. *Theoretical Computer Science*, 139(1–2):207–242, March 1995.

[DM90]   P. Deransart and J. Małuszyński, editors. *Proccedings of the 2nd International Workshop on Programming Language Implementation and Logic Programming (PLILP)*, number 456 in Lecture Notes in Computer Science. Springer–Verlag, 1990.

[Fer90]   C. Ferdinand. Pattern Matching in a Functional Transformational Language using Treeparsing. In Deransart and Małuszyński [DM90], pages 358–371.

[Gol81]   W. D. Goldfarb. The Undecidability of the Second-Order Unification Problem. *Theoretical Computer Science*, 13(2):225–230, February 1981.

[Hec88]   R. Heckmann. A Functional Language for the Specification of Complex Tree Transformations. In H. Ganzinger, editor, *Proccedings of the 2nd International Symposium on European Symposium on Programming (ESOP)*, number 300 in Lecture Notes in Computer Science, pages 175–190. Springer–Verlag, 1988.

[HF92]   P. Hudak and J. H. Fasel. A Gentle Introduction to Haskell. Technical report, Department of Computer Science, 1992.

[HKMN95]   M. Hanus, H. Kuchen, and J. J. Moreno-Navarro. Curry: A Truly Functional Logic Language. In *Proc. ILPS'95 Workshop on Visions for the Future of Logic Programming*, pages 95–107, 1995.

[HL78]   G. Huet and B. Lang. Proving and applying Program Transformations Expressed with Second Order Patterns. *Acta Informatica*, 11:31–55, 1978.

[HPW92]   P. Hudak, S. L. Peyton Jones, and P. Wadler *et. al.* Report on the Programming Language Haskell — A Non-strict, Purely Functional Language. Research Report 1.2, Department of Computer Science and Department of Computing Science, March 1992.

[Hue75]   G. Huet. A Unification Algorithm for Typed λ-Calculus. *Theoretical Computer Science*, 1:27–57, 1975.

[Hug86]   R. J. M. Huges. A Novel Representation of Lists and Its Apllication to the Function "reverse". *Information Processing Letters*, 22(3):141–144, March 1986.

[KLMNRA96] H. Kuchen, R. Loogen, J.J. Moreno-Navarro, and M. Rodriguez-Artalejo. The Functional Logic Language BABEL and its Implementation on a Graph Machine. *New Generation Computing*, 14:391–427, 1996.

[Mil84] R. Milner. *The standard ML core language*. Dept Computer Science, University of Edinburgh, 1984.

[MT97] M. Mohnen and S. Tobies. Implementing Context Patterns in the Glasgow Haskell Compiler. Technical Report AIB-97-04, RWTH Aachen, 1997. to be published.

[OW97] M. Odersky and P. Wadler. Pizza into Java: Translating theory into practice. In *Proccedings of the 24th Symposium on Principles of Programming Languages (POPL)*, pages 146–159. ACM, January 1997.

[Pey87] S. L. Peyton Jones. *The Implementation of Functional Programming Languages*. Prentice-Hall, 1987.

[Pey96] S. L. Peyton Jones. Compiling Haskell by Program Transformations: A Report from the Trenches. In H. R. Nielson, editor, *Proccedings of the 6th International Symposium on European Symposium on Programming (ESOP)*, number 1058 in LNCS, pages 18–44. Springer–Verlag, 1996.

[Pre94] C. Prehofer. Decidable Higher-order Unification Problems. In A. Bundy, editor, *Proccedings of the 12th International Conference on Automated Deduction (CADE)*, number 814 in Lecture Notes in Computer Science, pages 635–649. Springer–Verlag, 1994.

[PS94] S. L. Peyton Jones and A. Santos. Compilation by Transformation in the Glasgow Haskell Compiler. In *Functional Programming, Glasgow 1994*, Workshops in Computing. Springer–Verlag, 1994.

[Que90] C. Queinnec. Compilation of Non-Linear, Second Order Patterns on S-Expressions. In Deransart and Małuszyński [DM90], pages 340–357.

[SG89] W. Snyder and J. Gallier. Higher Order Unification Revisited: Complete Sets of Tranformations. *Journal of Symbolic Computation*, 8(1 & 2):101–140, 1989. Special issue on unification. Part two.

[Thi93] P. Thiemann. Avoiding repeated tests in pattern matching. In P. Cousot, M. Falaschi, G. Filè, and A. Rauzy, editors, *Proccedings of the 3rd International Workshop on Static Analysis (WSA)*, number 724 in Lecture Notes in Computer Science, pages 141–152. Springer–Verlag, 1993.

[Wil90] R. Wilhelm. Tree Transformations, Functional Languages, and Attribute Grammars. In P. Deransart and M. Jourdan, editors, *Attribute Grammars and their Applications*, number 461 in LNCS, pages 116–129. Springer–Verlag, 1990.

The GRIN Project:
A Highly Optimising Back End for Lazy Functional Languages

Urban Boquist and Thomas Johnsson

Department of Computing Science
Chalmers University of Technology
Göteborg, Sweden
E-mail: {boquist,johnsson}@cs.chalmers.se

Abstract. Low level optimisations from conventional compiler technology often give very poor results when applied to code from lazy functional languages, mainly because of the completely different structure of the code, unknown control flow, etc. A novel approach to compiling laziness is needed.

We describe a complete back end for lazy functional languages, which uses various interprocedural optimisations to produce highly optimised code. The main features of our new back end are the following. It uses a monadic intermediate code, called GRIN (Graph Reduction Intermediate Notation). This code has a very "functional flavour", making it well suited for analysis and program transformations, but at the same time provides the "low level" machinery needed to express many concrete implementation concerns. Using a heap points-to analysis, we are able to eliminate most unknown control flow due to evals (i.e., forcing of closures) and applications of higher order functions, in the program. A transformation machinery uses many, each very simple, GRIN program transformations to optimise the intermediate code. Eventually, the GRIN code is translated into RISC machine code, and we apply an interprocedural register allocation algorithm, followed by many other low level optimisations. The elimination of unknown control flow, made earlier, will help a lot in making the low level optimisations work well.

Preliminary measurements look very promising: we are currently twice as fast as the Glasgow Haskell Compiler for some small programs. Our approach still gives us many opportunities for further optimisations (though yet unexplored).

1 Introduction

Although the execution speed of programs written in a lazy functional language, like Haskell, have increased substantially since these languages first appeared, it is still the case that they are slower and consume more memory than imperative programs, in almost all cases.

The reason for functional programs being so slow, is, of course, that functional languages in general, and lazy languages in particular, are so abstract and "far from the machine". Thus, it is very hard for the compiler to optimise the program with good results. Put in another way, we can say that the laziness has a, not negligible, runtime cost.

One of the purposes of this paper is to show how this cost can be reduced by doing more aggressive optimisations than current compilers do. As part of that we will attack the well known problem that conventional (imperative) compiler optimisations do not apply very well to code produced from a lazy functional language, or, if they apply, produce far from satisfactory results. As we will later show, one important reason for this is the laziness, or rather those properties of the generated code that encode the lazy evaluation strategy (e.g. building and forcing *delayed computations*).

Our first, and most important, principle for solving this problem is to do *interprocedural* optimisation, i.e., we let the compiler optimise several procedures together (currently the whole program at once). This should be seen in contrast to the standard method of *global* optimisation, where only one procedure is optimised at a time,[1] a method that is often quite sufficient for imperative programs. This will be explained in more detail in section 2.

In this paper we will describe a novel back end for a compiler for a lazy functional language. The most interesting features of this back end are:

- It is interprocedural, aiming at much more aggressive optimisations than current compilers do.
- The intermediate code, called GRIN (Graph Reduction Intermediate Notation), has a very "functional flavour", which makes it well suited for analysis and program transformations. But, at the same time, it has the "low level control" that is needed.
- Using a two step process: a heap points-to analysis + a single GRIN program transformation, we are able to eliminate most *unknown control flow* (or actually give a good approximation to the real control flow), by inlining calls of eval and apply, in the program.
- The GRIN code is compiled (and optimised) using a series of, each very simple, GRIN source-to-source program transformations, which taken together will produce greatly simplified code.
- With the GRIN transformations as a basis, the resulting (machine) code will be of a form that is suitable for conventional optimisation techniques. In particular we use an interprocedural register allocation algorithm, developed especially with *call intensive* languages in mind.

The organisation of the rest of this paper is as follows. In section 2 we elaborate on the problem of implementing lazy evaluation, and try to motivate why interprocedural compilation is so important. Then, in section 3, we describe the overall structure of our compiler, and back end. In sections 4 to 7 we introduce the intermediate code, GRIN, and describe how it is compiled and optimised using program transformations. The particular heap analysis used is discussed

---

[1] We use these terms as found in most compiler literature, i.e. *global* does not really mean global...

```
main = sum (upto 1 10)

upto m n = if m > n then []
                     else m : upto (m+1) n

sum l = case l of  []     -> 0
                   (x:xs) -> x + sum xs
```

Fig. 1. A small program, summing the numbers from 1 to 10.

in section 8. After all GRIN transformations, the code is translated into real machine code, described in section 9, and a number of low level optimisations are applied; the register allocation is described in section 10 and an overview of the other optimisations is given in section 11. We present some preliminary results in section 12. Finally, we conclude with related work and further development of our back end.

2 Lazy evaluation

To explain why lazy evaluation hinders optimisation and to show how interprocedural compilation can be a first step in solving this we will discuss a small example, the program in figure 1. This program will also be used as the running example throughout this paper.

The program is written using a syntax similar to Haskell. If we had written this program in an imperative language (and using an imperative style) we would most certainly have used real **loops** to sum the numbers, because we know that imperative compilers are good at optimising loops, and often rather poor at optimising procedure calls.

If we imagine the program as written in a *strict* functional language, its execution would result in a *call graph* as the one in figure 2.

We define a node in the call graph as the union of all invocations of the corresponding function. An arc in the call graph means that a function call may occur in the direction of the arrow. Note that call graphs are approximations to what will happen in an execution of the program (but always safe approximations).

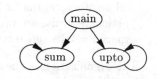

Fig. 2. The "strict" call graph

Returning to our example program, the strict call graph illustrates what will happen in a strict execution of the program. The main function will call the upto function which will produce a list of numbers. The upto function will create this list using recursion (i.e. a kind of loop). It will eventually return to main, which will directly call sum. The sum function will consume the list, also using recursion, and sum up the numbers (i.e a second loop). In this strict version of the program, the two loops are still quite "visible". We could imagine a compiler noticing that both sum and upto make recursive calls, and try to optimise this "as a loop".

However, if we turn to the call graph for the same program when executed in a lazy language it will look quite different, and much less attractive from a compilers point of view (figure 3).

Here, we imagine a standard implementation of lazy evaluation using *graph-reduction*. One additional procedure is added to the call graph, the special eval procedure. This is the procedure used to *force* (or evaluate) a suspended computation. Even though this is normally hidden in the runtime system of an implementation, we can think of eval as an ordinary procedure, which will turn its argument into *weak head normal form*. If, in the call graph, a particular procedure calls eval it will mean that the

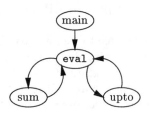

Fig. 3. Original "lazy" call graph

procedure needs the value of a *closure* (which might be a suspended computation). On the other hand, if eval calls a procedure, it means that a suspended computation of that procedure was forced (by someone else).

There are a number of different ways to implement and optimise this "forcing" (see for example [Joh84,PJ92]), but they all have one thing in common: the code will have to do an "unknown call" when it is faced with a suspended computation. By this we mean that it is *unknown at compile time* to which procedure such a call will jump. In our call graphs this will be seen as first a "call" to eval, and then a new call from eval to the suspended procedure.

Unfortunately, these unknown calls are one of the main reasons why conventional compiler optimisations will give so poor results for lazy functional languages. When the compiler is faced with an unknown call (i.e. unknown control flow), it will normally have to make the most pessimistic assumptions possible, like for example not allowing any values to be held in registers. And, since the functional programming style encourages "small" functions, it is not surprising that a global optimiser, that can only optimise the code between two calls at a time, will give so poor results in most cases.

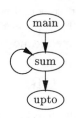

Fig. 4. Improved "lazy" call graph

The consequence of this is that if we want to use conventional optimisations effectively, we will **have to** eliminate most (or all) of the "unknown control flow". The way we do this is described in section 5. Seen in the call graph, it will have the effect of completely eliminating the eval procedure, and replacing each arc to eval with a safe superset of "real" calls, i.e., arcs to ordinary procedures. After this, we will get the call graph in figure 4.

This illustrates the "looping" behaviour that will actually happen in a lazy evaluation of this program. The loop will be in the sum function (using recursion) and, once each iteration, it will call the upto function to produce the next number (i.e. a new cons cell). The call graph also makes clear the producer/consumer relationship, that is so typical of lazy evaluation, between the upto and sum functions. An aggressive optimiser that is allowed to optimise the sum and upto functions together could take advantage of this knowledge and produce much better code compared to the original program (with eval).

3 Our compiler

To be able to compile real Haskell programs, we use our back end in conjunction with an already existing front end, hbcc, by Lennart Augustsson [unpublished]. Hbcc is a state of the art Haskell front end. Using hbcc we get well optimised code in a "low level functional" style, comparable to for example the *Core* language [PJ96] used by the Glasgow Haskell compiler. The code is lambda lifted, i.e., has only super combinators, and most "high level" Haskell constructions, like overloading, have been transformed away.

The structure of the back end (extended with hbcc) can be seen in figure 5. The front end, i.e., hbcc, uses standard separate compilation. Our back end (which is a stand alone program) will collect the code produced from all hbcc-compiled files (for a program spread over several files) and optimise the whole program at once. Thus, the entire system uses separate compilation in the front end, whereas the GRIN back end (currently) need the whole program at once.

The first part of the back end uses the intermediate code, GRIN, and gradually transforms and optimises the code into a very simple form. After that, the code is translated into machine code for a hypothetical RISC machine, and the second part of the back end uses this RISC code. After the low level optimisations, the RISC code is finally "pretty printed" as assembler code for the Sparc processor. However, the RISC code is not very Sparc-specific, so it would not be a large project to generate code for a different processor. Also, the optimisations done are mostly "generic" in nature, and would apply to any RISC processor.

4 GRIN - the intermediate code

The purpose of the GRIN intermediate code is the same as for the G-machine [Joh84] code: to provide a framework and vehicle for compilation of lazy functional languages. Thus, GRIN provides similar primitives as the G-machine does, but does it on a slightly higher level. GRIN can be thought of as a procedural language, where statements inside procedure bodies are essentially three-address code. GRIN is quite flexible: it is possible to compile lazy functional languages in a variety of ways, with different forms of tagging, unboxing, etc. The GRIN code is actually quite a general form of intermediate language, which could be a suitable intermediate form for compilers of many 'heap based' languages (e.g. Lisp, SML, possibly even languages like Smalltalk), although GRIN has some special provisions to accommodate for lazy evaluation.

We will continue to use the program in figure 1 as our running example. Figure 7 shows how it can be translated into GRIN code.

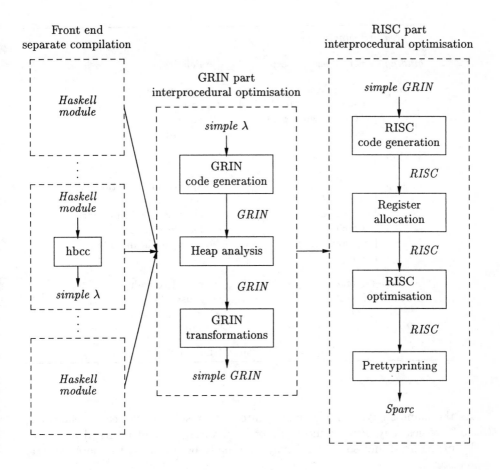

Fig. 5. Overview of the compiler

Sooner or later in the translation process, one has to be confronted with the issue of updating due to call-by-need. We have chosen to make updating explicit in the GRIN language. We currently fancy writing the GRIN programs as *state monadic* [Wad92], *first order, strict, functional programs*[2]. A simplified GRIN syntax is given in figure 6.

The **unit** operation corresponds to the unit in the monad, and ; is the bind operator. **store**, **fetch** and **update** are operations particular to this monad. Compilers often represent the code with "three address statements", and so do we: assume the existence of primitive operators for basic values, like **int_add**, **int_gr**, etc. By convention, the names of basic valued variables end with ' .

First a note on terminology: A *node value* (or just *node*) is a **tag** (e.g., **CInt**, **CNil**, **Fupto**) possibly followed by some arguments (pointers or basic values).

---

[2] Although monads normally are higher order constructs, we consider the GRIN monad as "built-in". All other operations in GRIN are first order.

$$prog \rightarrow \{ \; binding \; \}+$$

$binding \rightarrow var \; \{ \; var \; \} = exp$	definition

$$
\begin{array}{ll}
exp \rightarrow sexp \; ; \; \lambda val \; \text{->} \; exp & \text{sequencing} \\
\quad | \;\; \texttt{case} \; var \; \texttt{of} \; alt_1 \; || \ldots || \; alt_n & \text{case} \\
\quad | \;\; \texttt{if} \; var \; \texttt{then} \; exp \; \texttt{else} \; exp & \text{conditional} \\
\quad | \;\; sexp & \text{operation}
\end{array}
$$

$$alt \rightarrow val \; \text{->} \; exp$$

$$
\begin{array}{ll}
sexp \rightarrow var \; \{ \; val \; \}+ & \text{application, function call} \\
\quad | \;\; \texttt{unit} \; val & \text{return value} \\
\quad | \;\; \texttt{store} \; val & \text{allocate new heap node} \\
\quad | \;\; \texttt{fetch} \; var & \text{load heap node} \\
\quad | \;\; \texttt{update} \; var \; val & \text{overwrite heap node} \\
\quad | \;\; (\; exp \;)
\end{array}
$$

$$
\begin{array}{ll}
val \rightarrow (\; tag \; \{ \; val \; \} \;) & \text{complete node} \\
\quad | \;\; literal & \text{constant} \\
\quad | \;\; var & \text{variable} \\
\quad | \;\; () & \text{empty}
\end{array}
$$

Fig. 6. GRIN syntax (simplified)

As the name suggests, node values quite often reside in the heap — however, node values may also be the value of local variables, and returned as values by procedures, and so on (and may eventually be allocated to one or several registers).

The GRIN language itself does not make any *a priori* interpretation of the different node values, it is the GRIN program which interpret them as representing either ordinary constructor values of the source language (the tags CInt, CNil, CCons) or unevaluated expressions (Fupto, Fsum). As a naming convention, we use node tag names beginning with C and F to denote ordinary data constructors and unevaluated function applications, respectively.

Although the hbcc front end does a fair amount of strictness analysis, unboxing, etc, for the sake of the exposition here, we assume a rather unsophisticated translation, essentially in the same style as in the G-machine (ie, no fancy tagging or unboxing, nor is any strictness analysis assumed).

In our basic translation scheme, each supercombinator becomes a GRIN procedure. Arguments of functions, evaluated or unevaluated, are put in 'boxes' in the heap, and pointers to these boxes are passed as the actual arguments. Procedures return node values as a result (*not* a pointer to one in the heap!).

An essential feature of our approach is that eval, which is normally hidden in the runtime system (or e.g. done as a 'tagless' pointer dispatch) can be written as an ordinary GRIN procedure — and thus also is susceptible to transformation! Figure 8 shows the accompanying eval procedure for our example.

```
main =      store (CInt 1)      ; \t1 →
            store (CInt 10)     ; \t2 →
            store (Fupto t1 t2) ; \t3 →
            store (Fsum t3)     ; \t4 →
            eval t4             ; \(CInt r') →
            int_print r'

upto m n = eval m        ; \(CInt m') →
           eval n        ; \(CInt n') →
           int_gr m' n' ; \b'→
           if b' then
               unit CNil
             else
               int_add m' 1        ; \m1'→
               store (CInt m1')     ; \m1 →
               store (Fupto m1 n) ; \p →
               unit (CCons m p)

sum l =     eval l ; \l2 →
            case l2 of
                CNil ->        unit (CInt 0)
                CCons x xs ->  eval x       ; \(CInt x') →
                               sum xs       ; \(CInt s') →
                               int_add x' s' ; \ax'→
                               unit (CInt ax')
```

Fig. 7. GRIN code for the program in figure 1.

```
eval l = fetch l ; \l2 →
         case l2 of
             CInt x'    -> unit l2
             CNil       -> unit l2
             CCons x xs -> unit l2
             Fupto m n  -> upto m n   ; \v →
                           update l v ; \() →
                           unit v
             Fsum  l    -> sum l      ; \v →
                           update l v ; \() →
                           unit v
```

Fig. 8. GRIN code for the accompanying eval procedure.

The standard eval takes a pointer to a node, and in the case of an unevaluated function application, makes sure the node gets evaluated and updated; eval finally returns the value thus pointed at. This means that eval must fetch the node pointed at, and perform case scrutinisation. This case must enumerate all possible nodes that eval might ever encounter (which without flow analysis is easiest done by enumerating all nodes ever named). eval either returns the C-node so encountered, or calls the appropriate procedure to evaluate an application, and updates the F-node with the value returned.

5 The heap points-to analysis result

The transformation of the GRIN code, especially inlining of eval, is greatly aided by a program analysis, which gives a safe approximation to what possible nodes pointers might point to, at all points in the GRIN program. In this section we describe more precisely *what* this analysis returns, for our running example. Later we we describe *how* this analysis is implemented (section 8).

The main aim of our analysis is to determine, for each call of eval, a safe approximation to what different nodes, eval might get when it fetches a node via its argument pointer. But in effect, the heap analysis determines the abstract values of all variables in the GRIN program, as well as an abstract description of the heap.

In the concrete semantics, the value of a variable is either a basic value, a pointer into the heap, or an entire node value (as returned by a procedure or

$$
\begin{array}{lll}
\text{t1} \to \{\,1\,\} & \text{m'} \to \{\,BAS\,\} & \text{l2} \to \{\,\text{CNil}[\,], \text{CCons}[\{1,5\},\{6\}]\,\} \\
\text{t2} \to \{\,2\,\} & \text{n'} \to \{\,BAS\,\} & \text{x} \to \{\,1,5\,\} \\
\text{t3} \to \{\,3\,\} & \text{b'} \to \{\,BAS\,\} & \text{xs} \to \{\,6\,\} \\
\text{t4} \to \{\,4\,\} & \text{m1'} \to \{\,BAS\,\} & \text{x'} \to \{\,BAS\,\} \\
\text{r'} \to \{\,BAS\,\} & \text{m1} \to \{\,5\,\} & \text{s'} \to \{\,BAS\,\} \\
\text{m} \to \{\,1,5\,\} & \text{p} \to \{\,6\,\} & \text{ax'} \to \{\,BAS\,\} \\
\text{n} \to \{\,2\,\} & \text{l} \to \{\,3,6\,\} &
\end{array}
$$

Fig. 9. Abstract environment of the analysis result.

$$
\begin{array}{l}
1 \to \{\,\text{CInt}[\{BAS\}]\,\} \\
2 \to \{\,\text{CInt}[\{BAS\}]\,\} \\
3 \to \{\,\text{Fupto}[\{1\},\{2\}], \text{CNil}[\,], \text{CCons}[\{1,5\},\{6\}]\,\} \\
4 \to \{\,\text{Fsum}[\{3\}], \text{CInt}[\{BAS\}]\,\} \\
5 \to \{\,\text{CInt}[\{BAS\}]\,\} \\
6 \to \{\,\text{Fupto}[\{5\},\{2\}], \text{CNil}[\,], \text{CCons}[\{1,5\},\{6\}]\,\}
\end{array}
$$

Fig. 10. Abstract heap of the analysis result (*without* sharing analysis).

$1 \to \{\,\text{CInt}[\{BAS\}]\,\}$	shared
$2 \to \{\,\text{CInt}[\{BAS\}]\,\}$	shared
$3 \to \{\,\text{Fupto}[\{1\},\{2\}]\,\}$	unique
$4 \to \{\,\text{Fsum}[\{3\}]\,\}$	unique
$5 \to \{\,\text{CInt}[\{BAS\}]\,\}$	shared
$6 \to \{\,\text{Fupto}[\{5\},\{2\}]\,\}$	unique

Fig. 11. Abstract heap of the analysis result (*with* sharing analysis).

eval). In the abstract semantics, all basic values are abstracted to a single one, *BAS*.

For abstract locations we use a bounded domain of locations $\{1, 2, \ldots maxloc\}$ where *maxloc* is the total number of `store` statements in the GRIN program. Each occurrence of a `store` statement generates the same abstract location every time it is executed. It is as if each `store` statement had its own little heap (a feasible implementation), and the abstract pointer is simply the identity of the heap, thus abstracting away from the relative position in this 'little' heap. The abstract values of pointer valued variables, and arguments of nodes, are sets of abstract locations. See also section 8 and figure 16.

Figure 9 shows the abstract environment derived for our running example (the GRIN program in figure 7). The `store` statements of the program have been numbered $1 \ldots 6$, thus the abstract values of variables t1, t2, t3, t4, m1, and p are $\{1\}$, $\{2\}$, ..., $\{6\}$.

The analysis also returns an *abstract heap*, which maps abstract locations to abstract node values. Figure 10 show a possible abstract heap derived for our running example (this will be refined shortly).

Consider the `eval` of m in the `upto` procedure. The abstract value derived for m is $\{1, 5\}$. Both 1 and 5 in the abstract heap are CInt nodes; thus this `eval` is trivial, the value is already evaluated.

Now consider the `eval` of l in the `sum` procedure. The abstract value derived for l is $\{3, 6\}$, and according to figure 10 both these locations might be either Fupto, CNil, or CCons nodes.

It has turned out to be quite easy to incorporate a sharing analysis into the points-to analysis. Not only does this provide useful information for update avoidance, it also serves to improve the precision of the points-to analysis as such!

Thus, in actual practice our analysis also returns a third component, a sharing table, which maps abstract locations to its sharing properties: True if the abstract location is shared, i.e., if a concrete instance of the abstract location may be subject to a `fetch` more than once, False otherwise. In our example, and in general at the stage of compilation where points-to analysis is currently applied, it is only `eval` that performs `fetch` operations; however, we might also want to analyse the program later in the process where `fetch` operations can occur explicitly.

Figure 11 shows the abstract heap the analysis derived for our running example, together with its sharing information. Thus we can see that abstract locations 3 and 6 now only contain Fupto nodes, and that these locations are unique (non-shared). The explanation for this is that both these nodes are born as Fupto nodes, and even though `eval` might update such a concrete location with either a CNil or a CCons, this will never be visible. A location may only become shared if it is a possible value of a nonlinear variable (i.e., used more than once). The nonlinear variables in our example are: m, n, and m'.

The abstract environment of our running example does not become modified by the use of a sharing analysis part; but in general it might well be.

6 GRIN transformations

6.1 EVAL inlining

After the heap points-to analysis, the next step in the compilation process is to inline all calls of `eval`. In general, one might replace a call of `eval` by its entire body (see figure 8). This would, however, in most cases be blatantly wasteful, since at each `eval` point only a (small) subset of the nodes can be present — the result of the points-to analysis gives a safe subset. Further, one may also omit the accompanying `update` operations if according to the sharing information the corresponding abstract locations are unshared.

Let us discuss the most general cases first, from the point of view of our running example. Consider the `eval l` in the `sum` procedure, and let us assume for a moment that we do not have any sharing information, and that according to the analysis the possible nodes encountered here are `Fupto`, `CNil` and `CCons`. The code:

```
eval l ; \l2 → rest
```

could then be expanded into (by replacing the call by the body of `eval`, substituting actual arguments for formal ones, and deleting impossible cases):

```
(fetch l ; \l2 →
  case l2 of
      CNil        -> unit l2
      CCons x xs -> unit l2
      Fupto m n  -> upto m n   ; \v →
                    update l v ; \() →
                    unit v
) ; \l2 → rest
```

However, as can be seen from figures 9 and 11, the information actually derived by the analysis for this case is that `l` points to a `Fupto` node, and it is unique (unshared). This information can be used for two things:

- since there is only one node, `Fupto`, no case analysis needs to be done,
- since the pointer in known to be unshared, no updating needs to be done.

So, the "`eval ; \l2 → rest`" can actually be inlined into the much better:

```
( fetch l ; \(Fupto m n) →
  upto m n
) ; \l2 → rest
```

The second `eval` appearing in `sum`, the `eval x`, is much simpler in character. Since all the nodes that `x` might point to (in fact there is only one, `CInt`) are ordinary value nodes, `eval` does not have to call any evaluation procedure to get the actual value, instead a simple `fetch` will do. Figure 12 shows the complete `sum` procedure with both `eval`s inlined accordingly.

The inlining of `eval` does not actually happen in one ad-hoc step as indicated here. Rather, the resulting inlining of `eval` shown above is the result of a large number of small transformations — see next section.

```
sum l = (fetch l ; \(Fupto m n) →
          upto m n
        ) ; \l2 →
        case l2 of
            CNil ->         unit (CInt 0)
            CCons x xs ->   fetch x        ; \(CInt x') →
                            sum xs         ; \(CInt s') →
                            int_add x' s' ; \ax'→
                            unit (CInt ax')
```

Fig. 12. The procedure sum with its evals inlined.

6.2 The GRIN transformation machinery

Although the eval inlining above is a very important transformation, it is, in fact, only a small part of a large number of GRIN program transformations. The main idea behind the GRIN transformation machinery is to use many, each very simple, GRIN source-to-source transformations. Each transformation is of course correctness-preserving and hopefully performance-improving. Even though each single transformation will make only a very small change, they will, taken together, produce greatly simplified and optimised GRIN code.

Many of the transformations are very "local" in the sense that they will try to find a small sub-expression, of a larger GRIN expression, that matches a certain pattern, and if found, transform it to a slightly different sub-expression. Other transformations are a bit more involved. Remember also that we assume that the front end has already transformed the program "as much as possible' on the functional level, and hbcc does indeed implement most "standard" functional transformations.

6.3 Example transformations

Rather than going through all transformations, we will concentrate on a few examples. Some transformations are rather general in nature, some are more specialised. We will show a few of each kind.

Monad unit laws – copy propagation. Since we use a monad to structure GRIN we can directly use the *monad laws* [Wad92], that all monads must satisfy, as transformation rules. The *left unit* monad law is usually written as (we use ; as the bind operator, as in GRIN):

(unit x) ; m   ≡   m x

We can get a more useful transformation (denoted ⇒) by instantiating m as a binding:

```
(unit x) ; m
  ⇒   { instantiate m }
(unit x) ; (\v -> k)
  ⇒   { use unit law }
(\v -> k) x
  ⇒   { β reduction }
k[x/v]
```

I.e., we can always delete a `unit` to the left of a binding and simply do a substitution instead, i.e., we have eliminated a "copy". Note that x and v above must not necessarily be variables, they could equally well be complete nodes:

```
unit (CInt a') ; \(CInt b') -> k   ⇒   k[a'/b']
```

There is also a corresponding *right unit* monad law, which will give rise to the following transformation:

```
m ; \v -> unit v   ⇒   m
```

Bind associativity. In any monad the bind operator must be associative [Wad92], and this turns out to
be very useful for transformation purposes. During the
transformation process it is a good idea to keep the
GRIN code normalised, i.e., keep the GRIN syntax tree
"right skewed" with only bind operations as its spine. Unfortunately this property can be destroyed by any transformation that introduces new code, for example inlining
a call to `eval`. Say, for example, that we have the code
"g ; h" and we want to replace g by the sequence, "m ;
k". Then, we would like to restructure the code as shown
in figure 13, to keep the right skewed property.

But this is exactly what the associativity monad law
tells us! Shown in GRIN terms, the general transformation is:

Fig. 13. Normalisation

```
(m ; \a -> k a) ; \b -> h b   ⇒   m ; (\a -> k a ; \b -> h b)
```

Unboxed values. Our current front end, hbcc, uses the *unboxing* methods described in [PJL91]. It is often very good at transforming strict function arguments and function results to unboxed representations. However, it has some shortcomings. The method in [PJL91] cannot unbox a function that returns a value of a datatype whose (single) constructor takes more than one argument, like for example a pair. There is simply no way to express that in functional code, a function must always return exactly one value. Unboxing function arguments of such types (single constructor, more than one argument) is mentioned in [PJL91], but unfortunately not implemented in hbcc. As an example, a strict pair argument that is unboxed can be replaced by two arguments, one for each component of the pair, a transformation sometimes called *arity raising*. A final shortcoming of the unboxing done by hbcc is that it is only attempted in rather restricted contexts (sufficiently strict etc).

In GRIN there is no problem handling any of the cases above. As an example, we can express that a function returns an unboxed pair, i.e. simply returns the two components of the pair (in the final code, this will be done using two registers). To show our transformation, we will give an example of how a function that returns a boxed integer can be changed to return an unboxed integer. In GRIN, a function that *returns* an integer will do it using the unit operation. This means that the actual tag is visible, so we can simply remove it:

```
unit (CInt x')   ⇒   unit x'
```

Of course, we will now also have to change all calls to the function. Assuming the function we have just unboxed was called f, we will transform all calls to f (in any context):

```
f as   ⇒   f as ; \y' -> unit (CInt y')
```

Many of the "extra" units and lambdas that might get inserted are trivially eliminated using the monad law transformations described above. As an example, assume that the above call to f appeared right before a lambda pattern:

```
f as ; \(CInt a') -> m
   ⇒   { unbox f }
(f as ; \y' -> unit (CInt y')) ; \(CInt a') -> m
   ⇒   { associativity + left unit laws }
f as ; \y' -> m[y'/a']
```

The effect of this will be to eliminate all "tagging costs" associated with calls to f. Some special care has to be taken with tail calls, but they can be handled as well. Unboxing procedure arguments, and types where the node have several arguments can be done in a completely analogous way.

Simplifying nodes. Some of the GRIN transformations have more the nature of *simplifications* rather than *optimisations*. An example of the former is a transformation we call *vectorisation*. The aim of vectorisation is to make GRIN variables that contain node values (i.e. a tag possibly with arguments), more concrete by transforming to multiple variables, each containing a simple value (basic value or pointer). Consider the following:

```
foo l = fetch l ; \l2 ->
          case l2 of
              CNil         -> nil_ body
              CCons x xs -> cons_ body
```

This could be a function with a single list argument, where the points-to analysis has shown that the argument will always be evaluated (so all that remains of the eval is a fetch). If we look at the l2 variable above, it will contain a complete node, either a CNil tag or a CCons tag and two arguments. We will now replace l2 with three simple variables (this is what we call a *vector*):

```
foo l = fetch l ; \(t' a as) ->
          case (t' a as) of
              CNil         -> nil_ body
```

```
CCons x xs -> cons_body
```

In fact, we consider the actual tags to be basic values. Hence the variable t',
it will bind the tag itself. Note that if t' is CNil, then a and as are undefined.
This will hopefully be a bit more clear after the right hoisting transformation
below. Before that, though, we will simplify the vectors (variable nodes) that we
just introduced. The case expression in our example depends only on the tag, so
let us make that explicit:

```
foo l = fetch l ; \(t' a as) ->
        case t' of
            CNil  -> nil_body
            CCons -> cons_body[a/x,as/xs]
```

After this transformation, all case expressions will be only a "case test", they will
not bind any variables.

Right motion hoisting. The fetch operation above will load a complete node
from memory, and bind its various components to the three variables.[3] To further
simplify the GRIN code, we now split the fetch into its three components:

```
foo l = fetch l[0] ; \t' ->
        fetch l[1] ; \a  ->
        fetch l[2] ; \as ->
        case t' of
            CNil  -> nil_body
            CCons -> cons_body[4]
```

By the notation "l[n]" we mean the n:th component of the node pointed to
by l. We now see that since a and as are not used in the CNil branch of the
case expression, their corresponding fetch operations can be moved (or hoisted)
into the CCons branch:

```
foo l = fetch l[0] ; \t' ->
        case t' of
            CNil  -> nil_body
            CCons -> fetch l[1] ; \a  ->
                     fetch l[2] ; \as ->
                     cons_body
```

We call this transformation *right motion hoisting*. It is interesting to compare this
to the *let-floating* described in [PJPS96]. One of the let-floating variants, where a
let-binding is floated into a case branch, does look quite like our transformation
(one difference is of course that a let will allocate storage in the heap, whereas
our fetch will only read from the heap). However, the code above is an example

---

[3] Note that this does not imply anything about the way a node actually gets stored
in the heap! It only says that there should be some way to extract the tag, etc.

[4] We omit the substitution henceforth.

of a situation where we benefit from the extra "low level control" of the GRIN code. The transformation example above is not possible on the "functional level", because there is no way to distinguish between the different components of the value (the node variable 1 above).

A good thing about this transformation is that it can decrease memory *bandwidth*, by not fetching unnecessary values. However, the transformation might also have a negative impact on execution time. If the CCons branch is the most common one, and if the values a and as are needed early in *cons_ body*, it might, in fact, be better to *prefetch* them before the case test (for reasons of memory *latency*). On the other hand; if the tag is already loaded, the rest of the node is probably already in the cache, so subsequent loads will be cheap. More experiments are needed to determine if this optimisation really is beneficial.

More transformations. The effect of all GRIN transformations, of which we have only shown a few, is to gradually turn the GRIN code into a very simple form, with all operations made explicit. This will make the actual code generation (to real machine code) quite simple (see section 9).

7 Higher order functions

True to the GRIN philosophy, also function objects are represented by node values. Just like the G-machine and most other combinator-based abstract machines, function objects in GRIN programs exist in the form of curried applications of functions with too few arguments. Consider again the function upto of our running example, which takes two arguments. We represent the function object of upto by a node Pupto_2, and an application of upto to one argument by a node Pupto_1 e. The naming convention we use is that the prefix P indicates a partial application, and _2 etc. is the number of *missing* arguments.

In analogy with the generic eval procedure, programs which use higher order functions must also have a generic apply procedure, which must cover possible function nodes that might appear in the program. An example is shown in figure 14. apply returns the value of a function value (node) applied to one additional argument. Generally, apply just returns the next version of the function node with one more argument present, except when the final argument is supplied: then the call of the procedure takes place.

GRIN does not provide a way to do a function application of a variable in a lazy context directly, e.g., build a representation of f x where f is a variable, instead a closure must be wrapped around it; this is the purpose of the ap2 procedure.

In the further compiling of programs which uses higher order functions, also apply calls are inlined, in much the same way as eval calls.

If the application in the original program has more than one argument, several apply statements in sequence must be used. This arrangement is conceptually simple (a great advantage when it comes to the points-to analysis). Although it implies the unnecessary construction of intermediate function values,

```
apply f x = case f of
                Pupto_2    -> unit (Pupto_1 x)
                Pupto_1 y  -> upto y x
                    ⋮
```

Fig. 14. The apply procedure.

```
twice f x = store (Fap2 f x) ; \t1 →
            eval f ; \f2 →
            apply f2 t1

ap2 f x   = eval f ; \t2 →
            apply t2 x
```

Fig. 15. The GRIN code for the function twice f x = f (f x).

a sequence of inlined applys can easily be simplified to avoid these intermediate function values.

8 The innards of the points-to analysis

When we designed our points-to analysis, an overriding design goal was that it had to be very fast, in order to be able to analyse large entire programs at once — if it had to be done at the cost of some precision, then so be it! The result is an analysis which we think is no costlier than, e.g., live variable analysis. We accomplish this by the following means:

- a single abstract heap approximates the real heap at all times and at all program points: this makes the analysis flow insensitive,
- a single abstract environment approximates all local environments; this arrangement does not actually impose any extra approximation, since all local variables are uniquely named and an abstract local environment is always a subset of this 'global' abstract environment,
- the analysis is insensitive to calling context: a procedure parameter gets its abstract value by 'unioning' the corresponding actual parameters at the call sites, and the same abstract return value is returned as a result of all calls for each procedure.

As mentioned in section 5, we also include a sharing analysis into the points-to analysis machinery. Not only does this provide desired sharing information for update avoidance, it also serves to improve the precision of the points-to result! The analysis works in two steps:

- setting up a system of data flow equations, for the variables of the abstract environment and the abstract heap,
- solving the equations.

$$\widehat{Loc} = 1, 2, \ldots \qquad \text{"Cons points"}$$
$$\widehat{Val} = \{BAS\} + \widehat{Loc} \qquad \text{"Small" values}$$
$$\widehat{V} = \mathrm{P}(\widehat{Val})$$
$$\widehat{Node} = Con \times \widehat{V}^* \qquad \text{Node values}$$
$$\widehat{N} = \mathrm{P}(\widehat{Node})$$
$$\widehat{Heap} = \widehat{Loc} \rightarrow \widehat{N}$$
$$\widehat{VarVal} = \widehat{V} \cup \widehat{N} \qquad \text{Abstract values of variables}$$

Fig. 16. Abstract domains for the heap points-to analysis.

$$
\begin{array}{llll}
t1 = \{\,1\,\} & m' = \{\,BAS\,\} & x & = 12 \downarrow \mathtt{CCons} \downarrow 1 \\
t2 = \{\,2\,\} & n' = \{\,BAS\,\} & xs & = 12 \downarrow \mathtt{CCons} \downarrow 2 \\
t3 = \{\,3\,\} & b' = \{\,BAS\,\} & x' & = \{\,BAS\,\} \\
t4 = \{\,4\,\} & m1' = \{\,BAS\,\} & s' & = \{\,BAS\,\} \\
r' = \{\,BAS\,\} & m1 = \{\,5\,\} & ax' & = \{\,BAS\,\} \\
m = t1 \sqcup m1 & p = \{\,6\,\} & ru & = \{\,\mathtt{CNil}[\,], \mathtt{Ccons}[\,m, p\,]\,\} \\
n = t2 \sqcup n & l = t3 \sqcup xs & rs & = \{\,\mathtt{CInt}[\{BAS\}]\,\} \\
& 12 = EVAL(FETCH\,heap\,1) &&
\end{array}
$$

Fig. 17. Abstract environment equations.

$$
\begin{aligned}
heap = [\;\; & 1 \rightarrow \{\,\mathtt{CInt}[\{BAS\}]\,\} \\
& 2 \rightarrow \{\,\mathtt{CInt}[\{BAS\}]\,\} \\
& 3 \rightarrow \{\,\mathtt{Fupto}[\,t1, t2\,]\,\} \;\sqcup\; ru \\
& 4 \rightarrow \{\,\mathtt{Fsum}[\,t3\,]\,\} \qquad \sqcup\; rs \\
& 5 \rightarrow \{\,\mathtt{CInt}[\{BAS\}]\,\} \\
& 6 \rightarrow \{\,\mathtt{Fupto}[\,m1, n\,]\,\} \;\sqcup\; ru \quad]
\end{aligned}
$$

Fig. 18. Abstract heap equations.

$$
\begin{aligned}
EVAL\,S &= \{tag\,L \mid tag\,L \in S \wedge \textit{is-value-node}\ tag\} \\
FETCH\,heap\,\{l_1, \ldots, l_n\} &= heap \downarrow l_1 \sqcup \ldots \sqcup heap \downarrow l_n \\
\{\ldots, tag\,[v_1, \ldots, v_i, \ldots], \ldots\} \downarrow tag \downarrow i &= v_i \\
\{\ldots tag[x_1, \ldots, x_i, \ldots], \ldots\} \sqcup \{\ldots\, &tag[y_1, \ldots, y_i, \ldots], \ldots\} = \\
\{\ldots\, &tag[x_1 \cup y_1, \ldots, x_i \cup y_i, \ldots], \ldots\}
\end{aligned}
$$

Fig. 19. Utility functions.

We first describe the basic machinery without the sharing analysis part, and then discuss the modifications needed to implement the sharing analysis, and to deal with higher order functions.

8.1 The basic analysis machinery

Deriving the equations. From the GRIN program, we set up a system of data flow equations which describes the values of the variables in the abstract environment, and the locations of the abstract heap. Figures 17 and 18 shows these equations for our running GRIN program example (figure 7).

The abstract domains are summarised in figure 16. We now proceed to explain each of the different forms of equations.

The abstract environment contains the variables of the GRIN program, plus one variable for each procedure, which denotes the return value of such a call: ru for upto, and rs for sum.

To begin with, quite a lot of the variables can immediately be seen to have the value {*BAS*}.

As mentioned, we use a single fixed abstract location for each store statement: hence the equations for t1, t2, t3, t4, m1, and p in the environment part. The *heap* variable has at each location the value of the corresponding store, possibly unioned with one more item. If an abstract location has the value of a node which represent an unevaluated function application, in our case Fupto or Fsum, we simply set these locations also to have the value of the corresponding return values, since such nodes will most likely be updated with these eventually: hence the union with ru and rs respectively.

Parameter variables, like m, n, and l, has the value of the union of all the actual arguments of the applications of the program, both direct calls, e.g., sum xs, or 'lazy calls' .e.g., store (Fupto m1 n). So for instance, m is the first argument of upto, and hence gets the value $t1 \sqcup m1$ from the two different stores of Fuptos.

The variable l2 holds the value of an eval: this is simply obtained by taking the union of the value of the abstract locations which l might point to (done by *FETCH*), and then extracting those nodes that represent value constructors (done by *EVAL*).

Values for variables which are bound in a case, like x and xs, get their abstract value by extracting out the corresponding component value for the variable being cased upon.

In taking the union ($\sqcup$) of sets of node values, these are unioned tag-by-tag so that in the resulting set there is only one element for each node tag (see figure 19). Unions of sets of abstract pointers are like ordinary unions.

Solving the equations. Having obtained the data flow equations for the points-to analysis, the natural way of solving these equations is by fixpoint iteration, starting with an empty abstract environment and an empty heap, and apply the equations until a fixpoint is reached.

In our implementation, convergence is speeded up by using a 'depth first ordering' [ASU86, sec. 10.9] of the variable equations. Using this for our example, it takes only 4 iterations to converge to a fixpoint.

8.2 Adding sharing analysis

As mentioned already in section 5, a sharing analysis can easily be incorporated into the points-to analysis by adding a third component, suitably called a *sharing heap*, a mapping from abstract locations to a boolean value: True if an instance of this abstract location might be shared, False if it cannot be.

The initial value of the sharing heap is all Falses. The value of the sharing heap is awkward to express in equational form, instead we do as follows: during an iteration, an abstraction location is set to shared, i.e. True, either if it might be pointed to by a nonlinear variable, or from another shared location.

In the abstract heap the return value part, e.g., ru of location 3, is only ⊔'ed if the same abstract location becomes shared.

The semantic function *EVAL* also needs to be modified: it cannot just take the subset of the node values which represent proper values, but needs to extract 'by itself' from elsewhere what the values of an `Fupto` application, etc, might be. We omit those details here.

8.3 Higher order functions

Higher order functions cause no fundamental difficulties to add into our analysis — only practical ones!

The abstract value of an `apply f a` depends, obviously, on the abstract value of `a`: if the value of `f` contains e.g., a `Pupto_2` node, then the `apply` contains `Pupto_1 a` where a is the abstract value of `a`; if the value of `f` contains e.g., a `Pupto_1 b` node, then the value of the `apply` contains whatever upto returns since the application becomes saturated at that point (c.f. figure 14).

Previously, a parameter of a procedure gets its abstract value from the union (⊔) of some other variables – for example $l = t3 \sqcup xs$. Unfortunately, due to the `apply` calls, the equations for the variables are no longer this static. Now, if a call of some procedure occurs as a result of an `apply` call, then the actual arguments of those call need to be ⊔'ed with the abstract values of the corresponding parameter variables.

We have solved that problem practically as follows. A single variable, let us call it `aa` here, is used to collect all the possible 'extra' arguments as a result of the `apply`s in the program. It is convenient to represent these extra arguments by closure nodes for those applications, e.g., `Fupto` x_1 x_2. If there is an `apply a b` in the GRIN program, then there is also an *APPLICATONS a b* being ⊔'ed to the rhs of `aa`. If a call of, e.g., upto could occur as a result of that `apply` (in which case the value of a need to contain a `Pupto_1 c` node), then the value of *APPLICATIONS a b* should contain a `Fupto c b` node. Finally, the variable for the parameter need to extract the relevant part of `aa`: the first argument of upto, for example, need to add $aa \downarrow Fupto \downarrow 1$ to the right hand side of its equation.

9 RISC code generation

After all GRIN transformations, the resulting code is translated into machine code for a hypothetical RISC machine (load-store architecture) assuming an infinite number of available *virtual* registers. These virtual registers will later be mapped onto real machine registers by the register allocator. The translation to RISC code is rather straightforward, since the final GRIN code is in a very simple form.

Each procedure is represented as a flow graph of *basic blocks*. The (intraprocedural) flow graphs are at this stage always DAGs, since GRIN can not represent (intraprocedural) loops. Later in the compilation, tail recursion optimisations will indeed, turn tail calls (to the same function) into "real loops" in the flow graph. On the interprocedural level, i.e., between procedures, the flow graphs are linked together using *call* and *return* edges.

Throughout the entire back end we do a lot of book keeping and analysis aimed at determining enough information about what registers contain *root pointers*, i.e., need to be followed during GC. For space reasons we will have to postpone a description of how this is done to a future paper.

10 Interprocedural register allocation

We believe good register allocation to be a vital optimisation. For reasons explained in section 2, we also believe it to be important to do *interprocedural* register allocation for lazy functional languages. Or, put in another way, what we need, to implement these languages efficiently, is to minimise the procedure *call and return overhead*, and doing interprocedural register allocation can be a good method for achieving that [Cho88].

Our register allocation algorithm was described in [Boq95a,Boq95b], and, for space reasons we will not explain it in detail here (although it has changed a bit since then). In summary, it is an interprocedural *graph colouring* algorithm, based on *optimistic* graph colouring [BCKT89], but with several additions; e.g. interprocedural *coalescing* and a restricted form of *live range splitting*.

Cheap procedure calls. The register allocator helps reducing the procedure call penalty in the following ways:

- It is very successful in passing procedure *arguments* in registers, using tailor-made argument registers for each procedure.
- It often achieves good *targeting*, i.e., a value that later will be used as argument in a call, will actually be *calculated* in the correct register. In most cases, no extra "register shuffling" will be necessary at the call site.
- Likewise with procedure *return values* (we will often use more than one register to return a result).
- Local variables that are *live*[5] across a call site, can often be kept in a register during the call. This should be seen in contrast to a global register allocator, which normally will have to save and then restore certain registers around each call site, if they risk being clobbered by the callee.

Graph colouring. The main task of the register allocation algorithm is to build an *interference graph* (conflict graph) for the complete program, and then *colour* it. We initially assume that all variables are allocated to *virtual* registers.

---

[5] A variable is said to be *live* at a certain point if its value may be used on some execution path leading from that point.

If the allocator fails to find a colour for some variable it will be *spilled*, i.e., the value kept in memory instead, or *splitted*, i.e. kept in different registers during different periods. The "variables", that participate in the colouring are: procedure arguments and return values, local variables and all kinds of temporaries introduced by the compiler.

11   RISC optimisations

The RISC optimiser implements a number of different low level optimisations. Naturally, we implement the "standard" optimisations for lazy functional languages, like heap pointer and tail call optimisations. We also optimise stack usage (the stack pointer, frame building and the return address) using a *shrink-wrap* technique similar to the one used in [Cho88] to optimise the use of callee-saves registers. For example, the return address register,[6] can be seen as a callee-saves register, i.e. we need not save it until we are certain to do a new procedure call. In a similar way, we can avoid creating a stack frame,[7] until it is absolutely needed. The different stack optimisations, together with tail call optimisations, often succeed very well in creating small tight loops for tail recursive functions.

Other optimisations are of a more general kind, like instruction scheduling and branch optimisations. The Sparc processor is a *delayed-load* architecture with call and branch *delay slots*, which means that it is important to separate loads instructions and uses of the loaded result, and to fill delay slots with useful instructions. We use a rather standard instruction scheduler to accomplish this, in the style of [GM86].

Currently, most our RISC optimisations are placed *after* the register allocation (see figure 5), which might seem a bit odd in comparison with conventional compilers where normally many optimisations are done *before* the register allocation. However, in our case it turns out that many of the standard optimisations are subsumed by transformations already done at the GRIN level.

12   Measurements

We have compared our back end to the Chalmers and Glasgow Haskell compilers, hbc and ghc, respectively. Our implementation is still rather experimental, and unfortunately we have not been able to compile any large programs. Therefore, the measurements shown here should be taken for what they are, only toy programs experiments. On the other hand, one positive thing about having small test programs is that it is possible to examine the code produced in various stages of the compilation, to get "fair" tests between compiler "sub-parts". The measurements in figure 12 show four example programs: nfib 32, sieve2 (summing all primes below 10000), fqueens (the queens problem of size 10, a first order program) and hqueens (ditto, but using higher order functions). The

---

[6] Assuming a RISC style jump-and-link instruction used for doing procedure calls.

[7] On the Sparc we use the standard system stack.

		hbc[a]	GRIN	hbcc+GRIN	ghc[b]
nfib	instructions	341.9	123.4	81.1	-
	stack	84.6	28.2	21.1	-
	time	7.6	4.6	**1.8**	2.2
sieve2	instructions	72.9	24.2	24.2	-
	stack	17.2	3.1	3.1	-
	time	3.2	**1.7**	1.9	3.5
fqueens	instructions	174.3	49.4	48.9	-
	stack	44.6	3.0	3.0	-
	time	5.1	2.0	**1.9**	4.4
hqueens	instructions	198.3	-	57.8	-
	stack	50.8	-	3.3	-
	time	5.0	-	**2.0**	4.1

[a] hbc-0.9999.1 -O -msparc8
[b] ghc-0.29 -O2 -fvia-C -O2-for-C

Fig. 20. Performance of some small programs.

column marked just GRIN means that handwritten GRIN code is input to our back end. The intention of this is to create a fair comparison of hbc's and our back ends. We have made sure that this code is written exactly as what is input to hbc's back end, i.e., the same strictness and boxity, and it reads and writes exactly the same nodes in the heap. In other words, the hbc and GRIN columns will perform exactly the same graph reduction.

The column marked hbcc+GRIN shows our back end together with the hbcc front end, and is supposed to be a more fair comparison against the ghc column. Ghc and hbcc should be roughly comparable as front ends.

Our main measurements are done using a tool to collect dynamic instruction counts.[8] We show the total instruction count and the total number of stack references (loads + stores), all in millions of instructions. We also include some timings.[9] However, given how hard it is to accurately measure time on a UNIX system, especially for such small programs, these should be seen mainly as a reference. Garbage collection times are not included (for any compiler).

If we look at the total instruction count, we can see that the GRIN column is roughly 3 times as fast as hbc, i.e. our back end compared to the hbc back end. Moving to the hbcc+GRIN column, we see that we get slightly better yet, around 3-4 times fewer instructions executed compared to hbc. The total instruction count also correlate rather well with the timings. Comparing hbcc+GRIN with ghc, we are roughly twice as fast as ghc for all the examples except nfib.

We have included stack reference counts as a measure on how well our register allocator succeeds, since good register allocation typically means that stack allocated variables (including temporaries and function parameters and results), have been allocated to registers instead. Looking at the figures, we see a dra-

---

[8] Unfortunately, we have not yet been able to make this tool work for ghc binaries.
[9] User times on a 40MHz SuperSparc with 1Mb external cache and 80Mb memory.

matic reduction in the number of stack references for our back end compared to hbc, ranging from 70% to 95% eliminated stack references.

13   Related work

Interprocedural optimisation. Recently, various interprocedural optimisations have gained increasing popularity, simply because they are much more powerful than their corresponding global (i.e., per procedure) optimisations. Practical difficulties with whole-program optimisation can be reduced by the use of an integrated programming and optimisation environment, like the $\mathbf{R}^n$ environment [CKT86].

For a lazy language like Haskell, compilers typically compile one *module* at a time. At first sight, this might appear as a good opportunity to optimise several procedures at once. However, it seems as if this does not apply very well to low level optimisations, like those presented in this paper, where the actual *dynamic* control flow is important, as explained in section 2. In a lazy language, a function that is *local* to a module in the source code, might very well *escape* from the module at run time (if it is built into a closure) and then be called from somewhere else (using `eval`).

GRIN and transformations. Our intermediate code, GRIN, is in its essence not very different from any other intermediate code used to implement lazy functional languages (usually called code for a particular *abstract machine*); e.g. the G-machine [Joh84], the ABC-machine [SNvGP91] and TIM [FW87]. In some sense, GRIN is on a slightly "higher level" than the machines mentioned above. On the other hand, compared to the STG language [PJ92], GRIN is more "low level" which has proven itself useful in some transformations (see section 6).

The idea of "compilation by transformation" is not new, see for example [KH89,App92]. In particular, the idea of using a large number of very small transformations is similar to what is used by the *simplifier* [PJ96] in the Glasgow Haskell Compiler. The main difference compared to our transformations is that the GRIN code is a low level code compared to both the Core and the STG language used by ghc (they are both essentially 2:nd order λ-calculus, the STG language is on a slightly lower level). A typical example of the difference is that we, in GRIN, can "inspect" a node value (closure) without having to force (evaluate) it, something which is not expressible in the STG language.

It may be an illusion, but the monadic presentation of GRIN code gives it a very "functional flavour", and hence a nice framework for doing analysis and transformations.

The relationship between GRIN and *Continuation Passing Style* (CPS) [AJ89], can be compared to programming using either monads or continuations, i.e., it is probably mainly a matter of taste. One might also compare GRIN to *Static Single Assignment* (SSA) code [CFR+91], which has received recent popularity for implementing imperative languages (mainly Fortran). In GRIN, we will get single assignment "for free", i.e. all variables in a GRIN program are only assigned once, yet another example of the "functional flavour" discussed before.

Heap points-to analysis. A great deal of work has been done on points-to analysis of more conventional languages – see, for example, the overview in [SH97]. However, with the notable exception below, none other seem to have addressed the problem in the context of lazy graph reduction.

The work by Karl-Filip Faxén [Fax95,Fax96] is quite similar in scope to ours, and he addresses many of the same problems as we do. Central to his work is a type based program analysis, called *flow inference*, which analyses programs expressed in his intermediate language, *Fleet* (Functional Language with Explicit Evals and Thunks). As the name suggests, he analyses programs on a higher level than our GRIN code. His flow inference derives information quite similar to ours, and he uses the information to eliminate `eval`s and thunks, to do unboxing, and update elimination.

Register allocation. To our knowledge, interprocedural register allocation has not been applied previously to code generated from a lazy functional language. It has been applied to other kinds of languages though, e.g. to Lisp [SH89] and to C [Cho88,Wal86].

14 Conclusions and further work

Our preliminary results look very promising, but there is a lot of implementation work that needs to be done before we can say if our back end really can be made practical. We can not yet say how our interprocedural approach will scale up to large programs. Two possible problem areas are the heap points-to analysis and the interprocedural register allocation. Although there are various methods for trading exactness for speed in both these cases, it is difficult to predict exactly how the code quality will be affected by less precise program information.

The GRIN back end described in this paper constitutes quite a heavy basic machinery. But once that has come off the ground, many other opportunities for further optimisations present themselves:

So far, the only use of inlining in our GRIN transformations are to unfold calls to `eval` and `apply`, but we plan to experiment with more aggressive methods. Inlining of conventional calls, together with simplification of the resulting GRIN code, might effectively give a compile-time version of the vectored return mechanism of the STG machine [Joh91].

As an area for further work, we would like to investigate which of the transformations usually done closer to the front end, e.g., ghc's (or hbcc's) "functional" transformations, that could be profitably done on the GRIN level: for example unboxing, deforestation, firstification, possibly even strictness analysis!

The simplifier in ghc is a kind of "transformation engine" that will apply (and repeat) transformations rather automatically. We plan to implement a similar machinery in our back end.

Doing aggressive optimisations like the ones described here might very well turn out to be impractical to do on large entire programs. We might consider a profiling based approach, where the optimisation effort is spent where it really matters for the overall execution speed of the program.

Acknowledgements. The second author, Johnsson, visited the Glasgow Functional Programming Group 1989-90, on an SERC fellowship: the first ideas [Joh91] concerning the GRIN approach occured in that inspiring environment.

References

[AJ89]   A.W. Appel and T. Jim. Continuation-passing, closure-passing style. In *Conference Record of the 16th Annual ACM Symposium on Principles of Programming Languages*, pages 293–302, Austin, TX, January 1989.

[App92]   A. W. Appel. *Compiling With Continuations*. Cambridge University Press, 1992.

[ASU86]   A. V. Aho, R. Sethi, and J. D. Ullman. *Compilers: Principles, Techniques, Tools*. Addison-Wesley Publishing Company, Reading, Mass., 1986.

[BCKT89]   Preston Briggs, Keith D. Cooper, Ken Kennedy, and L. Torczon. Coloring heuristics for register allocation. In *Proceedings of the ACM SIGPLAN '89 Conference on Programming Language Design and Implementation*, volume 24, pages 275–284, Portland, OR., June 1989.

[Boq95a]   Urban Boquist. Interprocedural Register Allocation for Lazy Functional Languages. In *Proceedings of the 1995 Conference on Functional Programming Languages and Computer Architecture*, La Jolla, California, June 1995. URL: http://www.cs.chalmers.se/~boquist/fpca95.ps.

[Boq95b]   Urban Boquist. Interprocedural Register Allocation for Lazy Functional Languages. Licentiate Thesis, Chalmers University of Technology, Mars 1995. URL: http://www.cs.chalmers.se/~boquist/lic.ps.

[CFR+91]   Ron Cytron, Jeanne Ferrante, Barry K. Rosen, Mark N. Wegman, and F. Kenneth Zadeck. Efficiently computing static single assignment form and the control dependence graph. *ACM Transactions on Programming Languages and Systems*, 13(4), October 1991.

[Cho88]   Fred C. Chow. Minimizing Register Usage Penalty at Procedure Calls. In *Proceedings of the SIGPLAN '88 Conference on Programming Language Design and Implementation*, June 1988.

[CKT86]   Keith D. Cooper, Ken Kennedy, and Linda Torczon. The impact of interprocedural analysis and optimizations in the R(n) programming environment. *ACM Transactions on Programming Languages and Systems*, 8(4):419–523, October 1986.

[Fax95]   Karl-Filip Faxén. Optimizing lazy functional programs using flow-inference. In A. Mycroft, editor, *Static Analysis Symposium (SAS)*, volume 883 of *LNCS*. Springer Verlag, September 1995. URL: http://www.it.kth.se/~kff/fvSAS.ps.

[Fax96]   Karl-Filip Faxén. Flow Inference, Code generation, and Garbage Collection for Lazy Functional Languages. Licentiate Thesis, Department of Teleinformatics, Royal Institute of Technology, Stockholm, January 1996. URL: http://www.it.kth.se/~kff/TRITA-IT-9601.ps.

[FW87]   J. Fairbairn and S. C. Wray. TIM: A simple, lazy abstract machine to execute supercombinators. In *Proceedings of the 1987 Conference on Functional Programming Languages and Computer Architecture*, Portland, Oregon, September 1987.

[GM86]   P.B. Gibbons and Steven S. Muchnick. Efficient instruction scheduling for a pipelined architecture. In *Proceedings of the ACM SIGPLAN '86*

Symposium on Compiler Construction, volume 21, pages 11–16, Palo Alto, CA, June 1986.

[Joh84]   T. Johnsson. Efficient Compilation of Lazy Evaluation. In *Proceedings of the SIGPLAN '84 Symposium on Compiler Construction*, pages 58–69, Montreal, 1984. Available from http://www.cs.chalmers.se/~johnsson.

[Joh91]   Thomas Johnsson. Analysing Heap Contents in a Graph Reduction Intermediate Language. In S.L. Peyton Jones, G. Hutton, and C.K. Holst, editors, *Proceedings of the Glasgow Functional Programming Workshop, Ullapool 1990*, Workshops in Computing, pages 146–171. Springer Verlag, August 1991. Available from http://www.cs.chalmers.se/~johnsson.

[KH89]   R. Kelsey and P. Hudak. Realistic compilation by program transformation. In *Conference Record of the 16th Annual ACM Symposium on Principles of Programming Languages*, pages 281–292, Austin, TX, January 1989.

[PJ92]   S. L. Peyton Jones. Implementing lazy functional languages on stock hardware: the Spineless Tagless G-machine. *Journal of Functional Programming*, 2(2), April 1992.

[PJ96]   Simon Peyton Jones. Compiling Haskell by program transformation: a report from the trenches. In *Proceedings of the European Symposium on Programming*, Linköping, April 1996.

[PJL91]   Simon L. Peyton Jones and John Launchbury. Unboxed values as first class citizens in a non-strict functional language. In *Functional Programming and Computer Architecture*, Sept 1991.

[PJPS96]   Simon Peyton Jones, Will Partain, and André Santos. Let-floating: moving bindings to give faster programs. In *Proceedings of the International Conference on Functional Programming*, Philadelphia, 1996.

[SH89]   Peter A. Steenkiste and John L. Hennessy. A Simple Interprocedural Register Allocation and Its Effectiveness for LISP. *ACM Transactions on Programming Languages and Systems*, 11(1):1–32, January 1989.

[SH97]   Marc Shapiro and Susan Horwitz. Fast and Accurate Flow-Insensitive Points-To Analysis. In *Conference Record of POPL'97: 24nd ACM SIGPLAN-SIGACT Symposium on Principles of Programming Languages*, Paris, France, January 1997.

[SNvGP91] Sjaak Smetsers, Erik Nöcker, John van Groningen, and Rinus Plasmeyer. Generating efficient code for lazy functional languages. In *Proceedings of the 1991 Conference on Functional Programming Languages and Computer Architecture*, Cambridge, Massachusetts, July 1991.

[Wad92]   P. Wadler. The essence of functional programming. In *Proceedings 1992 Symposium on principles of Programming Languages*, pages 1–14, Albuquerque, New Mexico, 1992.

[Wal86]   David W. Wall. Global Register Allocation at Link Time. In *Proceedings of the SIGPLAN '86 Symposium on Compiler Construction*, pages 264–275, New York, 1986.

On Programming Scientific Applications in Sac - a Functional Language Extended by a Subsystem for High-Level Array Operations

Sven-Bodo Scholz

Dept of Computer Science, University of Kiel, 24105 Kiel, Germany
e-mail: sbs@informatik.uni-kiel.de

Abstract. This paper discusses some of the pros and cons of extending a simple functional language called Sac (for Single Assignment C) by array operations similar to those that are available in Apl. The array operations in Sac are based on the ψ-calculus, an algebra of arrays which provides a formalism for specifying and simplifying array operations in terms of index set manipulations.

The programming techniques made possible by Sac are demonstrated by means of a functional program for the approximation of numerical solutions of partial differential equations by multigrid relaxation. This application is not only of practical relevance but also fully exposes the flavors of using high-level array operations. In contrast to specifications in other languages, e.g. in Fortran or Sisal, the Sac program is well structured, reasonably concise, and - what is most important - invariant against dimensionalities and shapes. However, sophisticated compilation techniques are necessary to avoid, whenever possible, the creation of temporary arrays and to eliminate redundant operations.

The paper also includes performance figures for a Sac implementation of the NAS-mgrid-benchmark which are competetive with those of a Sisal implementation.

1 Introduction

Scientific computations often require numerical approximations for solutions of partial differential equations, using sophisticated relaxation methods, which usually involve arrays of 10^6 .. 10^8 elements. Many of the applications such as fluid dynamic problems or weather forecasts must also be stepped through time, taking days or even weeks to run on todays supercomputers, and requiring enormous memory capacities. Clever algorithms and programming techniques must be complemented by optimizing compilers to obtain efficiently executable code which, whenever possible, avoids the creation of intermediate data structures and immediately re-claims memory that is no longer needed.

There is no doubt that the low-level programming style of imperative languages is highly suited for this purpose. Explicit control over the allocation (and de-allocation) of memory space is more or less directly placed in the hands of the programmer and can be adapted exactly to the needs of a given applications. The concept of multiple assignments allows to overwrite arrays no longer needed (and thus to re-use space that is already allocated), and iteration loops can be made to traverse, by properly chosen starts, stops and strides, exactly the array entries which contribute to the desired results.

Most of the efficiency of imperative programs derives from the rigorous exploitation of side-effects due to multiple assignments. Unfortunately, side-effects stand in the way of splitting large programs into concurrently executable parts. Since variables may be shared among them, it is the responsibility of either the programmer or of the compiler to organize the entire computation in a way that produces deterministic results irrespective of varying execution orders.

Functional languages are free of side-effects and therefore appear to be ideal candidates for non-sequential processing which in scientific computations is highly desirable to keep program runtimes within reasonable limits. The absence of side-effects, however, causes considerable problems with the efficient implementation of array operations. Conceptually, they must consume their operand arrays and create new result arrays, rather than overwriting existing ones, which generally is very costly in terms of both memory space and execution time expended. Inferring by static analysis which operations may overwrite their operands is not in all cases decidable [AP95], doing it at runtime inflicts considerable overhead for reference counting.

Functional languages such as MIRANDA [Tur86] or ML [QRM+87] provide little direct support for arrays. HASKELL [HAB+95] includes arrays as data types, using ZF-expressions (comprehensions) to generate array entries, but performance of the compiled code so far is not very competitive. SISAL [BCOF91] and all major data flow languages, e.g., ID and VAL [Nik88, AD79], provide control constructs for the traversal of array entries very similar to those of imperative languages, but strictly enforce the single assignment rule. Owing to very sophisticated compilation techniques, SISAL programs are known to outperform equivalent FORTRAN programs on multiprocessor systems[Can92]. However, SISAL does not offer substantial advantages in terms of programming techniques. Other than introducing another syntax, the programmer is still asked to specify array operations as iteration loops whose index variables and index ranges must be strictly adapted to array dimensionalities and shapes.

Integrating into functional languages an array processing concept similar to that of Iverson's APL [Ive62] considerably improves high-level array processing. Work to this effect has been reported in [Sch86, SBK92], which describes how array operations may be supported by graph reduction machinery, and in [Tu86, TP86], which introduces a functional language FAC based on APL syntax and on a lazy semantics.

Arrays in APL are treated as conceptual entities which can be operated upon by high-level structuring and value-transforming primitives. Explicit specifications of iteration loops (which often are the source of annoying errors due to incorrectly chosen starts, stops or strides) can be avoided in many cases.

Beyond these pragmatic advantages, the APL approach has also stimulated the development of an algebra of arrays, called the ψ-calculus [Mul88, Mul91, MJ91]. It is based on a small set of absolutely essential array operations which are solely defined in terms of dimensionalities, shapes and indexing functions. By application of the rules of this algebra, complex array expressions can be consequently simplified prior to actually compiling them to code, thus avoiding intermediate arrays whenever possible. Extending the ψ-calculus by a subset of high-level structuring and value transforming primitives yields a full-fledged subsystem for array processing which can be smoothly integrated into functional languages.

This paper is to investigate the pros and cons of programming real life scientific applications in the functional language SAC[Sch94, GS95] (for Single Assignment C) which includes high-level primitives for array operations as in the ψ-calculus. SAC is specifically designed to

- provide a functional language with a syntax very similar to that of C in order to ease, for a large community of programmers, the transition from an imperative to a functional programming style;
- support high-level array operations which are invariant against dimensionalities and shapes, liberate programming, whenever possible, from tedious and error-prone specifications of starts, stops and strides for array traversals, and also allow for term simplifications which avoid the creation of intermediate arrays;
- facilitate compilation to host machine code which can be efficiently executed both in terms of time and space demand.

Section 2 gives a brief introduction into the basic language constructs of SAC, and Section 3 introduces the high-level array operations provided by SAC. As an application problem, a program for the approximation of numerical solutions of partial differential equations by multi-grid relaxation [Hac85, HT82, Bra84] is extensively studied in Section 4. This application is not only of practical relevance, but also of interest with respect to the programming techniques required for the array operations involved. Section 5 outlines how a compiler actually produces efficiently executable code from the the program specifications presented in Section 4. Section 6 compares the performance of a SAC implementation of the multigrid algorithm from the NAS-benchmarks [BBB+94] with that of equivalent SISAL and FORTRAN programs.

2   SAC - Single Assignment C

SAC is a strict, purely functional language whose syntax in large parts is identical to that of C. In fact, SAC may be considered a functional subset of C extended by high-level array operations which may be specified in a shape-invariant form. It differs from C proper mainly in that

- it rules out global variables and pointers to keep functions free of side-effects,
- it supports multiple return values for user defined functions, as usual in many dataflow languages[AGP78, AD79, BCOF91],
- it supports high-level array operations, and
- programs need not to be fully typed.

Fig. 1 illustrates the similarity to C by means of a SAC implementation of the Euclidian algorithm for computing the greatest common divisor of two integers, 22 and 27 in the particular case. It consists of three function definitions: a func-

```
int gcd( int high, int low)
{
  if (high < low) {
    mem = low;
    low = high;
    high = mem;
  };
  while( low != 0) {
    quotient, remainder = modulo( high, low);
    high = low;
    low  = remainder;
  }

  return(high);
}

int, int modulo( int x, int y)
{
  quot   = to_int( x/y);
  remain = x - quot*y;
  return( quot, remain);
}

int main ()
{
  return(gcd( 22, 27) );
}
```

Fig. 1. SAC program for computing the greatest common divisor.

tion `gcd` which implements the Euclidian algorithm, a function `modulo` which computes the quotient and the remainder of the division of two integer numbers, and the `main` function which specifies the goal expression to be computed.

Two differences to a C implementation can be observed: the absence of type declarations for local variables, e.g. for `mem`, `quotient`, and `remainder` in the definition of `gcd`, and the usage of two return values for the function `modulo`.

Type declarations for local variables are optional since SAC requires a sophisticated type inference system to deal with arrays of varying dimensionalities and shapes. However, type declarations for parameters and return values of functions are mandatory to aid the type system in resolving function overloading. Since SAC, in contrast to C, does not include pointers or records, there is no other way of returning multiple function values but to make them explicit.

Otherwise, this SAC program uses language constructs which syntactically are exactly the same as in C, i.e. assignments, conditionals, and loop constructs. SAC programs can be straightforwardly transformed into nestings of LET(REC)-expressions, conditionals and local function definitions as they typically occur in other functional languages, i.e. a functional semantics for SAC can be easily defined in terms of these constructs (see [Sch96]).

3 Array-Processing in SAC

The array concept supported by SAC is based on the ψ-calculus, an algebra of arrays [Mul88, Mul91] which provides a formal apparatus for specifying and simplifying array operations in terms of indexed memory accesses in a form that is independent of dimensionalities and shapes, treating arrays, whenever appropriate, as conceptual entities. An array is represented by a shape vector which specifies the number of elements per axis, and by a data vector which lists all entries of the array. For instance, a 2×3 matrix $\begin{pmatrix} 1\,2\,3 \\ 4\,5\,6 \end{pmatrix}$ has shape vector $[2,3]$ and data vector $[1,2,3,4,5,6]$. The set of legitimate indices can be directly infered from the shape vector as

$$\{[i_1, i_2] \quad | \quad 0 \le i_1 < 2, \quad 0 \le i_2 < 3\}$$

where $[i_1, i_2]$ refers to the position $(i_1 * 3 + i_2)$ of the data vector.

A small set of primitives suffices to express all structuring operations on arrays as modifications of their shapes. By introducing a function that converts array indices into offsets within data vectors, the translation of ψ-primitives into loops of data vector accesses can be specified in the ψ-calculus itself. In combination with dedicated transformation rules, this allows for a formal reduction of arbitrarily nested array operations to starts, stops, and strides of direct indexing schemes, from which efficiently executable code which avoids the creation of superfluous intermediate data structures can be directly generated.

In SAC, arrays are generally specified as expressions of the form

reshape(shape_vector, data_vector)

where *shape_vector* and *data_vector* are specified as lists of elements enclosed in square-shaped brackets. Since 1-dimensional arrays are in fact vectors, they can be abbreviated as

$[v_1, ..., v_n]$ $\equiv$ reshape([n], [$v_1, ..., v_n$])

Most of the primitives of the ψ-calculus are made available and defined as primitive functions, using the following syntax[1]:

---

[1] Note, that wherever in these definitions there is a vector or an array as argument, there may be expressions that evaluate to these data structures.

Let a, b denote arrays, let $v = [v_0, ..., v_{k-1}]$ denote a vector of k integers, then

dim(a) returns the dimensionality, i.e., the number of axes, of the array a;
shape(a) returns the shape vector of a;
psi(v, a) $\equiv$ a[v] returns the subarray of a selected by the index vector
   v, provided that $k \leq$ dim(a) and that v $\leq$ shape(a) component-wise over
   all indices $j \in \{[0], ..., [(k-1)]\}$, otherwise it is undefined;
take(v, a) returns the subarray of a with shape v from the front ends of the
   respective axes in a, provided that $0 \leq$ v $\leq$ shape(a) component-wise,
   otherwise it is undefined;
drop(v, a) returns the subarray of a with shape(shape(a)-v) from the
   back ends of the respective axes, provided that $0 \leq$ v $\leq$ shape(a) component-wise, otherwise it is undefined;
cat(k, a, b) catenates the arrays a and b along their k^{th} axis if the shapes
   along the other axes are same, otherwise it is undefined;

All binary operations defined on scalar values are extended to component-wise operations on pairs of arrays and scalar values, as well as on pairs of arrays of the same shapes. A few examples are given in fig. 2 to illustrate these operations.

Let a be a 2×3 matrix with a $= \begin{pmatrix} 1\ 2\ 3 \\ 4\ 5\ 6 \end{pmatrix}$, then the following holds:

```
reshape( [2,3], [1,2,3,4,5,6]) == a
shape(a) == [2,3]
dim(a)   == 2
psi( [1,2], a) == a[[1,2]] == 6
psi( [1], a)   == a[[1]]   == reshape( [3], [4,5,6]) == [4,5,6]
dim( psi( [1], a)) == 1
take( [2,1], a) == reshape( [2,1], [1,4]) != [1,4]
take( [1,1], a) == reshape( [1,1], [1])   != 1
drop( [1,1], a) == reshape( [1,2], [5,6]) != [5,6]
dim( take([2,1],a)) == dim( take([1,1],a)) == dim( drop([1,1],a)) == 2
dim( [1,4]) == dim( [5,6]) == 1
shape( [1,4]) == shape( [5,6]) == [2]
cat( 1, a, reshape( [2,1], [7,8])) == reshape( [2,4], [1,2,3,7,4,5,6,8])
2*a == a+a == reshape( [2,3], [2,4,6,8,10,12])
```

Fig. 2. Example applications of the primitive array operations of SAC.

The primitive functions introduced so far, in one way or another, affect all elements of the argument array(s) in the same way. Unfortunately, this may lead to rather awkward programs if only subarrays need to be operated on, or different operations need to be carried out on non-overlapping subarrays.

As a simple example, consider the problem of adding some constant value, say 1, to the inner elements of an array a of arbitrary shape. These elements are identified by index vectors i_vec from the interval 0*shape(a)+1 <= i_vec <= shape(a)-2. Expressing this computation in terms of an addition function which uniformly applies to all array elements requires that the array first be dismantled of all subarrays specified by index vectors with at least one zero or one maximal component, then the addition be performed on the remaining array, and finally the subarrays that have been taken off be attached again by catenation.

What needs to be cut off before and glued on after the addition of 1 in the special case of a two-dimensional array are the rows and columns with the lowest and highest indices. This leads to the following piece of SAC-program:

```
{ ...
  m = psi([0], shape(a));
  n = psi([1], shape(a));
  upper_row = take( [1,n], a);
  lower_row = drop( [m-1,0], a);
  left_col  = drop( [1,0], take( [m-1,1], a));
  right_col = take( [m-2,1], drop( [1,n-1], a));
  inner = take( [m-2,n-2], drop( [1,1], a));
  middle_section = cat( 1, left, cat( 1, inner+1, right));
  result         = cat( 0, upper, cat( 0, middle_section, lower));
  ... }
```

The disadvantages of this solution are obvious: The program is quite complicated and compilation to efficiently executable code is difficult, and last not least, it is dimension-specific: an adaptation to other dimensionalities requires extensive re-writing.

To overcome these programming problems (and the ensuing compilation problems as well), a more versatile construct for array operations is essential. For this purpose, SAC provides a variant of ZF-expressions called WITH-loops by which operations over pre-specified index ranges can be specified in a shape-independent form.

The syntax of WITH-loops is defined in fig. 3. They consist of three parts: a generator part, a filter part, and an operation part. The generator part defines lower and upper bounds for a set of index vectors and an 'index variable' which represents a vector of this set. The filter part consists of boolean expressions that usually depend on the index variable. They restrict the set of index vectors to those for which all filter expressions evaluate to true. The operation part finally specifies the operation to be performed on each element of the index vector set. Basically, three different kinds of operation parts are available (see *ConExpr* in fig. 3). Their functionality is defined as follows:

Let *shp* and *idx* denote SAC-expressions that evaluate to vectors, let *array* denote a SAC-expression that evaluates to an array, and let *expr* denote an arbitrary SAC-expression. Furthermore, let *fold_op* be the name of a binary commutative and associative function (*FoldFun* in fig 3) with neutral element *neutral*. Then

$WithExpr \quad \Rightarrow$ with ($Generator$ $\big[$, $Filter$ $\big]^{*}$) $Operation$

$Generator \quad \Rightarrow Expr$ <= $Identifier$ <= $Expr$

$Filter \quad \Rightarrow Expr$

$Operation \quad \Rightarrow \big[$ { $LocalDeclarations$ } $\big] ConExpr$

$ConExpr \quad \Rightarrow$ genarray ($Expr$, $Expr$)
$\qquad\qquad |$ modarray ($Expr$, $Expr$, $Expr$)
$\qquad\qquad |$ fold ($FoldFun$, $Expr$, $Expr$)

$FoldFun \quad \Rightarrow$ + | * | $Identifier$

Fig. 3. WITH-loops in SAC.

- genarray(shp, $expr$) generates an array of shape shp whose elements are the values of $expr$ for all index vectors from the specified set, and 0 otherwise;
- modarray($array$, idx, $expr$) returns an array of shape shape($array$) whose elements are the values of $expr$ for all index vectors from the specified set, and the values of $array$[idx] at all other index positions;
- fold($fold\_op$, $neutral$, $expr$) sets out with the neutral element $neutral$ to fold with the binary operation $fold\_op$ the values of $expr$ found in all index positions from the specified set. It is the responsibility of the programmer to make sure that the function $fold\_op$ is commutative and associative in order to guarantee deterministic results.

To increase program readability, local variable declarations may precede the operation part of a WITH-loop. They allow for the abstraction of (complex) subexpressions from the operation part.

Using these WITH-loops, the above example problem can be specified as

```
{ ...
  result = with( 0*shape(a)+1 <= i_vec <= shape(a)-2)
              modarray( a, i_vec, a[i_vec]+1);
... }
```

Apart from the fact that this specification is more concise and easier to understand, it is also invariant against the shape and the dimensionality of a.

4   Programming numerical Applications in SAC: an Example

To illustrate how SAC programs for real world application problems look like, we consider, as an example, approximations of numerical solutions for Poisson equations, i.e., for partial differential equations (PDEs) of the general form

$$\Delta u (x_0, \dots, x_{p-1}) = f (x_0, \dots, x_{p-1}) \mid (x_0, \dots, x_{p-1}) \in \Omega ,$$

where Δ denotes the Laplace-operator and Ω denotes the domain within which solutions for u are defined, given some specific boundary values. For the sake of simplicity, these boundary values are assumed to be

$$u\left(x_0,\ \ldots\ ,x_q^{min},\ \ldots\ ,x_{p-1}\right) = u\left(x_0,\ \ldots\ ,x_q^{max},\ \ldots\ ,x_{p-1}\right) = 0$$

for all $q \in \{0,\ldots,p-1\}$ throughout the example program, though in real world applications the boundary conditions may be more complicated.

Numerical solutions for Poisson equations are based on Gauss-Seidel or Jacobi relaxation algorithms. Both use discretizations of the PDEs on grids of some fixed mesh size h. They take the form

$$L\,u\left(i_0,\ldots,i_{p-1}\right) = h^2 * f\left(i_0,\ldots,i_{p-1}\right)$$

in which all $x_q \in \{x_0,\ldots,x_{p-1}\}$ are replaced by indices $i_q = \lceil x_q - x_q^{min}/h\rceil$ and the values of u and f are represented as p-dimensional arrays, with $i_q \in \{0,\ldots,n_q-1\}$ for all $q \in \{0,\ldots,p-1\}$. The discretizised Laplace operator L adds up, in every inner grid point $(i_0,\ldots,i_{p-1}) \in I_0 \times \ldots \times I_{p-1}$ with $I_q \in \{1,\ldots,n_q-2\}$, weighted values of u in all adjacent points and in the point itself, to compute a new p-dimensional array u'.

Using a p-dimensional array D of elements $D[i_0,\ldots,i_{p-1}]$ with $i_j \in \{0,1,2\}$ for all $j \in \{0,\ldots,p-1\}$, this relaxation step is formally specified as:

$$\forall i_0 \in \{1,...,n_0-2\}...\forall i_{p-1} \in \{1,...,n_{p-1}-2\}:$$
$$u'[i_0,...,i_{p-1}] = \sum_{j_0=0}^{2}\ ...\ \sum_{j_{p-1}=0}^{2} D[j_0,...,j_{p-1}] * u[(i_0+j_0-1),...,(i_{p-1}+j_{p-1}-1)]\ .$$

Both relaxation algorithms require that this computation be repeated several times until u' approximates the solution reasonably well, i.e. until a relaxation step changes the values in all grid points by less than some pre-specified threshold value.

With i_vec$=[i_0,\ldots,i_{p-1}]$ and j_vec$=[j_0,\ldots,j_{p-1}]$ denoting index vectors and a denoting an array , relaxation steps as above may be programmed in SAC in a completely shape-independent form as

```
{ ...
  new_u = with( shape(u)*0+1 <= i_vec <= shape(u)-2) {
             val = with( shape(D)*0 <= j_vec <= shape(D)-1)
                      fold( +, 0, D[j_vec] * u[ i_vec+j_vec-1 ]);
          } modarray( u, i_vec, val);
... }
```

The inner WITH-loop of this SAC-statement computes a new value **val** in grid point $[i_0,\ldots,i_{p-1}]$ by forming, with **fold**, the weighted sum of the values in all adjacent points (and in the point itself). The outer WITH-loop steps through all but the boundary grid points to update the values of **u** by **val**, and to assign the entire array thus computed to **new_u**.

Note that the number of components of the index vectors is solely determined by the shapes of the arrays whose elements must be traversed, i.e., by shape(u) for the outer loop, and by shape(D) for the inner loop. The term shape(u)*0+1 first multiplies all components of shape(u) by 0, and then adds 1, returning as the lower bound for i_vec a vector of p elements $[1,\ldots,1]$, and the term shape(u)-2 subtracts from all components $n_q \mid q \in \{0,\ldots,p-1\}$ of the vector shape(u) the value 2, returning as the upper bound for i_vec a p-dimensional vector $[n_0 - 2,\ldots,n_{p-1} - 2]$. Since shape vectors are part of the array specifications, this piece of program can be applied to arrays of any given shape.

Jacobi or Gauss-Seidel relaxation is known to reduce fairly quickly high-frequency error components but does poorly on low-frequency errors. This is due to the slow point-to-point propagation of corrected values through the entire grid, which in real life applications may have up to 10^4 points in each dimension. A well-established remedy for this problem are so-called multigrid methods which embed relaxation steps into a recursive fine-to-coarse grid approximation, followed by a coarse-to-fine grid correction [Hac85, HT82, Bra84].

Roughly speaking, multigrid relaxation applies the Jacobi or Gauss-Seidel relaxation algorithm recursively to grids of mesh sizes h_1, $\ldots$, h_k , $h_{(k+1)}$, $\ldots, h_m$ with $h_{(k+1)} = 2 * h_k$. It usually sets out with the finest grid and recursively works through some finite sequence of error approximations on increasingly coarser grids (which propagate errors in increasingly larger strides over the points of the original grid), followed by the passage of error corrections in the opposite direction (from coarser to finer grids). The mappings from finer to coarser grids and vice versa are done by calculating weighted averages of the values in adjacent grid points. To illustrate this, fig. 4 depicts two arrays of dimensionality two. The black dots are to represent grid points belonging to a coarse grid of

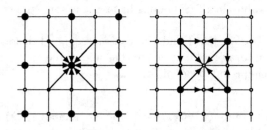

Fig. 4. The fine-to-coarse and coarse-to-fine grid mapping problem

mesh size $2 * h$, whereas both the blank and black dots represent the grid points that belong to a finer grid of mesh size h. The spider in the center of the left grid indicates how the elements of the coarser grid are calculated from those of the finer grid during a fine-to-coarse mapping. Conversely, the spider in the right grid shows from which elements of the coarser grid the elements of the finer grid are interpolated during a coarse-to-fine mapping.

Fine-to-coarse mapping, in fact, is very similar to relaxation: the value in a point of the coarser grid must be computed as a weighted sum over the values in all surrounding points, including the actual value in the point itself, of the finer grid. Let u_c, u_f and W respectively denote the arrays by which the coarser grid, the finer grid and the weight coefficients are represented, then the fine-to-coarse mapping may be specified in SAC in a shape-invariant form as

```
{ ...
  u_c = with( 0*shape(u_f)+1 <= i_vec <= shape(u_f)/2-1) {
          val = with( 0*shape(W) <= j_vec <= shape(W)-1)
                 fold( +, 0, W[j_vec] * u_f[ 2*i_vec+j_vec-1]);
        } genarray( shape(u_f)/2+1, val);
... }
```

with $shape(u\_c)=shape(u\_f)/2+1$, and with $shape(W)=[3,...,3]$ and $dim(W)= p$. For the two-dimensional case, a typical array of weight coefficients is

$$W = 1/4 * C \quad \text{with} \quad C = \begin{pmatrix} 1/4 & 1/2 & 1/4 \\ 1/2 & 1 & 1/2 \\ 1/4 & 1/2 & 1/4 \end{pmatrix} \quad ,$$

of which the value 1 in the center coincides with a point of the finer grid which maps directly into a point of the coarser grid (or coincides with the center of the spider in the left picture of fig. 4). This weight array lets the value in each point of the finer grid contribute with different weights to adjacent values of the coarser grid: 1/4 if it is in the center of the spider, 1/8 each to two points on each side if it is on a horizontal or vertical axis of the grid, and 1/16 each to four points if it is on the intersection between two diagonals.

The basic idea of specifying coarse-to-fine grid mapping in a shape-invariant form is to first initialize the array for the finer grid, which must have twice the shape of the coarser grid, in every other point along each axis with the respective values of the coarser grid, and all points in between with zero values. Then all values of the finer grid are computed in the same way as for the fine-to-coarse mapping, i.e., by adding up, in each point of the finer grid, weighted values of all points that are adjacent to it. This may be done with the same weight array as above, except that all its entities have to be multiplied by 4, i.e. we can use C as weight array for the coarse-to-fine grid mapping.

Thus, if the center of the weight array C coincides with a point of the coarser grid (see also the spider in the right picture of fig. 4), it reproduces the value in that point since it is multiplied by 1, and all surrounding points contribute zero values. Similarly, the values in points between two non-zero elements on a horizontal or vertical axis are computed as the sum of their values, multiplied by 1/2, and the values of points on the intersection between two diagonals are computed as the sum of four non-zero values, multiplied by 1/4. This algorithm can be implemented in SAC as follows:

```
{ ...
  u_f = with( 0*shape(u_c) <= i_vec <= shape(u_c)*2-3)
        genarray( shape(u_c)*2-2, 0);

  u_f = with( 0*shape(u_c) <= i_vec <= shape(u_c)-1)
        modarray( u_f, 2*i_vec, u_c[i_vec]);

  u_f = with( 0*shape(u_f)+1 <= i_vec <= shape(u_f)-2) {
          val = with( 0*shape(C) <= j_vec <= shape(C)-1)
                fold( +, 0, C[j_vec] * u_f[ i_vec+j_vec-1]);
        } modarray( u_f, i_vec, val);
... }
```

This piece of program, exept for the coefficients of the weight array, again remains invariant against changing dimensionalities and shapes. However, there is a simple algorithm by which the coefficients of the weight array may be computed dependent on the dimensionality p of the grid. Given that all entries of the weight array have p-dimensional index vectors within range

$$[0, \ldots, 0] <= \text{i\_vec} <= [2, \ldots, 2]$$

and that the entry in the center has index vector $\text{i\_vec}_C = [1, \ldots, 1]$, all there is to do is to compute $\text{i\_vec} - \text{i\_vec}_C = i_D$, count the number n of non-zero components in the vector i_D, and use the value 2^{-n} as entry $C[\text{i\_vec}]$:

```
{ ...
  C = with( shape(u)*0 <= i_vec <= shape(u)*0+2) {
        n=0;
        for( i=0; i<dim(u); i++) {
          if( i_vec[[i]] != 1)
            n++;
        }
        val = pow(2,-n);
      } genarray( shape(u)*0+3, val);
... }
```

Apart from the WITH-loops introduced sofar, the full multigrid program primarily consists of WHILE-loops which iterate through relaxation steps embedded in successive fine-to-coarse grid mappings followed by successions of coarse-to-fine grid mappings. As these iterations are quite straightforward and not directly related to the shapes of the arrays involved, they are omitted here.

5 A Note on Compilation

The program fragments specified in the preceding section are essential components of a SAC implementation of multigrid relaxation which can be uniformly applied to argument arrays (grids) of varying dimensionalities and shapes. However, this generality may have to be paid for by some penalty on runtime performance, unless compilation to executable code can be parameterized at least by dimensionalities, if not shapes, of actual argument arrays. For this purpose, the SAC compiler includes an elaborate type inference system to infer through a hierarchy of array types the most specific of these parameters statically. This enables the compiler to translate SAC function definitions into function codes or WITH-loops into nestings of FOR-loops that are exactly adapted to the array parameters which actually have to be dealt with. If necessary, the compiler may even generate several instances of function or WITH-loop codes to operate on arrays of changing dimensionalities and shapes.

To convey the basic idea of how the SAC compiler goes about converting WITH-loops into executable code, we consider, as an example, the program fragment which implements single relaxation steps.

For two-dimensional arrays with a shape vector of the form [n,n], it can be specialized at the SAC-level as

```
{ ...
  new_u = with( [1,1] <= i_vec <= [n-2,n-2]) {
            val = with( [0,0] <= j_vec <= [2,2])
                   fold( +, 0, D[j_vec] * u[ i_vec+j_vec-1 ]);
          } modarray( u, i_vec, val);
  ... }
```

simply by applying constant folding to the specifications of loop boundaries, which in the particular case are two-component vectors. Assuming

$$D = \begin{pmatrix} 0 & 1/4 & 0 \\ 1/4 & -1 & 1/4 \\ 0 & 1/4 & 0 \end{pmatrix}$$

to be the array of weight coefficients, the inner WITH-loop can be further specialized as

```
{ ...
  new_u = with( [1,1] <= i_vec <= [n-2,n-2]) {
            val = 0.25 * u[i_vec+[-1,0]] + 0.25 * u[i_vec+[0,-1]]
                  - a[i_vec]
                  + 0.25 * u[i_vec+[0,1] ] + 0.25 * u[i_vec+[1,0] ];
          } modarray( u, i_vec, val);
  ... }
```

by means of loop unrolling in combination with another constant folding step.

Following these high-level optimizations, the SAC-to-C compiler takes over to compile the remaining WITH-loop into two nested C-FOR-loops. Since SAC represents arrays by shape and data vectors, the index vectors i_vec which are to select array elements must be converted, by means of a function idx_to_off(i_vec,

shape) (with shape = [n,n] in the particular case), into offsets into the data
vector. Taking offset as a variable that carries actual values of idx_to_off(i_vec,
[n,n]) the C-code for the WITH-loop looks like this:

```
{ ...
  offset = 0;

  /* copy non-indexed elems of dim 0 */
  for(tmp=0; tmp <=n; tmp++)
    new_u_data[offset++] = u_data[offset];

  for(i_vec_data[0]=1; i_vec_data[0]<=n-2; i_vec_data[0]++) {
    /* copy non-indexed elem of dim 1  */
    new_u_data[offset++] = u_data[offset];
    for(i_vec_data[1]=1; i_vec_data[1]<=n-2; i_vec_data[1]++) {
      val = ... ;               /* compiled code for the weighted  */
                                /* summation of neighbors          */
      new_u_data[offset++] = val;
    }
    /* copy non-indexed elem of dim 1  */
    new_u_data[offset++] = u_data[offset];
  }

  /* copy non-indexed elems of dim 0 */
  for(tmp=0; tmp <=n; tmp++)
    new_u_data[offset++] = u_data[offset];
... }
```

In order to generate efficiently executable code for the expression that computes
val for each index vector i_vec, it is critically important to simplify as much as
possible accesses in the data vector representation u_data of u to the four elements adjacent to i_vec (whose values have to added up). To do so, we make use
of an optimization called index-vector-elimination which is based on the fact that
idx_to_off(i_vec + j_vec, shp)=idx_to_off(i_vec, shp)+idx_to_off(j_vec,
shp). This renders it possible to transform a selector term of the form, say, u[
i_vec + [0,-1]] into an access to u_data which is given as:

$$u\_data[idx\_to\_off(i\_vec + [0,-1], [n,n])]$$
$$= u\_data[idx\_to\_off(i\_vec, [n,n]) + idx\_to\_off([0,-1], [n,n])]$$
$$= u\_data[idx\_to\_off(i\_vec, [n,n]) - n]$$

Since the variable offset in the above piece of program already holds actual
values of idx_to_off(i_vec, [n,n]), the entire statement can, by similar transformation of the other four terms, be compiled to

```
{ ...
      val = 0.25 * u_data[offset-n] + 0.25 * u_data[offset-1]
            - u_data[offset]
            + 0.25 * u_data[offset+1] + 0.25 * u_data[offset+n];
      new_u_data[offset++] = val;
... }
```

as the body of the innermost FOR-loop. This optimization reduces the indexing arithmetic for accesses into the data vector to what is absolutely necessary.

Beyond that, the SAC-to-C compiler, of course, performs other optimizations which belong to the standard repertoire and, therefore, will not be outlined here.

6 Performance Figures

In this section we present some comparative performance measurements which show to which extend the SAC approach is competitive, in terms of program runtimes and memory space consumption, with FORTRAN and SISAL implementations. This comparison is based on the multigrid kernel MG of the NAS-benchmarks [BBB+94] which performs some prespecified number of complete multigrid cycles on a three-dimensional array of $2^n, n \in \{3, 4, ...\}$ entries per axis in the finest grid. Each cycle moves through a sequence of mappings from the finest to the coarsest grid of 4x4x4 entries, followed by a sequence of alternatingly doing relaxations and coarse-to-fine grid mappings back to the finest grid.

The FORTRAN implementation of this algorithm was directly taken from the benchmark[2], the SISAL program was hand-coded to perform the same elementary computations in the same order as the FORTRAN benchmark, whereas the SAC program uses the shape-invariant specifications of relaxation steps and of mappings between finer and coarser grids as outlined in Section 4.

The hardware platform used for this contest was a SUN ULTRASPARC-170 with 192MB of main memory. The FORTRAN program was compiled by the SUN FORTRAN compiler f77 version sc3.0.1 which generates native code directly. The SISAL and SAC programs were compiled by the SISAL compiler osc, version 13.0.2, and by the SAC compiler sac2c, respectively, both of which produce C-code as output. The GNU-C-compiler gcc version 2.6.3 was used to compile the C-code to native machine code. Program execution times and space demands were measured by the operating system timer and process status commands, respectively.

Fig.5 shows the time and space demands of all three multigrid implementations for three different problem-sizes, these being 32, 64, and 128 elements per axis. The bars in the left diagram depict execution times relative to that of the SAC program, with absolute times for one full multigrid cycle annotated inside the bars. For all three problem sizes the execution time of the SAC program is marginally shorter than that of the SISAL program, whereas the FORTRAN pro-

---

[2] We only simplified the initial array generation and modified the problem-size.

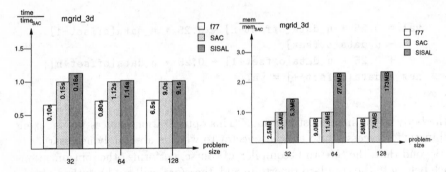

Fig. 5. Time and Space Demand for Multigrid Relaxation on 3 Dimensional Arrays

gram, on average, takes only 70% of the time for the SAC program. The reasons for the gap between the FORTRAN- and the SAC implementation are manifold.

Part of it may be attributed to the shape-independent specification of the coarse-to-fine mapping. As a comparison with a dimension-specific specification shows, the overhead due to additional additions/ multiplications causes about 10% of the slowdown. Also, the SAC compiler, as of now, uses the UNIX commands `malloc` and `free` to allocate and de-allocate heap space. Experiences from the implementation of the functional language KIR[Klu94] suggest that managing some program-specific heap from within the code can be expected to improve performance by another 10%. Last but not least, the C-code produced by the current compiler version is not yet fully optimized. Experiments with hand-coded improvements suggest that program execution times close to that of the FORTRAN implementation are within reach by integrating more elaborate optimizations.

The slightly poorer performance of the SISAL vs. the SAC implementation, despite the highly optimizing SISAL compiler [SW85, Can89, CE95, FO95], is presumably caused by the representation of arrays as vectors of vectors of data elements which inflicts a considerable overhead when accessing array entries that are adjacent to each other along other than the major axis.[3]

The diagram on the right of fig. 5 compares the relative space-demands of the three implementations. It shows that the FORTRAN program is the most space-efficient one, requiring on average only 80% of the space taken up by the SAC program. The additional space demand of the latter can be tracked down, by careful analysis of how both programs actually execute, to the coarse-to-fine grid mapping. Whereas the FORTRAN implementation needs to allocate only one instance of the finer array since it can do the interpolation of elements of the finer grid from those of the coarser grid directly, the SAC compiler version faithfully creates a second array into which the updated values are placed, as it is not yet equipped to fold WITH-loops whenever there is an opportunity to do so.

---

[3] For the next SISAL release (version 2.0)[BCOF91] an implementation of multi-dimensional arrays as continuous memory-blocks is intended [Old92].

The memory demand of the SISAL program significantly exceeds that of the SAC program, in the case of the largest problem size by more than a factor of two. We have not yet been able to identify the likely cause of this problem.

In order to dig a little deeper into the differences between the SAC implementation and the SISAL implementation, we also compared multigrid relaxation on two- and four-dimensional arrays. Whereas the SAC program could be used without changes, the SISAL program had to be re-written to adapt the FOR-loops to the actual dimensionalities of the arrays modified.

The performance measurements shown in fig. 6 nicely expose the overhead

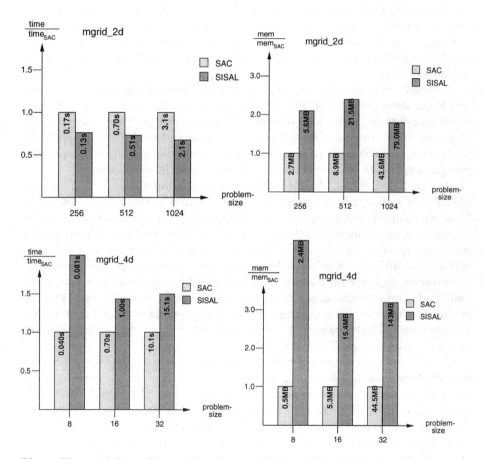

Fig. 6. Time and Space-Demand for Multigrid Relaxations on Different Dimensionalities

inflicted by the array representations of SISAL which grows with the dimensionality of the grid. While the two-dimensional SISAL program requires only 70% of the execution time of the SAC program, the situation is completely reverse in the four-dimensional case. Likewise, the space demand of the SISAL program increases relative to that of the SAC program with increasing grid dimensionality (from a factor of 2 for the two-dimensional case to a factor of 3 for the four-dimensional case).

7 Conclusion

This paper was to investigate, by means of a reasonably sophisticated array processing program (multigrid relaxation of PDEs), to which extent the integration of high-level array programming techniques into functional languages enhances program design and abstraction from problem-specific parameters, without paying too much of a performance penalty. The investigation is based on a performance comparison between a functional variant of C called SAC, whose design is focussed on the efficient support of high-level array operations, and SISAL, which is widely accepted to be the most efficient functional language for numerical applications.

SAC defines a set of structuring and value-transforming array operations which are invariant against dimensionalities and shapes, and apply uniformly to all elements (or subarrays) of arrays. They liberate programming from tedious and error-prone specifications of starts, stops and strides of iteration loops which prescribe traversals of array entries in a particular order, and also render programs applicable to arrays of different dimensionalities and shapes.

As this paper shows, elegant and concise programming can be achieved by the introduction of a high-level array concept similar to that of APL, extended by array comprehension constructs (WITH-loops) which, whenever necessary or appropriate, apply operations (functions) only to selected subsets of array entries which are specified in terms of index ranges and filter expressions. Of course, WITH-loop constructs, which have been frequently used in the multigrid program, re-introduce, as index ranges in conjunction with filter expressions, starts, stops and strides into programming through the back door. However, they may be specified in a shape-invariant form, and the filters may select entries from within the pre-specified index ranges by criteria other than equidistant index positions as they can be traversed with DO-loops.

As has been demonstrated for the example program, compilation to efficiently executable code of high-level programs which use a mix of array comprehensions and primitive array operations poses no major problems. Although the SAC compiler used for the performance measurements still lacks some advanced optimizations as they are integrated into the SISAL compiler [SW85, Can89, CE95, FO95], competitive performance is achieved through a type-inference system which generates dimension dependent specializations of function bodies and through a special optimization technique for the elimination of temporary index vectors.

Further improvements of the C-code generated can be expected by the application of the transformation rules of the ψ-calculus, which serves as a formal basis for the array concept of SAC. This does not only include simple optimizations of nested applications of primitive operations, e.g. take(v, (take(w, a))) = take(v, a) but the systematic simplification of complex expressions such as the folding of two WITH-loops which, in the example examined in this paper, can be expected to reduce the space-demand of the SAC implementation to that of the FORTRAN implementation.

References

[AD79]   W.B. Ackerman and J.B. Dennis: *VAL-A Value-Oriented Algorithmic Language: Preliminary Reference Manual.* TR 218, MIT, Cambridge, MA, 1979.

[AGP78]   Arvind, K.P. Gostelow, and W. Plouffe: *The ID-Report: An asynchronous Programming Language and Computing Machine.* Technical Report 114, University of California at Irvine, 1978.

[AP95]   P. Achten and R. Plasmeijer: *The ins and outs of Clean I/O.* Journal of Functional Programming, Vol. 5(1), 1995, pp. 81–110.

[BBB+94]   D. Bailey, E. Barszcz, J. Barton, et al.: *The NAS Parallel Benchmarks.* RNR 94-007, NASA Ames Research Center, 1994.

[BCOF91]   A.P.W. Böhm, D.C. Cann, R.R. Oldehoeft, and J.T. Feo: *SISAL Reference Manual Language Version 2.0.* CS 91-118, Colorado State University, Fort Collins, Colorado, 1991.

[Bra84]   A. Brandt: *Multigrid Methods: 1984 Guide.* Dept of applied mathematics, The Weizmann Institute of Science, Rehovot/Israel, 1984.

[Can89]   D.C. Cann: *Compilation Techniques for High Performance Applicative Computation.* Technical Report CS-89-108, Lawrence Livermore National Laboratory, LLNL, Livermore California, 1989.

[Can92]   D.C. Cann: *Retire Fortran? A Debate Rekindled.* Communications of the ACM, Vol. 35(8), 1992, pp. 81–89.

[CE95]   D.C. Cann and P. Evripidou: *Advanced Array Optimizations for High Performance Functional Languages.* IEEE Transactions on Parallel and Distributed Systems, Vol. 6(3), 1995, pp. 229–239.

[FO95]   S.M. Fitzgerald and R.R. Oldehoeft: *Update-in-place Analysis for True Multidimensional Arrays.* In A.P.W. Böhm and J.T. Feo (Eds.): High Performance Functional Computing, 1995, pp. 105–118.

[GS95]   C. Grelck and S.B. Scholz: *Classes and Objects as Basis for I/O in SAC.* In T. Johnsson (Ed.): Proceedings of the Workshop on the Implementation of Functional Languages'95. Chalmers University, 1995, pp. 30–44.

[HAB+95]   K. Hammond, L. Augustsson, B. Boutel, et al.: *Report on the Programming Language Haskell: A Non-strict, Purely Functional Language.* University of Glasgow, 1995. Version 1.3.

[Hac85]   W. Hackbusch: *Multi-grid Methods and Applications.* Springer, 1985.

[HT82]   W. Hackbusch and U. Trottenberg: *Multigrid Methods.* LNM, Vol. 960. Springer, 1982.

[Ive62]   K.E. Iverson: *A Programming Language.* Wiley, New York, 1962.

[Klu94]   W. Kluge: *A User's Guide for the Reduction System π-RED.* Internal Report 9419, University of Kiel, 1994.

[MJ91]   L.M. Restifo Mullin and M. Jenkins: *A Comparison of Array Theory and a Mathematics of Arrays.* In Arrays, Functional Languages and Parallel Systems. Kluwer Academic Publishers, 1991, pp. 237–269.

[Mul88]   L.M. Restifo Mullin: *A Mathematics of Arrays.* PhD thesis, Syracuse University, 1988.

[Mul91]   L.M. Restifo Mullin: *The Ψ-Function: A Basis for FFP with Arrays*. In L.M. Restifo Mullin (Ed.): Arrays, Functional Languages and Parallel Systems. Kluwer Academic Publishers, 1991, pp. 185–201.

[Nik88]   R.S. Nikhil: *ID Version 88.1, Reference Manual*. CSG Memo 284, MIT, Laboratory for Computer Science, Cambridge, MA, 1988.

[Old92]   R.R. Oldehoeft: *Implementing Arrays in SISAL 2.0*. In Proceedings of the Second SISAL Users' Conference, 1992, pp. 209–222.

[QRM⁺87] D. Mac Queen, R.Harper, R. Milner, et al.: *Functional Programming in ML*. Lfcs education, University of Edinburgh, 1987.

[SBK92]   C. Schmittgen, H. Blödorn, and W.E. Kluge: π-RED* - *a Graph Reducer for Full-Fledged λ-Calculus*. New Generation Computing, Vol. 10(2), 1992, pp. 173–195.

[Sch86]   C. Schmittgen: *A Datatype Architecture for Reduction Machines*. In 19th Hawaii International Conference on System Sciences, Vol. I, 1986, pp. 78–87.

[Sch94]   S.-B. Scholz: **S**ingle **A**ssignment **C** - *Functional Programming Using Imperative Style*. In John Glauert (Ed.): Proceedings of the 6th International Workshop on the Implementation of Functional Languages. University of East Anglia, 1994.

[Sch96]   S.-B. Scholz: **S**ingle **A**ssignment **C** - *Entwurf und Implementierung einer funktionalen C-Variante mit spezieller Unterstützung shape-invarianter Array-Operationen*. PhD thesis, Institut für Informatik und praktische Mathematik, Universität Kiel, 1996.

[SW85]   S. Skedzielewski and M.L. Welcome: *Data Flow Graph Optimization in IF1*. In FPCA '85, Nancy, LNCS, Vol. 201. Springer, 1985, pp. 17–34.

[TP86]   H-C. Tu and A.J. Perlis: *FAC: A Functional APL Language*. IEEE Software, Vol. 3(1), 1986, pp. 36–45.

[Tu86]   H-C. Tu: *FAC: Functional Array Calculator and its Application to APL and Functional Programming*. PhD thesis, Yale University, 1986.

[Tur86]   D.A. Turner: *An Overview of Miranda*. SIGPLAN Notices, Vol. 21(12), 1986, pp. 158–166.

The Implementation and Efficiency of Arrays in Clean 1.1

John H. G. van Groningen
Computing Science Institute, University of Nijmegen
Toernooiveld 1, 6525 ED Nijmegen, The Netherlands
e-mail: johnvg@cs.kun.nl

Abstract

We present a new approach to implementing arrays in a pure lazy functional programming language. The arrays can be updated destructively by using uniqueness typing, and the elements can be unboxed. We describe the implementation of these arrays in the functional programming language Clean 1.1. The performance of two sorting algorithms and a fast fourier transformation written in Clean using arrays is compared with similar programs written in C. The current implementation of Clean is on average about 25 percent slower than C for these programs.

1 Introduction

Until recently, most implementations of pure lazy functional programming languages had limited or no support for arrays. The main reason for this lack was that an implementation could not update arrays in place, but had to copy the array first before an element could be changed. This copying is necessary because there may be other references to the array in the program, and changing the array will cause a side effect, which of course is not allowed in a pure language.

This update problem also made implementation of efficient input/output very difficult. For example, writing to a file or to the screen can only be done without a side effect if there are no more references in the program to the old file (the file before the write) or the old screen.

A way to solve such problems is by using uniqueness typing [BaSm93]. Uniqueness typing tries to determine at compile time which objects are unique using a combination of reference counting, type checking and program analysis. An object passed as an argument to a function is *unique* if there is only one reference to it when the function is applied. An array update function on a unique array can now be implemented efficiently. When the update function is called at runtime, there is only one reference to the array, which can therefore be updated in place.

The remainder of this paper is organised as follows. In section 2 we describe lazy, strict and unboxed arrays in Clean. Section 3 combines these 3 kinds of arrays using a type constructor class. Section 4 discusses arrays of unique elements. In the next section the performance of unboxed arrays is compared with arrays in C. We give a few concluding remarks in section 6.

2 Lazy, Strict and Unboxed Arrays

The functional programming language Clean [PlaEe95] uses uniqueness typing, among other things, to implement destructively updateable arrays. There are three kinds of arrays in Clean: lazy, strict and unboxed. Lazy arrays are the most general ones, but also the most inefficient ones. Strict arrays are more efficient because the array elements are always evaluated (in root normal form). Unboxed arrays occupy less memory and are even more efficient. Lazy, strict and unboxed arrays are considered to be of different types. The overloading mechanism is used to handle arrays in a uniform manner. This is discussed is section 3.

2.1 Lazy Arrays

To manipulate (lazy) arrays the following functions have been predefined in the standard library of Clean 1.1:

```
createArray :: !Int e         -> .{e}
update      :: !*{.e} !Int .e -> .{.e}
select      :: !.{.e} !Int    -> .e
uselect     :: !u:{e} !Int    -> (e, !u:{e})
size        :: !.{.e}         -> Int
usize       :: !u:{.e}        -> (!Int, !u:{.e})
```

An array with elements of type e is denoted as {e}. Special symbols appear in the specification of a Clean type. For instance, ! is a strictness annotation. The other strange symbols have to do with uniqueness typing. A `*` before a type indicates that the type is unique. A u: before a type indicates that the type has a uniqueness attribute variable u. A type annotated with a uniqueness attribute variable can be unified with either a unique or a non-unique type. Usually, such a uniqueness attribute variable occurs several times in a function type. In an instance of a function type all types annotated with the same variable are either all instantiated with a unique type or all with a non-unique type. For example, the two u: before the array type in the uselect function indicate that if uselect is used on a unique array, the array returned in the tuple is also unique. Furthermore, if uselect is used on a non-unique array, the returned array will be non-unique as well.

Dots are used as an abbreviation to reduce the number of uniqueness attribute variables. A dot before a type variable v indicates that all type variables v annotated with a dot have the same anonymous uniqueness attribute variable. Prefixing a type, that is not a type variable, with a dot indicates that the type has an anonymous uniqueness attribute variable that does not occur anywhere else in the function type. A more detailed explanation of uniqueness attributes can be found in the Clean reference manual [PlaEe95].

`createArray` n e returns a one-dimensional unique array of n elements, all elements are initialised with e. The indices of the array are the integers from 0 to n-1.

`update` a i e returns an array which is identical to a, except that the element indexed by i of the array is updated with e. This function can only be used if a is a unique array.

`select` a i returns element i of array a.

`uselect` a i returns a tuple with the ith element of the array a and the array itself. This function is usually used to select elements from unique arrays, because we usually cannot use the `select` function to select an element from a unique array and then later use this array as a unique array as well. The compiler does not accept this because in such a case there would be more than one reference to the array. Because `uselect` also returns a 'new' array, which is identical to the array before the selection, we can select an element from a unique array and still use the (new) unique array.

`size` a returns the number of elements of array a.

`usize` a returns a tuple with the number of elements of array a and the array. Like `uselect`, this function is usually used to obtain the size of a unique array.

Clean 1.1 also includes the following syntactic sugar to manipulate arrays. Instead of `update` a i n, one may write {a & [i]=n}. Several updates at once are also possible, for example: {a & [i]=n,[j]=m}. `select` a i can also be written as: a.[i]. `uselect`'s can be done in patterns, for example:

```
swap a=:([i]=ai,[j]=aj}    =    {a & [i]=aj,[j]=ai}
```

is equivalent to:

```
swap __a = let! s=uselect _a j
              in   {a &[i]=aj,[j]=ai}
           where
              (ai,_a) = uselect __a i
              (aj,a)  = s
```

Selections in patterns are evaluated immediately to prevent space leaks (see section 2.2).

Arrays are stored in the heap. In a lazy context [PlaEe95] an array is represented by a node consisting of 2 machine words (a word consists of 32 bits in current implementations). The first word is an ARRAY descriptor, the second word is a pointer to another node in the heap. This other node consists of 3+n words, where n is the number of elements. The first word of these contains a descriptor and the second word the array size. The third word is 0 for lazy arrays. The remaining n words contain pointers to the elements of the array (nodes in the heap).

In a strict context the 2 word array indirection node is not used. In this case an array is represented only by the node of size 3+n. The compiler will create a new array indirection node if the array is later also used in a lazy context.

The advantage of this scheme is that we save an extra pointer indirection when we want to load or store information in the array. The disadvantage is that we sometimes have to create new array indirection nodes.

In the best case the code generated by the Clean compiler for a CISC processor for the update, select and size functions consists of only one machine instruction. This happens if the function is in a strict context, the compiler can determine that all arguments are evaluated, and the values of the arguments are already in registers. However, the compiler has to generate 3 instructions on most RISCs to do a selection or update instead of just one.

2.2 Inefficiency of Lazy Arrays

Although the array functions (except createArray) described above can be implemented in O(1), efficiency is still not as good as in (strict) imperative programming languages like C. This has the following reasons:

- More memory is required to store lazy arrays. For example, in an imperative language like C an array of n integers can be stored in n machine words. In Clean we need 3+3*n machine words. The elements of the array have to be pointers to nodes in the heap, because an element of an array can be unevaluated, and unevaluated expressions are stored in the heap as closures. So, even if an array contains evaluated integers, we still have to store them in the heap. To be able to recognise that an element is an evaluated integer we have to mark it. Therefore we store a descriptor just before the value of the integer. This descriptor is used by the garbage collector. So, for every evaluated element we have to store a pointer, a descriptor and a value. This means we have to store 3 words per element.
- Access to values in array elements is more expensive. For example, to select an integer, we first have to load a pointer, then load the descriptor, then examine the descriptor to find out if the integer has already been evaluated, and if it is evaluated, load the value. If the integer has not yet been evaluated, we have to call the evaluation code and later load the value. Only one load instruction is required to select an integer from an array in a language like C on a CISC processor.

We noticed that many programs using these lazy arrays use much more memory than expected. Even if all the extra costs of lazy arrays are taken into account. The most important reasons for this high memory use are:

- The update function does not evaluate the new array element. So, in most cases the update function will store a closure in the array. In many programs an array is updated many times before an element of the array is used. In such cases many elements of the array become closures, which are usually larger in size than an evaluated array element.

- A lazy array selector contains a reference to the whole array, not just to one element. The compiler creates closures for array selectors in a lazy context. Such a closure contains a pointer to the array and the index. The garbage collector generally cannot determine which element is selected from the array, because the index could still be unevaluated. So, even if there is just one reference to a selection closure of an array, the memory referenced by the whole array cannot be deallocated. For example, if a function creates a new vector by adding two vectors, the memory used by these two vectors cannot be deallocated as long as there are references to the new vector and only one element of this new vector is unevaluated.

2.3 Strict Arrays

To be able to write more efficient programs, Clean 1.1 also has strict arrays. A strict array with elements of type e is denoted with {!e}. The implementation stores strict arrays in the same way as lazy arrays, and the same kind of functions can be used for strict arrays as for lazy arrays. Different from the previous approach is that the update, createArray and uselect functions evaluate the array element to root normal form. The types of the functions now become:

```
createArray :: !Int !e          -> .{!e}
update      :: !*{!.e} !Int !.e -> .{!.e}
select      :: !.{!.e} !Int     -> .e
uselect     :: !u:{!e} !Int     -> (!e, !u:{!e})
size        :: !.{!.e}          -> Int
usize       :: !u:{!.e}         -> (!Int, !u:{!.e})
```

As a consequence, the select function for strict arrays can be implemented more efficiently than for lazy arrays, because it does not have to evaluate the element selected from the array. Also strict arrays cannot contain closures, so the memory use problem caused by the laziness of the update function does not occur with strict arrays. This high memory use caused by array selectors in a lazy context is still a problem, but happens less often. For example the vector add function will no longer build selection closures, because the sum of the vector elements is computed before it is stored in the new vector.

Unfortunately, the amount of memory occupied by a strict array is still as bad as for a lazy array with evaluated elements. For example, we still have to represent an array of integers by an array of pointers to integer nodes in the heap. However, the problem is now only caused by the fact that the predefined array functions are of polymorphic type. This means that the select function can be used to select an element from any type of array it is applied to. Therefore, array elements have to be represented in a uniform way as well.

This polymorphism also has its advantages. For example, one only has to write one function, like `swap`, `reverse` or `copy`, and one can use it for all types of arrays. In an imperative languages like C a function that swaps two integers in an arrays cannot be used to swap two reals. A swap function that can be used for all arrays can be implemented in C, if we pass the size of an element of the array to the function, and use it to calculate the addresses of the elements. But such a function is slower, and more difficult to use.

2.4 Unboxed Arrays

We now choose the most efficient representation for every type of array. So, an array of n integers is stored in n+3 machine words. The elements of such arrays are unboxed and strict. We denote such an unboxed array type with `{#e}`, where e is the type of the elements.

The Clean compiler stores the unboxed arrays in a strict context as follows: (we assume the sizes of integers and pointers are 4 bytes, and n is the number of elements of the array)
- `{#Char}`: 8+n bytes, a string descriptor, the size and the characters.

The first 12 bytes of all other unboxed array nodes are a descriptor, the size, and a descriptor that describes the elements, for example an integer descriptor for an `{#Int}`.
- `{#Int}`, `{#Real}` and `{#Bool}`: 12+es*n bytes, where es is the size of an element: 4, 8 or 1 bytes.
- Arrays of records: 12+es*n bytes, where es is the sum of the sizes of the elements of the record.
- Arrays of arrays: 12+4n bytes, for this array only. 'Unboxed' arrays of arrays are represented as arrays of pointers to arrays, without the extra array indirection node for the elements.

At most 3 align bytes follow a `{#Char}` or a `{#Bool}` to align the next node in the heap at a word aligned address (multiple of 4).

The problems caused by the different representations for different types of arrays can be solved using Clean's overloading mechanism. For every basic type, for example `Int`, we define:

```
createArray_int :: !Int !Int                 -> .{#Int}
update_int      :: !*{#v:Int} !Int !v:Int -> .{#v:Int}
select_int      :: !.{#v:Int} !Int           -> v:Int
uselect_int     :: !u:{#Int} !Int            -> (!Int, !u:{#Int})
size_int        :: !.{#.Int}                  -> Int
usize_int       :: !u:{#v:Int}                -> (!Int, !u:{#v:Int})
```

Of course, we don't want to write `select_int` when writing a program using integer arrays, so we define a class for every array function. For example for `select`:

```
class select e :: ! {#.e} !Int -> .e
```

and we define instances for all element types, for example:

```
instance select Int
where
   select a i = select_int a I

instance select Real
where
   select a i = select_real a i
```

Now we can still write select and the type checker will try to determine which instance of select should be used. If a programmer defines a function that uses overloaded array functions, the compiler will automatically generate specialised versions of this function, if the overloading of the array functions cannot be resolved while typing the function. In this way the compiler can remove nearly all overloading within a module. So the program will usually be just as efficient as it would have been without using overloading.

When such an overloaded function is exported, by specifying the function type in a definition module, and is called by a function in another module, the compiler cannot generate specialised versions. If this happens, the function will be very inefficient. To prevent this, the programmer can tell the compiler to generate specialised versions by adding an export statement in the definition module.

Using Cleans unboxed arrays as described above in combination with strictness annotations, we expect for most programs to be able to generate code which is about as efficient as code generated by imperative languages like C. We will compare the efficiency of some small Clean programs written in this way with similar programs written in C, this is done in section 5.1.

3 Combining Lazy, Strict and Unboxed Arrays

We have now defined three kinds of arrays: lazy arrays, strict arrays and unboxed arrays. So far we have used the same names for functions that manipulate each kind of array. We prefer to do this in this way, instead of having 3 different names for every function. We can then write a program using for example lazy arrays, and then later decide to change it to unboxed arrays without having to rewrite the whole program. All we have to do is change a few types. If we use a type synonym we may even have to change only one type.

We can achieve this by using Cleans type constructor classes, which are similar to Gofers type constructor classes [Jone95].

We define a type constructor class `Array` with instances lazy, strict and unboxed array with:

```
instance Array { }, {!}, {#}
```

For this class instances are defined for the predefined array functions for lazy, strict and unboxed arrays. The instances for unboxed arrays are:

```
class Array a
where
    createArray :: !Int !e            -> .(a e)          | createArray_u e
    update      :: !*(a .e) !Int .e-> .(a .e)            | update_u e
    select      :: !.(a .e) !Int      -> .e              | select_u e
    uselect     :: !u:(a e) !Int   -> (!e, !u:(a e))     | uselect_u e
    size        :: !.(a.e)             -> Int            | size_u e
    usize       :: !u:(a .e)        ->(!Int,!u:(a .e))   | usize_u e
```

The classes `createArray_u`, `update_u`, etc. are the same as the classes defined for unboxed arrays in section 2.4. So for example, class `select_u` is the same as class `select` in section 2.4.

So, the instance of `select` for unboxed arrays has type:
```
select :: !{# .e } !Int -> .e | select_u e
```

If the compiler cannot resolve the overloading in the type of the element, but can determine that it is an unboxed array, it will call this `select` with three parameters: the two normal parameters (the array and the index) and a `select_u` function added by the overloading mechanism. So, all the implementation of this function has to do is call the `select_u` function with the array and the index, and then return the result of this function application.

The implementation of the instances of the `select` function for lazy and strict arrays does not need the `select_u` function, because the implementation of these selects does not depend on the type of the elements of an array. So the instances for lazy and strict arrays for `select` are:

```
select :: !{ .e } !Int -> .e | select_u e
select a i = select_lazy_array a i

select :: !{! .e } !Int -> .e | select_u e
select a i = select_strict_array a i
```

where `select_lazy_array` is the `select` function for lazy arrays and `select_strict_array` is the `select` function for strict arrays.

We define the instances of the other predefined functions in the same way.

The instances of `createArray` and `update` are strict in the argument that passes the element for strict and unboxed arrays, but not for lazy arrays. The same goes for the element returned by `uselect`. The types defined in class `Array` for these instances are lazy in these arguments/results. To prevent loss of strictness information the compiler recognises these functions, and adds the strictness information for strict and unboxed arrays after typechecking.

We can now use the predefined array functions for all types of arrays, and the typechecker will determine the right instance. There are, however, also some disadvantages:
- When the compiler cannot determine whether an array is lazy, strict or unboxed or what the type of the array element is, and it cannot generate or use a specialised version, these array functions will be very inefficient.
- If the compiler cannot determine whether an array used by a function is lazy, strict or unboxed, the overloaded function type looks rather complicated.

4 Arrays of Unique Elements

With the array functions defined above we cannot create a unique array of which the elements are unique as well. It is also not possible to select a unique element from an array with the `uselect` function. Selection can be done with the `select` function, but this can be done only once: after the selection we no longer have a unique reference to the array.

The `createArray` function cannot create a unique array because it initialises all elements with the same value. If the array has more than 1 element, there will be more references to this initial value, therefore the elements cannot be unique.

So to create an array with unique elements, we have to compute a new value for every array element. We can do this by using an array comprehension [Wadl86,AnHu90] in Clean, which computes the value for every array element.

To compile such an array comprehension, the Clean compiler uses a function that creates an array of undefined elements, which may be unique, (`_createArray`). Since the compiler knows that all array elements will be updated immediately after the array has been created, it does not have to initialise the array, so this function is also faster. The current implementation does however initialise pointers in arrays with `Nil`, because the garbage collector cannot deal with such uninitialised structures.

Selecting a unique element from an array (without losing the array) is not possible, because after the selection we would have two references to the element: the element is returned by `uselect` and the returned array contains it as well.

The only way to make a selection of a unique element possible, seems to be by removing the element from the array. We can do this by replacing the selected array element by a new value with the function:

```
replace :: !*(a .e) !Int .e -> (.e, !*(a .e)) | Array a & replace_u e
```

which returns a tuple with the selected element and an array in which the selected element has been replaced by the third argument of `replace`.

With the `replace` and `update` functions we can compute a new unique element of an array that uses the old unique value in the computation in the following way. We use `replace` to select the element, then we compute the new value, and put it back in the array with `update`. This is of course slower than a modification using `select` and `update`, but an even more serious problem is that we temporarily need to create a unique element, which is inefficient or almost impossible for some types.

In a future version of the compiler we hope to make it easier to modify unique array elements in this way, may be by adding a function or special syntax.

4.1 Multidimensional Arrays

So far we have only looked at one-dimensional arrays. Multidimensional arrays are implemented in Clean as arrays of arrays.

Using arrays of arrays has certain advantages over implementing multi-dimensional arrays as a separate array type implemented by mapping two or more indices to one index in a one-dimensional array. For example, an array of strings (`{#Char}`) can be used as a one-dimensional array, but also as a two-dimensional array. A row of a matrix can be used as a vector without having to copy it, and the row may even be unevaluated. Without loop optimisations, updating an element of an array of arrays can usually be done faster than updating an element of a flat two-dimensional array, because the multiplication that is required for the index calculation is usually more expensive than loading the address of the row. There are also disadvantages: arrays of arrays occupy more memory. Multidimensional arrays can be accessed faster when certain loop optimisations are performed.

To be able to update such an array of arrays, all one-dimensional arrays have to be unique. For instance, to be able to update a lazy two-dimensional array of integers, we have to use an array of type `*{*{Int}}`.

To select an element from such an array, we would start by using `uselect` with the first index, which yields an array of type `*{{Int}}` and an array element of type `{Int}`. The elements of the returned array (of type `*{{Int}}`) are no longer unique, since the selection added a reference to an array element. Therefore we can no longer update this array after this selection.

To update a multidimensional array, we would start with a `uselect` with the first index. The elements of the returned array are no longer unique. The returned element is also not unique, so we cannot update it.

It is not possible to select or update a multidimensional array more than once with the `select`, `uselect` and `update` functions. So we have to invent a trick. Instead of just selecting an element, we select the element and also temporarily replace the selected element in the array by a dummy using the `replace` function. To select from a two-dimensional array of type `*{*{e}}` we need to create a temporary array, use `replace`, `uselect` and then use `update`. To update an element from an array of type `*{*{e}}` we need to create a temporary array, use `replace`, and then use `update` twice.

Clearly we don't want to write selections from and updates of multidimensional arrays in this complicated and inefficient way. We decided to extend the language with syntax for multidimensional selections and updates. The compiler transforms these selections and updates to several one-dimensional selections and updates.

The compiler uses the following functions to efficiently implement multidimensional selections: (they cannot be used by the programmer)

```
_uselect  :: !u:(a .e) !Int -> (.e,!u:(a .e))  |Array a & _uselect_u e
_uselectn:: !(!.(a .e),!.m) !.Int ->(.e,!.m)   |Array a & _uselectn_u e
_uselectl:: !(!.(a e ),!.m) !.Int -> (e,!.m)   |Array a & _uselectl_u e
_update  :: !(!*(a .e),!*m) !Int .e -> *m      |Array a & _update_u e
```

The `_uselect` function is similar to the `uselect` function, but returns a unique array element. Of course this element is not unique, but the compiler uses the function in such a way that this doesn't cause any problems.

The `_uselectl` function has two arguments. The first one is a tuple with an array and a value, this value is returned in a tuple by this function. The second argument is an index. The result of the function is the array element selected by the index and the value passed to the function as the second element of the tuple.

The `_uselectn` function is similar to the `_uselectl` function, but returns a unique array element. As for `_uselect`, this element is not unique, but the compiler uses the function in such a way that this doesn't cause any problems.

The first argument of the `_update` function is a tuple consisting of an array and a value that is returned by the function. The second argument is an index into the array. The last argument is the new array element. The function updates the element selected by the index with the new array element and returns the second element of the tuple.

A two dimensional selection a.[i,j] in a pattern is transformed by the compiler into:
```
_uselectl (_uselect a i) j
```

A two dimensional update {a & [i,j]=n} is transformed into:
```
_update (_uselect a i) j n
```

a.[i,j,k] is transformed into:
```
_uselectl (_uselectn (_uselect a i) j) k
```

{a & [i,j,k]=n} is transformed into:
```
_update (_uselectn (_uselect a i) j) k n
```

If there are more than 3 dimensions, for every extra dimension a _uselectn is added.

We can only compute the size of the first dimension of a multidimensional unique array with usize. So we also have to implement such a transformation to compute the size of the other dimensions.

The argument m passed to and returned by the _uselectn, _uselectl and _update functions is always an array. This array would normally be passed and returned with an extra array indirection node. The compiler recognises these functions and prevents this inefficiency.

5 Performance

5.1 Performance Results

To compare the performance of arrays in Clean 1.1 with C we wrote variants of the well-known quicksort, heapsort and fast fourier algorithms in Clean 1.1 and C. We used unboxed arrays in Clean and added strictness annotations to types of functions when necessary to make the functions strict in all arguments and tuple results. We then rewrote the programs in C using the same data structures. Tail recursive calls in C were manually optimised to while loops, because the C compilers did not perform this optimisation.

We used a PowerMacintosh 7100/80 with a 80 MHz PowerPC 601 cpu, 32 Mb of memory and 256 Kb secondary cache running system 7.5.3 without using virtual memory. We used the most recent version of the Clean 1.1 compiler. The compiler option to check whether array indices are in-range was turned off.

We compared the performance with two C compilers: Metrowerks CodeWarrior C 9, compiler version v1.5, and Apple's MrC version 1.0f4e1. We used maximum optimisation for both compilers. Global optimisation level 4, optimise for speed, peephole optimisation, instruction scheduling for 601, use FMADD & FMSUB for CodeWarrior and -opt speed for MrC.

quicksort and heapsort repeated the following 10 times: create a list of 200,000 integers, sort the list and check if the list was correctly sorted. The source code of these sorting programs can be found in the appendix. The fft and fftc programs create an array of 65536 complex numbers and then do a fast fourier transform followed by a reverse fast fourier transform on its result.

These are the results:

	Clean	CwC	MrC	Clean/CwC	Clean/MrC
quicksort	6.45	5.63	7.62	1.15	0.85
heapsort	12.13	8.55	7.60	1.42	1.60
fft	5.51	4.67	4.47	1.18	1.23
fftc	2.38	2.20	1.60	1.08	1.49

The first 3 columns contain execution times of PowerPC code, in seconds, of the Clean program, the C program compiled with Codewarrior C, and the C program compiled with Mr C. The last two columns are the execution time of the Clean program divided by the execution time of the C program for each C compiler.

There are two versions for the fast fourier program (fft and fftc). We first wrote fft. It was much slower than we expected. This was caused by a larger number of cache misses. We rewrote the program to use a recursive fft in the beginning that divided the array in two parts for every pass, did the other passes of the fft for the first part, then for the second part and then merged the two parts. When the parts were small enough to fit in the primary cache, we used the same algorithm as before. This reduced the number of cache misses and it was more than twice as fast.

5.2 Possible Improvements

On the PowerPC double precision floating point values have to be stored at double word aligned (multiple of 8) addresses for maximum performance. A misaligned floating point load from the cache usually takes 2 clock cycles instead of 1 to execute on a PowerPC 601, and a misaligned floating point store in the cache usually spends 5 clocks in the execution stage instead of 1. The current implementation of Clean does not store floating point values at double word aligned addresses, but only at word aligned addresses. To determine the cost of this inefficiency we changed the fft and fftc C programs to place the arrays at non double word aligned addresses. These programs (fftunalignc and fftcunalignc) were about 20 percent slower:

	Clean	CW	MrC	Clean/CW	Clean/Mrc
fft	5.51	4.67	4.47	1.18	1.23
fftunalignc	5.51	5.78	5.47	0.95	1.01
fftc	2.38	2.20	1.60	1.08	1.49
fftcunalignc	2.38	2.65	1.92	0.90	1.24

The `fft` and `fftc` C programs store the arrays always at double word aligned addresses. The `malloc` function of one of the C compilers did not return double word aligned addresses.

So for better performance we would have to change the Clean runtime system to allocate doubles at double word aligned addresses. Allocating arrays of reals at these addresses can be done easily. Changing the sliding compacting garbage collector to move these arrays to double word aligned addresses is more difficult.

Aligning doubles on the stack is also more difficult. We probably have to align all stack frames at double word addresses, which would result in higher use of stack space even for programs that do not use reals. Another option is to use a separate stack for reals. For the `fft` programs aligning reals on the stack is not important, because few reals are stored on the stack.

The code generated for loops can be improved easily. The test for the end of the loop is usually done in a pattern or guard. In such a case the current compiler generates code which looks like this:

```
function_entry:    cmp             index,size
                   beq             guard_false
guard_true:        do something
                   bra             function_entry
guard_false:
```

We can reduce the number of branches in the loop by changing this to:

```
guard_true:        do something
function_entry:    cmp             index,size
                   bne             guard_true
guard_false:
```

Applying this transformation to quicksort would reduce the number of branches in the most important loops from 3 to 2. A similar transformation would remove an incorrectly predicted branch from the most important loop of heapsort. C compilers do a similar transformation to reduce the number of branches in loops.

Another optimisation that C compilers perform, and has not yet been implemented in the Clean compiler, is common subexpression elimination of array index calculations. The Clean compiler generates 2 machine instructions on a RISC to calculate the address of an element in an array of integers or reals: a shift instruction and an `add` instruction. In the `quicksort` and `fft` programs the same index is used twice in the same basic block: when two elements are swapped and in the function `merge`. The addresses can be calculated once, and then used by more load or store instructions, saving 2 instructions per additional load or store.

We could also try to eliminate the add instruction in the address calculation. The compiler has to generate it because the first element of an array is not stored at offset 0 from the address of the array, but at offset 12 or 8. If an array is used several times, we could calculate the address of the element once, and use the address as the base for the indexed load or store instruction. This saves one instruction for every additional load or store of the same array.

We could remove this extra offset calculation in all cases, if we change the way we store nodes in the heap. In the current implementation we cannot pass the address of the first element of an array instead of a pointer to the node, because the descriptor has to be at offset 0 from the address. This is necessary because of the garbage collector and the way closures are evaluated.

In the current implementation the address of a node is the address of the descriptor of the node. If instead we would store the address of the word following the descriptor, we could remove the extra offset calculation for arrays, but we would have to change this for all nodes. We would have to change the compiler, the garbage collectors and other parts of the runtime system. Code that doesn't use arrays would probably still be just as efficient on a RISC after this modification.

The code generated for the fast fourier transform by the Clean compiler can probably be improved with a simple instruction scheduler. Instruction scheduling is not very important for the `quicksort` and `heapsort` programs.

5.3 Related Work

In Haskell, lazy arrays can be created using comprehensions, but in-place array updates are not possible. Several analyses and transformations are required to compile these comprehensions efficiently [AnHu90]. Currently none of the available Haskell compilers are able to do this.

The Glasgow Haskell compiler (GHC) has been extended with an array implementation based on monads [PeWa92]. Unboxed arrays (called Bytearrays) of basic types can be manipulated. For each basic type, functions are available to create, read or write an array. For example `writeIntArray` and `writeDoubleArray` are available, but there is no `writeArray` function that can be used for every Bytearray. [Serr96] compares the performance of both GHC's Bytearrays and monolothic arrays with Clean's unboxed arrays for a conjugate gradient algorithm, and Clean was always at least ten times as fast.

Using analyses, program transformations and reference counting strict pure functional languages like SISAL [FiOl95,Feo92] and SAC [MuKlSc96] achieve good performance for scientific applications using arrays.

The Clean compiler [SNGP91] inserts the necessary coercions to box or unbox basic types, tuples and records as described in [NöSm93]. Leroy [Lero92] also discusses automatic coercion of these data types. However, the transformation Leroy describes cannot unbox arrays. Unboxed (polymorphic) arrays are also not possible with unboxed types as described in [PeLa91]. This type system has as disadvantage that coercions have to be inserted by the programmer.

6 Conclusion

The efficiency of unboxed arrays in Clean 1.1 is good, and it can still be further improved with simple optimisations. Multidimensional arrays and array of unique elements are more difficult to use than one dimensional arrays. Strictness annotations, and sometimes small changes to the program, are still necessary to obtain the most efficient version of a Clean program.

References

[AnHu90] Andersen, S. and P. Hudak. 1990. Compilation of Haskell Array Comprehensions for Scientific Computing. In Proc. of the ACM SIGPLAN'90 Conf. on Programming Language Design and Implementation, New York, pp. 137-149.

[BaSm93] Barendsen E., and J.E.W. Smetsers. 1993. Conventional and Uniqueness Typing in Graph Rewrite Systems. In *proceedings 13th conference Foundations of Software Technology and Theoretical Computer Science*, Bombay, India, December 1993, pp. 41-51, LNCS 761.

[Feo92] Feo, J. A Comparative Study of Parallel Programming Languages: The Salishan Problems. 1992. North Holland, ISBN 0-444-88135-2.

[FiOl95] Fitzgerald, S.M. and R.R. Oldehoeft. 1995. Update-in-place Analysis for True Multidimensional Arrays. *High Performance Functional Computing*, pp. 105-118.

[Jone95] Jones, M.P. 1995. A system of constructor classes: overloading and implicit higher-order polymorphism. In *Journal of Functional Programming* 5(1) - January 1995, Cambridge University Press, pp. 1-35.

[NöSm93] Nöcker, E.G.J.M.H., and J.E.W. Smetsers. 1993. Partially strict non-recursive data types. In *Journal of Functional Programming* 3(2), pp. 191-215.

[Lero92] Leroy X. 1992. Unboxed objects and polymorphic typing. *Proc. 19th Symp. Principles of Programming Languages*, pp. 177-188.

[MuKlSc96] Mullin, L.R., W.E. Kluge and S. Scholz. 1996. On Programming Scientific Applications in SAC - a Functional Language Extended by a Subsystem for High-Level Array Operations. *Proc. of the 8th International Workshop on Implementation of Functional Languages*.

[PeLa91] Peyton Jones, S.L. and J. Launchbury. 1991. Unboxed values as first class citizens in a non-strict functional language. In *Proc. of Conference on Functional Programming Languages and Computer Architecture* (FPCA `91), Sept. 1991, Cambridge, LNCS 523.

[PeWa92] Peyton Jones, S.L. and P. Wadler. 1992. Imperative functional programming. *ACM Symposium on Principles of Programming Languages (POPL)*, pp.71-84.

[PlaEe95] Plasmeijer, M.J., and M.C.J.D. van Eekelen. 1995. Clean 1.1 Reference Manual. Technical Report. University of Nijmegen, The Netherlands.

[Serr96] Serrarens, P.R. A Clean Conjugate Gradient Algorithm. 1996. *Proc. of the 8th International Workshop on Implementation of Functional Languages.*.

[SNGP91] Smetsers, J.E.W., E.G.J.M.H. Nöcker, J.H.G. van Groningen and M.J. Plasmeijer. 1991. Generating Efficient Code for Lazy Functional Languages, In *Proc. of Conference on Functional Programming Languages and Computer Architecture* (FPCA '91) , Cambridge, MA, USA, Springer-Verlag, LNCS 523, pp. 592-617.

[Wadl86] Wadler. P. 1986. A new array operation for functional languages. In *Proc. Graph Reduction Workshop*, Santa Fe, Springer Verlag, LNCS 295.

Appendix: benchmark programs

1 Implementation of the Quicksort Algorithm in Clean

```
module quicksort;
import StdEnv;
:: SortElement:==Int;
:: SortArray:=={#SortElement};

quick_sort :: *SortArray -> .SortArray;
quick_sort a0
  = quick_sort1 0 (n_elements-1) a;
  {
    (n_elements,a) = usize a0;

    quick_sort1 b e a
      | b>=e
      = a;
    quick_sort1 b e a=:{[b]=ab,[m]=am}
      = find_large am (b+1) e {a & [m]=ab};
    { m=(b+e)>>1;

      find_large :: Int Int Int *SortArray -> .SortArray;
      find_large am l r a
        | l<=e && a.[l]<=am
        = find_large am (l+1) r a;
        = find_small_or_equal am l r a;

      find_small_or_equal :: Int Int Int *SortArray -> .SortArray;
      find_small_or_equal am l r a
        | r>b && a.[r]>am
        = find_small_or_equal am l (r-1) a;
        | l<r
        # (al,a)=uselect a l;
          (ar,a)=uselect a r;
        = find_large am (l+1) (r-1) {a & [l]=ar,[r]=al};
        | b==r
        = quick_sort2 (r-1) (r+1) {a & [b]=am};
        # (ar,a)=uselect a r;
        = quick_sort2 (r-1) (r+1) {a & [r]=am,[b]=ar};
```

```
      quick_sort2 l r a
        = if (l-b>=e-r)
          (quick_sort1 b l (quick_sort1 r e a))
          (quick_sort1 r e (quick_sort1 b l a));
    }
  }
unsorted_array n_elements
  = fill_unsorted_array 0 n_elements (createArray n_elements 0);
  { fill_unsorted_array i s a
    | i<s
      = fill_unsorted_array (i+1) s {a & [i]=(s-i-1) bitxor 0x2a};
      = a;
  }
check_sort :: !Int !Int !{#Int} -> Bool;
check_sort n n_elements a
  | n==n_elements = True;
  | a.[n]==n      = check_sort (n+1) n_elements a;
repeat_sort 0 = True;
repeat_sort n
  | check_sort 0 n_elements (quick_sort (unsorted_array n_elements))
    = repeat_sort (n-1);
  where { n_elements=200000; }
Start = repeat_sort 10;
```

2 Implementation of the Heapsort Algorithm in Clean

```
module heapsort;
import StdEnv;
:: SortElement:==Int;
:: SortArray:=={#SortElement};

heap_sort a0
  | n_elements<2
    = a
    = sort_heap max_index (make_heap (n_elements>>1) max_index a);
    { max_index=n_elements-1;

    make_heap :: Int !Int *SortArray -> *SortArray;
    make_heap (-1) max_index a = a;
    make_heap i max_index a=:{[i]=ai}
      = make_heap (dec i) max_index (add_to_heap i ((i<<1)+1) max_index ai a);

    sort_heap :: Int *SortArray -> *SortArray;
    sort_heap i a=:{[i]=ai,[0]=a0}
      | i==1
        = {a & [0]=ai,[i]=a0};
        = sort_heap deci (add_to_heap 0 1 deci ai {a & [i]=a0});
        with { deci=i-1; }

    add_to_heap :: Int Int !Int SortElement *SortArray->*SortArray;
    add_to_heap i j max_index ai a
      | j>=max_index
        = if (j>max_index)
          {a & [i] = ai}
          (if (ai<aj)
            {a` & [i]=aj,[j]=ai}
            {a` & [i]=ai});
        with { (aj,a`)=uselect a j; }
    add_to_heap i j max_index ai a=:{[j]=aj,[j1]=aj1}
      | aj<aj1
        = if (ai<aj1)
```

```
                (add_to_heap j1 ((j1<<1)+1) max_index ai {a & [i]=aj1})
                {a & [i]=ai};
          = if (ai<aj)
                (add_to_heap j ((j<<1)+1) max_index ai {a & [i]=aj})
                {a & [i]=ai};
        where { j1=j+1; }
    }
  where { (n_elements,a) = usize a0; }

repeat_sort 0 = True;
repeat_sort n
  | check_sort 0 n_elements (heap_sort (unsorted_array n_elements))
    = repeat_sort (n-1);
  where { n_elements=200000; }
Start = repeat_sort 10;
```

3 Implementation of the Quicksort and Heapsort Algorithms in C

```c
#include <stdlib.h>
#include <stdio.h>
static void quick_sort1 (int b,int e,int a[])
{ int m,l,r,ab,am;
  while (b<e){
    m=(b+e)>>1;
    ab=a[b]; am=a[m]; a[m]=ab;
    l=b+1; r=e;
    for (;;){
      while (l<=e && a[l]<=am)
        ++l;
      while (r>b && a[r]>am)
        --r;
      if (l<r){
        int al,ar;
        al=a[l]; ar=a[r];
        a[l]=ar; a[r]=al;
        ++l; --r;
      } else
        break;
    }
    if (b==r) a[b]=am;
    else { int ar; ar=a[r]; a[r]=am; a[b]=ar; }
    l=r-1; ++r;
    if (l-b>=e-r){
      quick_sort1 (r,e,a);
      e=l;
    } else {
      quick_sort1 (b,l,a);
      b=r;
    }
  }
}
static void quick_sort (int a[],int n_elements)
{ quick_sort1 (0,n_elements-1,a);
}
static void add_to_heap (int i,int j,int max_index,int ai,int a[])
{
  while (j<max_index){
    int j1,aj,aj1;
    j1=j+1; aj=a[j]; aj1=a[j1];
    if (aj<aj1){
      if (ai<aj1){
```

```
          a[i]=aj1;
          i=j1; j=(j1<<1)+1;
        } else {
          a[i]=ai;
          return;
        }
      } else {
        if (ai<aj){
          a[i]=aj;
          i=j; j=(j<<1)+1;
        } else {
          a[i]=ai;
          return;
        }
      }
    }
    if (j>max_index){
      a[i]=ai;
    } else {
      int aj;
      aj=a[j];
      if (ai<aj){ a[i]=aj; a[j]=ai; } else { a[i]=ai; }
    }
}
static void heap_sort (int a[],int n_elements)
{
  int max_index,i;
  if (n_elements<2)
    return;
  max_index=n_elements-1;
  for (i=n_elements>>1; i!=-1; --i)
    add_to_heap (i,i+i+1,max_index,a[i],a);
  i=max_index;
  while (i!=1){
    int ai;
    ai=a[i]; a[i]=a[0]; --i;
    add_to_heap (0,1,i,ai,a);
  }
  { int a0,ai; a0=a[0]; ai=a[i]; a[0]=ai; a[i]=a0; }
}
int main (void)
{
  long begin_time,end_time; int n_elements,*a,i,int count;
  n_elements=200000; a=malloc (n_elements*sizeof (int));
  if (a!=NULL){
    printf ("\n"); begin_time=TickCount();
    for (count=0; count<10; ++count){
      for (i=1; i<=n_elements; ++i)
        a[i-1]=(n_elements-i) ^ 0x2a;
      /* quick_sort (a,n_elements); */
      heap_sort (a,n_elements);
      check_sort (a,n_elements);
    }
    end_time=TickCount(); printf ("%g\n",(double)(end_time-begin_time)/60.0);
  }
  return 1;
}
```

Implementing the Conjugate Gradient Algorithm in a Functional Language

Pascal R. Serrarens

Computer Science Institute
University of Nijmegen, The Netherlands
e-mail: pascalrs@cs.kun.nl

Abstract. This paper evaluates the elegance and efficiency of functional programming in numerical scientific computing, an interesting area because time and space efficiency are important: many scientific programs work with large data sets and run for a long time. The example we use is the conjugate gradient algorithm, an iterative method to solve systems of linear equations. We investigated various implementations of the algorithm in the functional languages Clean and Haskell and the imperative language C. Good results are obtained when comparing the algorithm written in Clean with the same algorithm in C and Haskell.

The expressive power of functional programming languages seems to equal to that of traditional imperative languages, while many current compilers produce time- and space-efficient code, using various optimisations including the important update-in-place. Two traditionally weak points of functional language implementations are speed and memory usage, which are very important in numerical scientific computing. The "pseudoknot" paper [H+96] showed that, for a numerical algorithm, only a couple of functional-language compilers could produce code comparable with to that produced by C compilers.

In this paper we investigate writing the conjugate gradient algorithm in the general purpose lazy functional language Clean [PvE93] and compare it against similar implementations in C and Haskell [HPJW92]. In Section 1 we will look at the algorithm itself. We look how the choice of data structure influences the performance in Section 2. We describe some optimisations that yield an efficient implementation in Section 3. In Section 4 we compare our implementation in Clean with implementations in the languages C and Haskell, while Section 5 concludes.

1 The Conjugate Gradient Algorithm

An algorithm often used in scientific computing for solving a system of linear equations is the conjugate gradient algorithm [CSJ95] [EO94] [JDG92] [HS93]. The algorithm itself is an iterative approximation method to solve the linear equation $Ax = b$. A direct method is the gauss elimination. But, only when working with symbolic computation, which provides arbitrary precision integers, can we get an exact solution. Functional languages might be well suited for that. The conjugate gradient algorithm is used often because it is very fast and gives a good approximation of x.

The algorithm can be written down easily in Clean: it is close to what a mathematician would write. One limitation making the code less elegant is that the standard library defines that the overloaded *-symbol must have two arguments of the same type. Matrix-vector and scalar multiplications take the combination matrix-vector and scalar(real)-vector. To overcome this problem, we use the symbols #* and .* for matrix-vector and scalar multiplication respectively.

```
CG :: Matrix Vector Vector → Vector
CG a x b
    | delta0 < Epsilon = x
    | otherwise        = CGloop a x g delta0 d
    where
        g      = a #* x - b
        delta0 = InnerProd g g
        d      = ~ g
```

```
CGloop :: Matrix Vector Vector Real Vector → Vector
CGloop a x g delta0 d
    | delta1 < Epsilon = x'
    | otherwise        = CGloop a x' g' delta1 d'
    where
        h      = a #* d
        tau    = delta0 / InnerProd d h
        x'     = tau .* d + x
        g'     = tau .* h + g
        delta1 = InnerProd g' g'
        beta   = delta1 / delta0
        d'     = beta .* d - g'
```

Fig. 1. The conjugate gradient algorithm

The algorithm is called with the matrix A, the vector b and a rough approximation of vector x. After some initialisation in function CG, the recursive function CGloop runs until delta1 drops below the value of Epsilon, for which good values are between 10^{-8} and 10^{-12}. The returned x is a good approximation of the real value of x. A more detailed description of the algorithm can be found in [KGGK94].

1.1   The Matrix

The representation of the matrix we have chosen in this paper is not straight-forward. The conjugate gradient algorithm is used often to solve large sparse systems of linear equations. This implies two things: the first is that the matrix can be very large: matrices of size $100,000 \times 100,000$ for storing the data are not uncommon. With a direct representation it will take more than 74 gigabytes to store a matrix of that size.

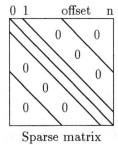

Sparse matrix

The second assumption is that the matrix is sparse, meaning that many matrix elements are zero. In this paper we use banded diagonal matrices with all non-zero elements aligned along five diagonals (see the picture on the left), just storing the diagonals is a good idea. We also assume that the matrix is symmetric, so we only have to store 3 diagonals. Now we need only a little more than 2 megabytes memory to store the matrix above.

The special representation of the matrix has its influence in the implementation of the matrix-vector multiplication. Normally, every value in the resulting vector is the result of an inner product of the vector element and the corresponding row of the matrix. In our situation we need only sum the products of the diagonals with the vector.

1.2   The problem sizes

We have tested the various implementations of the algorithm for up to five problem sizes, which are determined by the array size (see table 1).

Array size	Matrix + Vectors
625×625	35 Kb
2500×2500	140 Kb
10000×10000	560 Kb
40000×40000	2240 Kb
160000×160000	8960 Kb

Table 1. The problem sizes and their data sizes

The first column gives the array size. The second column lists the minimum data size of the matrix and vectors for every problem size. The minimum data size can be calculated easily: we need 3 vectors for the diagonals of the matrix and 4 vectors to store intermediate results during the computation: x, g, d and h. As we use 8-byte reals we need $s * (3 + 4) * 8$ bytes of memory, where s is the size of the array in one dimension.

2 Implementing the vectors and matrices

2.1 Vectors and matrices from lists

Why consider lists when time and space efficiency are so important? We have a number of reasons for that:

- Functional languages are designed with the list as the main linear structure, with list comprehensions, pattern matching and an extensive set of standard functions.
- In our algorithm lists can be used quite easily, because most of the time we simply walk over the structure. Indexing and updating can be avoided.
- We wanted to see the importance of good implementation of arrays in functional languages.

A number of operations are defined on vectors, like addition and inner product. Having list comprehensions, we can express those operations easily: (In Clean, when generators are separated with &, both lists are traversed simultaneously; each generated element is only combined with that at the same position in the other list. In Haskell, you would use zipwith)

```
instance + [ Real ]
where
    (+) v1 v2 = [ e1 + e2 \\ e1 ← v1 & e2 ← v2 ]


InnerProd :: [ Real ] [ Real ] → Real
InnerProd v1 v2 = foldl1 (+) [ e1 * e2 \\ e1 ← v1 & e2 ← v2 ]
```

The matrix-vector multiplication #* is the hardest part of the implementation, because of the representation of the matrix. First we have to extract the real five diagonals. The stored diagonals D0, D1 and D2 are the three upper diagonals of the matrix with respectively 0, 1 and *offset* zeros added to the front and back. From this all five real diagonals of the matrix can be created easily, by taking the correct ranges (see figure 2a).

We also add *offset* zeros to the front and back of the vector. Generating the result vector is now relatively easy: we multiply every diagonal of the matrix with the corresponding range of the vector (see figure 2b). Finally, we sum the results up for the result vector. The code for lists is shown below:

```
(#*) infixl 7 :: [[ Real ]] [ Real ] → [ Real ]
(#*) (offset, D0, D1, D2) v =
    [ d0e * v0e + d1e * v1e + d2e * v2e + d3e * v3e + d4e * v4e \\
```

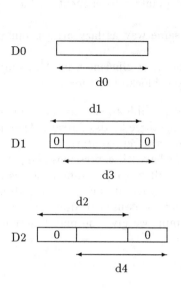

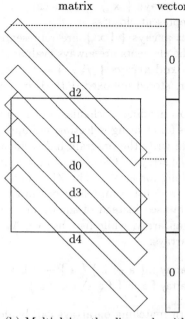

(a) Creating the five matrix diagonals dx from the stored three diagonals Dx

(b) Multiplying the diagonals with the vector. The dashed lines indicate which part of the vector is taken.

Fig. 2. The Matrix' diagonals

```
d0e ← D0 &
d1e ← drop 1 D1 &
d2e ← drop offset D2 &
d3e ← take 1 D1 &
d4e ← take offset D2 &

v0e ← v &
v1e ← drop (offset + 1) v' &
v2e ← drop (offset + offset) v' &
v3e ← drop (offset - 1) v' &
v4e ← v' ]
where
   v' = repeatn offset 0.0 ++ v ++ repeatn offset 0.0
```

2.2 Arrays

Clean provides three different kinds of arrays:

Lazy arrays { x } are basically a block of pointers to elements, which may represent closures.

Strict arrays { ! x } are represented the same way as lazy arrays, but now the elements are always evaluated.

Unboxed arrays { # x } are stored in the most efficient way. All elements are stored unboxed [PJL91] in a continuous block of memory.

The overloading mechanism of Clean makes it possible to use the same function names for creating, selecting and updating of the three kinds of arrays. Therefore we can write the program independent of the array representation.

The arrays of Clean are similar to lists, as we have ZF-expressions and pattern matching for arrays. The ZF-expressions are called array comprehensions and differ from list comprehensions in two things: to generate an array curly braces { } are used instead of square brackets [ ] and ←: is used to draw an element from an array, while lists use ←. As an example we give the map function on lazy arrays:

```
map_array :: ( a → b ) { a } → { b }
map_array f a = { f e \\ e ←: a }
```

Pattern matching on arrays can be done with the pattern a=:{[i] = x} , where x is taken from the i-th position of array a.

Besides generating and indexing of arrays, updating array elements is also possible in some cases. When the array type has the uniqueness attribute *, it is safe to perform an update in place. Uniqueness typing [BS93] is able to derive, or enforce, that functions have exclusive access to arguments with the uniqueness attribute. The expression { a & [i] = x } is an update of array a at position i with x.

2.3 Vectors and matrices from arrays

In [H+96] the remark was made that arrays were not well supported in most of the languages. Now that Clean supports arrays, we can see the importance of it. In this section we do not make use of update-in-place, with one exception for the matrix-vector multiplication. Update-in-place will be used in Section 3.2.

For the inner product we use indexing, which is more efficient than a combination of a map and a fold, because now we use only one loop (see also Section 3.1).

```
InnerProd :: { Real } { Real } → Real
InnerProd v1 v2 = InnerProd' (size v1 - 1)
where
    InnerProd' :: Int → Real
    InnerProd' 0 = v1.[0] * v2.[0]
    InnerProd' i  = v1.[i] * v2.[i] + InnerProd' (i - 1)
```

The matrix-vector multiplication with the array implementation is different from the list version, because we use indexing and updates. Going from the middle to the outside diagonals, we first multiply the middle diagonal with the given vector. Of the next two diagonals, the first $n-1$ elements of the upper upper diagonal are multiplied with the vector and added to the result vector. The treatment of the lower diagonal is similar, but uses the last $n-1$ elements. Next, we go to the outermost diagonals, where we take the first and last $n-offset$ elements of the vector argument respectively. This results in the following code:

```
(#*) infixl 7 :: {{ Real }} { Real } → { Real }
(#*) (offset, d0, d1, d2) v =
    Mul1 (n - offset) n d2 ( Mul1 (n - 1) n d1 ( Mul0 v ) )
where
    n = size v - 1

    Mul0 :: Vector → *Vector
    Mul0 v = { de * ve \\ de ←: d0 & ve ←: v }

    Mul1 :: Int Int Diagonal *Vector → *Vector
    Mul1 0 i2 d=:{[0]=de} u=:{[0]=e1, [i2]=e2} =
        { u & [0] = e1 + de * v.[i2],
              [i2] = e2 + de * v.[0] }
    Mul1 i1 i2 d=:{[i1]=de} u=:{[i1]=e1, [i2]=e2} =
        Mul1 (i1 - 1) (i2 - 1) d { u & [i1] = e1 + de * v.[i2],
                                        [i2] = e2 + de * v.[i1] }
```

2.4 Comparing lists and arrays

We were able to reuse the algorithm code presented in Section 1 for all list and array implementations. However, the implementation of simple operations like addition of vectors, must be implemented separately for arrays and lists. Multi-parameter type classes could avoid this [PJ96], but are not implemented at the moment.

For every problem size 10 test-runs were made, of which the best time was taken. All tests ran on a Sun Sparcstation 20 at 50MHz with 64Mb of memory and 1Mb cache running under Solaris 2.4. The compiler for Clean was Clean 1.1 for Solaris. For most implementations we tested for all problem sizes which could run efficiently in 32 Mb or less memory. The times were obtained by the built-in timer of Clean.

Table 2 lists from left to right the problem size and the execution times in seconds for lazy and spine-strict lists and lazy, strict and unboxed arrays. The spine-strict lists are user-defined and were to test the advantage of them over lazy lists. It showed that using spine-strict instead of lazy lists does not give a big speed advantage. The most remarkable thing is that lazy arrays are less efficient than all other implementations, including lists. This is because access to the array elements is much more expensive, as the elements may be unevaluated. Much time is also spent in the garbage collector, due to the high memory requirements.

Array size	Lists		Arrays		
	Lazy	Strict	Lazy	Strict	Unboxed
625^2	1.09	0.70	1.38	0.28	0.18
2500^2	9.06	7.51	15.10	3.23	1.45
10000^2		73.01		31.21	14.57
40000^2				318.45	159.13

Table 2. The execution times in seconds of the various list and array implementations

Array size	Real Data	Lists		Arrays		
		Lazy	Strict	Lazy	Strict	Unboxed
625^2	35 Kb	850 Kb	120 Kb	3790 Kb	80 Kb	60 Kb
2500^2	140 Kb	6170 Kb	480 Kb	29960 Kb	310 Kb	210 Kb
10000^2	560 Kb		1900 Kb		1220 Kb	810 Kb
40000^2	2240 Kb				4900 Kb	3230 Kb

Table 3. The minimum heap sizes for the various list and array implementations

Table 3 shows for every implementation and problem size the minimum heap size: we experimentally determined the size of heap just big enough for the program to run, by gradually reducing the heap size. Next to the problem size is the real data size we deduced in Section 1.1. The memory requirements of the strict and unboxed implementations of the list and the array are reasonable close to the minimal possible size of the data. The lazy versions have a bigger overhead, but again the lazy array is an exception: it uses a huge amount of memory to run. This is mainly because the elements in the array are closures pointing to other (older) arrays which also contain closures. The array elements are not evaluated when updated, but the closures created instead are not evaluated until needed, which is at the end of the program. In this way almost all intermediate vectors are kept in memory.

3 Optimisations

3.1 Map fusion

Among the inefficiencies in the implementation of the previous section are the loops and intermediate vectors introduced by expressions like tau .* d + x. With a straightforward implementation, this expression is built with two functions: + and .*. These operators are implemented with array comprehensions. The expression can then be reduced as follows:

```
        tau .* d + x
(+)    { ye + xe \\ ye ←: tau .* d & xe ←: x }
(.*)   { ye + xe \\ ye ←: { tau * de \\ de ←: d } & xe ←: x }
```

Now it is clear that the expression will be evaluated by the execution of two loops, represented by the two array comprehensions. This is not the most efficient way to implement the expression. One loop applying a function to the vector elements is better:

```
{ tau * de + xe \\ de ←: d & xe ←: x }
```

To test the significance of this we replaced three functions of the conjugate gradient specification by more efficient ones:

```
CGloop :: Matrix Vector Vector Real Vector → Vector
CGloop a x g delta0 d
    | delta1 < Epsilon = x'
    | otherwise        = CGloop a x' g' delta1 d'
    where
        h      = a #* d
        tau    = delta0 / InnerProd d h
        x'     = SAXPY tau d x
        g'     = SAXPY tau h g
        delta1 = InnerProd g' g'
        beta   = delta1 / delta0
        d'     = SAXMY beta d g'

SAXPY :: Real Vector Vector → Vector
SAXPY a x y = { a * xe + ye \\ xe ←: x & ye ←: y }
```

From table 4, we see that this change had a positive effect on the heap consumption. The minimal heap size decreased by 20% and the garbage collection times went down, because we had less intermediate vectors. The efficiency increased by 20-40%, because we did not have to create the extra vectors.

Array size	Min Heap size	Test run Heap size	Test run Exec time	Test run GC time
625^2	50 Kb	128 Kb	0.15	0.00
2500^2	170 Kb	512 Mb	1.16	0.05
10000^2	650 Kb	2 Mb	10.68	1.14
40000^2	2580 Kb	8 Mb	110.17	11.08

Table 4. Unboxed arrays with map fusion

Unfortunately, map fusion must be done completely by hand at the moment. There are a number of theories to do it automatically [Wad90] [SF93], but it is very hard to implement them. Only one implementation doing cheap deforestation exists at the moment [GLPJ93]. It only works for lists (and Haskell arrays, but those are based on lists, see Section 4.2) and cannot deforest more than one function argument.

3.2   Update in place

In our implementation of the conjugate gradient algorithm, we did not make an extensive use of the uniqueness typing and update-in-place of Clean. Instead of updating old ones, we created new vectors in every function. Using uniqueness typing for update-in-place has one disadvantage: one has to return every unique argument used, because it may be updated later on. If we want to introduce update-in-place with uniqueness typing in the version with map fusion of the previous section, we have to alter the specification again, losing the elegance of using the standard overloaded operators:

```
CGloop :: Matrix *Vector *Vector Real *Vector *Vector → *Vector
CGloop m x g delta0 d h
    | delta1 < Epsilon = x1
    | otherwise        = CGloop m x1 g3 delta1 d4 h3
    where
        (h1, d1)        = MatMulVec h m d
        (ip_dh, d2, h2) = InnerProd d1 h1
        tau             = delta0 / ip_dh
        (x1, d3)        = SAXPY tau d2 x
        (g1, h3)        = SAXPY tau h2 g
        (delta1, g2)    = InnerProd2 g1
        beta            = delta1 / delta0
        (g3, d4)        = SAXMY g2 beta d3
```

The vector and matrix functions change too. As an example, the implementation of SAXPY is given here:

```
SAXPY :: Real v:Vector *Vector → (*Vector, v:Vector)
SAXPY a x y = SAXPY' 0 x y'
where
    (n, y') = usize y

    SAXPY' :: Int v:Vector *Vector → (*Vector, v:Vector)
    SAXPY' i x y
        | i == n  = (y, x)
        | otherwise= SAXPY' (i + 1) x' { y' & [i] = a * xe + ye }
        where
            (xe, x') = uselect x i
            (ye, y') = uselect y i
```

Table 5 shows the performance when using update-in-place and map fusion. The code produced is approximately 2 times faster than the unoptimised version. We were able to set the heap size to its minimum, while garbage collection times are negligible, because when only using updates and tail recursions, no closures need to be built. Thus, except for the initialisation, the garbage collector is not used.

Another remarkable fact is that the minimal heap size is equal to that of the previous results with map fusion. The amount of 'live data', which determines the minimal heap size, is in both implementations the same. With a destructive update each live vector stays live. Without update-in-place, the old vector is copied and is eventually removed by the garbage collector, the copied vector will be the new live vector, so the amount of live data stays the same.

	Min	Test run		
Array size	Heap size	Heap size	Exec time	GC time
625^2	50 Kb	50 Kb	0.11	0.00
2500^2	170 Kb	170 Kb	0.91	0.00
10000^2	650 Kb	650 Kb	7.50	0.04
40000^2	2580 Kb	2580 Kb	76.24	0.24
160000^2	10350 Kb	10350 Kb	725.50	0.87

Table 5. Unboxed arrays with map fusion and update-in-place

4 Other languages

4.1 C

There have been quite a few claims that code produced by compilers for functional languages is comparable with code generated by compilers for imperative languages. Now that we have a fast code for this numerical algorithm, we can compare it against an equivalent C program.

The Clean program we compared with is the optimised version from the previous section. For the C code we used Sun's cc version 3.0.1, with -O4 optimisation. The process size is the memory size reported by UNIX command top. The execution times in second were obtained using the system function getrusage().

Table 6 shows that Clean is on average 30% slower than C. The difference in process size is caused by the stack of Clean: its default size is 512K. If we take that into account the process sizes are equal.

A big advantage of the Clean version over C is that it can be adapted easily: we did not change the program code for the algorithm when we used arrays

Array size	Clean		C	
	Process size	Exec time	Process size	Exec time
2500^2	1600 Kb	0.91	904 Kb	0.69
10000^2	2080 Kb	7.50	1432 Kb	5.20
40000^2	4008 Kb	76.24	3544 Kb	66.20
160000^2	12 Mb	725.50	12 Mb	608.75

Table 6. Comparing efficient Clean and C code for the CG algorithm

instead of lists. Using a different datatype for vectors in the C code has more effect on the C code of the algorithm.

4.2   GHC

We also compared the Clean code to Haskell code, using the Glasgow Haskell compiler (GHC). Two kinds of arrays were used: the Haskell array and the mutable _Bytearray, which is a non-Haskell extension of the Glasgow compiler.

The Haskell arrays, as implemented in GHC, are not primitive. It is a combination of a tuple for the boundaries and a list with associations between indexes and values. The type of a Haskell array is Array a b where a is the type of the index and b the type of the elements. The most important function for creating Haskell arrays is array:

array :: (Ix a) $\Rightarrow$ (a,a) $\rightarrow$ [(a,b)] $\rightarrow$ Array a b

It takes the boundaries of the new array and a list of associations from indexes to values and creates a new Haskell array. An association between index i and value x is denoted as i := x. Other functions on Haskell arrays are the operator !, for selecting an element from an array and // for incrementally updating an array. In the current implementation of GHC this updating is not in-place, a new array is created instead. In the future, the compiler could figure out where updates are possible, using update analysis and linear types.

Remarkable is the similarity of the Haskell code to the Clean code for arrays without updating (figure 3). The main difference is that Clean's array comprehensions are similar to list comprehensions, while Haskell uses the array function in combination with a list comprehension.

We tested this implementation with version 0.29 of GHC, with options -O -fvia-C -O2-for-C. The second optimisation level -O2 did not give an important speedup. As GHC's Haskell arrays are not primitive, the measured times are not so good (see table 7). We were only able to test for problem size 625^2. This makes the GHC implementation of Haskell arrays not suitable for numerical computing.

The mutable _Bytearray of the Glasgow compiler is a primitive array, comparable with the unboxed array of Clean. The elements of both arrays are stored

```
saxpy :: Double → Vector → Vector → Vector
saxpy a x y = array b [ i := a * x!i + y!i | i ← range b ]
   where b = bounds x


(#*) :: Matrix → Vector → Vector
(#*) (offset, d0, d1, d2) v =
   mul1 (n - offset) n d2 (mul1 (n - 1) n d1 mul0)
where
   b = bounds v
   n = snd b


   mul0 :: Vector
   mul0 = array b [ i := d0!i * v!i | i ← range b ]


   mul1 :: Int → Int → Diagonal → Vector → Vector
   mul1 0 i2 d u =
      u // [ 0 := u!0 + d!0 * v!i2, i2 := u!i2 + d!0 * v!0 ]
   mul1 i1 i2 d u = mul1 (i1 - 1) (i2 - 1) d
      (u // [ i1 := u!i1 + d!i1 * v!i2, i2 := u!i2 + d!i1 * v!i1 ])
```

Fig. 3. GHC code for the 'simple ax plus y' and matrix-vector multiplication functions

	Min	Test run		
Array size	Heap size	Heap size	Exec time	GC time
625^2	3950 Kb	16 Mb	67.38	41.62

Table 7. The performance of Haskell arrays for the algorithm

unboxed in one memory block and both can be updated in place. Where Clean uses uniqueness typing to do save update-in-place, GHC uses a monad [LPJ94]. Monads use a state to thread all functions using the state, which are called actions. Those actions are glued together using the combinator thenST :: ST s a → (a → ST s b) → ST s b: it executes the first action and passes the result, together with the updated state, to the second action. The result of the combination of the two actions is the result of the second action. The combinator seqST is similar to thenST, but now the second action does not get the result of the first action. Finally, the function returnST simply returns a value, without changing the world. All three combinators above have a variation which is strict in the state, respectively thenStrictlyST, seqStrictlyST and returnStrictlyST.

Monads have a big influence on the code:

```
saxpy :: Double → Vector s → Vector s → _ST s (Vector s)
saxpy a x y =
    case boundsOfByteArray x of {
        (p,q) → saxpy' p
            where
                saxpy' :: Int → _ST s (Vector s)
                saxpy' p
                    | p > q     = returnStrictlyST y
                    | otherwise =
                        readDoubleArray x p                      'thenStrictlyST' \xe →
                        readDoubleArray y p                      'thenStrictlyST' \ye →
                        writeDoubleArray y p (a * xe + ye) 'seqStrictlyST'
                        saxpy' (p + 1)
    }
```

While the implementations of Clean's unboxed and GHC Bytearrays are similar, but they do not give the same results (table 8). The remark from Glasgow was that the state monad was not fast enough and that they have not had time to make it faster.

	Clean			Glasgow Haskell		
Array size	Heap size	GC time	Exec time	Heap size	GC time	Exec time
625^2	50 Kb	0.00	0.11	256 Kb	0.19	1.83
2500^2	170 Kb	0.00	0.91	1 Mb	0.71	13.30
10000^2	650 Kb	0.04	7.50	4 Mb	5.21	103.54

Table 8. Comparing the time and space requirements for the most optimal Clean implementation for the conjugate gradient algorithm and one implemented with GHC's _Bytearray

The list implementation in GHC was as fast as we expected, with a performance comparable to the Clean version with lists. Remarkably, this version is also the fastest implementation we had with GHC (see table 9).

5   Conclusions

In this paper we investigated various implementations of the conjugate gradient algorithm. The first implementations in Clean with lists and arrays showed that the overhead imposed by the lazy data type is high, especially memory consumption can be extreme. List are only an alternative to arrays when speed is not important or when arrays do not give good performance.

A fast version of the implementation in Clean was obtained using an unboxed array and by the inclusion of map fusion and update-in-place. When compared

Array size	Clean			Glasgow Haskell		
	Min Heap	GC time	Exec time	Min Heap	GC time	Exec time
625^2	850 Kb	0.32	1.09	820 Kb	0.58	1.06
2500^2	6170 Kb	2.68	9.06	5900 Kb	1.80	7.97

Table 9. Comparing implementations of the conjugate gradient algorithm in Clean and GHC, both GHC with lazy lists. The heap size for the problem sizes are for both languages 2 Mb and 16 Mb respectively

to C, that code proved to be only 30% slower, while the amount of allocated memory was the same. The Clean program looks similar to the C version, but because of the absence of side-effects, program transformations are easier.

The GHC implementation of Haskell arrays proved to be less suited for scientific computing. The code which can be written with them is clean, but the speed and memory consumption are not good. The current implementation of the _Bytearray provided by the Glasgow Haskell Compiler gives better performance: the memory consumption was reasonable, but the execution time can be improved. The list implementation was the fastest we had with the GHC compiler.

References

[BS93]   E. Barendsen and J.E.W Smetsers. Conventional and uniqueness typing in graph rewrite systems. Technical Report CSI-R9328, Computer Science Institute, Faculty of Mathematics and Informatics, University of Nijmegen, December 1993.

[CSJ95]   S. Choi, T.K. Sarkar, and Choi J. Adaptive antenna array for direction-of-arrival estimation utilizing the conjugate gradient method. *Signal Processing (SIGPRO)*, 45(3):313–327, Sep 1995.

[EO94]   R.G. Ellis and D.W. Oldenburg. The pole-pole 3-d dc resistivity inverse problem: a conjugate gradient approach. *Geophysical Journal International*, 119:187–194, 1994.

[GLPJ93]   A. Gill, J. Launchbury, and S.L. Peyton Jones. A short cut to deforestation. In *Proceedings of the ACM Conference on Functional Programming Languages and Computer Architecture (FPCA'93)*, pages 223–232, April 1993.

[H+96]   P.H. Hartel et al. Benchmarking implementations of functional languages with "pseudoknot", a float-intensive benchmark. *Journal functional programming*, 6(4):621–655, July 1996.

[HPJW92]   P. Hudak, S.L. Peyton Jones, and P. Wadler. Report on the programming language haskell, a non-strict purely functional language (version 1.2). *SIGPLAN Notices*, Mar, 1992.

[HS93]   A.G. Hoekstra and P.M.A. Sloot. Implementation of a parallel conjugate gradient method for simulation of elastic light. *4th Physics Computing '92*, pages 345–346, 1993.

[JDG92]   E.M. Johansson, F.U. Dowla, and D.M. Goodman. Backpropagation learn-
           ing for multi-layer feed-forward neural networks using the conjugate gradi-
           ent method. *International Journal of Neural Systems*, 2(4), 1992.

[KGGK94] V. Kumar, A. Grama, A. Gupta, and G. Karypis. *Introduction to Parallel
           Computing, Design and Analysis of Algorithms.* The Benjamin/Cummings
           Publishing Company, Inc., California, 1994.

[LPJ94]   J. Launchbury and S.L. Peyton Jones. Lazy functional state threads. In
           Programming Languages Design and Implementation, Orlando, 1994. ACM
           Press.

[PJ96]   S.L. Peyton Jones. Bulk types with class. In *Proceedings of the 1996 Glas-
           gow Workshop on Fucntional Programming*, Ullapool, Scotland, July 1996.

[PJL91]   S.L. Peyton Jones and J. Launchbury. Unboxed values as first class citi-
           zens. In *FPCA'91 — Functional Programming Languages and Computer
           Architecture*, pages 636–666, 1991.

[PvE93]   M.J. Plasmeijer and M.C.J.D. van Eekelen. *Functional Programming and
           Parallel Graph Rewriting.* Addison-Wesley Publishers Ltd., 1993.

[SF93]   T. Sheard and L. Fegaras. A fold for all seasons. In *Proceedings of the ACM
           Conference on Functional Programming Languages and Computer Architec-
           ture (FPCA'93)*, pages 233–242, Orlando, April 1993. ACM Press.

[Wad90]   P. Wadler. Deforestation: Transforming programs to eliminate trees. *The-
           oretical Computer Science*, 73:231–248, 1990.

An Implementation of Eden on Top of Concurrent Haskell

Silvia Breitinger, Ulrike Klusik, Rita Loogen*

Philipps-Universität Marburg, Fachbereich Mathematik, Fachgebiet Informatik,
Hans Meerwein Straße, Lahnberge, D-35032 Marburg, Germany,
{breiting,klusik,loogen}@informatik.uni-marburg.de

Abstract. The functional concurrent language *Eden* is an extension of the lazy functional language Haskell by high level constructs for the explicit specification of dynamically evolving process systems. It employs stream-based implicit communication.

In this paper, we describe how Eden can be implemented on top of Concurrent Haskell, another concurrent extension of Haskell. This implementation provides valuable insights into the relationship between the two languages. Furthermore, an outlook on the parallel implementation on a distributed memory system is given.

1 Introduction

A widely accepted approach to concurrent programming is to use a standard sequential language as so-called *computation language* and extend it by a suitable *coordination language* (cf. [GC92]). Well-known approaches based on ML include Facile[TLP+93], Concurrent ML[Rep91] and LCS[Ber95]. The two languages analyzed in this paper, Eden and Concurrent Haskell (CH, for short), use the lazy functional language Haskell[PH96] as their foundation. Eden [BLO96] extends it by syntactic constructs for *explicitly* specifying and creating processes. These processes communicate by exchanging values via communication channels modelled by lazy lists. Communication is asynchronous and *implicit*, i.e. the exchange of messages is done automatically and need not be specified by the programmer using send and receive commands. In contrast to this, Concurrent Haskell [PJGF96] uses I/O monads to model processes and concurrent activities and thus encapsulates concurrency completely in monads.

Eden differs from other concurrent declarative languages in that it introduces processes, communication and nondeterminism on a much higher level of abstraction and that it is explicitly tailored for the programming of distributed memory parallel computers. Eden employs a declarative coordination language and uses a two-level structure: the level of *functions* (computation) and the level of *processes* (coordination) with nondeterminism being introduced at the process level only. This distinction and the maintenance of referential transparency for

---

* The authors are supported by the DAAD (Deutscher Akademischer Austauschdienst) in the context of a German-Spanish Acción Integrada.

functions and deterministic user-defined processes supports modularity. Existing reasoning techniques for functional languages can be retained without any modification. Moreover, Eden incorporates flexible constructs for the specification of time-dependent interactions and complex communication topologies. A predefined fair merge process is the only source of nondeterminism.

Due to its simplicity and its commonalities to Eden, Concurrent Haskell lends itself to a first concurrent implementation of Eden that does not incur the overhead of translating the full range of sequential Haskell constructs. Apart from this, our work provides valuable insights into the relationship of the two concurrent languages and several issues to be addressed in the parallel implementation.

Plan of the paper. Section 2 gives a short introduction to the key concepts of Eden. In Section 3, we present a short introduction to CH and describe the translation of Eden into CH. Section 4 discusses issues to be addressed in the parallel implementation of Eden. Finally, we mention related work and draw some conclusions.

2   Eden in a nutshell

In this section, we will explain how Eden extends Haskell by functional constructs for the definition and creation of processes and the specification of interconnections between processes. Eden provides *process abstractions*, which specify functional process schemes, and *process instantiations* in which process abstractions are supplied with parameters and inputs in order to create new processes.

The syntax of a process abstraction with parameters par_1, ..., par_k that maps inputs in_1, ..., in_m to outputs exp_1, ..., exp_n is shown below. In the part introduced by **where**, local definitions to be used in the output expressions can be given. In contrast to the Haskell **where** clause of an equation, the input variables $in_1, \ldots, in_m$ are visible in the local definitions.

$$p\ par_1 \ldots par_k = \texttt{process}\ (in_1, \ldots, in_m)\texttt{->}(exp_1, \ldots, exp_n)$$
$$\texttt{where}\ equation_1 \ldots equation_r$$

The right hand side of this definition is of type $\texttt{Process}\ (\tau_1, \ldots, \tau_m)\ (\tau'_1, \ldots, \tau'_n)$ where $\texttt{Process}$ is a predefined binary type constructor and $\tau_1, \ldots, \tau_m$ and $\tau'_1, \ldots, \tau'_n$ are the types of the inputs and outputs of the process, respectively.

A process is created using a *process instantiation*, i.e. the application of a process abstraction to parameter expressions and a tuple of input expressions, yielding a tuple of output channels for the newly created process. # is a predefined infix operator which applies a process abstraction to its input.

$$(out_1, \ldots, out_n) = p\ e_1 \ldots e_k \texttt{\#}\ (input\_exp_1, \ldots, input\_exp_m)$$

Example. The following process abstraction par_op uses a function given as parameter op to combine all values between two given boundaries. Only if the number of values is larger than the parameter threshold, the evaluation of subexpressions is performed in parallel.

```
par_op :: (Int -> Int -> Int) -> Int -> Process (Int,Int) (Int)
par_op op threshold
  = process (low,high) -> result
    where result
            = if high - low < threshold
              then (seq_op low high)
              else let res1 = (par_op op threshold) # (low,mid)
                       res2 = (par_op op threshold) # (mid+1,high)
                   in (op res1 res2)
          mid = (low + high) 'div' 2
          seq_op :: Int -> Int -> Int
          seq_op l h = foldr1 (op) [l .. h]
```

In Eden, process abstractions are first class values which can be passed as arguments to functions or other process abstractions. However, the duplication of *running* processes is neither desirable nor possible because they are dynamic entities with an internal state. The type of a process instantiation is simply the type of the results generated. There is no type that represents a running process.

Every output channel will be evaluated by a separate *concurrent thread* of execution. Each channel provides a transmission buffer into which fully evaluated objects are transferred by the sender process. Only the transmission of streams (i.e. list channels) is done piecemeal and does not have to be delayed until the whole list is fully evaluated. A concurrent thread will be suspended when trying to read from an inport with empty channel buffer.

As soon as a value of the channel's type has been transmitted in full, the channel is closed and the communication ports are abolished. A user process with all its outputs closed will terminate immediately. On termination, its input channels will be eliminated and the corresponding outports in the sender processes will be closed.

Basically, the whole computation of a process is driven by the evaluation of its outport expressions to normal form. This rule overrides lazy evaluation in favour of parallelism. Moreover, each process immediately evaluates all *top level* process instantiations, i.e. all that occur directly as the right hand side of an equation in the body, without any surrounding function definition or other expression. These two exceptions are essential in order to achieve maximum parallelism in Eden programs.

The *operational semantics* of Eden comprises two levels of transition systems: a lower level that models local effects with Haskell's operational semantics and an upper level that describes global effects on the whole process system by special 'actions'. For further details on Eden the reader is referred to [BLOP96].

3 Eden on top of Concurrent Haskell

The programming language Concurrent Haskell is, just like Eden, an extension of Haskell. Its primary application area is the programming of graphical user interfaces, and as a result it is well-suited to express concurrency, but not to speed up programs by evaluating subtasks in parallel. CH uses I/O monads to describe concurrent behaviour. It provides a `forkIO :: IO () -> IO ()` primitive for performing I/O actions concurrently. Communication between concurrent activities can be implemented using shared mutable variables. The primitive type `MVar` is used to introduce such mutable locations which may be empty or contain a value of type a. The following primitive operations on `MVar`s are provided:

- `newMVar :: IO (MVar a)` creates a new `MVar`.
- `takeMVar :: MVar a -> IO a` blocks until the location is non-empty, then reads the location leaving it empty and returns the value.
- `putMVar :: MVar a -> a -> IO ()` writes a value to the specified location which must be empty.

Another mutable variable type is `IVar`, a variant of `MVar`, which can be written only once:

- `newIVar :: IO (IVar a)` creates a new `IVar`.
- `readIVar :: IVar a -> IO a` blocks until the location is non-empty and then reads the value.
- `writeIVar :: IVar a -> a -> IO ()` writes a value the specified location which must be empty. Afterwards all processes can read the location without being blocked.

3.1 How to model Eden channels

On top of the primitives shown above, more abstract concurrency constructs can be built, e.g. `MVar`s can be used to define a channel with unbounded buffering with the following interface (see [PJGF96])[2]:

```
type Channel a
newChan :: IO (Channel a)
putChan :: Channel a -> a -> IO ()
getChan :: Channel a -> IO a
```

`Channel`s model infinite streams of values. In order to read all values transmitted via a channel, a function `getChanContents :: Channel a -> IO [a]` is provided which lazily reads the contents of a channel and puts them into a list. It returns immediately with a suspension without waiting for values on the channels. This action may cause unwanted nondeterministic effects since it changes the execution order of the actions in a program. For our purpose it is safe, since a channel is only read by one process.

---

[2] In the GHC, this data structure is called `Chan`, whereas `Channel` represents a POSIX channel.

```
type EChan a = Channel (Message a)
data Message a = EndMarker
     | Contents a

readEChan :: EChan a -> IO [a]
readEChan strm = getChanContents strm >>= \ mList ->
                  return (fromMessageList mList)
                  where fromMessageList (EndMarker:r) = []
                        fromMessageList (Contents x:r)
                                       = x: (fromMessageList r)

class NormalForm a where
               force :: a -> a
writeEChan :: (NormalForm a) => Echan a -> [a] -> IO ()
writeEChan strm l
  = sequence (map ((strict (putChan strm)).(strict Contents).force) l) >>
    putChan strm EndMarker
```

Fig. 1. Modeling Eden's finite streams in Concurrent Haskell

In order to work with finite streams, one has to extend the type of transmitted values by a special endmarker which indicates the closing of a stream. A corresponding specification is given in Fig. 1.

The infix combinators `>>` and `>>=` are used to combine actions of type IO a in sequence, `return` is used to convert values to actions, and `sequence` takes a list of actions and performs them sequentially. The action `delayIO` delays an action and returns a suspension for the return value of the action. When this value is requested, the delayed action is executed.

```
(>>)      :: IO a -> IO b         -> IO b
(>>=)     :: IO a -> (a -> IO b) -> IO b
return    :: a -> IO a
sequence  :: [IO a] -> IO ()
delayIO   :: IO a -> IO a
```

For the evaluation of output expressions in Eden programs, we need an evaluation to *normal form*. The method `strict` $:: (a \rightarrow b) \rightarrow a \rightarrow b$ in the class Eval (provided in Haskell from version 1.3 on) evaluates its second argument only to *head normal form* and therefore does not suffice for our purposes. Instead, we use instance declarations of a new class NormalForm (see Fig. 1) for all data types to be transmitted via streams:

```
instance NormalForm type where
    force (C a₁ ... aₙ) = force a₁ 'seq' ... force aₙ 'seq' (C a₁ ... aₙ)
```

Such instance declarations can automatically be inserted by the compiler. The definition of seq is as follows:

```
x 'seq' y = case x of
              _ -> y
```

With class `NormalForm`, `writeEChan strm l` writes the normal form of list `l` to stream `strm` by applying `force` to each element of the list.

Eden and Concurrent Haskell greatly differ in the underlying memory model and in their level of abstraction: while Eden processes can have arbitrary Haskell data types as their result, the concurrent agents of CH can only perform I/O actions. Moreover, Eden processes communicate via message passing, whereas in Concurrent Haskell shared mutable variables are used. The idea of the transformation presented in the following is to model Eden processes by concurrent I/O actions. For that purpose the implicit message passing of Eden must be explicitly simulated by finite stream channels (`EChan`). One value channels will be treated as "singleton" streams. In the program this is done by sending and receiving lists with one element instead of the element itself.

3.2 How to transform Eden programs

On process generation, the following steps have to be carried out:

1. `EChans` for the communication with the child must be created.
2. The child process must be forked.
3. Inputs for the child process must be written using separate threads, as these are new outports of the parent process.
4. Outputs from the child process must be read lazily.

For each process, the following behaviour has to be implemented:

5. Inputs are read on demand.
6. The *strict* evaluation of output values is initiated in `writeEChan` and the outputs are written by separate threads.

Example 1. In the following, we show how the process abstraction `par_op` from Section 2 can be translated. The numbers in brackets correspond to the steps listed above:

```
par_op :: (Int->Int->Int)->Int->(EChan Int,EChan Int)->EChan Int->IO ()
par_op op threshold (inlow,inhigh) out
  =  readEChan inlow >>= \ low ->           -- (5)
     readEChan inhigh >>= \ high ->
     if (high-low) < threshold
     then writeEChan out [seq_op low high]
     else (newEChan >>= \ inlow1 ->          -- (1) create in/out channels
           newEChan >>= \ inhigh1 ->         --      for 1st child process
           newEChan >>= \ res1 ->
           forkIO (par_op op threshold (inlow1,inhigh1) res1) >> -- (2)
           forkIO (writeEChan inlow1 [low]) >>   -- (3) write inputs
           forkIO (writeEChan inhigh1 [mid]) >>
           readEChan res1 >>= \ [arg1] ->    -- (4) read result on demand
```

```
        newEChan >>= \ inlow2 ->          -- handle 2nd child proc.
        newEChan >>= \ inhigh2 ->
        newEChan >>= \ res2 ->
        forkIO (par_op op threshold (inlow2,inhigh2) res2) >>
        forkIO (writeEChan inlow2 [mid+1]) >>
        forkIO (writeEChan inhigh2 [high]) >>
        readEChan res2 >>= \ [arg2] ->
        writeEChan out [op arg1 arg2] )  -- (6) write result
where mid = (low + high) 'div' 2
      seq_op :: Int -> Int -> Int
      seq_op l h = foldr1 (op) [l .. h]
```

In this example the spawning of threads for writing the output channels does not pay off, because the value is an integer given as a simple arithmetic expression. But in the general case the output expression can be arbitrarily complex, so that for interleaving we need an extra thread for the expression's evaluation to normal form.

In the following, we present more Eden programs in order to show some problems with the simple transformation approach developed so far. The next example shows a process instantiation embedded in a purely functional environment. The transformation of the process instantiation into an I/O action imposes the same transformation on all enclosing expressions since I/O actions cannot be encapsulated in CH. Thus, purely functional expressions in the context of a transformed expression must be transformed, too. The transformation into I/O monads is one-way and influences the context of expressions.

Example 2. The following function generates a pipeline of processes from a given list of process abstractions.

```
pipe :: [Process a a] -> a -> a
pipe p_list values = case p_list of
                          []     -> values
                          (p:ps) -> let mid = p # values
                                    in pipe ps mid
```

The type of the parameter processes will be transformed into
$$\text{EChan a -> EChan a -> IO ()}.$$
Using the above method for transforming process instantiations, mid = p # values will be translated into the following CH code:

```
midA :: IO [a]
midA = newEChan >>= \ valC ->
       newEChan >>= \ resC ->
       forkIO (p valC resC) >>
       forkIO (writeEChan valC values) >>
       (readEChan resC)
```

mid becomes an I/O action midA with type IO [a]. The list type results from the transmission. To access its value, the action has to be executed. Hence we have to perform the action before the recursive call of pipe. As the **let** expression is the second alternative of a **case** expression, we have to transform the first purely functional alternative into an I/O action, too, in order to obtain a correctly typed program. This is done by using the function *return*. The resulting program looks as follows:

```
pipe :: [ EChan a -> EChan a -> IO () ] -> [a] -> IO [a]
pipe p_list values
        = case p_list of
              []      -> return values
              (p:ps) -> let midA = ...
                        in midA >>= \ mid -> (pipe ps mid)
```

This example shows that the transformation process is not purely compositional. If at least one alternative of a **case** expression is transformed into an I/O action, the whole expression becomes an I/O action and additionally it is necessary to convert all other alternative expressions into actions.

In the following, expressions that will be transformed into I/O actions or the transformation of which yields I/O monads will be referred to as *interactions*. In the compiler, we use a so-called *interaction analysis* (see Subsection 3.4) in order to find the expressions which must be transformed.

In the next example we consider mutually recursive definitions.

Example 3 Ring topology. We can use **pipe** to produce a ring of processes by connecting the ends of the pipeline of processes.

```
ring :: [Process a a] -> a
ring (p:ps) = let link = p # next
                  next = pipe ps link
              in  link
```

Let $\mathcal{T}[\![x]\!]$ denote the transformation of Eden expression x (see Section 3.5). If we transform the program as shown before, we get:

```
ring (p:ps)                         linkA
  = let                             ⊢ nextA >>= \ nextV ->
      linkA = nextA >>= \ nextV ->      T[p # nextV]
                T[p # nextV]        ⊢ linkA >>= \ linkV ->
      nextA = linkA >>= \ linkV ->     pipe ps linkV >>= \ nextV ->
                pipe ps linkV           T[p # nextV] >>
    in linkA                        ⊢ nextA >>= \ nextV' ->
                                       T[p # nextV'] >>= \ linkV ->
                                       pipe ps linkV >>= \ nextV ->
                                       T[p # nextV] >>
                                    ⊢ ...
```

This program does not show the desired behaviour: The evaluation of `linkA` (see the reduction sequence above) produces an infinite sequence of process instantiations of p. The reason is that `linkA` is a composed action, the first action of which is `nextA`, and vice versa. So the execution of `linkA` only unfolds the composed actions, without finding a primitive action to execute. This recursion does not terminate and no process is created.

The problem is caused by the mutual dependency of the inports and outports link and next, which are values in the Eden version (as contents of channels), but are transformed into I/O monads in CH. The difference between I/O actions and values is that values are never evaluated more than once but actions are evaluated every time their return values are requested. Hence we have to ensure that such actions are performed only once.

This can be achieved with a kind of multicast using the "write once variables" IVars. The idea is to substitute an action by a read operation on a corresponding IVar. In order to model the reading of IVars on demand, we will use the operation:

```
lazyReadIVar = delayIO . readIVar
```

The IVars have to be created outside the declaration and to be written at the beginning of the declaration's body. This ensures that they are known within the declaration and the values of the actions can be assigned to them. In order to allow the interleaved computation of their values, link and next have to be spawned in separate threads.

```
ring :: [EChan a -> EChan a -> IO ()] -> IO [a]
ring (p:ps) = newIVar >>=  linkI ->
              newIVar >>=  nextI ->
          let next  = lazyReadIVar nextI
              link  = lazyReadIVar linkI
              linkA = next >>= \ nextV ->
                      T[p # nextV]
              nextA = link >>= \ linkV ->
                      pipe ps linkV
           in forkIO (linkA >>= \ val1 ->
                      writeIVar linkI val1) >>
              forkIO (nextA >>= \ val2 ->
                      writeIVar nextI val2) >>
              link >>= \ linkV' ->
              (return linkV')
```

An alternative solution is to implement a somehow parallel creation of mutually dependent processes: common channels are created first. Thus it is possible to use the output channel nextC of the pipeline as input channel for p.

```
ring :: [EChan a -> EChan a -> IO ()] -> EChan a -> IO ()
ring (p:ps) outc = newEChan >>= \ linkC ->
                   newEChan >>= \ nextC ->
                   forkIO (p nextC linkC) >>
                   readEChan linkC >>= \ link ->
                   forkIO ( pipe' ps link nextC) >>
                   writeEChan outC link
```

This transformation leads here to a correct program, but it is restricted to mutually recursive process instantiations. The function pipe has been replaced by a function pipe' which returns its result via a channel, i.e. its result type is

EChan a -> IO () instead of IO [a]. We decided to use the first variant as we need not introduce any new function there.

Finally we will discuss the treatment of higher order functions.

Example 4. Consider a slightly more complex pipeline: The outports of the processes are still connected to an inport of their successor. Additionally, processes have another inport for additional inputs from the parent process. The connection of the pipe processes is built via a higher order fold function.

```
aPipe :: (Process (a,b) a) -> [b] -> (Process a a)
aPipe p listb = process (in -> foldl f in listb)
                where   f x y = p # (x,y)
```

As the transformation of the function f to a function f' changes the type to a -> b -> IO [a], and foldl has type (x -> y -> x) -> x -> [y] -> x, foldl cannot be applied to f'. There are two possibilities to produce a well typed expression: either to use a specialized foldl or to introduce a function f'' of type IO [a] -> b -> IO [a]. The first method is not practicable as we would have to generate arbitrary specializations of (primitive) functions. The other method requires the transformation of other arguments into interaction functions, which in general is a quite complex task, too.

These issues are specific to the monadic representation of processes and will not be encountered in the parallel implementation. Therefore the handling of higher order functions which contain interactions in their body has not been investigated further. In the transformation there is no special handling for such cases. They are rejected by the interaction analysis.

3.3 Source and target language for the transformation

Within the compiler, simpler intermediate languages are used: *CoreEden* and *CoreCH* are the source and target languages of the transformation pass.

The output of the parser is a syntax tree of a slightly more complex language, that has to be transformed into *CoreEden*. Accordingly an extra compiler pass called *Desugaring* is needed to do some simplifications. In order to keep the transformation rules simple, only unary function applications and lambda abstractions are used here. The definition of *CoreEden* is given in Figure 2.

CoreCH is nearly the same as *CoreEden* except that Eden's coordination constructs (process abstractions and instantiations) are excluded. Moreover, new data structures (e.g. IO a, IVar a) and predefined functions (e.g. return, >>, >>=) are added.

3.4 Interaction analysis

In order to translate Eden programs in full, we have to perform a program analysis called *interaction analysis*, that infers which expressions have to be transformed into I/O actions, i.e. which are so-called "interactions" (cf. Section 3.2).

Expressions:

Exp	$\rightarrow$ Exp :: Type	type annotation
	| Exp$_1$ Exp$_2$	application
	| \ Pat -> Exp	lambda abstraction
	| **case** Exp **of**	
	{ Pat$_1$ -> Exp$_1$; ...; Pat$_n$ -> Exp$_n$ }	case expression, $n \geq 0$
	| **let** Var = Exp **in** Exp	non-rec. def.
	| **letrec** Var$_1$ = Exp$_1$; ... Var$_n$ = Exp$_n$ **in** Exp	rec. def., $n \geq 1$
	| Pat	pattern
	| Fun	predefined function
	| **process** (Var$_1$, ..., Var$_n$) -> (Exp$_1$, ..., Exp$_n$)	process abstraction
	| pabs # (Exp$_1$, ..., Exp$_n$)	process instantiation

Patterns:

Pat	$\rightarrow$ Con Pat$_1$ ... Pat$_n$	constructor term, $n \geq 0$
	| Var | Const	variable, basic value

Types:

Type	$\rightarrow$ Integer | Bool | Char | ...	predefined type
	| TVar	type variable
	| TCon Type$_1$ ... Type$_n$	algebraic data type
	| Type$_1$ $\rightarrow$ Type$_n$	function type

Fig. 2. Core Eden

In nearly all cases, this decision can be made bottom-up during the transformation, the only exceptions being mutually recursive declarations. In order to translate the right hand sides of the declarations correctly, it has to be known of which type the variables defined using mutual recursion will be after the transformation. Hence we need a method to infer this information before the transformation of such declarations.

This can be done by means of a type inference not on the Eden types, but on the types of the resulting Concurrent Haskell expressions, called *CH Types*. This type inference is defined by an extension of the Haskell type inference by some special type conversion rules that reflect the transformation done in the program transformation pass. The inference is described with the following kind of typing rules:

$$\Gamma \triangleright e :: \tau$$

which indicate that in the context Γ the expression e has CH Type τ, where CH Types differ from Eden types in the presence of monad types IO τ. The context $\Gamma :: Var \rightarrow CH\ Type$ provides the CH Type of variables. The inference rule

$$\frac{\Gamma \triangleright e_1 :: \tau_1, \ldots, \Gamma \triangleright e_n :: \tau_n}{\Gamma' \triangleright e :: \tau}$$

means: if the expressions e_i have types τ_i in the context Γ then the expression e has type τ in a context Γ'. As usual, $\Gamma[x/\tau]$ denotes the context Γ' with $\Gamma' x = \tau$ and $\Gamma' y = \Gamma y$ for variables $y \neq x$.

For the transformation, we prohibit that I/O monads are encapsulated in data structures. Therefore we extract monads out of a structure and compose a new action that first performs the extracted actions lazily and then returns the data structure. Corresponding to this, we apply in the inference the function *extract* in order to extract the component type from monadic types. For non-monadic types this function is the identity. Additionally we need a function *isIO* that checks for I/O monadic types:

$$
\begin{array}{ll}
extract \;\; (\text{IO } \tau) \;=\; \tau & isIO \;\; (\text{IO t}) \;=\; \text{True} \\
extract \;\; (\tau) \quad\;=\; \tau & isIO \;\; \_ \qquad\;\; =\; \text{False}
\end{array}
$$

Now all preliminaries are provided so that we can explain the type inference rules for the different Eden expressions:

Variables are assigned the type given in the context: $\qquad \Gamma[x/\tau] \rhd x :: \tau$

Constructors and predefined functions keep their type: $\qquad \Gamma \rhd C :: \text{type}(C)$

Process abstractions are assigned a CH Type which reflects that they are transformed into a function taking the input and output channels and returning an I/O monad which performs the process:

$$
\frac{\Gamma[x_1/\tau_1,\ldots,x_n/\tau_n] \rhd \texttt{let body in } (y_1,\ldots,y_m) :: (\sigma_1,\ldots,\sigma_m)}{\begin{array}{l} \Gamma \rhd \texttt{process } (x_1,\ldots,x_n) \to (y_1,\ldots,y_m) \texttt{ where } body :: \\ (EChan\,\tau_1,\ldots,EChan\,\tau_n) \to (EChan\,\sigma_1,\ldots EChan\,\sigma_m) \to \texttt{IO } () \end{array}}
$$

Process instantiations get a monadic type. The input expressions may contain interactions and thus have a monadic type. We extract their component type before checking type consistency with the process abstraction, because we want to transmit values and not I/O monads via the channels. Thus, the type *extract* (τ_i') of the input values e_i needs to be an instance of the type τ_i in the process abstraction.

$$
\frac{\begin{array}{l} \Gamma \rhd pabs :: (EChan\,\tau_1,..,EChan\,\tau_n) \to (EChan\,\sigma_1,..,EChan\,\sigma_m) \to \texttt{IO } (), \\ \Gamma \rhd e_i :: \tau_i' \text{ with } extract\,(\tau_i') = \tau_i\vartheta, \quad (1 \le i \le n) \text{ for a type substitution } \vartheta \end{array}}{\Gamma \rhd pabs \mathbin{\#} (e_1,\ldots,e_n) :: \texttt{IO } (\sigma_1',\ldots,\sigma_m') \quad \text{ where } \sigma_i' = extract\,(\sigma_i\vartheta)}
$$

Lambda abstractions are handled in the same way as in normal Haskell type inference.

$$
\frac{\Gamma \rhd pat :: \tau_1, e :: \tau_2}{\Gamma \rhd \backslash pat \to e :: \tau_1 \to \tau_2}
$$

Function applications can consist of functions or arguments which are transformed into I/O monads. Such I/O actions have to be performed prior to the application.

Additionally we must ensure that the transformed application is type correct. For this the type τ_2 of e_2 has to be an instance of the type σ_1 over which the function e_1 is defined, i.e., there must exist a substitution ϑ such that: $extract\,(\tau_2) = \sigma_1\vartheta$.

$$\frac{\Gamma \triangleright e_1 :: \tau_1,\, extract\,(\tau_1) = \sigma_1 \to \sigma_2 \qquad}{\Gamma \triangleright e_2 :: \tau_2,\, extract\,(\tau_2) = \sigma_1\vartheta,\ \text{for some substitution } \vartheta}$$
$$\Gamma \triangleright e_1 e_2 :: \begin{cases} \mathtt{IO}(\sigma_2\vartheta), & \text{if } isIO(\tau_i) \text{ for some } i \\ \sigma_2\vartheta, & \text{otherwise} \end{cases}$$

Local declarations require that the type of their right hand side has to be inferred first. Subsequently, the type of the body expression e_2 can be computed with a suitably extended environment. We extract the type of the variable x when inferring the type of e_2, because the translation guarantees that interactions in e_1 will be performed before the evaluation of e_2.

$$\frac{\Gamma \triangleright e_1 :: \tau_1 \qquad \Gamma[x/extract\,(\tau_1)] \triangleright e_2 :: \tau_2}{\Gamma \triangleright \mathbf{let}\ x = e_1\ \mathbf{in}\ e_2 :: \begin{cases} \mathtt{IO}\ (extract\ \tau_2), & \text{if } isIO(\tau_1) \\ \tau_2, & \text{otherwise} \end{cases}}$$

Mutually recursive declarations require that the types of the variables defined this way are determined as fixed points.

$$\frac{\Gamma[x_1/\tau_1,\dots,x_n/\tau_n] \triangleright e_1 :: \tau_1;\dots;e_n :: \tau_n,}{\Gamma[x_1/\tau_1,\dots,x_n/\tau_n] \triangleright e :: \tau}$$
$$\Gamma \triangleright \mathbf{letrec}\ x_1 = e_1, .., x_n = e_n\mathbf{in}\ e :: \begin{cases} \mathtt{IO}\ (extract\ (\tau)), & \text{if } isIO(\tau_i) \text{ for some } i \\ \tau, & \text{otherwise} \end{cases}$$

Case expressions will be assigned an I/O type if at least one of the alternatives is of I/O type. It has to be ensured that the type of the scrutinee e is an instance of the type *ptype* of the patterns $pat_1,\dots,pat_n$.

$$\frac{\Gamma \triangleright e :: \tau,\, extract\ \tau = ptype\ \vartheta,\, \Gamma_i \triangleright pat_i : ptype\ \vartheta\ (1 \le i \le n)}{\Gamma + \Gamma_1 \triangleright alt_1 :: \tau_1, \cdots, \Gamma + \Gamma_n \triangleright alt_n :: \tau_n,}$$
$$\tau' = extract\ (\tau_i\rho)\ \text{for some most general unifier } \rho \text{ of } \{\tau_1,\dots,\tau_n\}$$
$$\Gamma \triangleright \mathbf{case}\ e\ \mathbf{of}\ pat_1 \to alt_1; ..; pat_n \to alt_n :: \begin{cases} \mathtt{IO}\ \tau', & \text{if } isIO(\tau) \\ & \text{or } isIO(\tau_i) \text{ for some } i \\ \tau', & \text{otherwise} \end{cases}$$

The above type inference system allows to derive the CH Types of most *CoreEden* programs. This information will be exploited in the transformation algorithm, which will be presented subsequently.

3.5 Program transformation

For the transformation algorithm, we assume that the program to be transformed is fully CH typed. The auxiliary transformation functions *toIO* and *extractcode* take these types as arguments.
The transformation algorithm is given as the function

$$\mathcal{T}[\![.]\!] \;::\; CoreEden \rightarrow CoreCH$$

Note that parts written in *italic* belong to the meta language. The function *toIO* converts an expression into an I/O action. If it already was one, the execution of the action is delayed by the use of `delayIO`.

$$
\begin{aligned}
toIO \quad &e \;(\texttt{IO t}) \;=\; \texttt{delayIO e} \\
toIO \quad &e \;\_\; \qquad\;\;\; =\; \texttt{return e}
\end{aligned}
$$

extractcode produces code to perform the actions from a list of expressions and to return their values. Non-action expressions in the list are returned as they are.

$$
\begin{aligned}
&extractcode \quad [\texttt{e}_1 \!::\; \sigma_n, \ldots,\; \texttt{e}_n \!::\; \sigma_n] \\
&= toIO \quad \mathcal{T}[\![\texttt{e}_1]\!] \;\sigma_1 \;\texttt{>>= } \backslash\; \texttt{var}_1 \;\rightarrow \\
&\qquad\qquad \cdots \\
&\quad\;\; toIO \quad \mathcal{T}[\![\texttt{e}_n]\!] \;\sigma_n \;\texttt{>>= } \backslash\; \texttt{var}_n \;\rightarrow \\
&\quad\;\; \texttt{return (var}_1, \;\ldots, \;\texttt{var}_n\texttt{)}, \; \textit{if } isIO(\sigma_i) \textit{ for some } 1 \le i \le n \\
&= \texttt{return (}\mathcal{T}[\![\texttt{e}_1]\!], \;\ldots, \;\mathcal{T}[\![\texttt{e}_n]\!]\texttt{)}, \; \textit{otherwise}
\end{aligned}
$$

The main idea of the transformation is to adapt expressions in such a way that their monadic subexpressions are extracted out, if possible, and to convert the whole expression into an I/O monad. We define the transformation for Eden core expressions with fully CH-type annotated subexpressions.

For *variables, constants and constructors*, nothing has to be changed.

$$
\begin{aligned}
\mathcal{T}[\![\texttt{var}]\!] \quad &= \texttt{var} \\
\mathcal{T}[\![\texttt{const}]\!] \;\;&= \texttt{const} \\
\mathcal{T}[\![\texttt{C}]\!] \qquad\;&= \texttt{C}
\end{aligned}
$$

Process abstractions are transformed into functions that take inport and outport channel names and return an I/O action which spawns a thread for each outport. The threads then compute the output values and write them to the outports.

As the outport values may become I/O actions, we use *extractcode* to perform the actions and to get their values.

$$
\begin{aligned}
&\mathcal{T}[\![\textbf{process }(\texttt{var}_1 \!::\; \tau_1, \;\ldots, \;\texttt{var}_n \!::\; \tau_n) \rightarrow (\texttt{e}_1 \!::\; \sigma_1, \;\ldots, \;\texttt{e}_m \!::\; \sigma_m) \\
&\quad \textbf{where body}]\!] \\
&= \backslash\; (\texttt{inCh}_1, \;\ldots, \;\texttt{inCh}_n) \rightarrow \backslash\; (\texttt{outCh}_1, \;\ldots, \;\texttt{outCh}_m) \;\rightarrow \\
&\quad\;\; \texttt{readEChan inCh}_1 \;\texttt{>>= } \backslash\; \texttt{var}_1 \;\rightarrow \\
&\qquad\quad \vdots \\
&\quad\;\; \texttt{readEChan inCh}_n \;\texttt{>>= } \backslash\; \texttt{var}_n \;\rightarrow \\
&\quad\;\; \textbf{let } \mathcal{T}[\![\textbf{body}]\!] \\
&\quad\;\; \textbf{in } extractcode \quad [\texttt{e}_1 \!::\; \sigma_1, \;\ldots, \texttt{e}_m \!::\; \sigma_m] \;\texttt{>>= } \backslash\; (\texttt{out}_1, \;\ldots, \;\texttt{out}_m) \;\rightarrow \\
&\qquad\quad \texttt{forkIO (writeEChan outCh}_1 \;\texttt{out}_1\texttt{)} \;\texttt{>>} \\
&\qquad\qquad \cdots \\
&\qquad\quad \texttt{forkIO (writeEChan outCh}_m \;\texttt{out}_m\texttt{)}
\end{aligned}
$$

Process instantiations: The types of the output channels of the child process are derived from the type of the process abstraction.

$\mathcal{T}[\![$pabs:: $(\sigma'_1, \ldots, \sigma'_n) \to (\tau_1, \ldots, \tau_m) \to$ IO () #

  $(e_1:: \sigma_1, \ldots, e_n:: \sigma_n)]\!]$

= *extractcode* $[e_1:: \sigma_1, \ldots, e_n:: \sigma_n]$ >>= \ $(var_1, \ldots, var_n) \to$

createEChan >>= \ $inCh_1 \to$

  . . .

createEChan >>= \ $inCh_n \to$
createEChan >>= \ $outCh_1 \to$

  . . .

createEChan >>= \ $outCh_m \to$
forkIO $(\mathcal{T}[\![$pabs$]\!]$ $(inCh_1, \ldots, inCh_n)$ $(outCh_1, \ldots, outCh_m))$ >>
forkIO (writeEChan $inCh_1$ var_1) >>

  . . .

forkIO (writeEChan $inCh_n$ var_n) >>
readEChan $outCh_1$ >>= \ $out_1 \to$

  . . .

readEChan $outCh_m$ >>= \ $out_m \to$
return $(out_1, \ldots, out_m)$

For *applications*, we have to check if a subexpression e_i is transformed into an I/O action. In this case we have to extract the I/O action and use its result in the application. Then the application will be transformed into a sequence of I/O actions, the last of which returns the application's result.

$\mathcal{T}[\![(e_1:: \sigma_1 \ e_2:: \sigma_2)]\!]$
  = *extractcode* $[e_1:: \sigma_1, e_2:: \sigma_2]$ >>=
    \ $(var_1, var_2) \to e,$ *if* $isIO(\sigma_1)$ or $isIO(\sigma_2)$
      where e = var_1 var_2,   *if extract* σ_1 = ta $\to$ (IO te)
          = return $(var_1$ $var_2),$ *otherwise*
  = $\mathcal{T}[\![e_1]\!]$ $\mathcal{T}[\![e_2]\!],$ *otherwise*

Lambda abstractions are not changed:

$$\mathcal{T}[\![\backslash \ pat \to e:: t]\!] = \backslash \ pat \to \mathcal{T}[\![e]\!]$$

In *let expressions* the local declaration can be replaced by the lazy execution (introduced in *extractcode*) of the I/O action, the result of which can then be used within the body. This ensures that named actions are only performed once.

$\mathcal{T}[\![$let x = $e_1:: \sigma_1$ in $e_2:: \sigma_2]\!]$
  = *extractcode* $[e_1:: \sigma_1]$ >>= \ $var_1 \to$
    toIO $\mathcal{T}[\![e_2]\!]$ $\sigma_2,$ *if* $isIO(\sigma_1)$
  = let x = $\mathcal{T}[\![e_1]\!]$ in $\mathcal{T}[\![e_2]\!],$ *otherwise*

(Mutually) recursive declarations are the most involved case, because we have to ensure that I/O actions defined by mutual recursion are only performed once. This can be done as shown in Example 3 by the usage of IVars. For each such action we create a new IVar and then lazily read its value, so that we can use the value in the letrec. In the body of the letrec the actions are started in their own threads, such that they can simultaneously perform their results. In order to avoid a renaming of the variables x_i in the right hand sides e_i and the body e, we introduce new variables x_i' for the declared I/O actions and assign the actions for reading the IVars their original variable names x_i.

$$\mathcal{T}[\![\texttt{letrec } x_1 = e_1 :: \sigma_1; \ldots; x_n = e_n :: \sigma_n \texttt{ in } e :: \tau]\!]$$

```
= newIVar >>= \ ivar₁ →
     ⋮
  newIVar >>= \ ivarₖ →
  let  x_{i_1} = lazyReadIVar ivar₁
     ⋮
  in let x_{i_k} = lazyReadIVar ivarₖ
  in letrec y₁ = 𝒯[e₁] ; ...; yₙ = 𝒯[eₙ]
  in forkIO (delayIO x'_{i_1} >>= \ var → writeIVar ivar₁ var) >>
     ⋮
     forkIO (delayIO x'_{i_k} >>= \ var → writeIVar ivarₖ var) >>
     (toIO  e::τ) ,          if isIO(σ_{i_j})
                              for  1≤ i_j ≤ n, 1 ≤ j ≤ k
  where  yᵢ = x'ᵢ,   if isIO(σᵢ)
            = xᵢ,    otherwise
= letrec x₁ = 𝒯[e₁]; ...; xₙ = 𝒯[eₙ]  in 𝒯[e],          otherwise
```

In *case expressions*, we can extract I/O actions out of the scrutinee, but not out of the alternatives. Hence if at least one alternative becomes an I/O action, all right hand sides of the alternatives must be converted into I/O actions.

```
𝒯[case e:: τ of { pat₁ → e₁:: σ₁; ...; patₙ → eₙ:: σₙ}]
  = extractcode  [e :: t] >>= \ var →
    case var of alts,              if isIO(t)
  = case 𝒯[e] of alts,            otherwise
    where alts = { pat₁→toIO 𝒯[e₁] σ₁; ...; patₙ→toIO 𝒯[eₙ] σₙ},
               if isIO(σᵢ) for some 1 ≤ i ≤ n  or  isIO(τ)
             = { pat₁ → 𝒯[e₁]; ...; patₙ → 𝒯[eₙ]}, otherwise
```

This completes the specification of the transformation algorithm.

3.6 Overview of the compiler

↓ *Eden-Script*
Parser (generated by Happy)
↓ *syntax tree, synt. correct*
"Desugaring"
↓ *CoreEden*
Interaction Analysis
↓ *fully CH-typed program*
Program Transformation
↓ *CoreCH*
"Pretty Printer"
↓ *CH-script*
GHC
↓ *executable*

The Eden to Concurrent Haskell Compiler is written in Haskell and organized in the phases shown in the table on the left. The Eden script is parsed by a LALR(1)-Parser which was generated with Happy, a YACC-like parser generator which yields Haskell code. The parser produces a syntax tree of the given program and checks the scoping of the identifiers used. Only a restricted subset of the Haskell syntax is parsed. This excludes for example modules and type classes. The parsed syntax tree is simplified to a core language program in the "desugaring" phase. Now the interaction analysis can be performed on the *CoreEden* program.

Afterwards the transformation can be performed according to the type annotations added in the analysis phase. Finally, a pretty printer is used to produce a Concurrent Haskell script which can be translated by the Glasgow Haskell Compiler.

Runtime behaviour: As the compiler described here generates code for uniprocessors, it is inappropriate to expect speedups. Nevertheless one can estimate the quality of the CH code generated. For most example programs, the ratio of the runtimes of compiled Eden programs to hand-written Concurrent Haskell programs is less than two. The main overhead is due to the simulation of eager finite stream channels, especially the embedding of one value channels in streams. Moreover, the Eden to Concurrent Haskell compiler performs no optimizations at all. In comparison to plain Haskell, there is an additional overhead caused by the concurrent runtime system.

4 Eden's parallel implementation

Eden's parallel implementation will be based on a parallel abstract machine, DREAM (DistRibuted Eden Abstract Machine) implemented on an IBM SP-2 using the Message Passing Interface (MPI) Standard to coordinate parallel execution. In the same way as Eden extends the lazy functional language Haskell by coordination constructs, DREAM extends the underlying abstract machine of the Glasgow Haskell compiler, the STGM (Spineless Tagless G-Machine), by mechanisms for the treatment of the additional constructs. The table below indicates how the main coordination constructs are handled on the level of the parallel abstract machine. Process abstractions are static objects which will be represented by closures within the extended STG-machine. Process instantiations lead to the creation of new processes and the implicit stream-based communication must be handled by explicit message passing at the level of DREAM.

Eden $\implies$	DREAM
= Haskell	= STGM
+ *Coordination Constructs:*	+ *Extensions:*
– process abstractions	– process representation
– process instantiations	– process creation
– implicit stream-based communication	– message handling

In principle, DREAM is organized in a way similar to parallel implementations of functional languages which exploit implicit parallelism within functional programs. I.e., it maintains a workpool with the process descriptors of spawned processes which have not been allocated to processors yet, access to remote data (inports in Eden) leads to the suspension of computations until the data is available, and so on. But due to Eden's explicit treatment of parallel processes there are some new aspects on which we want to comment shortly.

A process with several output channels consists of a system of concurrent threads. On process creation the creator process also has to spawn new threads for the evaluation of the values that have to be sent to the new process. A difficulty that arises here is that the destination of the messages will only be known after the newly created process is assigned to a processor. This aspect does not occur in implementations which exploit implicit parallelism. There it does not matter where a parallel process is going to be evaluated because the only communication that takes place is the transfer of the result from the child process to the parent process. Transfer of information from the parent's location to the child's location is only performed in the form of remote memory accesses by explicit request messages by the child. In the Eden implementation a newly created and allocated process has to inform its creator process about its location and the addresses of its input channel buffers.

Eden channels are implemented in such a way that the channel buffers are located at the inport locations. Although on the level of the source program, there is only unidirectional communication from outports to inports, on the level of the system, messages will flow in both directions. System messages are sent from inports to outports in order to establish their connection after the allocation of a new process and in order to control the demand for outports on the side of the producer and thus to avoid an overflow of the buffers. To this end, a scheme similar to the one described in [Aßm96] can be implemented that additionally handles the propagation of termination.

5 Related work

Most concurrent functional languages have been implemented on single processor systems by extending sequential implementations of pure functional languages:

Concurrent Haskell has been implemented as an extension to the Glasgow Haskell compiler. It runs as a single UNIX process, performing its own scheduling internally. Each process has a heap-allocated stack. Access to shared data is organized in an ordinary way by suspending processes which access data currently under evaluation.

CML [Rep91] and Facile [TLP+93] have both been implemented on top of ML using continuations in order to model the concurrency constructs. Facile's implementation even supports true distributed computing on networks of homogeneous hardware.

For Erlang there exist various implementations which are based on abstract machines, see e.g. [Sah96]. As Erlang processes are dynamically spawned and killed during the execution, each process has its own stack and heap area and the abstract machines provide scheduling and suspension mechanisms. A distributed implementation of Erlang where Erlang nodes execute as single UNIX processes which internally contain many Erlang processes has been introduced in [Wik94].

Other approaches to the extension of functional languages by coordination constructs have been presented in [Aßm96] and [GH96]. In [Aßm96] Petri nets are used to specify the interaction of functional processes. A prototype implementation of this approach uses PVM to dynamically create and delete processes. ProFun [GH96] extends a subset of ML by a coordination language based on process algebras. Currently, there exists a compiler for a subset of the language which uses C++ as its target language and makes use of the multithreading facilities of Solaris in order to model concurrency.

Parallel implementations of functional languages usually exploit only implicit parallelism. Most of them are based on parallel abstract machines, see e.g. [KLB91], [AJ89], [LKID89], [vEP93], [THM+96], the basic ideas of which can be adopted in the parallel implementation of Eden. But as pointed out in the previous subsection, additional mechanisms have to be incorporated in order to implement the more general way of communication within Eden's dynamically evolving process networks.

6 Conclusions

Eden is a concurrent functional language which facilitates a flexible declarative style of parallel programming. It is based on the lazy functional language Haskell. The use of a widespread standard language proves to be advantageous for both programming and implementation. Especially, it was possible to use the implementation of Concurrent Haskell as the basis of the prototype implementation described in this paper.

This implementation of Eden provides a detailed comparison of the coordination constructs of the two languages involved. It is shown that that Eden's coordination constructs are higher-level and more expressive than those of Concurrent Haskell. This is due to the restricted usability of I/O actions in Concurrent Haskell which have been introduced to encapsulate side-effecting operations within functional programs. Consequently I/O actions are not allowed within functional expressions but can only be used on the top level of programs. In Eden, process instantiations may occur everywhere within expressions, as their type corresponds to the type of their output channels. Nevertheless referential transparency is kept in the functional world as nondeterminism introduced by the predefined process merge is allowed within processes only. One can distinguish between functions, deterministic and nondeterministic processes.

The transformation of Eden processes into I/O actions requires a detailed analysis of the context of coordination constructs because the whole context must be embedded in I/O actions. A similar analysis is necessary to determine the determinacy properties of Eden programs mentioned above.

Eden's parallel implementation currently under development relies on an orthogonal extension of Haskell's STG-machine implementation. It will use MPI in order to implement the coordination of parallel processes on a distributed memory computer.

Acknowledgements: We are grateful to our Spanish colleagues within the Acción Integrada: Yolanda Ortega-Mallén, Ricardo Peña, Pedro Palao Gostanza and Manuel Núñez García for valuable comments on a previous version of this paper. Thanks go also to the anonymous referees.

References

[AJ89]   Lennart Augustsson and Thomas Johnsson. Parallel Graph Reduction with the $\langle v, G \rangle$-machine. In *FPCA '89, Functional Programming Languages and Computer Architecture*, pages 202–213. ACM Press, 1989.

[Aßm96]   Claus Aßmann. Coordinating Functional Processes using Petri Nets. In Werner Kluge, editor, *Workshop on the Implementation of Functional Languages, Bonn, Germany*. Christian-Albrechts-University Kiel, September 1996. (also in this volume).

[Ber95]   B. Berthomieu. Process calculi at work — an account of the LCS project. In *PSLS*, LNCS 1068, Springer, 1995.

[BLO96]   Silvia Breitinger, Rita Loogen, and Yolanda Ortega-Mallén. Towards a declarative language for concurrent and parallel programming. In David N. Turner, editor, *Functional Programming, Glasgow 1995*. Springer, 1996.

[BLOP96]   Silvia Breitinger, Rita Loogen, Yolanda Ortega-Mallén, and R. Peña. Eden — Language Definition and Operational Semantics. Technical Report 96-10, Philipps-Universität Marburg, 1996.

[GC92]   David Gelernter and Nicolas Carriero. Coordination languages and their significance. *Comm. of the ACM*, 35(2), 1992.

[GH96]   T. Gehrke and M. Huhn. ProFun – a language for executable specifications. In *International Symposium on Programming Languages: Implementations, Logics, Programs (PLILP)*, LNCS 1140, Springer, 1996.

[KLB91]   H. Kingdon, D. R. Lester, and G. L. Burn. The HDG-machine: a highly distributed graph-reducer for a transputer network. *Computer Journal*, 34(4):290–301, 1991.

[LKID89]   Rita Loogen, Herbert Kuchen, Klaus Indermark, and Werner Damm. Distributed implementation of programmed graph reduction. In *Proc. PARLE*, LNCS 365, Springer, 1989.

[PH96]   John Peterson and Kevin Hammond (eds). Report on the programming language Haskell: a non-strict, purely functional language, version 1.3. Technical Report YALEU/DCS/RR-1106, Yale University, 1996.

[PJGF96]   Simon Peyton Jones, Andrew Gordon, and Sigbjorn Finne. Concurrent Haskell. In *ACM Symposium on Principles of Programming Languages (POPL) 96*. ACM Press, 1996.

[Rep91]   John H. Reppy. CML: A higher-order concurrent language. In *ACM SIG-PLAN Conference on Programming Language Design and Implementation (PLDI)*, 1991.

[Sah96]   D. Sahlin. The concurrent functional programming language Erlang - an overview. In *Multi Paradigm Logic Programming*, pages 9–12, 1996.

[THM⁺96]   P. W. Trinder, K. Hammond, J. S. Mattson, Jr., A. S. Partridge, and S. L. Peyton Jones. GUM: A portable parallel implementation of Haskell. In *ACM SIGPLAN Conference on Programming Language Design and Implementation (PLDI)*, 1996.

[TLP⁺93]   B. Thomsen, L. Leth, S. Prasad, T.-S. Kuo, A. Kramer, F. Knabe, and A. Giacalone. Facile antigua release – programming guide. Technical Report ECRC-93-20, European Computer-Industry Research Centre, 1993.

[vEP93]   Marco van Eekelen and Rinus Plasmeijer. *Functional Programming and Parallel Graph Rewriting*. Addison Wesley, 1993.

[Wik94]   Claes Wikström. Distributed programming in Erlang. In Hoon Hong, editor, *PASCO'94: First International Symposium on Parallel Symbolic Computation*, pages 412–421. World Scientific Publishing Company, 1994.

Coordinating Functional Processes Using Petri Nets

Claus Aßmann

Dept of Computer Science, University of Kiel, 24105 Kiel, Germany,
e-mail: ca@informatik.uni-kiel.de

Abstract. Functional programs are well suited for concurrent execution due to the Church-Rosser property. However, for many applications there is still need to explicitly specify process systems instead of relying on compilers. Coordination languages provide one viable solution to the problem of specifying concurrent process systems, since they do not interfere with the properties of the language used for the algorithmic specification of the processes. The coordination language K2 to be proposed in this paper is based on a variant of colored Petri nets. It primarily defines process systems with deterministic behavior, but also allows for controlled forms of non-determinism. Specifications based on Petri nets offer several advantages. An underlying net calculus facilitates formal analysis and verification of basic safety and liveness properties. Graphical representations clearly expose structural dependencies among system components. Our variant of colored Petri nets provides several forms of net abstractions which facilitate the systematic construction of complex systems from small subsystems by composition. Recursive specifications can be used to adapt the structure of a process system to actual problem sizes or to varying input parameters.

1 Introduction

Though functional languages are well suited for concurrent program execution, it has become increasingly clear that "the problem of selecting the useful parallelism in functional programs is (almost) as difficult as detecting the possible parallelism in imperative programs" [Sch93]. As long as compilers are not mature enough to generate efficient code for general applications, it is up to the programmers to explicitly specify concurrent computations. This can be either done by just giving hints to the compiler, or by providing means for the specification of processes and their communication structure. The first solution is not considered here, since it depends too much on the quality and facilities of the compiler. Coordination languages [CG89,CG92,Arb96] pursue the latter approach. According to Gelernter and Carriero [CG92], a programming model consists of a coordination model and a computation model. They argue that a strict separation of these two models has several advantages, e.g., portability and heterogeneity. Linda is a well-known example which uses a tuple space (an associative object memory) as coordination model. Notwithstanding this line of reasoning, realizations like C-Linda embed the coordination part into the computation language. Mixing communication and computation complicates the understanding of both, and may cause dependencies which complicate the re-use of modules in other settings [Arb96]. Communication protocols may be buried deep under the application code, making it next to impossible to use them in other programs.

In order to be useful, coordination languages and supporting tools should in our opinion

- provide a completely separate level for the specification of communications that must be established among processes;
- be based on process calculi which provide formal methods for analyzing and reasoning about basic safety and liveness properties;
- be compositional to allow for the systematic construction of complex systems from simpler subsystems;
- support controlled forms of non-determinism which are necessary to realize, say, client/server interactions;
- allow for recursive process structures which, at runtime, may be dynamically expanded depending on actual problem sizes, available resources, etc.;
- support graphical specifications of process structures;
- allow for high-level debugging and performance analysis, e.g., by animated execution;
- provide the means to re-use existing (sequential) code;
- be portable to different, possibly heterogeneous hardware platforms.

Higher-order Petri nets [Rei85] are a good model for process specification languages. They combine the advantages of comprehensible graphical representations of process communication structures with consistent textual inscriptions of net elements by which computations on the objects communicated among the processes may be specified. Petri nets provide a clear-cut interface between both specification levels: communication coincides with the firing of transitions, which is a much stronger separation than in other coordination models that allow for communication during computation.

A well-known tool for system modeling with colored Petri nets is Design/CPN [Jen92,Jen95]. It consists of a graphical net editor, an interactively controlled simulator, and an analysis tool. Design/CPN supports net abstraction mechanisms for the hierarchical design of complex systems, but lacks the means to specify dynamically expanding (e.g., recursive) process structures. Moreover, since no restrictions are imposed on the net design, reasoning about structural and behavioral properties may become unmanageable. For instance, invariants must be specified by the users, they cannot be inferred from given net structures and annotations. The system can only verify whether pre-specified invariance properties hold.

It turns out that specifying systems of cooperating computational processes, for almost all practical purposes, does not require the full generality of the colored Petri nets used in Design/CPN. Communication among processes can safely be restricted to a small set of well-defined interaction schemes with deterministic behavior, and to a few primitives which realize good-natured forms of non-determinism. These interaction schemes ensure well-behaving systems largely by construction. They also considerably facilitate formal reasoning about the intended system behavior, e.g., by verifying the existence of certain invariance properties which are essential prerequisites for safety and liveness properties.

An earlier version of such a process coordination language has been implemented in the programming system GRAPH [Sch91,Sch92]. It consists of a graphical net editor, a runtime system which supports interactively controlled stepwise execution of process systems for validation purposes, and tools to verify invariance properties. It uses the functional language $\mathcal{KiR}$ [Klu94] for the algorithmic specification of the computations that are to be performed by the processes. However, GRAPH has several drawbacks: it does not support a sufficiently general concept of recursion, it is based on high-level interpretation of the process interactions, and it only runs on an operating system and on a hardware platform that are no longer available. Therefore, a complete redesign was considered necessary.

The result of this redesign is the coordination language $K2$ which satisfies all of the requirements listed above. It provides abstraction mechanisms for subsystems of cooperating processes similar to code abstractions as they are available in conventional programming languages, including recursive process specifications and client/server interactions. The computations within the processes may be specified either in a functional language like $\mathcal{KiR}$ or in an imperative language like C, so that existing conventional code may be migrated. $K2$ is currently being implemented on widely available (de-facto) standard software (PVM [GBD$^+$94], X Window system) for easy portability to different platforms. $K2$ specifications are compiled to dedicated code for efficient execution.

The remainder of the paper is organized as follows: in the next chapter, the basic concepts underlying $K2$ and its abstraction mechanisms are described. The means available to verify and validate system invariants are explained in chapter 3. Chapter 4 gives an overview of the implementation of a prototype system, which is currently in progress. The last chapter summarizes the current work and outlines further directions of research.

2   The Coordination Language $K2$

$K2$ is a coordination language for cooperating processes which is based on a variant of colored Petri nets. A Petri net is a directed, bipartite graph composed of transitions and of places which in the context of $K2$ stand for processes and for streams of objects to be communicated among processes, respectively. Directed arcs represent the communication structure. Streams are realized as FIFO-queues of finite capacities. They establish finite synchronic distances[1]

---

[1] A synchronic distance generally defines the number of occurrences by which one of two or more concurrent events can get ahead of the others before they must catch up.

within which producing and consuming processes may operate concurrently. A process is enabled iff there are enough objects – in the following also referred to as tokens – on every input stream, and there is sufficient free space on every output stream. An enabled process may fire, in which case it consumes the first tokens from all its input streams, performs a computation on them, and produces a set of result tokens which are placed into the output streams. Legitimate interaction schemes among processes are in *K2* restricted to those which can be modeled by so-called synchronization graphs, i.e., a stream connects just one producing and one consuming process. This restriction excludes conflict situations as enabled processes can never be de-activated by the firing of other processes, which considerably simplifies the problem of establishing a stable system behavior. Though synchronization graphs allow to model only deterministic systems, controlled forms of non-determinism may be introduced into *K2* specifications by careful use of primitive MERGE processes (see section 2.1).

The elements of colored Petri nets are inscribed with components of a functional calculus, i.e., with variables assigned to arcs, constant terms carried along with the tokens (the colors), and functional abstractions specifying the transformations to be performed by the transitions on the token inscriptions. Graphical *K2* specifications require essentially the same inscriptions as colored Petri nets. These inscriptions specify the computations which are to be carried out by the individual processes:

- streams need to be inscribed with capacities;

- arcs are inscribed with product terms of the form W×U, where W is a weight coefficient and U denotes a variable;

- tokens carry constant terms;

- the inscriptions of processes are programs whose formal parameters coincide with the variables of the incoming and outgoing arcs of the respective transitions.

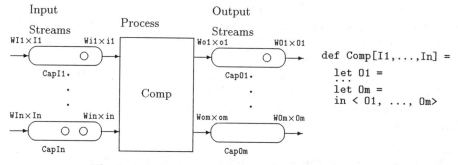

Fig. 1. Atomic process with input and output streams

Fig. 1[2] shows a so-called atomic process `Comp` together with its input and output streams. Tokens are represented as circles within the streams. The process inscription is given as a $\mathcal{KiR}$ program on the right. The function `Comp` will be called with the first tokens from all input streams. If the weight `Wi` assigned to an arc is greater than one, the corresponding parameter is a list of that length. The function must return as value a list of `m` elements which are assigned to the output parameters. Upon completion of the computation the result values are sent to the output streams. In principle, it does not matter which programming language is used for the process inscription. The only requirement is that the parameter passing mechanism and the format of the parameters must be known to the *K2* compiler. There are no further restriction on the program: it can be of arbitrary complexity, undergo eager or lazy evaluation, and it can even be written in an imperative language. The program must just be available as an executable and it must conform to some known parameter passing convention. Due to the strict separation of communication and computation, the program has no access to the connected streams. It cannot request further values from an incoming stream, or send tokens to some outgoing stream. The program just acts as a stand-alone function, which gets some input values and is expected to return some output values.

Having weights assigned to arcs slightly complicates the analysis of nets. However, it allows to re-use functions in different contexts. For example, if a producer process returns a number on each invocation, it cannot be used in a situation where a consumer process needs a list of several numbers on each call. So, a new function would have to be written which produces such a list. Using weights, the individual numbers can be collected in a stream and transformed into a list of the required length without changing any participating function. Moreover, without weights modeling real systems may become awkward as the number of occurrences of different processes in relation to each other is difficult to define otherwise.

In addition to these atomic processes whose internal behavior is specified by program code, *K2* provides several other process types: primitive processes, which have a predefined behavior, process abstractions in the form of hierarchical processes, and state-based processes which have a special token balance, all of which will be explained in the following sections.

The abstract behavior of each process type in *K2* is defined by a corresponding Petri net. These definitions are required for two purposes: first, to verify some basic invariance properties, and second, to formally define the semantics of the specified process system.

The Petri net description of atomic processes is very simple. It consists of a single transition for the process and places for the connected streams. The places do not model the FIFO behavior of the streams in *K2* which, however, is irrelevant wrt analysis purposes.

---

[2] In most figures, inscriptions of net components that are irrelevant in the particular context are omitted.

2.1 Primitive Processes

K2 provides three primitive process types which do not comply with the afore-mentioned firing rule. There are two deterministic primitive process types: SPLIT sends tokens from one input stream to one of several output streams, and SE-LECT routes tokens from one of several input streams to one output stream, both depending on the values of a control token.

Another primitive process is MERGE which non-deterministically routes to-kens from several input streams to a single output stream. This process type can be used to merge token streams whenever a particular order of tokens in output streams is neither desired nor necessary. A typical application is the interaction between multiple clients and a server. Fig. 2 shows a client/server system as it must be specified in *K2*. The MERGE process non-deterministically selects a token from one of its inputs streams and sends it to its output stream. These tokens originate at the clients and contain tags which are used by the server to identify the clients. The SPLIT process passes tokens from its input stream to either of its output streams selected by control tokens. These control tokens are generated by the server and depend on the tag of the tokens sent from the client processes. The control tokens are passed through the lower of the two streams which connect the **Server** process and the SPLIT process.

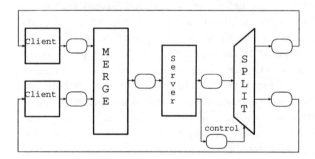

Fig. 2. Client/server example

2.2 Hierarchical Processes

For the specification of complex process systems *K2* provides a general abstrac-tion mechanism similar to that available in conventional programming languages. It allows for the construction of process hierarchies and of recursive processes. This gives the desired compositionality of process systems which is essential for the design of large systems whose components may be validated or verified independently.

Fig. 3 depicts two representations of a hierarchical process PH. On the left, it is defined as a composition of four processes which may be atomic or hierarchical, with arcs connecting to input streams I1, I2, I3 and to output streams O1,

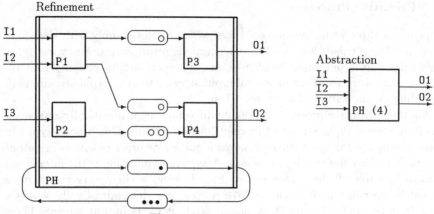

Fig. 3. A hierarchical process

O2. On the right, the same process is shown as an abstraction with the same connections. The name PH can be used to refer to this process definition somewhere else, e.g., in other hierarchical or recursive processes, or in libraries. The vertical double bars on both sides may be considered firewalls, or plain transitions which conceptually synchronize input tokens before entry into and output tokens before exit from this subnet. Such a hierarchical process must conceptually behave exactly as an atomic process, i.e., it consumes a set of input tokens from the input streams, performs a computation on them, and produces a set of result tokens to be placed in the output streams. This behavior ensures the required compositionality. However, hierarchical processes may be operated, without loss of this property, as pipelines of some pre-specified maximum depth which may also be referred to as a synchronic distance between input and output. This synchronic distance specifies the number of token sets that can be processed simultaneously. It may be modeled by the two complementary streams[3] which in the lower part of the box on the left hand side cyclically connect with the firewalls. The number of plain tokens circulating about these two streams defines a synchronic distance between input and output in terms of the number of token sets that may be within the firewalls. Stream capacities inside the firewalls which are smaller than this synchronic distance enforce tighter synchronization among the processes, and may even reduce this distance. The synchronic distance, which in this example is 4, translates into an inscription in the abstraction on the right.

2.3 State-based Processes

There is need for processes which consume a sequence of token sets before they produce one single set of tokens and which produce a sequence of token sets

---

[3] These streams do not belong to the specification, they are shown here just for explanation purposes.

after they consumed one initial token set. The former are required for so-called consumer processes: they take an unspecified number of token sets to combine them into a single result set of tokens, or they filter out tokens according to some criteria. The latter are necessary for so-called producer processes: they generate a number of token sets which may depend on parameters supplied by some initial tokens.

$K2$ supports a process type called state-based (all previously introduced process types are called state-free) to realize the required behavior. Processes which make use of this feature can be in one of three states: INITIALIZATION, COMPUTATION, and C-OR-T (compute or terminate). For each state there is a corresponding stream type: INIT, unmarked, and TERMINATE streams, respectively. The unmarked streams are the same as those found in state-free processes. This corresponds to the fact that state-based processes in the state COMPUTATION behave exactly as state-free processes do.

State-based processes are initially in the state INITIALIZATION. They consume tokens from all input streams marked with the keyword INIT, and thereupon switch to the state COMPUTATION. In the states COMPUTATION and C-OR-T the other (unmarked) streams are used just as in state-free processes for input and output. A process can switch from the state C-OR-T back to INITIALIZATION if a designated embedded function returns the pre-defined value TERMINATE, which is the first element of the result list. In this case, output tokens are produced for the streams marked with the keyword TERMINATE.

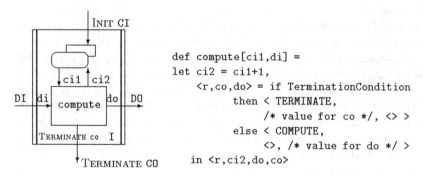

```
def compute[ci1,di] =
let ci2 = ci1+1,
    <r,co,do> = if TerminationCondition
        then < TERMINATE,
               /* value for co */, <> >
        else < COMPUTE,
               <>, /* value for do */ >
in <r,ci2,do,co>
```

Fig. 4. A State-based process and the program inscription for `compute`

Fig. 4 shows a simple state-based process I. It has one INIT stream CI, one input stream DI, one output stream DO, and one TERMINATE stream CO. The icon denotes an initialized stream. This stream can be either directly initialized by writing values into the rectangle, or it can be connected to an external INIT stream. In the latter case, the contents of the initialized streams are replaced by tokens read from the external INIT streams in the INITIALIZATION state. Now the internal processes can consume tokens from their input streams in the usual manner. Without this, processes connected to INIT streams are but activated in the INITIALIZATION state.

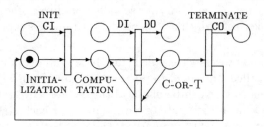

Fig. 5. Petri net model for a state-based process

The plain Petri net model of this state-based process is given in fig. 5 which describes the behavior of a state-based process reasonably well. First, the process is in state INITIALIZATION, which is denoted by a token (the black dot) in that place. Now only the transition INIT can fire. After that, the state changes to COMPUTATION, in which the input transition for DI is the only one which can fire. Next, it has to be decided whether the process will stay in the state COMPUTATION or whether it will terminate. This is modeled by a non-deterministic choice in the plain Petri net (place C-OR-T). In a colored Petri net, this choice depends on the result of a designated function, which is `compute` in the example specified in fig. 4.

To exemplify how state-based processes can be used, we specify a simple producer process as given in fig. 6. This process generates all integer values within the boundaries supplied through the INIT streams `lower` and `upper`. The function `cprod` gets the values `f` and `t` from its input streams and returns values for `fo,to,` and `r`. This producer process does not have TERMINATE streams. It returns the value TERMINATE just to change its state back to INITIALIZATION. The producer completely terminates if its INIT streams `lower` and `upper` are empty. This happens after the first invocation: the process produces all numbers from 2 to 33. Thereafter the process terminates completely and information to this effect is propagated to its consumer.

Another example is a filter as shown in fig. 7. This process does not have an INIT stream. It consumes tokens from its input stream `v`; if the value is less than zero, no output is produced. Otherwise, it is placed into the stream `r` and the process starts over.

2.4 Recursive Process Abstractions

In many cases, it is necessary to define a computation in terms of process templates which can be replicated in order to adapt the number of processes to

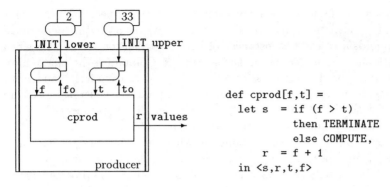

```
def cprod[f,t] =
  let s  = if (f > t)
               then TERMINATE
               else COMPUTE,
      r  = f + 1
  in <s,r,t,f>
```

Fig. 6. Producer process

```
def filter[v] =
  if (v ge 0)
      then < TERMINATE, v>
      else < COMPUTE, <> >
```

Fig. 7. Filter Process

actual problem sizes or to the number of processing sites available in the system. It may also be used to balance dynamically evolving workload. The basic concept to achieve these ends are recursive process abstractions, similar to recursive procedures in conventional languages. Expansion of recursive hierarchies may be terminated by means of the primitive process types SPLIT and SELECT. Termination conditions may be expressed in terms of problem-specific parameters or in terms of system parameters such as number of processing sites or actual workload distribution.

Straightforward recursive insertion of processes in themselves results in process hierarchies with communication structures that pass argument tokens from father to son processes and result tokens in the opposite direction. A well-known example of this kind is the sieve of Erastosthenes which filters out all prime numbers from a stream of monotonically increasing natural numbers, starting from 2 and up to some upper bound. The solution presented in fig. 8 consists of a recursive process S, which contains an atomic process Filter, and a recursive reference to itself, embedded in SPLIT and SELECT processes. The program inscription of Filter is given on the right hand side of fig. 8. Filter receives a number N as input. Moreover, it has a side-condition MyPrime which holds the prime number for this filter. Initially, MyPrime is 0 since the stream is initialized with this value. Therefore, the first comparison in Filter succeeds and the value supplied for the parameter N is the result value for MP which yields the prime number for this filter process. On all later invocations, the value for MyPrime stays the same. In these invocations, the value N is divided by MyPrime and if the remainder is 0, then N is not a prime and hence marked as negative. Otherwise, it is sent to the recursive invocation of S, which is selected by the value 2 on the control outputs c1 and c2. The recursive expansion of the hierarchical process S unfolds a cascade of instances of it. This expansion terminates when consuming the last prime number in the stream IN. Combining the hierarchical process S with the producer process and the filter process from figs. 6 and 7, respectively, yields the complete sieve program. The producer generates a stream of numbers for the input IN and the filter removes all non-primes (which are marked as negative numbers) from the output stream OUT.

This solution differs from those found elsewhere, e.g., in ordinary data flow graphs [Klu92], in order to comply with the firing rule of state-free processes that are available in K2. The recursive process S as well as the process Filter that is used inside S require that tokens be consumed from all input streams and produced in all output streams. Hence, there is no way of filtering tokens out of a stream other then by a consumer process, which cannot be made part of process S.

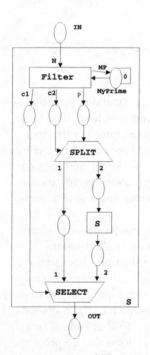

```
def Filter[N,MyPrime]=
  if (MyPrime eq 0)
  then <1,1,N,N>
  else if ((N mod MyPrime) eq 0)
       then <1,1,-N,MyPrime>
       else <2,2,N,MyPrime>
```

Fig. 8. Sieve of Erastosthenes

To allow for more general forms of interactions, e.g., among peer processes, another approach is necessary. To generate such communication structures by means of recursion, the processes cannot obey the general firing rule since two different types of input and output streams are required. One type is used to control the expansion and termination of the processes, the other is used for data communication after expansion. This can be accomplished by state-based processes.

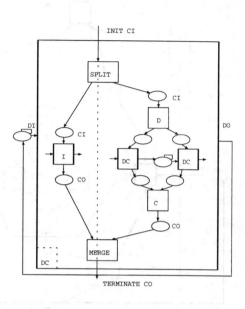

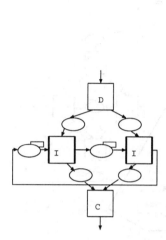

Fig. 9. Desired process system

Fig. 10. Specification of a recursive process system

A simple example of a process structure is given in fig. 9. Arcs connecting the process boxes horizontally represent the communication streams, vertical input (output) streams are INIT (TERMINATE) streams. This process system specifies a divide-and-conquer expansion in which the processes I, which do the actual computations, can communicate directly with each other to exchange data. The process system divides a problem by means of process D between two processes I. The structure of the state-based process I is the same as in fig. 4 (see previous section). The result of the computation is assembled by process C and placed into an output stream. Since communication in $K2$ occurs only at process invocations and process termination, the program specification must follow the general scheme for state-based processes given in fig. 4. First, the process I gets a token from CI to initialize the internal stream. Next, I changes its state to COMPUTATION. Now, the internal process **compute** receives tokens from di and ci1. Depending on some termination condition, **compute** may either send data to its neighbor via **do** or it may return its result via co. In the latter case, I switches its state back to INITIALIZATION and waits for new data to arrive on CI.

To dynamically build such a structure with varying numbers of processes, the specification of a recursive process system as in fig. 10 must be used. The re-

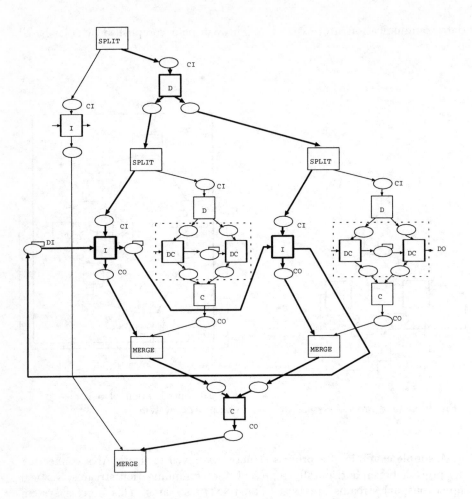

Fig. 11. Sketch of a recursive process system

cursive process named DC consists of two different parts separated by the dashed line. The recursion is controlled by the token passing through the INIT stream CI to the SPLIT process. Depending on the value of the token, it is either passed to the iterative process I on the left or to the process system on the right, in which two references to the recursive process are made. If the token is passed to the right, the complete process system DC is recursively inserted for the two references to it, thus creating a process system as given in fig. 11. This structure corresponds to the desired process structure of fig. 9. Considering only the processes which are connected with thick arcs, it is identical to that of fig. 9 if the SPLIT and MERGE processes are removed. These processes are just for creating the process structure, so they can be ignored. The recursive processes DC are instantiated iff tokens are routed to them, i.e., processes are created only on demand in order to avoid recursive expansion without end.

3 Verifying and Validating System Invariants

Due to the clear-cut interfaces between process and program specification, system properties can be verified or validated on both levels independently.

On the program specification level it primarily suffices to show that the programs with which the process templates are inscribed interface correctly with the incoming and outgoing streams, and that the computations are bound to terminate. Correct algorithmic implementations may either be verified by formal methods or validated by interactively controlled stepwise execution and inspection of intermediate states.

On the process communication level a stable system behavior can be formally verified on the basis of invariance properties. There are basically two structural invariants which must hold: S-invariants and T-invariants, which are invariants in places and in transitions, respectively.

To explain these invariants, a formal definition of Petri nets is required. A plain Petri net can be defined as a tuple (S, T, F, W) with a set of places S, a set of transitions T (where $T \cap S = \emptyset$), a flow relation $F \subseteq S \times T \cup T \times S$ which specifies a set of arcs that connect places with transitions and vice versa, and a weight assignment function to arcs $W : F \to \mathbb{N}$. Let $X = T \cup S$; the *preset* of $x \in X$ is $\bullet x = \{y \in X \mid (y, x) \in F\}$, its *postset* is $x\bullet = \{y \in X \mid (x, y) \in F\}$. The incidence matrix $I : S \times T \to \mathbb{Z}$ is defined by the token changes in places $s \in S$ upon occurrences of transitions $t \in T$, i.e.,

$$I(s, t) = \begin{cases} -W(s, t) & \text{if } s \in \bullet t \setminus t\bullet \\ W(t, s) & \text{if } s \in t\bullet \setminus \bullet t \\ W(t, s) - W(s, t) & \text{if } s \in t\bullet \cap \bullet t \\ 0 & \text{otherwise} \end{cases}$$

An S- (T-)invariant is defined as a vector $\mathbf{w}$ in places ($\mathbf{r}$ in transitions) that is a minimal, positive, integer solution of the set of homogeneous linear equations $I^T \times \mathbf{w} = 0$ ($I \times \mathbf{r} = 0$). An S-invariant guarantees that the weighted sum of the tokens within the net remains invariant against re-distribution due to occurrences of transitions. A T-invariant guarantees the reproduction of token distributions after as many occurrences of the transitions as are specified by the components of the vector $\mathbf{r}$, which is therefore referred to as a reproduction vector.

One application of invariance properties is the verification of the proper behavior of hierarchical processes. With the help of these invariance properties, it can be shown that hierarchical processes behave like atomic processes wrt the token balance. Since it is possible to erroneously specify process abstractions with a different behavior, this requirement must be verified. This is done by a so-called feedback net: the firewalls of the Petri net model H of a hierarchical process are connected via two places to a single transition t_f. There must exist a T-invariant with $\mathbf{r}(t_f) \neq 0$, which means that for each token set consumed the hierarchical process produces one token set. If there exists a transition t_p in H such that $\mathbf{r}(t_p) = 0$ for all T-invariants $\mathbf{r}$ of H, then the firing of t_p destroys the required behavior of the process.

Take for example the process system for the sieve of Erastosthenes from section 2.4. Its Petri net representation is shown in fig. 12, the incidence matrix of this net is given in fig. 13. This example shows how the Petri net models for SPLIT, SELECT, and hierarchical processes look like. SPLIT is modeled by $s2, s3, t3, t4$, SELECT is modeled by $s4, s5, s7, t6, t7, s8$ (both are enclosed by dashed boxes). The model for the hierarchical process consists of the plain transitions $t1, t8$ surrounding the (Petri net models of the) local processes and two places $s9, s10$ which define the depth of the pipeline.

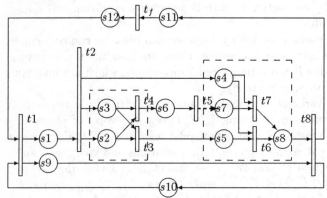

Fig. 12. Petri net model for **Erastosthones** process

	$t1$	$t2$	$t3$	$t4$	$t5$	$t6$	$t7$	$t8$	t_f
$s1$	1	−1	0	0	0	0	0	0	0
$s2$	0	1	−1	−1	0	0	0	0	0
$s3$	0	1	−1	−1	0	0	0	0	0
$s4$	0	1	0	0	0	−1	−1	0	0
$s5$	0	0	1	0	0	−1	0	0	0
$s6$	0	0	0	1	−1	0	0	0	0
$s7$	0	0	0	0	1	0	−1	0	0
$s8$	0	0	0	0	0	1	1	−1	0
$s9$	1	0	0	0	0	0	0	−1	0
$s10$	−1	0	0	0	0	0	0	1	0
$s11$	0	0	0	0	0	0	0	1	−1
$s12$	−1	0	0	0	0	0	0	0	1

Fig. 13. Incidence matrix of the plain Petri net shown in fig. 12

Verification for hierarchical recursive processes proceeds in two steps:

1. The recursive reference is replaced by a transition ($t5$) without outgoing arcs (i.e., the dashed arc ($t5, s7$), which corresponds to the bold **1** in the incidence matrix, is not used in this step) to check that the non-recursive part of the

process behaves like an atomic process. If the resulting Petri net has a T-invariant, the next step can be performed. For the example the T- and S-invariance vectors are $(1, 1, 1, 0, 0, 1, 0, 1, 1)$ and $(1, 0, 0, 1, 0, 0, 0, 1, 1, 1, 1, 1)$, respectively. So the non-recursive part $(t2, t3, t6)$ behaves like an atomic process, since the T-invariant covers the full cycle composed of the transitions $t2, t3, t6$, the plain transitions $t1, t8$, and the feedback transition t_f.

2. The recursive reference is replaced by a transition including an outgoing arc (i.e., the dashed arc) since the first step has verified that the process behaves as expected and it is assumed that the recursion eventually terminates. The checks for invariants are repeated with this new Petri net model. They yield $(2, 2, 1, 1, 1, 1, 1, 1, 2)$ and $(4, 1, 1, 2, 2, 2, 2, 4, 2, 2, 4, 4)$ as T- and S-invariance vectors, respectively.

The entire net is therefore S-invariant (token-conserving), and also T-invariant (reproducing), i.e., the net does not contain structural deadlocks or livelocks.

A similar check can be performed for the divide-and-conquer process system. However, the Petri net model for this system is significantly more complex than the one given above and is therefore not explained here.

The existence of S- and T-invariants is a necessary but by no means a sufficient prerequisite for a stable system behavior. Both are purely structural properties which give some confidence in the proper workings of the system, but they are no guarantee that it may not fail for other reasons. They ensure that the number of tokens neither decreases to the extent that the system deadlocks, i.e., no transition can be enabled, or monotonically increases to the extent that it deadlocks due to exhaustion of the capacities in the places.

Establishing the existence of these invariants requires the solution of the above sets of equations. This can be done as part of an interactive specification process in which net elements are in incremental steps added to or removed from an existing net. Whenever the user demands a verification, the necessary checks are performed. Elements which corrupt existing invariants can be immediately identified and rejected. The invariants of net abstractions which satisfy the properties of transitions can be taken for granted without proof on the next higher specification level.

With appropriate system support, the correct functioning of net-based process systems may also be validated by interactively controlled stepwise execution and inspection of intermediate token distributions. This may be done on any level of net abstractions and in any local context, e.g., by selecting a single process, a local subnet, or the entire system for one or several process occurrences, provided they can be enabled.

Another important property in distributed process systems is the absence of deadlocks. A Petri net is called live if at least one transition is enabled under every reachable token distribution (at least one process can take place). This liveness property must be distinguished from that used in system theory, where it means that "something good happens" [AS85], which for example includes termination. Liveness in Petri nets falls under the category of safety properties in system theory. Though there exists a formal apparatus to prove liveness, its complexity is generally exponential in time. However, the problem is considerably simplified in the case of synchronization nets, which are Petri nets with $W(f) = 1$ for all arcs $f \in F$ and $|s \bullet| = 1 \wedge |\bullet s| = 1$ for all places $s \in S^4$. Such nets are live iff on each path through it there is at least one place occupied by a token. This property can be algorithmically proved by removing all marked places from the net and by showing that the remaining net contains no more cycles, which is a fairly simple problem that can be solved with well-known methods of graph theory.

4 Implementation of a Prototype

A first compiler for $K2$ has been implemented. It makes use of available software as much as possible to minimize the time required for the implementation. PVM [GBD+94] has been chosen as basis for the runtime system, since it is available on almost all UNIX based platforms, and even on many multiprocessor systems with proprietary operating systems. Moreover, PVM allows to dynamically create and delete processes. This feature, which is currently not available under the proposed message passing standard MPI [MPI93], is essential to support the concept of recursive processes. PVM also provides hooks to dynamically control the allocation of processes to processing sites. This allows the use of dedicated algorithms for load balancing and process allocation based on decisions made either by the compiler or by the programmer.

Each user-specified process is embedded in a simple wrapper; together they constitute a PVM process. Each process has an identifier PId which is used for internal purposes, e.g., to maintain the communication channels between processes. The wrapper manages the input and output streams connected to it, checks whether the user-specified process is activated, in which case it calls it with the input values supplied, and sends the result values to the output streams.

Since the communication structure of $K2$ is restricted to synchronization graphs, it is possible to include input streams of processes into the wrappers as exemplified by fig. 14. Thus a wrapper has direct access to the input parameters of the user-specified process, which is essential for fast process invocation. The output streams of a process are part of the wrappers of the respective consuming processes, to which they are input streams.

In the following, we will explain how a wrapper checks the activation condition, how it ensures that stream capacities are never exceeded, and give a brief outline of the algorithm realized by a wrapper. This explanation mainly refers to atomic processes; for other process types slightly different algorithms and data are required.

Table 1 shows excerpts of the C structure definitions of the stream data types as used by a wrapper. The input stream data type Istream_str contains all necessary data to manage a stream, e.g., its capacity, the number of tokens actually in the stream, and the identifier of the producing process to which it

---

[4] $K2$ graphs are not in the strict sense synchronization nets, since the weights may be different from one.

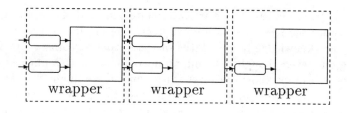

Fig. 14. Wrappers in a simple process system

is connected. There is also a so-called flow control counter whose purpose will be explained below. The output stream data type **Ostream_str** requires the equivalent of the flow control counter, and the subset of data that identifies the stream, since the wrapper does not have to manage the buffer by which the stream is implemented.

```
typedef struct Istream_type {
  int  Capacity;                    /* stream capacity                  */
  int  Occupied;                    /* number of tokens in stream       */
  void **data;                      /* pointer to list of values        */
  int  I_FC;                        /* flow control counter             */
  int  PId;                         /* Id of producing process          */
} Istream_str, * pt_Istr;

typedef struct Ostream_type {
  void *data;                       /* pointer to value                 */
  int  O_FC;                        /* flow control counter             */
  int  PId;                         /* Id of consuming process          */
} Ostream_str, * pt_Ostr;

typedef struct my_Streams {
  int       I_number,O_number;      /* number of I,O streams            */
  pt_Istr *I_str;                   /* pointer to list of I streams     */
  pt_Ostr *O_str;                   /* pointer to list of O streams     */
  int     not_I_rdy,not_O_rdy;      /* number of I,O streams for which  */
                                    /* ready condition is not fulfilled */
} Streams_str, * pt_Streams;
```

Table 1. Excerpt from C definitions for streams

A stream is called ready iff it is an input stream and there are enough tokens on it, or it is an output stream and there is sufficient free space on it. A process is activated iff all of its streams are ready. The wrapper maintains two counters not_I_rdy and not_O_rdy to detect these conditions with minimal overhead. One counts the number of input streams which do not contain enough tokens, and the other counts the number of output streams which may likely not have sufficiently many free slots left. There are two counters instead of one, since some of the special processes require separate counters. The producing process does not have an exact knowledge of the status of the output streams, neither has the consuming one, even though both maintain counters for this purpose. The consuming process cannot know the exact status since there might be tokens on their way to it; the producing process does not know the exact status since the other process might have already consumed an unknown number of tokens. So none of them knows for sure whether a stream can accept another set of tokens. Therefore, the processes maintain flow control counters by which the producing process can guarantee that the stream never exceeds its capacity, and hence the ready condition for the output streams will be based on their values. The algorithm to compute these counters is explained in the next paragraph. The token re-distributions which must be accounted for by not_I_rdy and not_O_rdy are those which change the ready condition of a stream. The ready condition for an input stream changes from **FALSE** to **TRUE** iff the number of tokens increases from below the weight of the outgoing arc to above it; for an output stream it changes in the same way iff the number of free slots increases from below the weight of the incoming arc to above it. Thus, rather than checking every stream upon token changes, only these counters have to be checked as to whether or not the process becomes activated. The process is activated iff both counter values are down to zero.

There must also be a flow control mechanism which ensures that the finite capacities of the streams are not exceeded. To minimize communication overhead, both wrappers connected to a particular stream maintain their own so-called flow control counters which are initialized with the stream capacity. The counter I_FC belongs to the wrapper of the consuming process and is decremented whenever a token is received by the stream; the counter O_FC belongs to the wrapper of the producing process and is decremented whenever a token is sent out to the stream. If O_FC decreases below the weight assigned to the connecting arc, which means that the output stream can presumably not accept another set of tokens, the producing process is disabled by incrementing its counter not_O_rdy. If I_FC reaches some lower threshold, which depends on the weight assigned to the arc and on the capacity of the stream, the wrapper computes the number of slots that are actually free in the stream. This number may differ from the counter value, since some tokens may have been consumed by the process. The wrapper sends the difference between the number of slots that are actually free and its own flow control counter to the wrapper of the producing process which adds it to the counter O_FC, and sets the counter I_FC to the number of slots that are actually free. The new counter value O_FC now gives the number of tokens which can be sent out by the producing process without further exchange of control flow data.

The algorithm realized by the wrapper is outlined below:

```
while not terminated:
  get input from any connected process
  extract MsgType and StreamNumber from tag of input
```

```
switch on MsgType
  IsData? put received data into buffer for StreamNumber
          decrement I_FC of StreamNumber
          decrement not_I_rdy if necessary
  IsControl? add received value to O_FC of StreamNumber
          decrement not_O_rdy if necessary

while process enabled:
  get data from stream buffers
  increment not_I_rdy if necessary
  perform flow control
  perform computation
  send results to output streams
  decrement O_FC
  increment not_O_rdy if necessary
```

This algorithm has two interlocked loops. The outer loop terminates whenever it can be made sure that this process will not be activated anymore. This includes the case that the entire process system comes to a halt. The inner loop is executed as long as the user-defined process remains enabled, i.e., iff the counters not_I_rdy and not_O_rdy are both down to zero. In the outer loop, tokens and control information are received, which are distinguished by their tags. These tags also include the number of the corresponding stream at the receiving process. Tokens that are received from producing processes are placed in the buffer of the input stream. Flow control data are received from consuming processes and are added to the output flow control counter belonging to the stream. These data may decrement one of the counters not_I_rdy or not_O_rdy so that the inner loop will be entered iff both counters are zero. In this case the wrapper consumes the first values (depending on the weight of the arcs) from its input streams, which are handed over as input parameters to the user-defined process. Upon completing the function call, the result values are sent to the output streams. Consuming the values from the input streams and sending the results to the output streams may cause one of the counters not_I_rdy or not_O_rdy to be incremented. As long as this does not occur, the process remains activated and can be immediately invoked with the next values.

To aid programmers in developing, debugging, and verifying *K2* programs, a graphical editor is currently being implemented. It will allow to graphically construct process systems, and will provide easy means for the creation of process abstractions and for the verification of structural invariance properties. The editor will also act as a front-end of a debugger which performs stepwise execution of a process system. A single step corresponds to the firing of a process which consumes tokens from the input streams and sends tokens to the output streams. After each sequence of steps the resulting token distribution, the activation status of processes, and the contents of the streams may be displayed, and inscriptions of selected tokens may be inspected. The programmer may freely select any part of the net for execution, i.e., a pre-specified number of steps may be carried out in the entire net, in local subnets, or by individual processes. This provides simple means for the stepwise validation of the process system.

5 Conclusion

Design/CPN, GRAPH, and *K2* are coordination languages based on high-level Petri nets. Design/CPN offers the most general specification of static process structures, but does not allow for dynamically expanding process structures. GRAPH and *K2* are based on a more restrictive approach which simplifies the verification and validation of some basic system properties. At least some of these validations can be performed in Design/CPN too, but with much greater computational complexity [Jen95]. *K2* addresses the deficiencies of GRAPH without giving up its advantages. Most importantly, it offers a more general concept of recursive processes than GRAPH. State-based processes can be used to specify flexible recursive process structures, and producer or consumer processes. *K2* is portable to different platforms since it is based on widely available software. Instead of using an interpreted runtime system, a compiler generates code for the efficient execution of the specified programs on distributed systems.

However, none of these approaches currently has means to dynamically create process communication structures which do not follow a pre-specified pattern. While both GRAPH and *K2* have recursive process structures, they do not allow to create connections between completely unrelated processes. For example, there is no simple way for a (client) process to ask some name server for a service and to dynamically establish a connection to a (server) process which provides that service. All these process structures must either exist or they must be generated from recursive specifications. Whether this constraint can be removed without giving up the advantages of simple verification will be a topic of further research.

The restriction of the process communication in *K2* to a small set of well-defined interaction schemes ensures safety and liveness properties within the system largely by construction. The disadvantage is the restriction of the degree of freedom of specifying process systems. Communication coincides with process invocation and termination; while executing, a user-defined process does not communicate. This sometimes requires the re-formulation of an algorithm to adhere to this restriction.

References

[Arb96]   F. Arbab. The IWIM Model for Coordination of Concurrent Activities. In P. Ciancarini and C. Hankin, editors, *Proc. 1st Int. Conf. on Coordination Models and Languages*, volume 1061 of *LNCS*, pages 34–56, Cesena, Italy, April 1996. Springer-Verlag, Berlin.

[AS85]   Bowen Alpern and Fred B. Schneider. Defining liveness. *Information Processing Letters*, 21(4):181–185, October 1985.

[CG89]   N. Carriero and D. Gelernter. Linda in context. *Communications of the ACM*, 32(4):444–458, April 1989.

[CG92]   N. Carriero and D. Gelernter. Coordination languages and their significance. *Communications of the ACM*, 35(2):96–107, February 1992.

[GBD+94]   Al Geist, A. Beguelin, J. Dongarra, W. Jiang, R. Manchek, and V. S. Sunderam. *PVM: Parallel Virtual Machine A Users' Guide and Tutorial for Network Parallel Computing*. Scientific and Engineering Computation Series. MIT Press, Cambridge, MA, 1994.

[Jen92]   K. Jensen. *Coloured Petri Nets: Basic Concepts, Analysis Methods and Practical Use*, volume 1 of *Monographs on Theoretical Computer Science*. Springer-Verlag, 1992.

[Jen95]   K. Jensen. *Coloured Petri Nets: Basic Concepts, Analysis Methods and Practical Use*, volume 2 of *Monographs on Theoretical Computer Science*. Springer-Verlag, 1995.

[Klu92]   W.E. Kluge. *The Organization of Reduction, Data Flow and Control Flow Systems*. MIT Press, 1992.

[Klu94]   W.E. Kluge. A User's Guide for the Reduction System π-RED. Technical Report 9409, Institut für Informatik und praktische Mathematik, Universität Kiel, 1994.

[MPI93]   MPI Forum. MPI: A message passing interface. In *Proceedings of Supercomputing '93*, pages 878–883, Portland, OR, November 1993. IEEE CS Press.

[Rei85]   W. Reisig. *Petri Nets*, volume 4 of *ETACS Monographs on Theoretical Computer Science*. Springer–Verlag, 1985.

[Sch91]   J. Schepers. Using Functional Languages for Process Specifications. In *Proc. Int. Workshop on the Parallel Implementation of Functional Languages, Southampton, UK*, 1991. CSTR 91–07.

[Sch92]   J. Schepers. Invariance properties in distributed systems. In *CONPAR 90–VAPP IV: Joint International Conference on Vector and Parallel Processing*, pages 145–156. LNCS 457, Springer-Verlag, 1992.

[Sch93]   W. Schreiner. Parallel Functional Programming, An Annotated Bibliography (2nd Edition). Technical Report 93-24, Research Institute for Symbolic Computation (RISC-Linz), Johannes Kepler University, Linz, Austria, 1993.

Making a Packet:
Cost-Effective Communication
for a Parallel Graph Reducer

Hans-Wolfgang Loidl[1] and Kevin Hammond[2]

[1] Department of Computing Science, University of Glasgow, Scotland, U.K.
E-mail: `hwloidl@dcs.glasgow.ac.uk`
[2] Division of Computer Science, University of St. Andrews, Scotland, U.K.
E-mail: `kh@dcs.st-and.ac.uk`

Abstract. This paper studies critical runtime-system issues encountered when packing data for transmission in a lazy, parallel graph reduction system. In particular, we aim to answer two questions:

- *How much graph should go into a packet?*
- *How aggressively should a processor look for work after requesting remote data?*

In order to answer the first question, we compare various *packing schemes*, of which one extreme packs just the node that is demanded ("incremental fetching"), and the other packs all the graph that is reachable from that node ("bulk fetching"). The second question is addressed by considering various mechanisms for latency hiding during communication, ranging from fully synchronous communication with no attempt to mask latency, to full thread migration during asynchronous communication.

In order to make our results as general as possible, we have used the GranSim simulator to study a wide variety of parallel machine configurations. Based on these measurements we propose concrete improvements for parallel graph reducers such as the GUM implementation of Glasgow Parallel Haskell.

1 Introduction

Our motto for parallel functional programming is: the more implicit the better. Thus, it is our goal to hide most of the details of a parallel system in the runtime system. This enables the programmer to work on a more abstract level by only annotating potential parallelism in the program and to ignore machine-specific details. However, in order to achieve good parallel performance the runtime system must be able to perform efficient communication without additional hints by the programmer. Since we wish to achieve good performance on a variety of architectures, it is essential to consider communication schemes that can take advantage of the available bandwidth in order to mask network latency for slow networks, as well as schemes aimed at low latency networks.

In this paper we study the performance of parallel algorithms when different schemes are used to pack graph into a communication packet (*packing schemes*) and when different schemes are used to hide latency costs during communication (*rescheduling schemes*). We show that it is important to study both kinds of schemes in order to achieve high performance.

In order to measure the impact of packing and rescheduling schemes we use a set of non-trivial Glasgow Parallel Haskell (GPH) programs. As these programs exhibit fairly complex communication patterns the results obtained from these measurements should also be applicable for the large-scale parallel programs that we are currently working on.

We have chosen to use the *GranSim* [HLP95, Loi96] simulator as the testbed for our measurements. This gives us a high degree of flexibility in simulating a wide range of parallel machines. GranSim has been designed to yield an accurate simulation for machines with very different communication characteristics using state-of-the art compilation technology. The visualisation tools accompanying GranSim have also proved extremely useful both for monitoring performance and detecting possible performance bottlenecks.

To date we have not repeated our experiments on the actual GUM implementation. There are two main reasons for this:

- such results can only confirm individual points on the parallel machine spectrum, rather than explore the entire design space;
- a major objective for GranSim is to drive the implementation priorities for GUM, in order to save implementation effort — the results reported here reflect part of the study that is needed to achieve that priority setting.

In due course, we do expect to report comparisons for those techniques that do prove worth implementing, however.

The rest of the paper is structured as follows: Section 2 discusses principles of parallel graph reduction. Section 3 introduces the notions of packing and rescheduling schemes, discussing advantages and disadvantages of individual schemes. Section 4 compares the efficiency of different packing schemes. Section 5 compares the efficiency of different rescheduling schemes. Section 6 discusses related work. Finally, Section 7 draws conclusions from the measurements and discusses future work.

2 Parallel Graph Reduction

We use Glasgow Parallel Haskell (GPH), a parallel version of Haskell [PH+97]. GPH specifies parallelism using `seq` and `par` combinators, which act as sequential and parallel composition, respectively (see [THL+96] for details). Our computation model is one of parallel graph reduction [Pey89]. This section discusses the most important aspects of the model we are using.

Sparks. In GPH expressions that should be evaluated in parallel have to be marked with a `par` combinator. Currently these annotations must be added by the programmer. The construct

```
x `par` e
```

creates a *spark* for evaluating x and then proceeds with the evaluation of e. The result of the whole construct is the result of e. Typically x is a variable that occurs in the expression e. A spark represents potential parallelism and basically consists of a pointer to a *thunk* (an unevaluated closure). All sparks are put into a distributed spark pool. When a processor is idle the runtime-system tries to get a spark from the local spark pool. If successful, it turns the spark into a *thread*. If there is no local spark available, however, the system then tries to obtain work from a remote processor. An important design decision, which is examined in this paper, is how aggressive to be when looking for remote work while other threads are blocked waiting for remote data.

Evaluate-and-die. The specific variant of parallel graph reduction we are using is an *evaluate-and-die* model of computation [PCS89]. In this model a parallel thread simply picks up a spark, reduces a thunk to normal form and updates it with its result. No explicit notification of the parent process is necessary. Synchronisation between threads will only occur when one thread tries to access a value that is under evaluation by another thread. In this case the thread is put into a blocking queue that is attached to the thunk being evaluated. When overwriting the thunk with its result the threads in the blocking queue are reawakened.

It is important to note that the runtime-system is free to discard sparks. This means that one parallel thread can subsume potentially parallel computations for which sparks have been created. Therefore, this mechanism is able to automatically increase the granularity in a system with many sparks. This behaviour is similar to a lazy task creation mechanism [MKH90] with sparks taking the role of lazy futures.

Communication. Our communication mechanism is described in detail in the following section. Two basic design decisions are worth mentioning at this point, however: in order to avoid duplicating reduction work, we preserve all graph sharing; and we always move data to the processors running the threads that need it rather than moving threads to the processor where the data happens to reside.

A consequence of the latter decision is that thunks are evaluated on the processor that needs the result of the thunk. The alternative approach of offloading the thunk to the processor that holds the data it needs would improve data locality, but might increase communication costs if the thunk were small but the result large. This decision would repay further study.

It is worth noting in passing that because thunks are just normal graph nodes, the same communication method is used to transfer both data and work, and even for thread migration.

At present we make no attempt to combine consecutive packets sent between the same two processors into a single message. It seems unlikely that this would have a significant effect on performance, however, unless the packet creation overhead was high. It also seems unlikely that our system would generate such patterns of communication except in rare instances.

3 Packing and Rescheduling Schemes

3.1 Packing Schemes

Packing schemes prescribe how much of the graph to transfer to a processor that demands the value of a node. In our model the same scheme is used when transferring a sparked closure in response to a request for work. For convenience we will classify both data transfer mechanisms as *fetching*. Two contrasting packing schemes are *incremental fetching* and *bulk fetching*.

For incremental fetching, only the closure that is requested is sent to the processor that demanded it. This scheme aims to minimise the total number of closures that are sent during the execution of the program ("lazy fetching"). The fixed overhead for this scheme is small because exactly one closure is sent for every fetch request. The cost is that many messages will need to be sent if large parts of the graph need to be shared across processors, and this may prove to be inefficient in a high-latency system.

In contrast, bulk fetching transfers a group of related nodes in a single packet ("eager fetching"). The per-packet overhead is higher because packet construction/deconstruction is much more complicated. The gain is in reduced latency, because many nodes will be transferred in a single packet, and so will not need to be transferred individually if they are needed.

In our implementation of bulk fetching, packets are constructed by traversing the graph to be transmitted in a breadth-first fashion. Each closure is given a global address which is used to preserve sharing both across the system and within the packet. When packing a thunk the original closure is overwritten with a *FetchMe* closure, which acts as a global indirection to remote data. Communication of data is triggered if a thread enters such a *FetchMe* closure during evaluation. Unlike thunks, normal form closures are simply copied. See [THM+96] for a more detailed discussion of this communication mechanism.

In this paper we are interested in refinements of the basic bulk fetching scheme that limit the amount of the graph being sent. We investigate two possibilities: specifying a bound on the packet size or specifying a bound on the number of thunks that can be packed into a single packet. If neither limit is specified, all the graph that is reachable from the requested node will be packed into the packet. Note that packing multiple thunks into one packet essentially amounts to eager work distribution, which may consequently lead to an uneven distribution of sparks. For reference, the GUM implementation [THM+96] currently uses a full-subgraph packing scheme but imposes a limit on the packet size.

Figure 1 depicts the bulk fetching mechanism in action on a simple graph that involves sharing. The left hand side shows the graph before packing takes place, the right hand side shows the graph as it has been updated following packing. The centre of the diagram shows the packet that is constructed to transmit the graph. Shading is used to depict thunks, normal form closures are left unshaded. Note that thunks are replaced by *FetchMe* closures (lightly shaded) in the packed graph whereas normal form closures are left unchanged (and so duplicated on

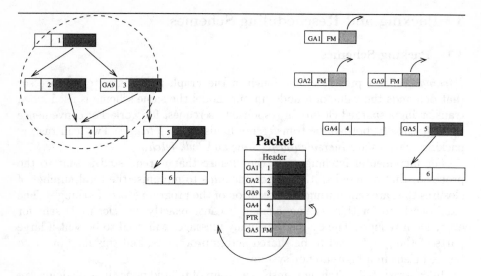

Fig. 1. The bulk fetching mechanism (with 3 thunks per packet)

the remote processor). Since this example shows a packing scheme that packs a maximum of 3 thunks into a packet, one thunk is left behind on the original processor (referenced by a *FetchMe* in the packet).

As closures are added to the packet, they are assigned global addresses (*GAs*) if they were previously held entirely locally. Otherwise their existing *GA* is used. Sharing is preserved within the packet by using special small *PTR* indirection nodes.

3.2 Rescheduling Schemes

Rescheduling schemes prescribe what the processor should do while communication is taking place. The two basic choices are between *synchronous* and *asynchronous* communication.

With synchronous communication, the processor will be idle until it receives a response to its fetch request. If asynchronous communication is used, however, another thread can be executed in the interim. This amounts to latency hiding, since useful work can be performed until the requested data arrives. In high latency systems latency hiding is usually advantageous, effectively reducing processor idle time. However, in low latency systems the overhead attached to descheduling one thread and scheduling another may well be greater than the wasted time, and synchronous communication should be used. Some recent approaches have attempted to use lightweight threads and active messages to mask latency [Ost93, Cha97]. Such an approach may be beneficial for high latency systems (primarily by allowing multiple data fetch messages to be transmitted as soon as a closure that needed several remote closures was activated), but would require significant changes to our implementation in order to support the notification model.

A refinement of the asynchronous rescheduling scheme is to specify how aggressive the system should be in acquiring new work while waiting for the answer of a fetch request. We compare four rescheduling schemes:

1. only execute another runnable thread;
2. turn a spark into a thread if no runnable threads are available;
3. try to acquire a remote spark if the processor has no local sparks;
4. try to migrate another runnable thread if no remote sparks can be found.

These schemes are cumulative, so that thread migration will only be attempted if the three previous schemes have failed, etc. Note that the third and fourth 'global' rescheduling schemes will involve communication in order to obtain new work. In particular, the fourth scheme may introduce gratuitous thread migration towards the end of the computation, when the system load is low.

The rescheduling scheme is only relevant when there are outstanding fetch requests to process. If the processor is idle, it will attempt to use all four schemes to obtain work regardless of the rescheduling scheme in force.

4 An Evaluation of Packing Schemes

In order to evaluate the quality of the different packing and rescheduling schemes it is important to use realistic programs. In particular, it is not likely that simple programs with simple communication patterns will yield meaningful performance measurements for the schemes considered here. We therefore use the following set of example programs:

- coins (ca. 30 lines), a divide-and-conquer program that, given a set of coins and a value, will compute the number of ways this value can be paid using those coins;
- linsolv (ca. 500 lines), a linear system solver based on a multiple homomorphic images approach, which is typical for many algorithms in symbolic computation;
- determinant (ca. 100 lines), a determinant computation, which is the main component of the above linear system solver (both linsolv and determinant have a divide-and-conquer structure);
- cfd (ca. 800 lines), a computational fluid dynamics program, exhibiting an iterative transformation structure typical for many applications in numerical computation.

The principal data structure for the coins program is a list of integers, for linsolv and determinant is a list of lists of integers, and for cfd is an array of floating point values. All of these programs, in particular cfd, perform a large amount of communication involving these data structures.

Our test programs are already quite efficient. The purpose of the measurements reported here is to show the extent to which a *tuned* parallel algorithm

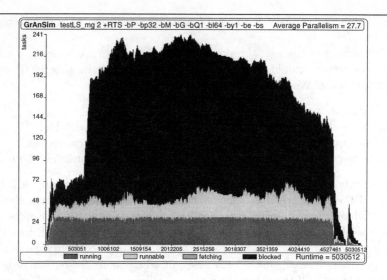

Fig. 2. Activity profile of `linsolv`

can be improved using runtime-system techniques, rather than to show maximal improvements. As an example, Figure 2 shows the overall activity profile for the `linsolv` example program running on 32 processors. Note that the number of running threads is almost always at the maximum (32 in this case). Only at the end does the CPU utilisation drop before showing a final peak of parallel threads. This indicates that there is a minor sequential bottleneck in the final combination stage of this otherwise very efficient divide-and-conquer algorithm.

4.1 Bulk versus Incremental Fetching

First we compare the performance of basic bulk fetching (as used in GUM) with incremental fetching (as used in GRIP [PCSH87]). In order to obtain results that are applicable for a wide range of machines we perform each of the measurements for a number of widely varying latencies.

In order to allow comparisons to be drawn for several different cases, each graph plots relative speedup over a sequential program for a range of latencies. Time is measured in terms of abstract machine cycles. This allows low-level details such as the clock frequency of the processor to be abstracted.

Since small differences are more important for lower latencies, the use of a logarithmic scale allows these differences to be more easily seen. The graphs cover the spectrum of parallel machines from shared-memory machines (about 10–20 cycles) through fast distributed-memory machines like GRIP (about 400 cycles) to workstation networks (between 50,000–100,000 cycles). No attempt is made to model network topology, however, and we also assume that sufficient bandwidth

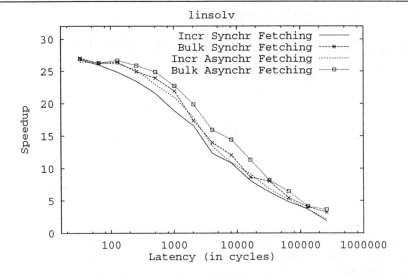

Fig. 3. Bulk vs incremental fetching for `linsolv`

is available to avoid communication bottlenecks. The communications latency is therefore effectively constant throughout the computation.

When comparing bulk and incremental fetching, it is also necessary to consider the most extreme rescheduling schemes. The absolute performance of the resulting four combinations is shown in Figure 3 using `linsolv` as our example program. Overall a bulk fetching scheme with asynchronous communication performs best for all latencies, whereas the incremental synchronous fetching scheme is worst. This is not an entirely obvious result: the speculative nature of bulk fetching may result in unnecessary data being transmitted, or in the same thunks being packed repeatedly, and synchronous communication carries less task rescheduling overhead at low latencies.

Figure 4 shows the same relative runtimes for the same four configurations treating incremental synchronous fetching as the base case. Up to latencies of about 100 cycles, all schemes have almost exactly the same performance. For latencies exceeding 500 cycles, however, bulk asynchronous fetching yields a significant improvement over the other schemes. We observe a reduction of the total runtime of 17% and 28% for latencies between 1,000 and 50,000 cycles. For higher latencies the relative runtimes vary significantly since data locality becomes crucially important. Bulk asynchronous fetching is still consistently the best scheme with a runtime improvement of about 50% at a latency of 260,000 cycles.

The relative runtime graph for `coins` on the right hand side of Figure 4 shows a similar overall picture with the bulk fetching schemes performing best. However, this graph shows a problem that can occur for incremental asynchronous

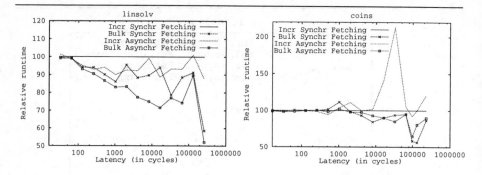

Fig. 4. Bulk vs incremental fetching for `linsolv` and `coins`

fetching: performance can drop drastically if many threads simultaneously compete for the same remote data ("data stealing"). Normally, the communication cost is within a factor of 2 of that for incremental synchronous communication but it exceeds a factor of 3 for the spike shown in the graph. Despite this problem with incremental fetching, there is, somewhat surprisingly, no evidence that data stealing has affected any of the bulk fetching results. This is perhaps because bulk fetching creates duplicates of those normal form closures that are likely to be required by several tasks.

4.2 Bounded Packet Size

One way to reduce communication costs is to impose a limit on the size of graph that is transmitted in response to a fetch request. The graph is packed in a breadth-first manner, with the fringe of the graph replaced by *FetchMe* closures if the packet is too small for the complete graph. Measurements taken from the GUM system [THM+96], which uses a similar mechanism, show a significant performance improvement as the packet size limit is increased from 16 words up to the default value of 1024 words.

While the average packet size in the GUM measurements was quite large, the average size for the example programs reported here was, in contrast, quite small. Even with full-subgraph packing the average packet size for `coins` is between 3 and 4 closures, for `linsolv` it is between 5 and 15 closures (the largest we recorded), and for `cfd` it is between 4 and 10 closures. The average closure size in these examples is also very close to the minimum size for updatable closures: four words. This explains why limiting the packet size has little effect on performance for our programs.

4.3 Limited Number of Thunks

Another way to throttle the communication is to limit the number of thunks that can be packed in one packet. Since thunks represent potential work, specifying such a limit intuitively increases the resistance against moving work to other processors. In a lazy fetching scheme, except for the root of the graph, only normal form closures are packed. As there is no danger of duplicating work, normal forms can always be copied without destroying data locality. However, this might result in very small packets and hence in a rather high relative overhead for packing the graph.

The other extreme is the scheme used, for example, in GUM: no limit on the number of thunks in a packet. This increases the average packet size but runs the risk of offloading thunks which may be needed later by the current processor. This *"thunk stealing"* effect will cause additional communication if a thunk must subsequently be returned to the originating processor. Although this behaviour has been observed in the GUM system for several programs that communicate heavily, its overall effect on performance has not been measured precisely.

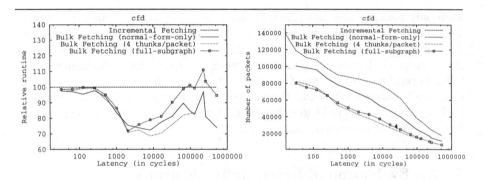

Fig. 5. Relative runtimes and number of packets sent for `cfd`

Figure 5 compares the runtimes for the full-subgraph and normal-form-only packing schemes using bulk fetching, against those for incremental fetching for `cfd`. Interestingly, for most latencies a full-subgraph packing scheme does not give the best performance. For this example program it is better to use a normal-form-only packing scheme. For very high latencies (greater than 100,000 cycles) full-subgraph packing is worse even than incremental fetching, and normal-form-only packing yields a performance improvement of about 20%. The communication graph on the right hand side of Figure 5 shows that full-subgraph packing does not in fact generate the least number of packets, as might be expected. Choosing a limit of 4 thunks per packet actually results in least communication, because it reduces the probability of thunks being stolen while still allowing reasonable work distribution. This compromise between large packet sizes and low probability of thunk stealing shows the best performance for `cfd`.

In Figure 6 we show the relative runtime of the `linsolv` program using packing schemes with different numbers of thunks per packet (left hand side) and the corresponding amount of communication (right hand side). In this case normal-

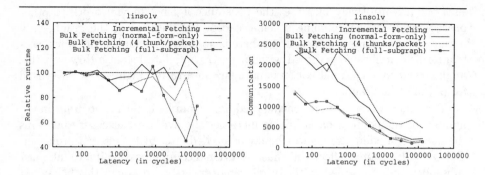

Fig. 6. Relative runtimes and number of packets sent for `linsolv`

form-only packing does not generally achieve an improvement in performance. The amount of communication is close to the incremental fetching scheme and much higher than for the other bulk fetching schemes. However, when increasing the number of thunks per packet to 4 we can surpass the performance of the full-subgraph packing scheme for some latencies. The number of packets sent in this case is consistently below the number of packets sent with a full-subgraph packing scheme. This indicates that thunk stealing is occurring in this program, too. However, it is less harmful than in `cfd`.

5 An Evaluation of Rescheduling Schemes

The different rescheduling schemes introduced in Section 3.2 have a direct influence on the distribution of work and on the locality of data in the system. The first and second ("local") rescheduling schemes only try to access work present on the local processor and are therefore refinements of asynchronous communication. The second rescheduling scheme is slightly more aggressive than the first in that it also creates new work if the processor is idle. Therefore, this scheme is likely to increase the overall workload on the machine and would be advantageous for programs creating a rather small number of threads under the default scheme, but for which there is a potential reserve of parallelism. The third and fourth ("global") rescheduling schemes are most aggressive in attempting to acquire work from other processors while awaiting a response to a message.

These schemes can consequently be seen as an alternative way to distribute the system workload. However, in doing so they also increase the total amount of communication. Since these schemes only make a difference if no local work is available, they are not generally very effective in creating an even workload. They should be seen as a cheap form of load distribution that comes as part of a refined asynchronous communication scheme.

Figure 7 compares the speedups (left hand side) and the relative runtimes (right hand side) for `linsolv` using different rescheduling schemes. The base

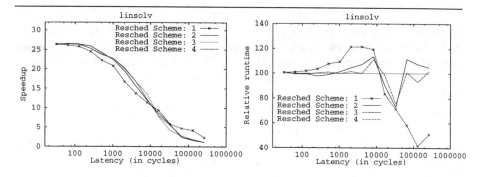

Fig. 7. Speedups and relative runtimes with different rescheduling schemes for `linsolv`

case for the relative runtimes is the third rescheduling scheme, which is the one used in GUM. The packing scheme is fixed to be full-subgraph packing.

The quality of the rescheduling schemes clearly depends on the latency. For low latencies the more aggressive global schemes perform best since there is little cost associated with fetching work from remote processors. The improved load distribution outweighs the increased communication caused by a deteriorated locality of the data. However, for high latencies the dominant cost becomes that of moving data between processors. In this case, data locality is more important than an even load distribution. Therefore, the local rescheduling schemes usually perform better than the more aggressive schemes.

It is also worth noting that the difference between the rescheduling schemes is smaller for full-subgraph packing. This is because there are fewer fetch requests if such a packing scheme is used, and hence the more aggressive rescheduling schemes do not have many opportunities to acquire remote work while waiting for remote data to arrive. The relative runtimes given on the right hand side of Figure 7 show that the runtime for the least aggressive scheme lies between 120% (medium latencies) and 40% (high latencies) of the base case. For latencies higher than about 15,000 cycles this scheme yields a clear improvement in overall runtime.

6 Related Work

The importance of packing schemes on distributed memory machines has already been observed in systems such as Alfalfa [Gol88], where poor data partitioning was cited as the main reason for the poor performance of matrix multiplication and other programs. Goldberg suggested that compiler controlled data partitioning could overcome this problem by ensuring a good initial data distribution. However, our experience with large application programs such as Lolita [MSS94] and the programs studied here shows that parallel symbolic programs operate mainly on large dynamic data structures. This suggests that a more sophisticated dynamic management of the distributed heap is required.

In his PhD thesis, Kesseler [Kes96] examines different "copying strategies" (corresponding to our packing schemes) for the Concurrent Clean system. The main difference from our work is that his schemes have to maintain uniqueness information attached to a graph. Thus, in his case a copying strategy that violates this uniqueness information might change the semantics of the program. This complication does not arise in our work.

Since his lazy normal form copying strategy only copies those non-normal-form closures that are suitably annotated, this is close to our normal-form-only packing scheme. Kesseler also considers data locality and its effect on performance, an area that we have not yet studied in detail.

As already mentioned, the GUM system [THM$^+$96] uses a full-subgraph packing scheme with a default packet size of 1024 words. The rescheduling scheme that is used corresponds very closely to our third scheme: a processor may turn a spark into a thread while waiting for remote data and may try to find a remote spark. GUM does not support thread migration. The GRIP system [PCSH87] uses incremental synchronous communication. This is motivated by the low latency of this machine (around 400 cycles).

In [TD94] Toyn and Dix give an algorithm for the efficient lazy transfer of arbitrary pointer structures. The structure of this algorithm is similar to that of a copying garbage collector and therefore closely related to our graph traversal during packing. The invariants of the algorithm are similar to those in our packing schemes: sharing and cycles have to be preserved during the packing processes. This is achieved by using two kinds of special nodes similar to our *FetchMe* and *PTR* nodes. However, in our model the original graph is updated with *FetchMe* closures whereas Toyn and Dix's algorithm leave it unchanged. They also only consider a lazy packing scheme without discussing variants for tuning the granularity of the transfer.

In the pHluid [FN96] distributed memory implementation of a shared memory parallel functional language a key issue for achieving good performance is to avoid distributing work unnecessarily. This is achieved by handling a queue of stealable threads in a LIFO manner and stealing work from the old end of the queue (similar to the mechanism used in the HDG machine [KLB91]).

The pHluid heap is partitioned into pages that are owned by processors. These pages act as units for communication. A simple cache coherence algorithm without invalidation is used to manage communication. Thus, in this model no thunk stealing will happen because the result of an evaluation is always sent to the original processor. This enforces good locality of data in the long run but may cause more communication than our model if many updates need to be performed on a remote page. Overall, the packing and rescheduling schemes that correspond most closely to the pHluid model are bounded packet size packing and aggressive asynchronous rescheduling.

The abstract TAM dataflow machine [CGS93] also emphasises latency tolerance by using asynchronous communication, implemented in this case via split-phase memory access operations. As in the work by Ostheimer [Ost93] and Chakravarty [Cha97], TAM uses multi-threading and active messages. Performance thus depends on the source program providing large amounts of multi-threaded parallelism. Only data that is needed immediately is transferred, similarly to our incremental fetching scheme.

7 Conclusion

We have studied communication issues in a parallel graph reduction system, covering machines with widely varying latencies. We have proposed methods for limiting the amount of communication (*packing schemes*) and for distributing work during the idle time caused by communication (*rescheduling schemes*).

The results in this paper are representative for our measurements of all possible combinations of packing and rescheduling schemes on a set of non-trivial programs that exhibit a significant amount of communication using fairly complex communication patterns. The structure of the parallelism in and the communication behaviour shown by these programs lead us to believe that these results can be applied in the ongoing parallelisation of very large programs. The programs that we are currently studying include a program that determines accident blackspots based on a large database of traffic accident reports [WH96] and Lolita [MSS94], a large scale natural language engineering system (about 60,000 lines of Haskell).

From our measurements we draw the following conclusions:

- *Rescheduling schemes:* For low latencies, where an even load distribution is more important than good locality of data, aggressive rescheduling schemes deliver good work distribution and therefore good performance. For high latencies, however, the improved load distribution does not compensate for reduced data locality. The crossover point usually lies between 15,000 and 30,000 cycles, i.e. loosely-coupled multiprocessors.
- *Packing schemes:* In general, full-subgraph packing proves to be the best packing scheme. In practice, there is little danger that such a packing scheme will cause a disastrously uneven load distribution.
- *Thunk stealing:* Occasionally the full-subgraph packing scheme causes *thunk stealing*: the gratuitous offloading of thunks that will be needed later. This increases communication costs and hence reduces performance. We believe that thunk stealing is the reason for full-subgraph packing sometimes being worse than those schemes that pack a limited number of thunks per packet (e.g. cfd). This does not happen very frequently, however.
- *Bulk vs incremental fetching:* For low latencies (up to about 100 cycles) there is no difference in the performance of bulk and incremental fetching. Especially for very high latencies (more than about 50,000 cycles) bulk fetching achieves significant runtime improvements compared to incremental fetching even when using asynchronous communication for latency hiding.
- *Bounded packet size:* The average packet size is in general very small, even for full-subgraph packing (in our example programs it is almost always smaller than 15 closures). Therefore, changing the packet size, as has been previously

suggested for improving communication performance, has hardly any effect on the runtime of the program.

From these observations taken from our simulation results, we can make the following suggestions for improving the runtime-system of a parallel graph reduction machine such as GUM:

- Choosing a small packet size is not an effective means of tuning the granularity of the communication. This is due to the small average number of closures per packet in most programs.
- For programs with a high degree of communication a *normal-form-only packing* scheme should be used in order to reduce the amount of thunk stealing. It is probably not worthwhile implementing a more general scheme that allows the user to specify the number of thunks per packet because good values for such a parameter are very hard to predict.
- When running on a high-latency system (more than about 15,000 cycles) a *less aggressive rescheduling scheme* should be used in order to maintain good data locality. Our recent measurements with Lolita seem to underline the importance of data locality in large application programs. Currently, GUM uses a global rescheduling scheme similar to our third rescheduling scheme.

As further work we plan to quantify the impact of thunk stealing on the performance of larger parallel programs exhibiting a less regular structure of parallelism. Our initial results indicate that limiting the number of thunks per packet is an effective way of avoiding thunk stealing. Another aspect we would like to investigate is the impact of our rescheduling schemes on the total heap consumption of the parallel program. For large programs a too aggressive rescheduling scheme might unnecessarily create threads that hold on to a large partition of the heap increasing the total heap residency. It would also be interesting to compare our rescheduling schemes, which influence the load distribution, with other work on load balancing.

References

[Cha97] M. Chakravarty. *On the Massively Parallel Execution of Declarative Programs.* PhD Thesis, Technical Univ. of Berlin, Feb. 1997.

[CGS93] D.E. Culler, S.C. Goldstein, K.E. Schauser, T. von Eicken. TAM — A Compiler Controlled Threaded Abstract Machine. *Journal of Parallel and Distributed Computing,* 18:347–370, Jun. 1993.

[FN96] C. Flanagan and R.S. Nikhil. pHluid: The Design of a Parallel Functional Language Implementation on Workstations. In *ICFP'96 — Intl. Conf. on Functional Programming,* pp. 169–179, Philadelphia, PA, May 24–26, 1996. ACM Press.

[Gol88] B. Goldberg. Multiprocessor Execution of Functional Programs. *Intl. Journal of Parallel Programming,* 17(5):425–473, Oct. 1988.

[HLP95]   K. Hammond, H-W. Loidl, and A. Partridge.   Visualising Granularity
           in Parallel Programs: A Graphical Winnowing System for Haskell. In
           HPFC'95 — Conf. on High Performance Functional Computing, pp. 208–
           221, Denver, CO, Apr. 10–12, 1995.

[Kes96]   M. Kesseler. *The Implementation of Functional Languages on Parallel Ma-
           chines with Distributed Memory*. PhD thesis, Univ. of Nijmegen, Apr. 1996.

[KLB91]   H. Kingdon, D. Lester, and G. Burn.   The HDG-machine: a highly dis-
           tributed graph-reducer for a transputer network. *The Computer Journal*,
           34(4):290–301, 1991.

[Loi96]   H-W. Loidl. *GranSim User's Guide*. Dept. of Computing Science, Univ. of
           Glasgow. Jul. 1996.

[MKH90]   E. Mohr, D.A. Kranz, and R.H. Halstead Jr. Lazy Task Creation: A Tech-
           nique for Increasing the Granularity of Parallel Programs. In *LFP'90 —
           Conf. on Lisp and Functional Programming*, pp. 185–197, Nice, France, Jun.
           27–29, 1990.

[MSS94]   R.G. Morgan, M.H. Smith, and S. Short. Translation by Meaning and Style
           in Lolita. In *Intl. BCS Conf. — Machine Translation Ten Years On*, Cran-
           field Univ., Nov. 1994.

[Ost93]   G. Ostheimer. *Parallel Functional Programming for Message-Passing Mul-
           tiprocessors*. PhD thesis, Univ. of St Andrews, Mar. 1993.

[PCS89]   S.L. Peyton Jones, C. Clack, and J. Salkild.   High-Performance Parallel
           Graph Reduction. In *PARLE'89 — Parallel Architectures and Languages
           Europe*, LNCS 365, pp. 193–206. Springer-Verlag, 1989.

[PCSH87]   S.L. Peyton Jones, C. Clack, J. Salkild, and M. Hardie. GRIP — a High-
           Performance Architecture for Parallel Graph Reduction. In *FPCA'87 —
           Intl. Conf. on Functional Programming Languages and Computer Archi-
           tecture*, LNCS 274, pp. 98–112, Portland, OR, Sep. 14–16, 1987. Springer-
           Verlag.

[Pey89]   S.L. Peyton Jones. Parallel Implementations of Functional Programming
           Languages. *The Computer Journal*, **32(2)**:175–186, Apr. 1989.

[PH⁺97]   J.C. Peterson, K. Hammond (eds.) *et al.*   *Haskell 1.4 — A Non-Strict,
           Purely Functional Language*, Apr. 1997.

[TD94]   I. Toyn and A.J. Dix. Efficient Binary Transfer of Pointer Structures. *Soft-
           ware – Practice and Experience*, **24(11)**:1001–1023, Nov. 1994.

[THL⁺96]   P. Trinder, K. Hammond, H-W. Loidl, S.L. Peyton Jones, and J. Wu. A
           Case Study of Data-intensive Programs in Parallel Haskell. In *Glasgow
           Workshop on Functional Programming 1996*, Ullapool, Scotland, Jul. 8–10.

[THM⁺96]   P. Trinder,   K. Hammond,   J.S. Mattson   Jr.,   A.S. Partridge,   and
           S.L. Peyton Jones. GUM: a portable parallel implementation of Haskell.
           In *PLDI'96 — Programming Languages Design and Implementation*, pp.
           79–88, Philadelphia, PA, May 1996.

[WH96]   J. Wu and L. Harbird. A Functional Database System for Road Accident
           Analysis. *Advances in Engineering Software*, **26(1)**:29–43, 1996.

The Results of: Profiling Large-Scale Lazy Functional Programs

Stephen A. Jarvis[1] and Richard G. Morgan[2]

[1] Oxford University Computing Laboratory, Wolfson Building,
Parks Road, Oxford, England.
Stephen.Jarvis@comlab.ox.ac.uk
[2] Department of Computer Science, Durham University,
South Road, Durham, England.
R.G.Morgan@durham.ac.uk

Abstract. At the High Performance Functional Computing conference in Denver [MoJ95] a new approach to profiling was presented, this allowed the complete set of program costs to be recorded in so-called cost centre stacks. It was proposed that these program costs could then be manipulated using a post-processor which would speed up the task of profiling a Haskell program and would also produce more accurate profiling results.

This paper presents the results of using this new profiling tool in the analysis of a number of Haskell programs. The overheads of the scheme are discussed and the benefits of this new system are considered. The paper also outlines how this approach can be modified to trace and debug Haskell programs.

1 Introduction

One would like to think that most programmers understand what a profiler is by now and that they use a profiler in everyday programming. Even when a program appears to be efficient, an inquisitive programmer will run a program and study the profiling results. In doing so he may find that parts of his code are not as efficient as he hoped, and, as a consequence of this, the code may be changed, re-compiled, and profiled once more. The results, one hopes, are an improvement on the original.

There are a number of reliable profiling tools now available to Haskell programmers, of these the York heap profiler [RuW93] supplied with the Chalmers Haskell compiler and the Glasgow cost centre profiler [SaP95] supplied with the Glasgow Haskell compiler are probably the most well-known. Each measures heap usage during the execution of a Haskell program. At regular intervals during program execution the amount of heap used by each function is recorded; these results can then be viewed as a graph of total heap usage over execution time. The cost centre profiler also displays time profiling results for the program. The results of the profiler show, in tabular form, the percentage of the total execution time spent in each of the program's functions.

There are many variations on this theme: the heap profiler can display the results in terms of the producers or constructors; the cost centre profiler can also display a serial time profile, similar to the heap graphs; there is also the possibility of limiting the number of functions which the programmer profiles, allowing him to concentrate on only that part of the code which he believes is inefficient.

The aim is to supply the programmer with enough material with which to identify possible bottlenecks in the program, to identify space leaks, or to locate those parts of the code which use a disproportionate amount of time or memory.

One large programming project which has made considerable use of these profiling tools is the LOLITA natural language processing system at the University of Durham. This system consists of over 50,000 lines of Haskell source code, written in over 180 different modules. The development of the system began in 1986 and there are currently 20 developers working on it [LGa94]. In June 1993 the LOLITA system was demonstrated to the Royal Society in London.

LOLITA is an example of a large system which has been developed in a lazy functional language purely because it was felt that this was the most suitable language to use. It is important to note the distinction between this development, where the choice of a lazy functional language is incidental, and projects which are either initiated as experiments in lazy functional languages or have a vested interest in functional languages. Because of this, conclusions drawn regarding the effectiveness of functional languages, and in particular their profilers, were based on real experience. The following problems with the heap and cost centre profilers were identified:

- Profiling takes a long time — Compiling and running programs with the profiling options takes longer than without, due to the extra bookkeeping needed. Programmers also have a tendency to select and reselect functions a number of times before they are completely satisfied with the results. This may require the code to be re-compiled and re-run a number of times. For this reason profiling a large program can conceivably take a number of weeks!
- Profiling results can be misleading — Once the results of a large program have been produced the programmer is then faced with the separate problem of interpreting what they mean. Often the programmer will want to display the results at a high level in the code and then decompose them to constituent functions; alternatively the results may be displayed at a low level in the code and inherited to functions higher in the functional dependency of the program. Previous methods of inheritance (see section 2) have either been inaccurate (statistical inheritance) or limited to a fixed number of generations, because the overheads were considered to be too high to make such a scheme feasible. The cost centre profiler has no inheritance at all; profiling results may therefore be restricted and problems difficult to identify.

These problems were compounded by the scale of the LOLITA system and it was necessary to design a new method of profiling. This is described in the next section.

2 The Cost Centre Stack Profiler

2.1 Cost centres

As the name suggests, the cost centre stack profiler is based on the Glasgow cost centre profiler. There were two reasons for extending the cost centre profiler rather than the heap profiler. Firstly, the cost centre profiler produces time as well as heap profiles and secondly, with the cost centre profiler the programmer can annotate the code by hand or automatically and is therefore given more control over which part of the code he wishes to profile.

A *cost centre* is a label to which costs are assigned. To profile a piece of code, the programmer is required to annotate the code with an scc expression (set cost centre) followed by the cost centre name. For instance

```
function x = scc "costs" (map expensive x)
```

will assign to the cost centre cost the costs of evaluating the mapping. So that the task of annotating large programs does not become tiresome, the programmer is also able to select all top-level functions for profiling.

Costs are allocated to a single cost centre which is currently in *scope* according to a set of cost attribution rules. Such rules state that given an expression, "scc *cc exp*", the costs attributed to *cc* are the entire costs of evaluating the expression *exp* as far as the enclosing cost centre demands it, excluding, firstly the costs of evaluating the free variables of *exp*, and secondly the cost of evaluating any scc expressions within *exp* (or within any function called from *exp*).

This means that any costs incurred by functions within the scope of the enclosing cost centre are aggregated (subsumed) and that the results are independent of the evaluation order, that is, lazy evaluation is respected. The results of the cost centre profiler are flat or non-inherited; this means that the cost of a function is only assigned to its enclosing cost centre.

Many of the problems experienced with the cost centre profiler have been due to the inability to inherit program costs. Consider the following example program:

```
a = (b [1..20]) ++ (c [1..10000])
b x = c (c (c x))
c = foldl (flip (:)) []
```

A flat profile of the program produced by the cost centre profiler is:

COST CENTRE	MODULE	GROUP	scc	subcc	%time
c	Main	Main	280	268	100.0
MAIN	MAIN	MAIN	1	0	0.0
a	Main	Main	3	5	0.0
b	Main	Main	2	9	0.0
PRELUDE	Prelude	Prelude	0	0	0.0

This is what the programmer might expect, as all of the work is done in function c. The programmer would be aware of two ways of improving this program. Function c could be re-written to make it more efficient, or the code calling the function c could be made more efficient. In this particular example it is not easy to see how c (a reverse function) could be improved and unfortunately the flat profile does not give the programmer any more detail regarding those functions calling c. The only other information which the programmer has to go on is the number of annotated sub-expressions which attribute their costs to another cost centre, subcc. This information is in fact a red herring in this particular case as the programmer might think that b, having more subccs, is responsible for more of the computation in c - this is not true.

There is a solution to this problem. The program can be profiled once again with the shared function c deselected. This allows the costs of c to be subsumed by its parents; the programmer would find that function a was responsible for more of cs costs. Experience has shown that this solution is inadequate as firstly, this requires the program to be re-compiled and re-profiled, which takes a long time, particularly in a large program, and secondly, it is not always easy to see which functions should be selected or deselected in a large piece of code. The programmer may end up repeating this exercise a number of times before the results begin to make any sense. A solution is offered by using cost centre stacks.

2.2 Cost centre stacks

Cost centre stacks record the sequence of cost centres for a piece of code, so rather than having an enclosing cost centre there is an enclosing stack of cost centres. This shows the precise order of function calls and allows the run-time costs to be recorded in more detail. This extra detail means that a program need only be profiled once and that results can be accurately inherited if required. The cost centre stack results for the above program might be:

COST CENTRE STACK	MODULE	GROUP	scc	subcc	%time
<c,a,MAIN,>	Main	Main	278	266	99.4
<c,b,a,MAIN,>	Main	Main	2	2	0.6
<MAIN,>	MAIN	MAIN	1	0	0.0
<a,MAIN,>	Main	Main	3	5	0.0
<b,a,MAIN,>	Main	Main	2	9	0.0

At the head of the cost centre stack is the current cost centre to which the costs of program execution have been assigned. The remainder of the stack shows the order in which cost centres were encountered in the evaluation required to reach this current cost centre. The results are not only more revealing but are also, as will be seen, amenable for post-processing. This makes the task of profiling quicker and also allows the production of accurate inherited results. An extension of this example can be seen in the first set of results, see section 3.1.

2.3   Efficient solution

Previous attempts had been made at producing these accurate inheritance results [GKK82] [CCP95], but all of them had been dismissed as being too costly in practice, or they had produced solutions which relied on statistical averaging and not raw data. For this reason the design of the cost centre stack profiler had to be based on an implementation which avoided excessively large overheads. To this end a number of design criteria were formulated:

- No duplication of cost centres — A method of stack compression is used which prevents the duplication of cost centres in a stack. This is particularly important in the case of recursive or mutually recursive function calls.
- Memoised stacks — A potentially expensive part of cost centre stack profiling is in building the stacks. For this reason once a stack had been created is will continue to exist throughout the execution of the program. Any sequence of function calls which matches an existing stack will have small profiling overheads as the existing stack will be re-used.
- Pointer implementation — The cost centre stack profiler makes use of the existing cost centres in the Glasgow Haskell compiler. The construction of the stacks at run-time is done using pointers. The only other information needed by the stack profiler is an extra level of cost information. The physical overheads are therefore quite small.

These design decisions endeavor to permit the collection of complete program results without excessive overheads. This is discussed in more detail in the next section. The reader is referred to [MoJ95] for more details on the implementation.

3   Results of the Profiler and Post-processor

In this section results from the cost centre stack profiler and the accompanying post-processor are presented. Case studies are used to compare the results of the cost centre profiler and the cost centre stack profiler. The results of both large and small programs are discussed.

The first example illustrates the effect which the cost centre stack profiler has on the results of shared functions. It is difficult to illustrate the benefits of accurate cost inheritance when working with larger programs; the quantity of code means that it is not always easy to see why the results are so different. Therefore, the first example program is only 15 lines long. The results gained from the cost centre profiler and the cost centre stack profiler are significantly different. This first example is also used to explain the post-processing procedure.

Results are then presented from the LOLITA system. This is a considerable example and contains hundreds of thousands of function calls. It is therefore a substantial test case with which to test the profiler. Attention is paid to the process of profiling using the inheritance results; this contains some different observations from those identified in previous methods of profiling.

The final set of results are from the `nofib` benchmark suite; this includes the traditional benchmark program `clausify`. From these results some general conclusions are drawn.

3.1 Introductory example

The first set of results are from a simple program designed to be computationally expensive. The program, which repeatedly reverses lists of numbers, makes use of a number of shared functions. These functions illustrate the difference in the results achieved using a method of cost inheritance, produced by the cost centre stack profiler, and a method of flat profiling, produced by the original cost centre profiler. The example is clearly contrived, but serves to illustrate the basic differences between the two sets of profiling results.
The program

```
module Main where
main = print (length a)
a = (b 1) ++ (c 1)
b x = (d x) ++ (e x)
c x = f x
d x = g (x - 10)
e x = g x
f x = (h x) ++ (i x)
g x = (j [x..100]) ++ (rev (rev (rev (rev [x..100])))) 
h x = j [-1000..100]
i x = rev (rev (rev (rev [x..100])))
j l = rev (rev (rev (rev (rev (rev l)))))

rev [] = []                     -- An O(n^2) reverse function
rev (x:xs) = (rev xs) ++ [x]
```

is depicted in the dependency graph in figure 1. The shared functions g and j serve to illustrate expensive functions, if called with suitably large arguments. It is a function call from h to j which causes the largest amount of computation; the function call from g to j causes significantly less. The arguments passed to the called function are shown in brackets in the figure; for example function e calls function g with the argument 1.

The program is time-profiled with the cost centre profiler[3] and the results are displayed in figure 2. As expected, the reverse function `rev` (from the program `Main`) accounts for nearly all of the execution time, 99.7% in total[4]. The remaining 0.3% of costs are attributed to the functions f (0.1%) and the prelude (0.2%). This last figure is due to the catenation function (++) used throughout the program.

---

[3] Compile-time flags: `-prof -auto-all`; Run-time flags: `-pT`.

[4] This $O(n^2)$ reverse function is included in the Main program to prevent costs from being assigned to the $O(n)$ reverse function defined in the PRELUDE library.

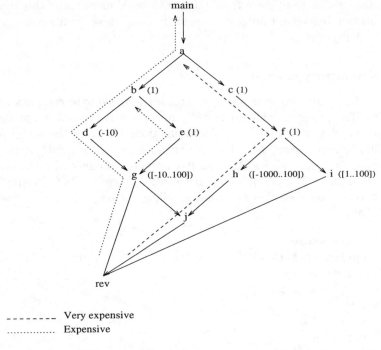

main

b (1)   c (1)

d (-10)   e (1)   f (1)

g ([-10..100])   h ([-1000..100])   i ([1..100])

j

rev

```
- - - - - - - -   Very expensive
................   Expensive
```

Fig. 1. Dependency graph of the first example program

The flat cost centre profile presented in figure 2 does not provide the programmer with very useful information. It is not clear which of the functions g, j and i, which share the function calls to the utility function rev, is responsible for the highest proportion of the costs. Without any recompilation and reprofiling further results are impossible to calculate.

The cost centre stack profiler produces two sets of results. Firstly, a flat profile is produced in the same way as for the cost centre profiler, figure 3. It is important to note that the results of the cost centre stack flat profile are almost identical to the results of the flat profile of the cost centre profiler. This is an important observation; it shows that the results of the original cost centre profile will not be distorted by the inclusion of the cost centre stacks in the compiler. The 0.3% error is due to sampling differences.

The cost centre stack profiler also produces the cost centre stacks found in figure 4. Each cost centre stack is displayed with the units of time spent computing values within its scope. These results are useful as they immediately indicate the cost stack of the most computationally expensive part of the program. As expected, function rev is at the head of this stack:

`<Main_rev,Main_j,Main_h,Main_f,Main_c,Main_a,Main_main> 1181 TICKs`

The reader will observe from figure **??** that the function rev is also at the head of five further cost centre stacks which show the path of cost centres to the

Thu Jun 20 14:46 1996 Time and Allocation Profiling Report   (Final)
                        (Hybrid Scheme)

            run +RTS -pT -H60M -RTS

COST CENTRE	MODULE	GROUP	scc	subcc	%time	%alloc
Main_rev	Main	Main	20867	20834	99.7	99.8
Main_f	Main	Main	3	2	0.1	0.0
Main_a	Main	Main	2	3	0.0	0.0
Main_b	Main	Main	2	2	0.0	0.0
Main_g	Main	Main	2	12	0.0	0.0
MAIN	MAIN	MAIN	1	0	0.0	0.0
Main_c	Main	Main	1	3	0.0	0.0
Main_d	Main	Main	2	1	0.0	0.0
Main_e	Main	Main	1	1	0.0	0.0
Main_h	Main	Main	1	2	0.0	0.0
Main_i	Main	Main	1	4	0.0	0.0
Main_j	Main	Main	6	21	0.0	0.0
PRELUDE	Prelude	Prelude	0	0	0.2	0.1
Main_main_CAF	Main	Main	0	0	0.0	0.0
CAF.Main	Main	Main	0	3	0.0	0.0
Main_h_CAF	Main	Main	0	0	0.0	0.0
Main_g_CAF	Main	Main	0	0	0.0	0.0
Main_i_CAF	Main	Main	0	0	0.0	0.0

Fig. 2. Results of the cost centre profiler

Total Number of Time Ticks = 1237

Cost centre	Ticks as head of CC stack	Total time ticks	%time
Main_rev	1237	1237	100.0
Main_main	0	0	0.0
Main_a	0	0	0.0
Main_b	0	0	0.0
Main_c	0	0	0.0
Main_d	0	0	0.0
Main_e	0	0	0.0
Main_f	0	0	0.0
Main_g	0	0	0.0
Main_h	0	0	0.0
Main_i	0	0	0.0
Main_j	0	0	0.0
Prelude	0	0	0.0

Fig. 3. Flat profile of the cost centre stack profiler

```
<Main_rev,Main_j,Main_h,Main_f,Main_c,Main_a,Main_main,>  1181 TICKs
<Main_j,Main_h,Main_f,Main_c,Main_a,Main_main,>              0 TICKs
<Main_f,Main_c,Main_a,Main_main,>                           0 TICKs
<Main_j,Main_g,Main_e,Main_b,Main_a,Main_main,>             0 TICKs
<Main_rev,Main_j,Main_g,Main_e,Main_b,Main_a,Main_main,>   16 TICKs
<Main_g,Main_e,Main_b,Main_a,Main_main,>                    0 TICKs
<Main_rev,Main_g,Main_e,Main_b,Main_a,Main_main,>          10 TICKs
<Main_a,Main_main,>                                         0 TICKs
<Main_b,Main_a,Main_main,>                                  0 TICKs
<Main_i,Main_f,Main_c,Main_a,Main_main,>                    0 TICKs
<Main_rev,Main_i,Main_f,Main_c,Main_a,Main_main,>           7 TICKs
<Main_main,>                                                0 TICKs
<Main_c,Main_a,Main_main,>                                  0 TICKs
<Main_g,Main_d,Main_b,Main_a,Main_main,>                    0 TICKs
<Main_rev,Main_g,Main_d,Main_b,Main_a,Main_main,>          11 TICKs
<Main_j,Main_g,Main_d,Main_b,Main_a,Main_main,>             0 TICKs
<Main_rev,Main_j,Main_g,Main_d,Main_b,Main_a,Main_main,>   12 TICKs
<Main_d,Main_b,Main_a,Main_main,>                           0 TICKs
<Main_e,Main_b,Main_a,Main_main,>                           0 TICKs
<Main_h,Main_f,Main_c,Main_a,Main_main,>                    0 TICKs
```

Fig. 4. Results of the cost centre stack profiler

function rev via d, e and i. The programmer is presented with a complete set of unambiguous results which avoids there being any misunderstanding when they are interpreted.

The first stage of post-processing involves the cost centre stacks being transformed, using a C script, into a format which can be interpreted by the graphtool. Cost centres in the stacks become graph *nodes* and adjacent cost centres in a cost centre stack are connected with directed *arcs*.

The total number of time ticks is calculated for each of the functions at the head of each cost centre stack. This figure is divided by the total number of time ticks recorded to obtain a percentage. This is equivalent to calculating a flat profile, as in figure 3.

The second stage of post-processing involves the programmer selecting those functions which he is interested in profiling. This activity has been moved from pre-profiling to post-profiling. For the sake of this initial example all functions are selected.

This task is implemented in a second C script, taking the graph-tool input file and producing an augmented input file depending on which cost centres are selected. The resulting file is then loaded into the graph-tool; this is the third stage of post-processing.

The structure of the program becomes clear when the results are displayed in the graph-tool. In this example the programmer is presented with the callgraph of the program containing all top-level functions. These results are shown in figure 5.

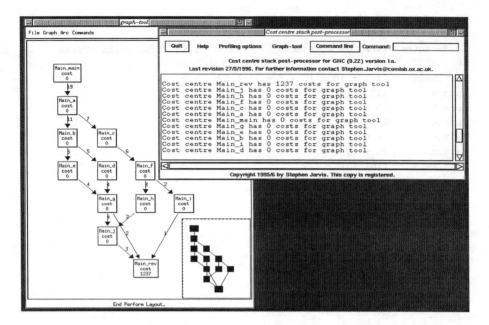

Fig. 5. Post-processor displaying non-inherited post-processed results

Each node in the graph contains the cost centre name and the associated costs (in time ticks or as a percentage; the figure shows the former). Each arc in the call-graph is annotated with a number. This number indicates in how many cost centre stacks this arc was found.

The results are also displayed textually in the cost stack post-processor. The programmer can view the cost centre stacks, select cost centres or choose different profiling options from this window. All functions are executed within a couple of seconds without any further execution or compilation of the program.

The post-processing tool is also able to perform inheritance of results, accurately inheriting the profiling results to all the selected functions. This is achieved by adding the costs associated with each cost centre stack to every function in the cost centre stack. This mechanism is demonstrated in figure 6.

These results can also be displayed by reloading the graph-tool with the new input file, see figure 7. If it was not already clear in the previous results, the expensive arm of the graph now becomes immediately obvious. To emphasise this fact, it is possible to highlight the expensive arm of the graph (or display this arm of the graph only). This proves to be a useful function in graphs which contain a large number of nodes.

There are two issues which must be addressed in the analysis of these results. The first is the *usefulness* of the cost centre stack data and the post-processing techniques for presenting this data. The second is that of the *overheads* involved in collecting this extra data.

Total Number of Time Ticks = 1237

Cost centre	Ticks in CC stack	Total time ticks	%time
Main_main	1181 + 16 + 10 + 7 + 11 + 12	1237	100.0
Main_a	1181 + 16 + 10 + 7 + 11 + 12	1237	100.0
Main_b	16 + 10 + 11 + 12	49	4.0
Main_c	1181 + 7	1188	96.0
Main_d	11 + 12	23	1.9
Main_e	16 + 10	26	2.1
Main_f	1181 + 7	1188	96.0
Main_g	16 + 10 + 11 + 12	49	4.0
Main_h	1181	1181	95.5
Main_i	7	7	0.6
Main_j	1181 + 16 + 12	1209	97.7
Main_rev	1181 + 16 + 10 + 7 + 11 + 12	1237	100.0

Prelude

Fig. 6. Inherited results of the cost centre stack profiler

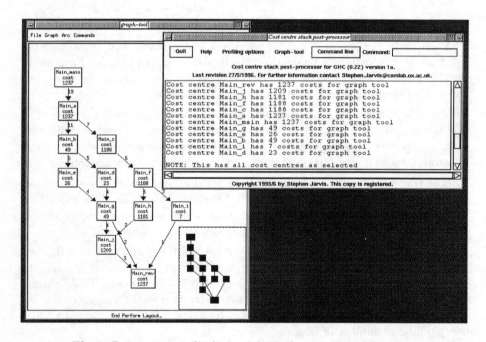

Fig. 7. Post-processor displaying inherited post-processed results

3.2 Usefulness

The cost centre stack information allows a dynamic call-graph of the program (such as those seen in figures 5 and 7) to be displayed. Even if the programmer is familiar with the code this makes the task of determining the relationships between parts of the code easier, particularly in the context of a large program. This information has not previously been shown in the profile of a program.

The dynamic call-graph constructed from compressed cost centre stacks may look different to a call-graph produced by static analysis of the program, particularly if the program contains many mutually-recursive function definitions.

Compressed stacks ensure that cost centres will only appear in a cost centre stack once, therefore removing the possibility of loops from the final call-graph. This may appear to the programmer to be different to the way in which the program is actually coded. It does not, however, affect the accuracy of the profiling results and the programmer is quickly able to adjust to the way in which the results are displayed. The simplified call-graphs may even make it easier for the programmer to identify expensive portions of the code.

Profiling with cost centre stacks allows the complete set of program costs to be recorded. They are an accurate record of the program's computational behaviour and therefore a true profile of the program in the sense that no statistical averaging has been used to produce the results.

The post-processor allows these results to be explored instantaneously and without any further execution or compilation of the program. This has not previously been possible when profiling a program. Figure 7 shows the complete set of inherited results. These results can be interpreted outside the context of the actual program code; the program graph allows the expensive portion of the code to be identified, leaving the programmer free to identify its cause.

There are a number of profiling and graph-tool options available to the programmer which allow, amongst other things, the most expensive arm of the graph to be displayed, functions to be selected, and flat and inheritance profiles of the program to be produced. None of these options take more than two or three seconds to execute.

The graph in figure 7 clearly shows the distribution of costs in the program, focusing the programmer's attention on the functions c, f, h and j. The programmer can quickly identify the function call from h to j as causing a significant amount of computation.

Using the post-processor it is also possible to select and de-select cost centres. In the example the programmer might have chosen to view the flat profile with the cost centre Main_rev de-selected. The post-processor would accurately subsume the costs of Main_rev to its calling functions, again highlighting Main_j as part of the expensive arm of the program. Repeating this exercise on Main_j would confirm that the call from Main_h to Main_j was instigating most of the program costs.

A similar top-down (as opposed to bottom-up) approach to profiling can be performed using the post-processor. This is easy to achieve without reprofiling and recompiling the program and the time benefits are considerable.

3.3 Overheads

The study of the overheads for the cost centre stack profiling scheme is important. Previous profiling literature has shown that earlier attempts at similar cost collection methods were abandoned because of the extremely high overheads. The success of the cost centre stack method of recording results relies on the fact that the overheads are low enough to make such a system practical. There are a number of overheads to consider:

- The size of the cost centre stack table should not become so large that cost centre stack profiling becomes impossible on normal workstations;
- The time that the program takes to compile and any extra heap space needed during compilation should be acceptable. That is, the extra compilation overheads should be small enough to make cost centre stack profiling preferable to repeated compilations of a cost centre profile. Although most of the changes to the Glasgow Haskell compiler are to the run-time system, the changes to the compiler optimiser and the generation of extra run-time code mean that the size of the executable file is slightly larger;
- Finally, the execution time costs should be small enough to make the collection of costs practical. The run-time overheads should not be unacceptably high and the extra heap needed for execution should not be unacceptably large.

These overheads are considered for the first example program:

Cost centre stacks: Execution of the first example program produces 20 cost centre stacks (when using the -prof -auto-all compile time option). There are a total of 12 cost centres in this program.

Analysing the structure of the cost centre stacks and calculating how many bytes are needed to store this information shows that the size of the cost centre stack table for this program is 528 bytes. Compared with the total size of the executable which GHC produces, 696320 bytes, these extra bytes are insignificant.

Compilation overheads: There is no detectable difference in the size of the heap needed for compilation between the two profilers. The GHC default of 4 Megabytes is used. The cost centre profiler takes a total of 94.3 seconds to compile and link the program. This time is taken from an average of ten compilations using the unix system time command. The cost centre stack profiler takes a total of 98.5 seconds to compile and link the code. This gives a time overhead of 5.57%. These compilation overheads are acceptable.

Executable differences: The cost centre profiler produces an executable file of 696320 bytes. The cost centre stack profiler produces an executable file of 712704 bytes. This gives a 2.35% size overhead when using the cost centre stack profiler.

The execution time measured using the unix time command is averaged over 10 executions of the program. The cost centre profiler produces an executable which runs in 130.5 seconds; the cost centre stack profiler runs in 133.5 seconds. These run-time overheads are 2.29%. The size of the heap needed to execute the program is the same for both profilers.

These results are encouraging for small programs, but the results of some larger programs must also be considered.

3.4   LOLITA results

The LOLITA system is one of the largest test cases available for profiling. The version of LOLITA which is profiled to gather these results contains 39094 lines of Haskell code and 10177 lines of C code. In addition, the system contains 6.79Mb of data.

First example

The LOLITA system is interactive and offers a number of operations to its user. These operations will invoke different parts of the system and consequently will produce different results during profiling. Before any of these operations can be performed the system must load its semantic-net data. At the end of an execution, the LOLITA system saves the semantic-network data structure. As these two operations are required each time the LOLITA system is run, they provide the first test case for the cost centre stack profiler.

When the cost centre stack results are produced, the programmer's attention is drawn to the cost centre stack with the highest costs:

```
<StaticNet_load_Ascii,StaticNet_sNetLoad,StaticNet_sInitData,
 Total_loadData,Okf_mapOKF,IMain_go,> with   157 TICKs
```

At the head of this stack is the cost centre StaticNet_load_Ascii. This cost centre stack alone accounts for 24.3% of the total execution time. These large costs are due to the loading of the LOLITA semantic-net data structure. The sequence of cost centres to this particular point in the program is clearly shown.

The investigation of the cost centre stack profile is facilitated by the use of the graph-tool and post-processor. There are a considerable number of cost centre stacks to analyse and perhaps only the most diligent programmer is prepared to look through the cost centre stack output to find the expensive stacks.

The output is loaded into the graph tool; it contains 66 different nodes and 83 arcs between these nodes. For this reason the graph is large and cannot be seen in a single window display. The programmer is able to use the virtual display window in the bottom right-hand corner to view the remainder of the results.

The programmer may find that the post-processing and graph-tool functions are an easier way of analysing the profiling results. Consider the following examples of post-processing:

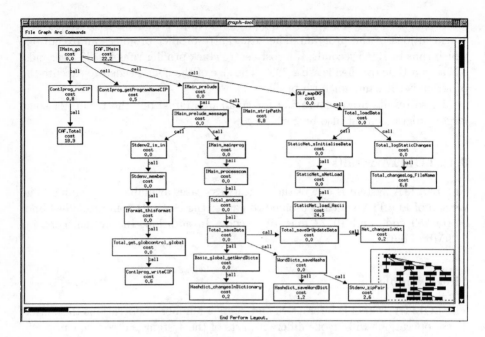

Fig. 8. Graph-tool view of all stacks with non-zero costs

– Using the post-processing tool the programmer can display only those parts of the graph which have non-zero costs. A reduction of the graph of the LOLITA system, to only those cost centre stacks with associated costs, is shown in figure 8. The graph is reduced by more than a half; it now contains 31 cost centres and 30 arcs. It is clearly easier to read the results in this form as they appear on a single screen. In general, a programmer will only be interested in a profile of the program which shows the actual program costs. Further, it is then possible for the programmer to select the cost centre stack with the highest associated costs, leading to a very rapid analysis of the profiling results.

– Post-processing also allows the programmer to select particular functions which he is interested in profiling. This facility is demonstrated on the LOLITA cost centre stack profile by selecting the following four cost centres: Total_loadData, IMain_go, IMain_prelude and Total_saveData. It may be useful for the programmer to gather profiling costs in terms of these four functions, as it allows the developers to see how much time is spent loading and saving the semantic net; how much time is spent in the prelude function of the IMain module and how much time is spent in the main function go. Those functions which are not selected have their costs subsumed by those functions which are selected; see figure 9. The results do not account for 100% of the overall execution costs as some of the results are attributed to constant applicative forms (CAFs); these are top-level values which are not functions, x=[1..], for example.

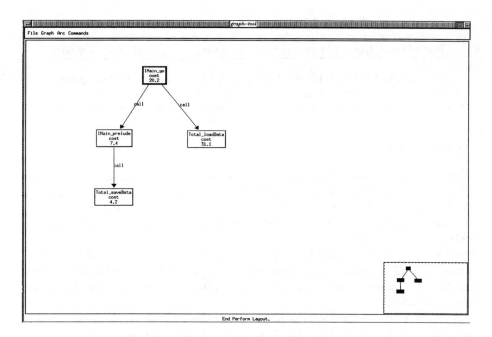

Fig. 9. Graph-tool view with selected cost centres

These post-processing facilities allow the programmer to explore the profiling costs after program execution. In this example, the programmer is able to see that loading the semantic-net data accounts for 31.1% of the total execution time. The LOLITA prelude accounts for 7.4% of the program costs; this involves formatting and printing the credit information and information regarding the authors of the system. At least 4.2% of the program's execution time is due to saving the semantic net structure. Some of the saving costs (18.9%) have been attributed to a CAF in the `Total` module; this can be seen in figure 8, but not in figure 9. It is expected that later versions of the cost centre stack profiler will improve this situation; later versions of the GHC cost centre profiler are more explicit regarding the cost information for CAFs[5]. A further 20.2% of the program costs are subsumed to the cost centre `go`; this corresponds to the `main` function of LOLITA.

These results show a clear mechanism by which a programmer can collect and view profiling results. The post-processing facilities are clearly useful in such a large example and the way in which they are able to filter large collections of results gives the cost centre stack profiling scheme potential.

---

[5] Now that the prototype has been tested and has provided satisfactory results, it is proposed that the cost centre stack profiler is implemented on GHC 2.02.

Table 1. LOLITA results for template analysis

Input	Comp. time	Exec. size	Run-time	#Stacks	Depth	#Push
(*i*)	50123.7 (10.2%)	41279488 (7%)	110.9 (70.6%)	1807	112	278081
(*ii*)	same	same	55.4 (130.8%)	1766	94	12321

Second example

The second example considers a LOLITA function which makes use of a far greater percentage of the total code. Template analysis takes as its input a passage of text. This is then parsed and semantically analysed to produce a network of semantic nodes from which information can be scanned to match a collection of templates.

Two sets of input data were tested. The first was a passage of text taken from the *Daily Telegraph* newspaper concerning an IRA terrorist incident (*i*); it contained 74 words. The second piece of data was the sentence "The cat sat on the mat" (*ii*).

The first set of data clearly required more processing than the second, though using these two sets of data allows the profiling overheads required for each to be compared. Most of the time taken in (*ii*) is due to the loading of the semantic network.

Table 1 shows: the input data used; the time taken to compile the LOLITA system using the cost centre stack profiler (the difference between this and the cost centre profiler is shown in brackets); the size of the executable file produced by the cost centre stack profiler (the difference is again shown in brackets); the template analysis runtime (again the difference is in brackets); the number of cost centre stacks produced as output; the depth of the largest cost centre stack and the number of times a cost centre was *pushed* onto a cost centre stack during program execution.

As expected the larger input causes more computation and as a consequence of this the mechanics of cost centre stack profiling are considerably more detailed - this is shown by the number of push operations performed during each execution. The depth of the largest cost centre stacks are similar for both sets of input; 112 and 94 cost centres respectively. Since large stacks are constructed for the small input as well as the large, many of the 265760 push operations (the difference between the two tests) will be performed on memoised stacks - this accounts for the reduction in overheads when considering a larger input. Overheads are covered in more detail in the next section.

As well as the post-processing functions shown above the cost centre stack profiler produces accurate inheritance results. These are particularly useful in the analysis of large graphs. There are two observations which can be made about inherited results:

– If a cost centre has a small number of inherited costs and is itself inexpensive then there is no way that any performance improvement made to this function will help to improve the program. This is not true of the cost centre profiler where cost centres with low or even zero costs may still contain a performance bug;

— Conversely, if a cost centre has a large inherited cost and is itself inexpensive then it may well be worth some attention, as this function may be the cause of large costs lower down in the program graph. This is different to the way in which the programmer would interpret a flat profile of the program.

Using these observations and the post-processing facilities, the programmer is able to perform a comprehensive analysis of his program. This will enable improvements to be made to parts of the program without any further compilation, execution or profiling of the code. The cost of post-processing, even for very large programs, is negligible.

3.5 nofib results

The previous results are further supported by the results of testing the cost centre stack profiler on the nofib benchmark [Par92]. The nofib benchmark suite specifically consists of:

— Source code for real Haskell programs which can be compiled and run;
— Sample inputs (workloads) to feed to the compiled programs, along with the expected outputs;
— Specific rules for compiling and running the benchmark programs and reporting the results; and
— Sample scripts showing how the results should be reported.

Those programs included in the nofib suite are divided into three subsets, Real, Imaginary and Spectral (between Real and Imaginary). The results displayed in this paper are of Real and Spectral programs; this means that they perform a useful task and are not implausibly small (or large). They are also written by someone trying to get a job done, not by someone trying to make a pedagogical or stylistic point. The results of Imaginary programs such as queens and fib etc. are specifically avoided.

The version of the nofib suite used in these tests dates from June 1996. All the tests were carried out on the same machine[6]. The standard optimiser (-O) was used during the compilation and the compile-time flags were set so that all top-level functions were profiled (-prof -auto-all). The compiled programs were run with the time profiler (-pT) and the stats option (-s) so that the heap and time usage could be recorded.

In the majority of cases the supplied input was used during program execution, although some of the input data was extended to increase the runtime of

---

[6] System Model : SPARCclassic, Main Memory : 96 MB, Virtual Memory : 353 MB, CPU Type : 50 MHz microSPARC, ROM Version : 2.12, OS Version : SunOS 4.1.3C.

Table 2. `nofib` benchmark results

Program	Comp. time sec. (diff.)	Run-time sec. (diff.)	Cost centres	#Push
Real subset				
ebnf2ps	2518.5 (13.5%)	3.9 (84.8%)	225	34335
gamteb	816.0 (13.2%)	216.3 (100.1%)	57	356142
gg	1097.7 (11.1%)	14.4 (73.2%)	133	76272
maillist	106.8 (3.8%)	20.1 (6.0%)	10	5367
mkhprog	476.3 (13.9%)	0.4 (42.8%)	30	134
parser	1331.9 (7.7%)	79.5 (384.7%)	78	1375957
pic	475.3 (6.5%)	11.9 (6.25%)	26	6885
prolog	442.0 (12.6%)	4.3 (358.3%)	64	40847
reptile	1116.2 (9.9%)	7.3 (38.0%)	253	30051
Spectral subset				
ansi	141.2 (5.7%)	0.7 (133.3%)	26	113
banner	265.6 (0.2%)	0.6 (10.9%)	9	3359
clausify	132.7 (16.6%)	14.8 (33.3%)	26	693542
eliza	284.2 (7.12%)	2.6 (144.8%)	17	24696
minimax	379.0 (6.6%)	5.0 (152.3%)	40	114384
primetest	216.6 (6.0%)	153.3 (2.4%)	21	24062

the programs. The only other changes made to the programs were for debugging purposes (incorrect Makefiles etc.). Not all of the programs included in the suite compiled correctly; some required a more up-to-date version of the compiler (0.24+) and some of the programs had files missing. All of the programs which compiled and ran correctly under GHC 0.22 are included, that is to say, this data was not selected on the basis that it produced favourable results.

For each program tested, the results of compiling and running the program under the cost centre stack compiler have been recorded. The difference in the overheads of the cost centre stack compiler and a standard version of GHC 0.22 (using the -prof -auto-all compiler flags) is shown in brackets. Statistics recorded include compile-time, runtime, the number of cost centres in the program and the number of push operations performed by the cost centre stack profiler. The difference in the total heap usage is not shown as in each case these overheads were negligible. The results can be seen in table 2. Analysis of the results shows the following:

Compile-time: Between 3.8% and 13.9% overhead. This is due to the time needed to produce the larger executable file. The size of the executable files was expected to be slightly larger because of the changes made to the compiler optimiser and to the run-time system.

Heap usage: No detectable difference, as expected, since most of the changes made to the compiler are to the run-time system.

Run-time difference: This is where the most overheads are anticipated, as most of the profiler changes are to the run-time system. These range from 2.4% to 384.7%. These overheads are dependent on the structure of the program (see section 4). Even when the run-time overheads are 384% (`parser`), this only means an extra 59 seconds of execution time, which accounts for just 4.4% of a single compilation of that program.

The relation between, the number of cost centres and push operations, and the overheads is discussed in the next section.

These results show that the cost centre stack profiler should be used if the cost centres are going to be moved one or more times in the analysis of a program. If this is the case, a substantial amount of time will be saved.

4 Complexity Analysis

How can the difference in run-time overheads found in the testing of the cost centre stack profiler be explained? The answer is that the run-time overheads are dependent on the structure and style of the program. For example,

- the complexity of the cost centre stack table will increase with the number of arcs in the call-graph. The greater the functional dependency, the greater the overheads involved in creating the cost centre stacks;
- the more cost centres there are per unit of code, the greater the overhead of managing the cost centre stacks. The number of top-level functions may be increased by the programmer's style, for example, if the programmer does not use many local function definitions.

It is important to note that it is not simply the size of a program which increases the overheads. This is shown by the LOLITA results, for example, where the overheads are lower than the overheads of programs hundreds of times smaller. It is the possibilities allowed in the call-graph, which are fulfilled at runtime, that increase the overheads.

Of course this analysis (as in the `nofib` results) is based on the assumption that all top-level functions are profiled (`-auto-all`). This need not always be the case. The cost centre stack profiling method is equally valid with less cost centres in the code, in fact the programmer might find high-level information, gained from a profile containing less cost centres, more informative at the early stages of profiling. It would also be the case that the use of less cost centres would reduce the overheads of the cost centre stack profiler.

A worst- and average-case analysis of the cost centre stack profiler may be found in [Jar96] - the analysis also considers the overheads of this profiling scheme according to different program structures. For example if the call-graph is a tree, where each function is called by only one other function, then the complexity of the algorithm is logarithmic over the number of cost centres in the program.

5 Debugging and tracing

There are a number of further applications of this cost centre stack technique, two of which are the debugging and tracing of Haskell programs.

There are two types of error found in Haskell programs which are particularly awkward for the programmer to detect:

- The first is non-termination as there is usually no helpful information given as to why this is the case.
- The second is the familiar head [] error. When this error is presented it is often very difficult to determine what the caller was. Part of the problem is that the programmer wants to know what built the thunk (head []) rather than the function which demanded it.

It is proposed that the cost centre stack profiler be modified so that it outputs the current stack of cost centres when an error occurs in a program. This means that the location of an error can be determined immediately; it is also possible to trace the path which the program took to that erroneous piece of code. This limits the search required by the programmer and in initial tests has provided invaluable information in the debugging of the LOLITA system.

It is also possible to output the cost centre stacks as the program is executing. Although this provides a lot of information it does allow the programmer to watch the order of evaluation of expressions in the execution of a program. Alternatively the programmer could stop the program, pressing control-C, and the current cost centre stack could be printed. In the past the only way to see the sequence of lazy evaluation was to watch the program stack. This was not easy and was difficult to interpret even for the experienced programmer.

The cost centre stack approach to debugging and tracing is very flexible as the programmer can insert cost centres into the code where he thinks it is necessary, therefore controlling the output of the debugger just as a C programmer might add printf statements to his code. Integrating the tracing and debugging functions with the post-processor may provide the programmer with a useful environment in which to profile, view and debug his Haskell programs.

6 Conclusions

The development of the cost centre stack profiler was based on the results of a series of case studies implemented over a three-year period. The case studies investigated the profiling of the LOLITA system, a large-scale lazy functional system written in 50,000 lines of Haskell code. This study highlighted a number of problems with the current profiling tools and in response to these the cost centre stack profiler was designed.

The cost centre stack profiler collects results which can then be post-processed after the execution of a program. The post-processor implements a scheme whereby the programmer can select and reselect cost centres in his code and view the results accordingly. This enables the results to be displayed at different levels in the program without any further compilation or execution of the code.

The implementation of the cost centre stack profiler and the post-processor provides a number of benefits to the programmer:

- The new method of profiling provides an opportunity for a reduction in the time needed to profile Haskell programs.
- The new method of profiling extends the results presented by previous profilers in so much as the accurate inheritance of shared program costs can be achieved without having to recompile and rerun the program.
- The new method of profiling provides these new facilities without imposing an unacceptable overhead on the compilation or execution of a Haskell program.

It is also considered that this method will offer assistance in the debugging and tracing of Haskell programs.

References

[CCP95] Clayman, S.; Clack, C.; Parrott, D. J.: Lexical Profiling: Theory and Practice, Journal of Functional Programming, Volume 5, Part 2, 1995

[LGa94] Long, D.; Garigliano, G.: Reasoning by Analogy and Causality: A Model and Application, Ellis Horwood, 1994

[GKK82] Graham, S. L.; Kessler, P. B.; Kusick, M. K.: gprof: a call graph execution profiler, ACM Sigplan Notices, 17(6):120-126, Symposium on Computer Construction, June 1982

[Jar96] Jarvis, S. A.: Profiling Large-scale Lazy Functional Programs, Ph.D. Thesis, University of Durham, 1996

[MoJ95] Morgan, R. G.; Jarvis, S. A.: Profiling Large-scale Lazy Functional Programs, In Proceedings of High Performance Functional Computing, A. P. W. Bohm and J. T. Feo Editors, Lawrence Livermore National Laboratory, USA, pp. 222-234, April 1995

[Par92] Partain, W.: The nofib Benchmark Suite of Haskell Programs, Department of Computer Science, University of Glasgow, 1992

[RuW93] Runciman, C.; Wakeling, D.: Heap Profiling of Lazy Functional Programs, Journal of Functional Programming, Volume 3, Part 2, 1993

[SaP95] Sansom, P. M.; Peyton Jones, S. L.: Time and space profiling for non-strict, higher-order functional languages, 22nd ACM Symposium on Principles of Programming Languages, San Francisco, California, January 1995

Two-Pass Heap Profiling:
A Matter of Life and Death

Colin Runciman and Niklas Röjemo

Department of Computer Science, University of York,
Heslington, York, YO1 5DD, UK
(e-mail: {colin,rojemo}@cs.york.ac.uk)

Abstract. A heap profile is a chart showing the contents of heap memory throughout a computation. Contents are depicted abstractly by showing how much space is occupied by memory cells in each of several classes. A good heap profiler can use a variety of attributes of memory cells to define a classification. Effective profiling usually involves a *combination* of attributes. The ideal profiler gives full support for combination in two ways. First, a section of the heap of interest to the programmer can be specified by constraining the values of *any* combination of cell attributes. Secondly, no matter what attributes are used to specify such a section, a heap profile can be obtained for that section only, and *any* other attribute can be used to define the classification.

Achieving this ideal is not simple for some combinations of attributes. A heap profile is derived by interpolation of a series of *censuses* of heap contents at different stages. The obvious way to obtain census data is to traverse the *live heap* at intervals throughout the computation. This is fine for static attributes (eg. What type of value does this memory cell represent?), and for dynamic attributes that can be determined for each cell by examining the heap at any given moment (eg. From which function closures can this cell be reached?). But some attributes of cells can only be determined retrospectively by *post-mortem inspection* as a cell is overwritten or garbage-collected (eg. Is this cell ever used again?). Now we see the problem: if a profiler supports *both* live *and* post-mortem attributes, how can we implement the ideal of unrestricted combinations? That is the problem we solve in this paper. We give techniques for profiling a heap section specified in terms of both live and post-mortem attributes. We show how to generate live-attribute profiles of a section of the heap specified using post-mortem attributes, and vice versa.

1 Variety and combination in heap profiling

We begin by reviewing the different kinds of memory-cell attributes on which heap profilers to-date have been based, and how these attributes have been combined.

1.1 Static attributes

The original heap profiler of the kind we are concerned with in this paper dealt with just two attributes of heap cells [RW93]. A *producer profile* classifies cells by the program components that created them; a *construction profile* classifies cells according to the kinds of values they represent. Both the producer and the construction of a cell are *static* attributes; they can be determined at compile-time and permanently recorded in each cell on allocation. The initial implementation took *censuses* of the *live heap* at fixed intervals, recording in a log-file the numbers of live cells with each different combination of attribute values. The log file was afterwards converted by a post-processor into a chart, also termed a *heap profile*.

In many instances, static heap profiles are quite effective as a means of locating space-faults. By taking slices through the heap in more than one dimension a programmer can often pin-point the reason for any excesses in demand for heap memory. *This is what makes heap profiles particularly effective: the possibility of combining attributes and profiling only a section of the heap.*

1.2 Dynamic attributes

Heap profilers can answer a wider range of questions about memory-use if they are extended to work also with *dynamic* properties of cells. For example, a *lifetime profile* classifies cells according to the total time for which they are part of the live heap. A cell's lifetime cannot be determined statically, but it is an *invariant* attribute of the cell. If live-heap census data includes creation-times, lifetime profiling can be implemented by post-processing [RuR96a], and combinations with static attributes are straightforward.

However, some important dynamic attributes of cells are *not* invariant. For example, the changing graph-structure of the heap is used in a *retainer profile* to classify cells according to the active program components that retain them. This is an *instantaneous* attribute: it can be determined for each cell by examining the heap at any given moment. So censuses of the live heap are sufficient to obtain information for a retainer profile of the full heap, or of a statically-specified section. But combining retainer and lifetime attributes is a problem: because the retainers of a cell can vary between censuses, there is no consistent way to record necessary counts for post-processing. Our earlier profilers [RuR96a] simply forbade this combination.

1.3 Post-mortem attributes

Some cell attributes useful for heap-profiling cannot be determined from live-heap censuses, even with post-processing. Complementary techniques based on *post-mortem censuses* are needed for such attributes: data is gathered from *dead cells* (as they are over-written or garbage-collected) instead of from the live heap. For example, a *biographical profile* [RöR96] puts each cell into one of four classes depending on the answers to two questions: has it been used (yet), and will it be used (again)? Like the lifetime and retainer attributes this classification is dynamic, but it is neither invariant nor instantaneous. If a creation time is recorded in each cell the post-mortem technique can also be used for static profiles, so combinations between post-mortem and static attributes are fine.

attributes	static	dynamic	
		live	dead
static	●	●	●
dynamic live	●	●	○
dynamic dead	●	○	●

Fig. 1. In previous heap profilers, though most combinations of cell attributes are supported (●), others are not (○).

Lifetime profiling is actually *easier* to treat as a post-mortem attribute. But combining a post-mortem attribute with one based on the instantaneous live-heap again poses a problem.

1.4 Why worry about missing combinations?

The ideal of unrestricted combination seems a natural design goal for profilers. For aesthetic reasons, at least, it would be desirable to eliminate the ○ entries in Figure 1. But do they really matter in practice?

We can answer this question from our experience of developing and applying a profiler that supports both retainer-sets and biographical phases, among other cell attributes, *but not in combination*. We have found that we often resort to some means of *approximating* a combination of retainer profiles and biographical profiles. For example, suppose a biographical profile reveals a large volume of *drag* cells — as defined in §2.2. We can use a (static) producer profile for the drag section of the heap to identify a set F of functions that create drag cells. Now a retainer profile for the (statically-specified) section of the heap produced by F *may* point to the retaining components that prevent drag cells from being reclaimed. But the technique fails if F produces many other cells apart from the problematic drag population. One ends up trying to gauge the degree of correlation between two separate heap profiles, one using static and biographical attributes and the other using static and retainer attributes. What is really needed is a *single* heap profile based on an *exact* combination.

2 Live-heap and post-mortem techniques

The combination of biographical and retainer profiling was the motivating example that prompted us to look for some way to combine live-heap and post mortem profiling. We shall use this example combination to provide a specific illustration of a more general technique. This section explains in a little more detail how the two different types of profile are implemented.

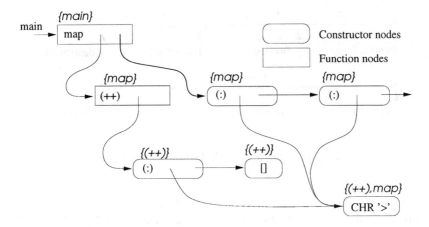

Fig. 2. Graph annotations during a retainer census. The sets above the nodes are retainer sets. Note that the character node is shared between map and (++).

2.1 Live-heap profiling of retainers

A census during retainer profiling involves traversing the live heap, annotating every cell with the set of its *retainers* — the active program components that have most immediate access to it. *Active program components* are function closures, either in the heap or on the stack, and named top level expressions. The annotations are *sets* of retainers because a cell can have more than one retainer due to sharing — see Figure 2 for an example. Because the retainers of a cell depend on the structure of a constantly mutating graph, the profiler must redetermine current retainer sets for each live cell at each census.

For fuller details of retainer profiling, and examples of its use, see [RuR96a].

2.2 Post-mortem profiling of biographical phases

Biographical profiling uses the times of four important events in a cell's lifetime: creation, first use, last use, and destruction. The intervals between these events are the phases used for a biographical classification of a cell. A cell in the live heap, but not yet used for the first time is in its *lag* phase. A cell that has been used, but not yet used for the last time, is in its *use* phase. A cell remaining in the live heap after its last use is in its *drag* phase until it is finally destroyed. A cell that is *never* used remains throughout its existence in a distinct *void* phase. The four different phases are illustrated in Figure 3.

As long as the cell remains part of the live graph it might or might not be used (again) which makes it impossible to distinguish between void and lag, or between drag and use. Only when the time comes for a cell to be detached from the live graph and garbage-collected, or over-written in a graph update, can its phase at *all earlier* points in the computation be determined. Biographical profiling is therefore implemented using post-mortem censuses.

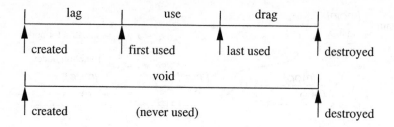

Fig. 3. The four biographical phases of a heap cell.

To support biographical profiling every cell is enlarged to accommodate three extra fields — its times of creation, first use (if any) and *latest* use (if any). During a census all garbage cells are collected and cell-counts for each combination of event times are written to a log file. Since these cells cannot play any further role in the computation, it is correct to interpret recorded times of their *latest* uses as the times of their *last* uses. All times are reckoned by the number of censuses that have occurred. This makes the time of the final event for a cell, its destruction, implicitly available in the immediately following post-mortem census. Cells overwritten between censuses are also treated as if they were garbage collected during the immediately following census. As usual, a postprocessor generates a heap profile from the census data.

For fuller details of biographical profiling, and an example of its use, see [RöR96].

3 Combination by two-pass profiling

3.1 Approaches to combination

How can the two forms of profile — those based on live-heap censuses, and those based on post-mortem censuses — be combined? There are two obvious alternatives:

1. We make retainer information available during a post-mortem census. This can be done, but only by attaching an *unbounded* auxiliary data structure to every cell in the heap. It would be necessary to maintain a list of each cell's retainer sets at every census during the cell's lifetime. Since the purpose of profiling is often to deal with a program that already uses too much space, a post-mortem reimplementation of retainer profiling does not seem to be a feasible option.
2. We make biographical information available during a live-heap census. Since full biographical information is not available until a cell is destroyed, taking this option requires a means of *looking into the future* to get the necessary biographical data. How can we know the future events of a computation? By rehearsing the whole computation in advance, and remembering all the

```
if cell has been used then
    if cell will be used (again) then use
    else                                drag
else
    if cell will be used        then lag
    else                             void
```

Fig. 4. Decision tree to determine the phase of a live cell. The *italic* parts are from the future.

critical events. This will roughly double execution time, but that is more tolerable than putting further strain on heap memory.

3.2 Back from the future — minimising the luggage

However it is done, we must expect time travel to be expensive! So it is important to restrict our requirements to the *essential* information we need about the future.

Suppose we observe a cell during a live-heap census involving retainers. What information is immediately available about the timing of the cell's main biographical events, in relation to this census? At least we know that the cell was created before this, and will only be destroyed some time later. We can also know whether it has yet been used for a first time by introducing a single marker-bit to the cell (and extra code to update the bit appropriately). Putting these pieces of information together it is possible to classify each cell as either use/drag or lag/void.

We need just one more piece of information to assign a cell to exactly one phase: will the cell be used (again) in the future? See Figure 4. It must be possible to answer this question for every cell at every census. It is necessary and sufficient to know for each cell the time of its last use (if any). That is the information we must fetch 'from the future'.

3.3 Implementing a time machine

So much for what we need. Next how to obtain it. As we have already indicated, the broad plan is to run the program twice. The first time, take post-mortem censuses and record essential information only. The second time, take live-heap censuses using the saved post-mortem data as a source of any information needed about future events.

Two aspects of the implementation need special attention. First, to be sure that the post-mortem data from the first run provides accurate information about events in the second, the two executions must correspond exactly. In a functional language, if we supply the same input then we will get the same computation. The implementation therefore saves all input to the program in a buffer file during the first run. For the second run, all input is taken from the buffer, and all output is suppressed.

Secondly, there must be some way to identify as *one and the same* a cell for which a time of last use is recorded in the first run, and a cell encountered in a census during the second run. Alternatives include:

1. Use cell addresses. This idea cannot work. The same memory location may be re-used many times by different cells.
2. Number each cell as it is allocated. This is excessive. Many cells are so short-lived that they are never seen by a live-heap profiler: they live and die between one census and the next.
3. Number cells lazily — by need. Allocate a number to a cell only when it is first seen during a live-heap census. For this to work, censuses must be taken in each execution at *exactly the same points in the computation*. Censuses timed by system clocks are not precise enough for this. The solution is to time the interval between censuses using memory allocations as clock-ticks.

Our implementation uses numbering by need. The information saved during the first run represents a partial function from cell numbers to times of last use. If t is the time of the last use of cell N, then $t + 1$ is stored in the Nth byte of the saved data. For cells never used, the byte is zero. Since every cell allocated a number contributes to the final heap profile, every offset in the saved data is accessed in the second run.

4 Results obtained

4.1 An example profile

As discussed in section 1, without access to the combination of retainer and biographical profiling a programmer is often left with two charts and a question. See Figure 5 for an example. Now we can also provide the answer! See Figure 6.

4.2 The cost of two-pass profiles

The obvious overhead of two-pass profiling is the extra time for a repeated computation. We also need extra space to store the input to ensure identical computations in each run of the program. Both of these extra costs are easy to estimate: profiling takes twice as long, and all input must be saved in an auxiliary file.

But what about the cost of storing post-mortem data between executions? In the worst case, every cell ever allocated is part of the live-heap for at least one census, so every cell must have a slot in the post-mortem data. In practice, however, none of the programs we have tested has been even close to this worst case behaviour. Table 1 gives examples of some typical figures. The programs here are: nfib 23, the usual (artificial) benchmark program; mastermind, which controls the board in the game with the same name; nhccomp, the heart of the nhc compiler; and diff, a file comparison program. Even for the least favourable example, less than 10% of allocated cells are numbered. For the largest and most complex application, the nhc compiler itself, the figure is less than 2%.

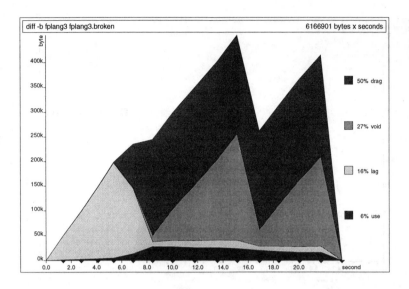

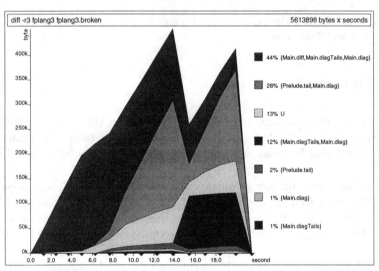

Fig. 5. A separate biographical profile (upper chart) and a retainer profile (lower chart) are not always easy to combine in one's head. For example, are the two void peaks populated by the same cells as the two peaks retained by `Prelude.tail` and `Main.diag`?

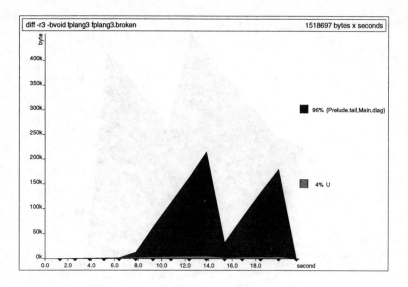

Fig. 6. The answer to the question in Figure 5. Yes, the void is retained by `Prelude.tail` and `Main.diag`.

5 Related work

This paper has concentrated on a specific problem in the *implementation* of heap profiling. See [RuR96b] for a series of tutorial *applications* illustrating various techniques. Applications are also discussed in [RW93,RuR96a,RöR96], for example.

Though many programming languages have heap-based implementations we know of little work apart from our own on tools to examine the make-up of heap memory during a computation. (We do not count profilers based on *allocation counts*, as these are not a reliable guide to the continuing size and content of the live heap.)

The earliest systems profiling heap contents gave only summary statistics. They were developed by researchers who mainly wished to understand and improve the memory characteristics of *implementation techniques*, not specific application programs. For example, there was a published study of this kind in the late '70s for a SNOBOL4 system[RGH78], and another a decade later for a fixed-combinator implementation of the lazy functional language SASL[HV88].

Various profiling tools have been developed as part of the ghc optimising compiler project at Glasgow, as described in [SPJ96,Sa94]. The ghc profiler assigns the costs of heap memory to the producing *cost centres* defined either implicitly (eg. each function is a cost centre) or by explicit annotation of expressions. But ghc does not support combinations of attributes of the kind we have considered in this paper.

	allocated cells	numbered cells	ratio (%)	censuses taken
nfib 23	812887	605	0.1	13
mastermind	275907	2480	0.9	20
nhccomp	4598625	67229	1.5	19
		75630	1.6	38
		85458	1.8	76
diff	1008757	49459	4.9	9
		54380	5.4	15
		66397	6.6	30
		90195	8.9	60

Table 1. Typically, information only has to be saved about a small percentage of allocated cells. The entries in the 'numbered cells' column also indicate the size of the saved file in bytes.

6 Concluding remarks

We have reported a specialised application of a common design principle: avoid unnecessary restrictions. Many computer programs are used to classify data in several ways. Such programs are often far more useful if classifications can be combined: naturally, users expect *all* combinations to be available, not just a restricted subset.

But what if a full implementation supporting every possible combination is expensive — at development-time, or at run-time, or both? Is it worth it? For our heap-profiler, yes it is. Finding and fixing space-faults in functional programs involves posing and answering a series of questions. The very abstractness of functional programs that makes them attractive also makes answering many of these questions impossible without implementation-based profiling tools. The more questions the tools can answer, the better the programmer can be informed. It is part of the ethos of heap-profiling to employ even *brute-force* methods to gather and sift data about how heap memory is used during a computation. The costs of double-execution, and of introducing (yet more) auxiliary files, are worth paying to provide a full range of live-heap and post-mortem sections and profiles in combination. The extra costs are only incurred when a combination of live and post-mortem profiling is needed. As we have shown, it is still practical to construct profiles of large programs such as compilers.

To illustrate the technique of two-pass profiling, we have concentrated on the example of combining retainer sets and biographical phases. But the approach is readily adapted for other combinations of live-heap and post-mortem attributes.

Current heap-profilers could be further refined in various ways. For example, there is scope for refining the precision of information in biographical profiles, since not all cells in the 'use' phase are used equally often. In constructor/closure profiles specific source-locations corresponding to individual occurrences of symbols would sometimes be more informative than references to entire bodies of functions. But whatever further additions or refinements are made to the repertoire of cell attributes, the principle of unrestricted combination should apply — even when it's a matter of life and death!

Acknowledgements

During the work reported here NR was supported by a post-doctoral scholarship from TFR, the Swedish Research Council for Engineering Sciences. Our thanks also to the referees.

References

[HV88]   Hartel, P.H., Veen, A.H.: Statistics on graph reduction of SASL programs. *Software — Practice and Experience*, 18:239–253, 1988.

[RGH78]   Ripley, G.D., Griswold, R.E., Hanson, D.R.: Performance of storage management in an implementation of SNOBOL4. *IEEE Transactions on Software Engineering*, SE-4:130–137, 1978.

[RuR96a]   Runciman, C. and Röjemo, N.: New dimensions in heap profiling. *Journal of Functional Programming*, 6(4):587–620, 1996.

[RuR96b]   Runciman, C. and Röjemo, N.: Heap profiling for space efficiency. In *2nd Intl. School on Advanced Functional Programming*, pages 159–183. Springer LNCS 1129, 1996.

[RW93]   Runciman, C. and Wakeling, D.: Heap profiling of lazy functional programs. *Journal of Functional Programming*, 3(2):217–245, 1993.

[RöR96]   Röjemo, N. and Runciman, C.: Lag, drag, void and use — heap profiling and space-efficient compilation revisited. In *Proc. Intl. Conf. on Functional Programming*, pages 34–41. ACM Press, 1996.

[Sa94]   Sansom, P.M.: *Execution profiling for non-strict functional languages*. Ph.D. thesis, Computing Science, University of Glasgow, UK, 1994.

[SPJ96]   Sansom, P.M., Peyton Jones, S.L.: Time and space profiling for non-strict higher-order functional languages. *Proc. ACM Conf. on Principles of Programming Languages (POPL'95)*, pages 355–366, ACM Press, 1995.

First Class File I/O

Marco Pil

Computing Science Institute, University of Nijmegen,
Postbus 9010, 6500 GL Nijmegen, The Netherlands
e-mail: marcop@cs.kun.nl

Abstract. In most functional languages little attention has been paid
to file I/O. The file system is poorly typed at best and some classes of
objects, in particular functions, cannot be stored on disk at all. In this
article we present a mature type system for typing files. We also discuss
briefly how we plan to implement the storage of functions in files. We
make use of the concept of dynamic types, as introduced in Abadi et
al., which provide an interface between statically and dynamically typed
parts of a program. We have modified the concept of dynamic types to
include polymorphic types in a natural way and we are implementing this
modified system of dynamic types in the functional language *Clean*. We
have developed a simple run-time matching algorithm for the dynamic
type checks. We present some of the problems we encountered when the
system of dynamic types is implemented to its full extent in a language
that already has an elaborate type system. Finally we show that the
same concepts that we used for constructing the file system can be used
for communication between independently running programs in general.

1 Introduction

In the framework of a functional operating system, an operating system that is
specified and implemented in a functional language, one of the main problems is
the communication between independent processes (programs). When programs
communicate with other programs, or possibly with incarnations of themselves,
flexibility is demanded. Programs do not have to know about their mutual existence and can be terminated before others are launched. Good examples of such
communication are asynchronous message passing and file I/O.

In this article we will focus mainly on file I/O, but the methods we discuss and
the tools we present will be equally applicable to other forms of communication
between independent programs.

When processes communicate, both sender and receiver must abide by the
same set of mutually known agreements: the communication protocol. The agree-
ment most commonly made for file I/O is that files consist of series of characters.
All data that is written to and read from files must be coded in a series of characters.

Obviously, this protocol is very primitive: for all datatypes the user has to
define encoding and decoding mechanisms. Furthermore it is hardly possible to
store functions in files.

In functional languages functions are viewed as 'first class citizens'. They can be passed to other functions or yielded as a result, just like any other 'first-order' value But, in contrast to their 'first class' status, they cannot be stored on disk like the basic datatypes. Overcoming this imperfection of the language would be a real improvement, not only for reasons of orthogonality. Functions in files occur often in everyday programming. An executable, for instance, can be viewed as just being a function: it would be nice to be able to apply the contents of one file — a compiler — to the contents of another file — the source program — yielding yet another file — a new executable.

In concept a function definition cannot be treated as an object in the program in which it is defined. To simulate function manipulation, we have to settle for a *description* of its function definition. This description can be read from file and must then be interpreted by the program. In fact, this principle holds for functions in memory too: only a description of the function has been stored, which is interpreted by the CPU. In order to make the interpretation by the program efficient, we can choose the representation of functions in files in such way that the interpretation does not have to be done by the program, but can be done by the CPU right away.

The type system might provide the more flexible protocol we are looking for. Types can ensure that an action such as the one described above is safe: the data that is interpreted as a function will at least be a representation of a function of the right type.

Clean has an elaborate static type system, based on a combination of Hindley-Milner and Mycroft typing, extended with uniqueness types, existential types, and type constructor classes. We would like to equip the file system with a comparably rich type system, in which objects can be stored without having to convert them to series of characters explicitly. This leads to the formulation of our goal: *the construction of a strongly typed file system in which any object may be stored that can be expressed in the* Clean *programming language*. The objects in memory should become fully interchangeable with objects in files.

n this article we present an extension of the type system of Clean with a form of dynamic typing such that the file system can be typed properly (section 3). Most of that is due to Abadi, Cardelli & Pierce [ACP89, ACP91] and Leroy & Mauny [LM93]; we simplified deduction rules and the matching algorithm and integrated dynamics in Clean's current type system. We discuss why 'dynamic' types serve our purposes best (section 2.1) and how we are implementing them in Clean (section 4). In section 4.2 we discuss how we plan to implement the storage of functions in files.

2 Typing the file system

Types can be used in a protocol for performing file I/O. For this we must make the types of the objects in the files explicit. In a file exactly one object can be stored. We say that the file has type File σ iff the object stored in the file has type σ. This type should be stored together with the file in some way. An object can only be read from a file if its type component matches the type that was expected by the context defined by the program.

Typing file I/O differs from typing ordinary expressions because there is no static link between the name of a file and its contents and thus its type. Due to this fact, types of the parts of a program that perform file I/O can only be checked at run-time, when reading or writing. For this reason a certain amount of dynamic typing is unavoidable.

Typing file I/O is not the only problem area in which dynamic typing is a necessity. In general, programs that communicate data with their environment cannot be typed statically.

But we do not want our entire language to become dynamically typed. Statically typed programming languages allow earlier error checking, and generation of more efficient object code than languages where all type consistency checks have to be performed at run-time.

We are looking for a *hybrid* type system in which both forms of type checking can coexist in a sound way, offering the advantages of both type systems. An interface has to be defined between the statically and dynamically typed parts of the program. The compiler must be able to distinguish between those values whose types may be needed in dynamic type checks during execution and those values whose types can be discarded after compilation.

In [ACP89], Abadi et al. introduce such an interface. It is based on the construction of pairs of an object and its type. Such a pair is called a 'dynamic'. Access to the components of a dynamic is limited to a pattern match, where the type component of the dynamic is compared with a given type pattern. The interface provides a carefully designed but subtle separation of the statically and dynamically typed parts of the program: pattern matches specify the dynamic checks, while the static checks ensure that a program is correctly typed, independent of the results of dynamic type checks in the pattern matches.

A type system that types the file system can also be used to solve other typing problems. In concept, message passing between independently running processes can be seen as a particular instance of file I/O. The messages can be viewed as short-lived files which are created by the sending process and destroyed by the receiving process. In this way, our typing mechanism for typing files can be reused to type message passing.

Although in the actual implementation messages are probably more efficiently transferred than through files, this analogy provides a good theoretical model for message passing and eases its implementation.

In section 3 we present the hybrid type system, which is very powerful but complex. Before going into thecnical details we first discuss why we need such a powerful and hence complex system in the first place.

2.1 Why dynamic types?

In this section we discuss why dynamic checks are unavoidable and why it is convenient to separate file access from dynamic type checking, as can be done with dynamics. We start with a less complex type system, in which file access and type checking are viewed as a single atomic action, and show that its power is insufficient to satisfy our demands.

We aim for a file system in which any file may contain any object that can be expressed in our language. A simple read or write statement should suffice to copy an object from memory to disk or vice versa. One could think of these functions as:

```
class store    a :: Filename a *Disk → (Status,    *Disk)
class retrieve a :: Filename   *Disk → (Status, a, *Disk)
```

The function store has a filename and an object as input and puts the object on disk, under the given filename. The retrieve function copies an object from disk to memory. Both functions return a Status value in with error messages can be found. The * before a type, in this case *Disk, expresses that the function demands unique (i.e. single threaded) access to this argument. Clean's type system takes care that at run-time the actual argument is indeed single threaded, i.e. there are no other references to that argument. In [BS93] more information about uniqueness types can be found.

Disk access should be type safe. This means that if a program is specified to read an object of a certain type, then it must be guaranteed that the object which is read during execution has that same type.

If we want to statically check this type requirement, we have to determine at compile-time which filename comes with which type during the execution of the program. As mentioned before, this generally cannot be determined at compile-time, since the filename of a file or its contents may change between compilation and execution of the program. Reliable information is only obtained during the execution of the program, when the file is read. This shows that run-time type checks are necessary when dealing with the file system.

Since Clean programs are compiled rather than interpreted, it is hard, some-times even impossible, to reconstruct the correct type of an object at run-time. For the purpose of dynamic type checks, it is therefore necessary to preserve some type information together with the object. This should be stored with the object, in the file. The type information must be supplied by the write function and used by the read function to perform a run-time type check.

In such a system, type checking and disk access cannot be seen separately. They are combined in one atomic action. This causes some problems. Consider the following function:

```
copyfile :: Filename Filename *Disk → *Disk
copyfile src_name dest_name disk = newDisk
    where
    (stat1, object, disk1) = retrieve src_name disk
    (stat2, newDisk) = store dest_name object disk1
```

The function copyfile specifies that an object (object) is copied from one file to another. The object can be of arbitrary type, the program poses no restrictions on the type of 'object'. This causes trouble for the store function. It cannot determine what type it has to write with its object unless some type information remains after transferring the object from disk to memory. Somehow the type information should be passed from the source file to the destination file.

Now consider the following function. It reads two objects from files and applies the first to the second:

```
apply :: Filename Filename *Disk → (Int, *Disk)
apply f_name x_name disk
    | (status1==OK) && (status2==OK) = (f x, disk2)
    | otherwise                      = (0,   disk2)
  where
  (status1, f, disk1)  = retrieve f_name disk
  (status2, x, disk2)  = retrieve x_name disk1
```

In contrast to the previous program, this one does pose restrictions on the types of the objects that are to be read. Static analysis shows that the object f should have a function type: $X \rightarrow Int$, and the object x should have that same type X, or an instance thereof. The type requirements for retrieving x depend on the type of f. Somehow the type information that is stored with f must be administered during the execution of the apply function, so that it can be compared with the type that is stored with x.

Both cases show that type information has to persist beyond the scope of the read and write functions. For some objects type information has to be dragged along during the execution of the program. Since Dynamic types consist of a pair of an object and its type, they are a perfect tool to accomplish this.

3 Introducing a Dynamic type

In this section we present a type called Dynamic, first introduced by Abadi et al. in [ACP89]. We modify its syntax a bit to fit into our language and extend it to cover polymorphism, much like Leroy and Mauny did in CAML [LM93]. Furthermore, we integrate the type in Clean's type system.

We first introduce the notion of dynamic types informally. Then we give a formal definition of its syntax (section 3.1) and we extend Clean's type system with new type rules (section 3.2). These new rules turn out to be very simple. Finally, in section 3.4 we specify the run-time semantics of the dynamic constructs. These too are simple.

The values of Dynamic are, roughly speaking, pairs of a value and a type, such that the value component can be typed with the type component. The access to objects of type Dynamic is limited. A *dynamic* (a value of type Dynamic) can be built from a value and its type using the "dynamic" construct, as shown in the following examples (Note that all four expressions are of type Dynamic, the

"::"-symbol is used to separate the value of the dynamic construct from its type argument):

```
dynamic 3 :: Int
dynamic (dynamic 3 :: Int) :: Dynamic
dynamic reverse :: [a] → [a]
dynamic reverse :: [Int] → [Int]
```

Statically it is checked that the specified value (e.g. 3) can indeed be typed with the specified type (e.g. Int). Note that this type may be polymorphic and/or an instance of the most general type of the value.

The value stored in a dynamic can only be retrieved after a successful match against the type component of the dynamic. When the match succeeds, the contents of the dynamic can be used in the expression which is guarded by the match.

The following functions are examples of such type pattern matches:

```
f :: Dynamic → Int
f (n::Int)  = n * n
f  dn       = 0


g :: Dynamic → [Int]
g (f::[a]→[a])  = f [1,2,3]
g  df           = [ ]


h :: Dynamic Dynamic → Dynamic
h (f::X→Y)  (x::X)  = dynamic (f x) :: Y
h  df       dx      = dynamic "Error" :: String
```

Each time the first function (f) is evaluated, it checks whether its dynamic argument contains an integer. If this is the case, the function returns the square of the integer value. Otherwise f yields 0.

The type [a]→[a] in the function g expresses polymorphism. In other formalisms this type is sometimes written as ∀a.[a]→[a]. The function g only enters the body of the first alternative if its Dynamic argument contains a polymorphic function that maps lists to lists. Otherwise it will return the empty list.

In the last example special variables are used (the uppercase variables X and Y). These are called "type-pattern variables". During the evaluation of the function these variables are bound to parts of the contents of the type field of its Dynamic argument. Type pattern variables have the same scope as the ordinary variables that occur on the left hand side of a rule alternative (i.e. the whole rule alternative).

The function h takes two dynamic values. It demands that the first one contains a function of type X→Y, for some X and Y. Then it checks (at run-time) that the second dynamic contains a value of the same type X. If both requirements are met, the function h builds a new dynamic whose value component is formed by the application of the value components of the arguments of h. The type component of the new dynamic is Y. Note that such a type pattern variable can only be used to form a new dynamic. It can never be used in the type of the function's result.

3.1 Formal syntax of 'dynamic' expressions

In this section we define the constructs formally, starting with their syntax. To link up with the Clean syntax we modified the syntax as specified in [ACP89].

$<dynamic\text{-}expr>$ = 'dynamic' $<expr>$ [':$:$' $<type>$]

$<type\text{-}pattern>$ = 'case' $<expr>$ 'of'
  '|' $<termvar_1>$ ':$:$' $<type_1>$ '$=$' $<expr_1>$
  $\vdots$
  '|' $<termvar_n>$ ':$:$' $<type_n>$ '$=$' $<expr_n>$

$<type>$ = $<type\text{-}variable>$
  | $<type\text{-}pattern\text{-}variable>$
  | $<type>$ '$\rightarrow$' $<type>$
  | $<type\text{-}constructor>$ $\{<type>\}^*$

Note that in the $<dynamic\text{-}expr>$ the specification of a type is optional. The type σ in the expression $(dynamic\ e :: \sigma)$ can be omitted, since Clean's type checker is able to derive the most general type for e. This will then be stored as the type component of the dynamic.

3.2 Extending the type system

The type rules for typing Clean expressions have to be extended with the new constructs for packing and unpacking dynamics. Clean's set of deduction rules consist of statements of the form:

$$\mathcal{F}, B \vdash e : \sigma$$

which states that the expression e can be typed with type σ, given a function environment $\mathcal{F}$ and a basis B. As usual, as basis B consists of type declarations. The function environment $\mathcal{F}$ consists of type declarations of function definitions. Contrasting the types appearing in the basis, the latter types are assumed to be universally quantified, which means that a proper instance of the given function type can be used each time the function is applied. (See [BS93] for more details.)

To Clean's set of rules, two new deduction rules are added for introducing and eliminating values of type Dynamic respectively.

An expression $(dynamic\ e :: \sigma)$ is of type Dynamic if the expression e can be typed with σ:

$$\frac{\mathcal{F}, B \vdash e : \sigma \qquad V(B) \cap V(\sigma) = \emptyset}{\mathcal{F}, B \vdash (\text{dynamic } e :: \sigma) : \text{Dynamic}} \text{(DynI)}$$

The type rule for eliminating a Dynamic is somewhat more complicated. This is due to the possible presence of type pattern variables. They are used to enable type information to persist beyond the scope of the read and write function.

A type pattern match is typed correctly if the selector-expression is of type Dynamic and each entry is correctly typed for every possible substitution of its type-pattern variables.

$$\frac{\mathcal{F}, B \vdash e : \text{Dynamic} \qquad \forall : (\mathbf{X}_i \to \mathbb{T}). \ \{\mathcal{F}, \ x_i : \widehat{\sigma}_i\}, B \vdash \widehat{e}_i : \tau}{\mathcal{F}, B \vdash \left(\begin{array}{l} \text{case } e \text{ of } | \ \{\mathbf{X_1}\}(x_1 :: \sigma_1) = e_1 \\ \qquad \vdots \\ | \ \{\mathbf{X_n}\}(x_n :: \sigma_n) = e_n \end{array} \right) : \tau} \text{(DynE)}$$

where i ranges over $\{1 \ldots n\}$. (Note that bold characters denote vectors.)

The expressions $\{\mathbf{X_i}\}$ in the branches of the case-expression do not belong to the syntax of the language. They are used in this type rule to make the type pattern variables that occur in σ_i and e_i visible. The function $\widehat{}$ maps the type pattern variables to types.

The assertion $x_i : \widehat{\sigma}_i$ is placed in the function environment rather than in the basis. In this way we handle polymorphism: a polymorphic pattern is treated in the same way as a polymorphic function. By placing the assertion in the function environment, the type becomes implicitly universally quantified. So for each application of x_i in e_i the free variables in $\widehat{\sigma}_i$ are taken fresh.

3.3 Uniqueness and Dynamic types

Treatment of Dynamic types in Clean's uniqueness type system is a subtle matter. With respect to uniqueness Dynamic types behave in the same way as higher-order functions do. A dynamic containing a unique expression must itself be unique as well. But more: it is *necessarily* unique. We cannot allow a unique dynamic to coerce to its non-unique variant. If we allow a dynamic which contains a unique expression to be copied, we can no longer guarantee that the object remains unique during evaluation.

3.4 Run-time type checks

The type rules above are used in static type checking. In this section we present a mechanism for dynamic type checks.

Each time the run-time system evaluates a type pattern match, it should perform a run-time type check as part of the match. The current contents of the type component of a dynamic value (Tag) are compared with the pattern specified in a type pattern match (Pattern). The run-time matching algorithm is specified by the Clean function below. For this purpose the types are encoded in an algebraic datastructure. The Environment is used to store substitutions for variables. The function sub stores a substitution in the Environment, and the function val retrieves a substitution again. The function unify takes care of the necessary run-time unification.

```
match :: Tag          Pattern       Env → (Bool, Env)
match    INT           INT           env = (True, env)
match    type          (PattVar X)  env = unify type (val X env) env
match    (Var a)       type          env = (True, sub a type env)
match    *A_T           *A_P          env = match A_T A_P env
match    (C A_T)        (C A_P)       env = match A_T A_P env
match    (A_T → B_T)   (A_P → B_P)  env = (b1 && b2, env2)
                       where
                       (b1,env1) = match A_T A_P env
                       (b2,env2) = match (val B_T env1) (val B_P env1) env
```

The algorithm ensures, amongst other things, that no substitution occurs for type variables in the pattern (which denote real polymorphism): the type tag must be polymorphic in at least the same positions as the pattern is. So the function

```
f :: Dynamic → [Int]
f (g::[a]→[a])  =  g [1,2,3]
f dg            =  [ ]
```

will only enter the first alternative if the actual argument of f is a polymorphic function whose type can be specialized to [a]→[a]. For example the expression f (dynamic I :: a→a) reduces to [1,2,3], but f (dynamic I :: [Int]→[Int]) reduces to [ ].

Type pattern variables can be used to write functions for dynamic values of arbitrary type. The function

```
f :: Dynamic → (Dynamic, Dynamic)
f (x,y)::(U,V)  =  (dynamic x :: U, dynamic y :: V)
f else          =  (dynamic "Error", dynamic "Error")
```

will choose the first alternative whenever the dynamic argument is a tuple. It poses no restriction on the types of the separate parts of the tuple.

Type pattern variables extend the expressive power of the language but they have a drawback. They induce, as specified in the match function, a run-time unification. This is the price that has to be paid for a flexible type system.

4 Implementation of Dynamics

In this section we discuss how dynamics can be implemented in Clean. Three things have to be accomplished: types have to be encoded; a mechanism is needed to preserve them during the execution of a program; and the matching algorithm has to be inserted in Clean's run-time system (section 4.1). Finally we discuss how we plan to implement file I/O with dynamics (section 4.2).

In the previous sections, no distinction was made between complex types (algebraic types, record types, list types, etc). They were all represented by the case *<type-constructor>* {*<type>*}*. In this section their difference is made explicitly, since the implementation of the various types differs slightly.

4.1 Encoding the types

The representation of a dynamic value consists of a representation of a value and a representation of its type. Thus for the construction of a dynamic, we have to encode types into a form which is preserved during execution. We should make a distinction between the use of dynamics within the boundaries of a single program and the use that goes beyond that boundary.

When we use dynamics within the boundaries of a single program, where all type definitions are known throughout the entire program, a simple encoding of types suffices. The following example shows such an encoding (not all types are listed, for reasons of brevity).

$$
\begin{aligned}
\text{Code(Int)} \quad &= \texttt{Int} \\
\text{Code(a)} \quad &= \texttt{Var a} \\
\text{Code(A}\rightarrow\text{B)} \quad &= \texttt{Arrow } \text{Code(A) } \text{Code(B)} \\
\text{Code([A])} \quad &= \texttt{List } \text{Code(A)} \\
\text{Code($*$A)} \quad &= \texttt{Unique } \text{Code(A)} \\
\text{Code(T } A_1 \ldots A_n) &= \texttt{Algebraic "T" } \text{Code}(A_1) \ldots \text{Code}(A_n) \\
&= \texttt{Record "T" } \text{Code}(A_1) \ldots \text{Code}(A_n) \\
&= \texttt{Abstract "T" } \text{Code}(A_1) \ldots \text{Code}(A_n)
\end{aligned}
$$

For user-defined types this form of coding is inadequate when the use of dynamics goes beyond the boundary of a single program. The representation of these types no longer contains enough information to decide outside an individual program whether two types should be considered to be equal. An algebraic datatype Colour, for example, can differ in definition from one program to another, it can be defined as, say,

Colour = Red | Blue | Green

in the first program, and

Colour = Red | Yellow | Blue

in the second. We do not want to consider these types equal.

Within one program it is sufficient to test type equality by equality of name. Beyond the boundaries of one program some information about the definition of the type is essential. This difference between *name equivalence* and *structural equivalence* is discussed extensively in [CBC90]. They conclude that both name and structural equivalence checks are needed for checking persistent types both adequately and efficiently.

A new version of the 'Code'-function incorporates both notions of equivalence:

$$
\begin{aligned}
\text{Code}(\text{Int}) &= \texttt{Int} \\
\text{Code}(a) &= \texttt{Var a} \\
\text{Code}(A{\rightarrow}B) &= \texttt{Arrow } \text{Code}(A) \ \text{Code}(B) \\
\text{Code}([A]) &= \texttt{List } \text{Code}(A) \\
\text{Code}(*A) &= \texttt{Unique } \text{Code}(A) \\
\text{Code}(T\ A_1 \ldots A_n) &= \text{Definition}(T)\ \text{Code}(A_1)\ \ldots\ \text{Code}(A_n)
\end{aligned}
$$

where "Definition(T)" is some representation of the definition of T.

For *abstract datatypes* a mechanism has to be implemented that obtains the actual implementation of the datatype from its defining module. The mechanism of overloading could provide a solution here. One can require that for all types a packing function must be available (i.e. for each datatype its definition must be somehow obtainable). A module that introduces an abstract datatype must provide a function that packs a value of that datatype as well.

The type T may depend on other datatypes. It may even depend (indirectly) on itself. Therefore the representation cannot be obtained by simply replacing the name of the type by its definition.

The functional language Clean is based on graph rewriting. It turns out to be profitable to represent the type component of a dynamic as a graph. Variables that occur more than once in a type can be shared. Representing types as graphs has two advantages.

Firstly, the representation of definitions of datatypes can be constructed easily with the use of graphs. Recursive dependency can be represented by cyclic pointer structures.

The second advantage is that all tools that are available for graph rewriting can now be used for handling the types as well.

The matching algorithm can be programmed directly into Clean's run-time system. Two graphs representing the types are compared with each other. Since the variables in a type are shared, a substitution of a variable during the match can be done in place. This means that in the actual implementation we get rid of the Environment as used in the matching algorithm.

4.2 Disk Access

A feature which we get almost for free now is writing and reading dynamics to and from disk. Since Dynamics are just graphs, it is possible to write and read files simply by copying graphs from memory to disk and vice versa. Copying a graph is a simple, basic operation in a graph rewrite system, which can be performed quickly, and uniformly for all representable objects.

For functions this mechanism does not work, however. This is because of the way functions are represented in the graph. They are again not treated as other types, in this respect. The graph that represents the function contains pointers into the *program store* (the part of Clean's run-time system that contains blocks of executable code).

If a function that is written by a program was only read by the same instantiation of the same program, this difference in representation would not lead to a problem. One could simply store the pointer into the program store as a representation of the function. But files are designed to outlive the instantiation of the program that created them. Moreover they tend to be shared by *more than one program*, possibly over *different platforms*. A solution must be found in more complex forms of representation.

We would like to stress here that we are only interested in efficient solutions. Clean's language and its compiler are focussed on an efficient implementation of the programs written in Clean. The representation of a function by its source code, which can be interpreted at run-time, is not a satisfactory solution. In our opinion, the interpretation of source code would have an unacceptable effect on the efficiency.

If files are known to be used on one kind of platform only, a function can be represented by its blocks of executable code. Mechanisms to copy those blocks of code are not yet available in Clean. A problem is that inside the block arbitrary jumps in the code can be made. It may turn out that the whole contents of the program store is necessary in order to evaluate one function. Furthermore, when blocks of code are to be read again, the executable code has to be linked dynamically to the existing program.

When files are used over different platforms, we have to settle for a less efficient representation. The function description must be sufficiently general to be dynamically translatable into proper executable code on any target machine. A suitable representation might be in the intermediate code of the abstract ABC-machine. This ABC-code can be compiled dynamically to the target machine. It is of course not very efficient, but a lot of flexibility is gained.

Although both solutions are hard to implement, we do not expect fundamental problems. Dynamic linking is daily business in almost every large operating system. Dynamic compilation might slow down the execution a bit, but the slowdown is negligible compared to the time that is spent due to sending the information over a network.

5 Related work and Conclusions

Abadi et al. present in [ACP89] a theoretical framework for Dynamic types, complete with an extensive review of the history of dynamic typing in statically typed languages. They also mention a large number of languages in which restricted use has been made of the dynamic concept. In [ACP91] this theoretical framework is extended to cover polymorphism. Higher order pattern variables are introduced to be able to match against polymorphic types. We decided to deal with polymorphism differently and use ordinary type variables to accomplish this (section 3).

Leroy and Mauny describe in [LM93] how a simple version of Dynamic is implemented in ML. They also specify a more complicated system of dynamics with universally and existentially quantified variables, which has not yet been implemented. It uses the existentially qualified types to specify dynamic matches with incomplete type information. These are basically the same as our type pattern variables. Their type system of "Mixed quantifications", in which they use both polymorphism and type pattern variables, is as powerful as the type system that is presented in this article, but our implementation, in particular the runtime matching algorithm, is much less complicated (section 3.4). Furthermore we showed how the type Dynamic can be integrated in a complex type system.

Morrison et al. present in [MBC89] the type system as implemented in Napier, a language which is specially developed to handle persistent objects. They use the type **any** to pack and unpack values with their types. The difference between this type **any** and our type Dynamic is in the fact in Napier, with **any**, the difference between statically and dynamically checkable values is left more implicit.

A nice feature of Dynamic types and our way of viewing the file system is that we can use the extended type system for typing message passing between independently running processes as well (section 2).

We have not reached our goal yet: *the construction of a strongly typed file system in which any object may be stored that can be expressed in the* Clean *programming language*. But we have made a lot of progress. We have designed a suitable extension of Clean's type system. We are able to type the file system, and we are extending the Clean compiler accordingly. Currently we are developing the mechanisms for storage of functions in files.

References

[ACP89] M. Abadi, L. Cardelli, B. Pierce, G. Plotkin. *Dynamic typing in a statically typed language,* ACM Transactions on Programming Languages and Systems 13(2):237–268, 1991.

[ACP91] M. Abadi, L. Cardelli, B. Pierce, D. Rémy. *Dynamic typing in polymorphic languages,* In: Journal of Functional Programming 5(1):111–130, Cambridge University Press 1995.

[BS93]   E. Barendsen and J. Smetsers. *Uniqueness Typing for Functional Languages with Graph Rewriting Semantics,* to appear in MSCS.

[CBC90] R. Connor, A.Brown, Q Cutts, A. Dearle, R. Morrison and J. Rosenberg. *Type Equivalence Checking in Persistent Object Systems,* In: Implementing Persistent Object Bases pp.151–164, Morgan Kaufman 1990

[PE93]   M. van Eekelen, M. Plasmeijer. *Functional Programming and Parallel Graph Rewriting,* Addison-Wesley 1993.

[PE97]   M. van Eekelen, M. Plasmeijer. *Concurrent Clean 1.0 language report,* Computing Science Institute, University of Nijmegen, http://www.cs.kun.nl/~clean/Clean.Cleanbook.html.

[LM93]   X. Leroy, M. Mauny. *Dynamics in ML,* In: Journal of Functional Programming 3(4), Cambridge University Press 1995.

[MBC89] R. Morrison, A.Brown, R. Carrick, R. Connor, A. Dearle, and M. Atkinson. *The Napier Type System,* In: Persistent Object Systems pp.3–18, Springer-Verlag 1989.

A Type-Based Algorithm for the Control-Flow Analysis of Higher-Order Concurrent Programs

Mourad Debbabi, Ali Faour, Nadia Tawbi

Computer Science Department,
Laval University,
Quebec, G1K 7P4, Canada.
E-mails: {debabi,faour,tawbi}@ift.ulaval.ca

Abstract. We address, in a type-based framework, the problem of control-flow analysis for concurrent and functional languages. We present an efficient algorithm that propagates automatically types, communication effects and call graphs. The algorithm comes with a logical characterization that consists of a type proof system. The latter operates on a Concurrent ML core-syntax: a strongly typed, polymorphic kernel that supports higher-order functions and concurrency primitives. Effects are represented as algebraic terms that record communication effects resulting from channel creation, sending and receiving. Call graphs record function calls and are captured by a term algebra that is close to usual process algebras. Types are annotated with effects and call graphs. For the sake of flexibility, a subtyping relation is considered on the type algebra. We present the language syntax together with its static semantics that consists of the typing rules and an inference algorithm. The latter is proved to be sound with respect to the typing rules.

1 Motivation and Background

Control-flow analysis is a traditional optimizing compiler technique. It aims to approximate, at compile time, dynamic function call graphs induced by program execution. Furthermore, control-flow analysis provides a static information that is valuable for debugging purposes. Control-flow analysis has been extensively studied for traditional imperative programming languages such as Fortran and C [ASU86]. However, very little seems to have been done about the control-flow analysis of higher-order programming languages such as Scheme and ML.

In this paper, we are concerned in the control-flow analysis of concurrent, functional and imperative languages. More accurately, the language considered here consists of a Concurrent ML core-syntax [Rep91a]. Consequently, the analysis will be done in the presence of first-class functions, higher-order processes, channels and references. The key idea underlying this work is to annotate types with structured approximations of call graphs. The annotated types are then propagated by an inference system and its corresponding algorithm. As mentioned by O. Shivers [Shi90], the call graph information is crucial for control and data-flow optimizations.

Lately, a great deal of interest has been expressed in the use of type inference system in program analysis. Such an interest is motivated by the fact that type systems caters for a natural separation of the analysis into three parts. First, a specification of the analysis is elaborated thanks to a proof system. Second, an inference algorithm is devised. It aims to reconstruct automatically the information needed by the analysis. Finally, the information gathered is used to perform the analysis. Such a separation is valuable especially when extending the analysis to deal with new language features. Furthermore, type-based analyses are suitable to the extension in presence of modularity and separate compilation. On the other hand, abstract interpretation [CC92] provides a powerful approach for static analysis. It performs very precise analyses but does not provide a clear separation between the specification and the implementation issues.

Annotated type systems emerged first from the idea of considering side effects as part of the static evaluation. They have been firstly used within the FX project [GJLS87]. Afterwards, many annotated type systems have been proposed. Among them one can cite the type and effect discipline of Talpin and Jouvelot [TJ92]. In this discipline, the static evaluation of an expression yields as a result not only its type, but also all the minimal side effects. Afterwards, various type systems have been devised by Bolignano and Debbabi [BD93b, BD93a, BD94, Deb94] as a generalization of the type and effect discipline in order to deal with concurrency. The generalization consists of an inference type system that propagates the communication effects that results from channel creation, sending and receiving. Nevertheless, similar type systems have been advanced independently by H. Riis-Nielson and F. Nielson [NN94b] and Thomsen [Tho93].

Here is the way the rest of the paper is organized. Section 2 is devoted to the state of the art in control-flow analysis. An informal description of the language is presented in Section 3. A full presentation of the static semantics is given in Section 4. The reconstruction algorithm comes in Section 5. Section 6 is devoted to the establishment of the soundness of the algorithm with regard to the typing rules. A few concluding remarks and a discussion of future work are ultimately sketched as a conclusion in Section 7.

2   Related Work

Control-flow analysis is a very well-known problem for compiler developers. A heavy machinery of various control-flow analyses is employed in traditional imperative compilers such as C and Fortran. These analyses contribute significantly to the efficiency of the corresponding compilers. The reader may refer to [ASU86] for a full account of such optimizations.

On the other hand, higher-order programming languages, such as ML, Scheme, Concurrent ML, etc., are very popular mainly for their widely recognized expressiveness power. However, the most up-to-date ML or Scheme compiler is still roughly as efficient as the non-optimizing traditional imperative compilers. One of the main reasons underlying this gap is the level of optimization applied.

It is well known since [Shi88], that in order to apply any data-flow optimization: common-subexpression elimination, loop invariant detection, induction variable elimination, etc, one has to know explicitly at compile-time an approximation of control-flow graph.

Since then, a great deal of interest has been expressed in the control-flow analysis problem usually referred to as the CFA problem. Shivers demonstrated in [Shi90] that one key problem in CFA is the static computation of call graphs. He proposed many algorithms for the static reconstruction of call graphs in Scheme. These algorithms have been formulated in the framework of abstract interpretation of P. Cousot and R. Cousot [CC92].

Later, in [TJ94, Tan94], Tang and Jouvelot proved that the control-flow analysis could be expressed either as a type and effect system or abstract interpretation.

The work reported here originates from the following observation: the control information gathered by the algorithms of both Shivers and Tang-Jouvelot consists of the set of function names possibly called during the evaluation of expression. By doing so, these algorithms lose the control structure of the program. Tang and Jouvelot decided to do so in order to preserve the decidability of their type and effect system.

In this paper, we will elaborate a new algorithm that gathers a much more precise and structured approximation of the control information. This will be accomplished by putting much more structure on the control information. Actually, this structure is a strong simulation relation on call graphs [Mil89]. Moreover, our algorithm operates on a multi-paradigmatic language that incorporates higher-order concurrency extensions. Furthermore, the information gathered by our algorithm is richer since it comes with a compile-time approximation of the communication effects. The presence of communication effects control the generalization of type variables in the let construct. The algorithm reported here, is firstly specified with a logical characterization that consists of a type and effect system. The latter is proved to be sound and complete with respect to the logical specification.

3 Syntax

In this section we present the Concurrent ML core-syntax considered in this work. We have kept the number of constructs to a bare minimum so as to facilitate a more compact and complete description of the static semantics. We consider:

– Literals, such as the boolean true and false, and a distinguished value () that belongs to the one-element type usually referred to as *unit*.

– Three binding constructs, the functional abstraction, the recursion and the let definition. The construct f where $f(x)= e$ stands for the definition of a function whose body is e. The construct rec f where $f(x)= e$ stands for the definition of a recursive function named f whose body is e. In fact the recursion operator rec is not part of the Concurrent ML syntax, since recursion is implicit in Concurrent ML. It has been included just to provide a semantics for recursive behaviors.

Table 1. The Core Syntax

Exp $\ni e ::= x \mid v \mid e\,e' \mid$ rec f where $f(x){=}\,e \mid$		**(Expressions)**
$\mid$ let $x{=}e$ in e' end $\mid$ if e then e' else e'' end		
Const $\ni c ::= ()$ $\mid$ true $\mid$ false $\mid$ channel $\mid$ spawn $\mid$ sync		**(Constants)**
$\mid$ receive $\mid$ transmit $\mid$ choose		
Val $\ni v ::= c \mid f$ where $f(x) = e$		**(Values)**

– Imperative aspects are supported in Concurrent ML through the notion of reference. The latter is not included in this core-syntax since it can be simulated easily using servers that communicate through typed channels, as shown in [BMT92, Rep91b]. Semantically, references are treated as communication channels.

– Expressions may communicate through channels. New channels are created by applying the built-in function channel to the trivial value (). The expression transmit(e_1,e_2) means evaluate the expression e_1 to get a channel value and then evaluate the expression e_2. The value returned afterwards is an "event" that stands for a potential communication that results from sending the value along the channel. Similarly, receive(e) means evaluate the expression e to get a channel value and then form an event that denotes the possibility of receiving a value on the channel. Events are activated using the construct sync.

– Parallel behaviors are supported through the unary operator spawn, which stands for the activation of its argument expression, meant to be executed in parallel with the rest of the program.

– We have a CCS-like choice operator, referred to as choose whose behavior amounts to the nondeterministic choice of some event. The reader should notice that we used a binary choice operator, as in [BMT92], for the sake of compactness.

More formally, the BNF syntax of the core language is presented in Table 1.

Notice that we have three syntactic categories. The category of expressions (Exp) ranged over by e, the category of constants (Const) ranged over by c and the category of values (Val) ranged over by v.

Along this paper, given two sets A and B, we will write $A \rightarrow\!\!\!\!\!\!{\scriptstyle m}\ B$ to denote the set of all mappings from A to B, having in mind that there is no overlap (that is, mappings are functions, not relations). A mapping (map for short) $m \in A \rightarrow\!\!\!\!\!\!{\scriptstyle m}\ B$ could be defined by extension as $[a_1 \mapsto b_1, ..., a_n \mapsto b_n]$ to denote the association of the elements b_i's to a_i's. We will write $dom(m)$ to denote the domain of the map m and $ran(m)$ to denote its range (co-domain). We will write $m_{x_1,x_2,...}$, the map m excluding the associations of the form $x_i \mapsto \_$. Given two maps m and m', we will write $m \dagger m'$ the overwriting of the map m by the associations of the map m' i.e. the domain of $m \dagger m'$ is $dom(m) \cup dom(m')$ and we have $(m \dagger m')(a) = m'(a)$ if $a \in dom(m')$ and $m(a)$ otherwise.

4 Static Semantics

The static semantics is based on an extension of the type and effect discipline. This allows us to control safely the type generalization in the presence of polymorphic channels. Actually types and effects are used to control the generalization of type and effect variables. As shown in [Ler92, TJ92], effect-based type systems outperform the other type systems when typing in the presence of mutable data. Furthermore, call graphs, communication effects, together with principal types capture a valuable static information on the dynamic behaviors of a program. The latter information may be of great interest in the static analysis of programs.

We need the following static domains:

– The domain of *regions*: regions are intended to abstract channels. Their domain consists in the disjoint union of a countable set of constants ranged over by r, and variables ranged over by ϱ. We will use ρ, ρ', etc., to represent values drawn from this domain.

– The domain of communication *effects*: it is defined inductively as follows:

$$\sigma ::= \emptyset \mid \varsigma \mid \sigma \cup \sigma' \mid create(\rho, \tau) \mid in(\rho, \tau) \mid out(\rho, \tau)$$

We use $\emptyset$ to denote an empty communication effect. We use ς to stand for a communication effect variable. The communication effect $create(\rho, \tau)$ represents the creation, in the region ρ, of a channel that is a medium for values of type τ. The term $in(\rho, \tau)$ denotes the effect resulting from receiving a value of type τ on a channel in the region ρ. The term $out(\rho, \tau)$ denotes an output of a value of type τ, on a channel in the region ρ. We introduce also a union operator $\cup$ intended to effect cumulation.

– The algebra of call *graphs*: it is defined as follows:

$$\gamma ::= nil \mid \delta \mid f.\gamma \mid \gamma + \gamma' \mid \gamma; \gamma' \mid fork(\gamma) \mid rec\ \delta.\gamma$$

The terms of this algebra stand for call graph approximation noted Call graphs in the sequel. We use nil to denote the empty call graph and δ to denote a polymorphic variable call graph. A term of the form $f.\gamma$ stands for a call graph recording an initial call of the function f and having γ as the corresponding unique subgraph. The term $\gamma + \gamma'$ is used to denote a call graph with two alternatives call graphs γ and γ'. One and only one of the two branches will be effective for some program execution. The notation $\Sigma_{i=0}^{n}\gamma_i$ will be used as an abbreviation of $\gamma_1 + \ldots + \gamma_n$. The call graph operator $+$ is associative, commutative, idempotent and has nil as a unit element. The term $\gamma; \gamma'$ denotes the sequencing of γ and γ'. The term $fork(\gamma)$ denotes the spawning of an expression having γ as a call graph. The term $rec\ \delta.\gamma$ denotes a recursively defined call graph. For instance, the term $rec\ \delta.(f.g.nil + h.t.\delta)$ denotes the call graph of a program that either calls the function f and then g, or makes a call to the function h, followed by a call to the function t, and then recurses.

– The domain of *types*: is inductively defined by:

$$\tau ::= unit \mid bool \mid \alpha \mid \tau \times \tau' \mid chan_\rho(\tau) \mid event_{\sigma,\gamma}(\tau) \mid \tau \xrightarrow{\sigma,\gamma} \tau'$$

Table 2. The Typing Rules

(cte)	$\dfrac{\tau \triangleleft TypeOf(\mathbf{cte})}{\mathcal{E} \vdash \mathbf{cte} : \tau, \emptyset, nil}$
(var)	$\dfrac{\tau \triangleleft \mathcal{E}(x)}{\mathcal{E} \vdash x : \tau, \emptyset, nil}$
(abs)	$\dfrac{\mathcal{E}_x \dagger [x \mapsto \tau] \vdash e : \tau', \sigma, \gamma}{\mathcal{E} \vdash f \text{ where } f(x) = e : \tau \xrightarrow{\sigma, f.\gamma} \tau', \emptyset, nil}$
(app)	$\dfrac{\mathcal{E} \vdash e : \tau \xrightarrow{\sigma, \gamma} \tau', \sigma', \gamma' \quad \mathcal{E} \vdash e' : \tau, \sigma'', \gamma''}{\mathcal{E} \vdash (e\ e') : \tau', \sigma \cup \sigma' \cup \sigma'', ((\gamma'; \gamma''); \gamma)}$
(let)	$\dfrac{\mathcal{E} \vdash e : \tau, \sigma, \gamma \quad \mathcal{E}_x \dagger [x \mapsto Gen(\mathcal{E}, \sigma, \gamma)(\tau)] \vdash e' : \tau', \sigma', \gamma'}{\mathcal{E} \vdash \mathbf{let}\ x = e \ \mathbf{in}\ e' \ \mathbf{end} : \tau', \sigma \cup \sigma', (\gamma; \gamma')}$
(if)	$\dfrac{\mathcal{E} \vdash e : bool, \sigma, \gamma \quad \mathcal{E} \vdash e' : \tau', \sigma', \gamma' \quad \mathcal{E} \vdash e'' : \tau'', \sigma'', \gamma''}{\mathcal{E} \vdash \mathbf{if}\ e \ \mathbf{then}\ e' \ \mathbf{else}\ e'' \ \mathbf{end} : \tau, \sigma''', \gamma'''} \left\{ \begin{array}{l} \tau' \preccurlyeq \tau \\ \tau'' \preccurlyeq \tau \\ \sigma \cup \sigma' \cup \sigma'' \preccurlyeq \sigma''' \\ \gamma; (\gamma' + \gamma'') \preccurlyeq \gamma''' \end{array} \right.$
(rec)	$\dfrac{\mathcal{E}_{x,f} \dagger [x \mapsto \tau, f \mapsto \tau \xrightarrow{\sigma, \delta} \tau'] \vdash e : \tau', \sigma, \gamma}{\mathcal{E} \vdash \mathbf{rec}\ f \ \mathbf{where}\ f(x) = e : \tau \xrightarrow{\sigma, rec\, \delta.\gamma} \tau', \emptyset, nil}$

unit is the type with only one element "()", *bool* the type of usual truth values true and false, α a type variable. The term $\tau \times \tau'$ stands for the type of pairs whose first component is of type τ and the second of type τ'. The term $chan_\rho(\tau)$ is the type of channels in the region ρ that are intended to be media for values of type τ. The term $\tau \xrightarrow{\sigma, \gamma} \tau'$ is the type of functions that take parameters of type τ to values of type τ' with a latent effect σ and a latent call graph γ. By latent effect (respectively call graph), we mean the effect (respectively call graph) generated when the corresponding function expression is applied to its arguments. The type $event_{\sigma, \gamma}(\tau)$ denotes inactive processes made of potential communications (latent effect σ) and function calls (latent call graph γ) that are expected to return a value of type τ once their execution terminated. The static semantics manipulates sequents of the form $\mathcal{E} \vdash e : \tau, \sigma, \gamma$, which state that under some typing environment $\mathcal{E}$ the expression e has type τ, effect σ and call graph γ. We also define type schemes of the form $\forall v_1, \ldots, v_n.\tau$, where v_i can be type, region, effect or call graph variable. A type τ' is an instance of $\forall v_1, \ldots, v_n.\tau$ noted $\tau' \triangleleft \forall v_1, \ldots, v_n.\tau$, if there exists a substitution θ defined over $v_1, \ldots, v_n$ such that $\tau' = \theta\tau$. Static environments, ranged over by $\mathcal{E}$, map identifiers to type schemes. The Table 2 presents the static semantics of our core language.

Table 3. Subtyping on Call Graphs

(Reflexivity) $\gamma \preccurlyeq \gamma$	**(;+ Distributivity)**	$(\gamma + \gamma'); \gamma'' \equiv (\gamma; \gamma'') + (\gamma'; \gamma'')$
(Transitivity) $\dfrac{\gamma \preccurlyeq \gamma' \quad \gamma' \preccurlyeq \gamma''}{\gamma \preccurlyeq \gamma''}$	**(+ 1st law)**	$\gamma \preccurlyeq \gamma + \gamma'$
(Pre-cong. 1) $\dfrac{\gamma \preccurlyeq \gamma'}{f.\gamma \preccurlyeq f.\gamma'}$	**(+ 2nd law)**	$\gamma \preccurlyeq \gamma' + \gamma$
(Pre-cong. 2) $\dfrac{\gamma \preccurlyeq \gamma'}{rec\ \delta.\gamma \preccurlyeq rec\ \delta.\gamma'''}$	**(+ 3nd law)**	$\gamma + nil \preccurlyeq \gamma$
(Pre-cong. 3) $\dfrac{\gamma \preccurlyeq \gamma' \quad \gamma'' \preccurlyeq \gamma'''}{\gamma + \gamma'' \preccurlyeq \gamma' + \gamma'''}$	**(Idempotence)**	$\gamma + \gamma \preccurlyeq \gamma$
(Pre-cong. 4) $\dfrac{\gamma \preccurlyeq \gamma'' \quad \gamma' \preccurlyeq \gamma'''}{\gamma; \gamma' \preccurlyeq \gamma'; \gamma'''}$	**(; Associativity)**	$\gamma; (\gamma'; \gamma'') \equiv (\gamma; \gamma'); \gamma''$
(Pre-cong. 5) $\dfrac{\gamma \preccurlyeq \gamma'}{fork(\gamma) \preccurlyeq fork(\gamma')}$	**(Unwinding)**	$rec\ \delta.\gamma \equiv \gamma[rec\ \delta.\gamma/\gamma]$
(EmptyGraph 1) $\gamma \equiv nil; \gamma$	**(EmptyGraph 2)**	$\gamma; nil \equiv \gamma$
(Renaming) $rec\ \delta.\gamma \equiv rec\ \delta'.\gamma[\delta'/\delta]$ where $\delta' \notin fv(\gamma)$		

Type generalization in this type system states that a variable cannot be generalized if it is free in the type environment $\mathcal{E}$ or if it is present in the inferred effect or call graph. The first condition is classical while the other is due to the fact that types are annotated by effects and graphs. Concerning the effect part, the reader should refer to [TJ92, BD93a] for a detailed explanation of this issue.

$$Gen(\mathcal{E}, \sigma, \gamma)(\tau) = \mathbf{let}\ \{v_1, \ldots, v_n\} = fv(\tau) \backslash (fv(\mathcal{E}) \cup fv(\sigma) \cup fv(\gamma))$$
$$\mathbf{in}\ \forall v_1, \ldots, v_n.\tau\ \mathbf{end}$$

where $fv(\_)$ denotes the set of free variables:

$$
\begin{aligned}
fv(\mathcal{E}) &= \cup\{fv(\mathcal{E}(x)) \mid x \in dom(\mathcal{E})\} & fv(\gamma + \gamma') &= fv(\gamma) \cup fv(\gamma') \\
fv(\forall v_1, ..., v_n.\tau) &= fv(\tau) \backslash \{v_1, \ldots, v_n\} & fv(\gamma; \gamma') &= fv(\gamma) \cup fv(\gamma') \\
fv(unit) &= \{\} & fv(fork(\gamma)) &= fv(\gamma) \\
fv(bool) &= \{\} & fv(rec\ \delta.\gamma) &= fv(\gamma) \backslash \{\delta\} \\
fv(\alpha) &= \{\alpha\} & fv(\emptyset) &= \{\} \\
fv(\tau \times \tau') &= fv(\tau) \cup fv(\tau') & fv(in(\rho, \tau)) &= fv(\rho) \cup fv(\tau) \\
fv(chan_\rho(\tau)) &= fv(\rho) \cup fv(\tau) & fv(out(\rho, \tau)) &= fv(\rho) \cup fv(\tau) \\
fv(event_{\sigma,\gamma}(\tau)) &= fv(\sigma) \cup fv(\gamma) \cup fv(\tau) & fv(create(\rho, \tau)) &= fv(\rho) \cup fv(\tau) \\
fv(\tau \xrightarrow{\sigma,\gamma} \tau') &= fv(\sigma) \cup fv(\gamma) \cup fv(\tau) \cup fv(\tau') & fv(\varsigma) &= \{\varsigma\} \\
fv(nil) &= \{\} & fv(\sigma \cup \sigma') &= fv(\sigma) \cup fv(\sigma') \\
fv(\delta) &= \{\delta\} & fv(r) &= \{\} \\
fv(f.\gamma) &= fv(\gamma) & fv(\varrho) &= \{\varrho\}
\end{aligned}
$$

The function $TypeOf$, defined in Table 6, allows the typing of built-in primitives.

Since types may be annotated by effects and call graphs, the typing context may lead occasionally to a type mismatch between subexpressions that have similar type structure but different graph annotations. This may appear when typing applications and conditionals. Generally, two techniques may be considered to get rid of this problem:

Table 4. Subtyping on Types

(Reflexivity) $\tau \preccurlyeq \tau$	(Pre-cong. 2)	$\dfrac{\tau \preccurlyeq \tau' \quad \tau'' \preccurlyeq \tau''' \quad \sigma \preccurlyeq \sigma' \quad \gamma \preccurlyeq \gamma'}{\tau' \xrightarrow{\sigma,\gamma} \tau'' \preccurlyeq \tau \xrightarrow{\sigma',\gamma'} \tau'''}$
(Transitivity) $\dfrac{\tau \preccurlyeq \tau' \quad \tau' \preccurlyeq \tau''}{\tau \preccurlyeq \tau''}$	(Pre-cong. 3)	$\dfrac{\tau \preccurlyeq \tau'}{chan_\rho(\tau) \preccurlyeq chan_\rho(\tau')}$
(Pre-cong. 1) $\dfrac{\tau \preccurlyeq \tau' \quad \tau'' \preccurlyeq \tau'''}{\tau \times \tau'' \preccurlyeq \tau' \times \tau'''}$	(Pre-cong. 4)	$\dfrac{\tau \preccurlyeq \tau' \quad \sigma \preccurlyeq \sigma' \quad \gamma \preccurlyeq \gamma'}{event_{\sigma,\gamma}(\tau) \preccurlyeq event_{\sigma',\gamma'}(\tau')}$

Table 5. Subtyping on Effects

(Reflexivity)	$\sigma \preccurlyeq \sigma$	(Idempotence) $\sigma \cup \sigma \preccurlyeq \sigma$
(Transitivity)	$\dfrac{\sigma \preccurlyeq \sigma' \quad \sigma' \preccurlyeq \sigma''}{\sigma \preccurlyeq \sigma''}$	($\cup$ 1st law) $\quad \sigma \preccurlyeq \sigma \cup \sigma'$
(Precong.)	$\dfrac{\sigma \preccurlyeq \sigma' \quad \sigma'' \preccurlyeq \sigma'''}{\sigma \cup \sigma'' \preccurlyeq \sigma' \cup \sigma'''}$	($\cup$ 2nd law) $\quad \sigma \preccurlyeq \sigma' \cup \sigma$
(EmptyEff. 1)	$\sigma \equiv \emptyset \cup \sigma$	(EmptyEff. 2) $\quad \sigma \cup \emptyset \equiv \sigma$
(ElemEffe)	$\dfrac{\tau \preccurlyeq \tau'}{\mu(\rho,\tau) \preccurlyeq \mu(\rho,\tau')} \; \mu \in \{create, in, out\}$	

– The first technique, usually referred to as *subeffecting* consists in computing larger annotations so as to avoid type clashes. This technique remains acceptable as far as programming is the issue. Nevertheless, in the case of static analysis, the use of subeffecting may result in a significant loss of information that affects the analysis precision.

– The second technique consists in introducing a *subtyping* relation on the type and annotation algebras. In other words, appropriate preorders are defined on types and annotations. Consequently, different types are tolerated during the pattern-matching as far as the difference concerns only annotations. For instance, in a conditional construct we allow the types of the branches to be dissimilar and only require them to be subtypes of a common and explicitly given type. By doing so, the information gathered by the type system is kept intact and then no loss of information is reported. However, subtyping introduce a significant complexity at the level of the type system as well as the inference algorithm.

In this work, we adopt the second technique, subtyping, since the issue is static analysis. Accordingly, we begin by introducing preorder relations on types, effects and graphs. First of all, these preorders will all be written $\preccurlyeq$ ($\preccurlyeq$ is overloaded) and the corresponding kernel will be written $\equiv$ which is equivalent to $\preccurlyeq \cap \succcurlyeq$. It is defined by: $t \equiv t'$ if and only if $t \preccurlyeq t'$ and $t \succcurlyeq t'$.

Table 3 axiomatizes the subtyping relation on the algebra of call graphs. The rules stipulate that such a relation is a preorder (reflexive and transitive) and a precongruence ($\preccurlyeq$ is closed under the different operations on graphs). The rules also state that the operator ; is associative, commutative and idempotent and admit *nil* as a neutral element. The call graph operator ; is right-distributive

Table 6. The Initial Static Basis

$TypeOf = [$

$() \mapsto unit,$

$true \mapsto bool,$

$false \mapsto bool,$

$channel \mapsto \forall \alpha, \varrho.\ unit \xrightarrow{create(\varrho,\alpha),channel.nil} chan_\varrho(\alpha),$

$receive \mapsto \forall \alpha, \varrho.\ chan_\varrho(\alpha) \xrightarrow{\emptyset,receive.nil} event_{in(\varrho,\alpha),nil}(\alpha),$

$transmit \mapsto \forall \alpha, \varrho.\ chan_\varrho(\alpha) \times \alpha \xrightarrow{\emptyset,transmit.nil} event_{out(\varrho,\alpha),nil}(unit),$

$choose \mapsto \forall \alpha, \varsigma, \varsigma', \delta, \delta'.\ event_{\varsigma,\delta}(\alpha) \times event_{\varsigma',\delta'}(\alpha) \xrightarrow{\emptyset,choose.nil} event_{\varsigma \cup \varsigma', \delta+\delta'}(\alpha),$

$spawn \mapsto \forall \varsigma, \delta.\ (unit \xrightarrow{\varsigma,\delta} unit) \xrightarrow{fork(\varsigma),spawn.fork(\delta).nil} unit,$

$sync \mapsto \forall \alpha, \varsigma.\ event_{\varsigma,\delta}(\alpha) \xrightarrow{\varsigma,sync.\delta} \alpha$

$]$

---

with respect to the call graph operator +. The unwinding property states that it is always possible to fold and unfold a recursion. Finally, the renaming rule states that it is possible to rename bound call graph variables. Notice that such an axiomatization is close to some extent to the strong simulation notion of Park and Milner [Mil91, Mil89]). Table 4 axiomatizes subtyping on the type algebra. The rules stipulate that such a relation is a preorder (reflexive and transitive) and that is monotonically closed under all the type constructors not including the arrow type constructor (function). The latter is contravariant on the first argument and covariant on the second. Table 5 axiomatizes subtyping on effects. The rules stipulate that such a relation is a preorder (reflexive and transitive) that is closed under effects union. The rules also define the $\cup$ operator as being associative, commutative, idempotent and admitting $\emptyset$ as a neutral element.

Now, let us turn to the explanation of the typing rules of Table 2. The typing of constants is standard and is dictated by the basis environment. It stipulates that any instance of the corresponding type scheme is accepted as a type together with an empty effect and a *nil* call graph. The same explanation applies to the typing of variables. For function abstraction, the resulting type, effect and call graph indicate that neither effect is reported nor function call is performed when defining the function. Effects and function calls are latent and take place when the function is applied. For an application expression, the overall inferred effect and call graph express eager left-to-right evaluation: first, the function expression e is evaluated into a function abstraction, then the argument e' is evaluated and finally the function is applied to the argument. For the pair and sequencing rules, the corresponding inferred types, effects and call graphs are straightforward. The typing rule for recursive function definition is similar to the rule for abstraction except that we need to extend the type environment with assumptions about the recursive function. Finally, the rule for conditional allows the types of the branches to be dissimilar and only requires them to be subtypes of a common and explicitly given type. The effect inferred is the union of the three effects produced by both the boolean expression and the two branches, while the resulting call graph should report at first the boolean expression call graph γ followed by the call graph that results from evaluating either the then-branch or the else-branch. Since the inference is done at compile-time, it is undecidable to know which branch will be executed. Accordingly, both call graphs are reported using the $+$ operator on call graphs i.e. $(\gamma' + \gamma'')$.

5 Inference Algorithm

The present section is dedicated to the algorithm of type, effect and call graph inference. This algorithm is inspired by the type inference discipline of Damas-Milner [DM82]. However, it deviates from the Damas-Milner schema by propagating inequations (constraints) on types, effects and call graphs and also by using a constrained unification instead of a syntactic unification.

Definition 5.1. (Model) Given a constraint set φ and a substitution θ, we say that θ is a model of φ and we write $\theta \models \varphi$, if and only if, $\forall t, t'$ such that $t \preccurlyeq t' \in \varphi$ we have $\theta t \preccurlyeq \theta t'$.

5.1 Constraint Resolution

When typing an expression, the constraints collected by the inference algorithm should be resolved in order to get a substitution. When the latter is applied to the corresponding produced type, effect an call graph, it will yield respectively, the type, the minimal effect and the minimal call graph of the original expression.

Actually, the constraint resolution is performed in 3 steps: splitting, flattening, and resolving. The explanations as well as the formalizations of these 3 phases are given hereafter.

Flattening: This step aims to simplify the constraints generated during the inference process. Such a simplification consists in removing trivial constraints and in decomposing complex ones into simpler constraints. This transformation is formally captured by the semantic function $\mathcal{F}$ defined in Table 7. The definition of $\mathcal{F}$ is inductive on to the structure of type expressions.

Splitting: This step aims to partition the collected constraint set into two separate sets: one that corresponds to type constraints and the other reports effect and call graph constraints. This is done by the function S described in Table 8.

Resolving: To resolve a constraint set, first, one has to simplify it thanks to the function $\mathcal{F}$ (flattening). Second, the simplified constraint set is partitioned into two different sets (splitting): one for type constraints, and the other one for effect and call graph constraints. Third, the effect and call graph constraint set is subjected to a resolution procedure and the resulting substitution is reported in the resolution of the type constraint set.

Table 7. Constraint Flattening

$\mathcal{F}(\varphi) \quad = \cup\{\mathcal{F}(x \preccurlyeq y)|x \preccurlyeq y \in \varphi\}$
$\mathcal{F}(\sigma \preccurlyeq \sigma') = \{\sigma \preccurlyeq \sigma'\}$
$\mathcal{F}(\gamma \preccurlyeq \gamma') = \{\gamma \preccurlyeq \gamma'\}$
$\mathcal{F}(\tau \preccurlyeq \tau') = \mathbf{case}\ (\tau, \tau')\ \mathbf{of}$

$\qquad\qquad\qquad (\tau, \alpha) \Rightarrow \{\tau \preccurlyeq \alpha\}$
$\qquad\qquad (chan_\rho(\tau), chan_\rho(\tau')) \Rightarrow \mathcal{F}(\tau \preccurlyeq \tau')$
$\qquad\quad (\tau_i \xrightarrow{\sigma,\gamma} \tau_f, \tau_i' \xrightarrow{\sigma',\gamma'} \tau_f') \Rightarrow \mathcal{F}(\tau_i' \preccurlyeq \tau_i) \cup \mathcal{F}(\tau_f \preccurlyeq \tau_f') \cup \{\sigma \preccurlyeq \sigma'\} \cup \{\gamma \preccurlyeq \gamma'\}$
$\qquad\quad \mathbf{else\ if}\ \tau = \tau'\ \mathbf{then}\ \{\}\ \mathbf{else}\ fail\ \mathbf{end}$
$\qquad\quad \mathbf{end}$

Table 8. Constraint Splitting

$\mathcal{S}(\varphi) = \mathbf{let}\ f\ =\ \lambda\varphi'.\lambda\varphi_\tau.\lambda\varphi_{\sigma\gamma}.$
$\qquad\qquad \mathbf{case}\ \varphi'\ \mathbf{of}$

$\qquad\qquad\qquad\qquad \{\ \} \Rightarrow (\varphi_\tau, \varphi_{\sigma\gamma})$
$\qquad\qquad\qquad\qquad \{\sigma \preccurlyeq \varsigma\} \cup \varphi'' \Rightarrow f(\varphi'')(\varphi_\tau)(\varphi_{\sigma\gamma} \cup \{\sigma \preccurlyeq \varsigma\})$
$\qquad\qquad\qquad\qquad \{\gamma \preccurlyeq \delta\} \cup \varphi'' \Rightarrow f(\varphi'')(\varphi_\tau)(\varphi_{\sigma\gamma} \cup \{\gamma \preccurlyeq \delta\})$
$\qquad\qquad\qquad\qquad \{\tau' \preccurlyeq \alpha\} \cup \varphi'' \Rightarrow f(\varphi'')(\varphi_\tau \cup \{\tau' \preccurlyeq \alpha\})(\varphi_{\sigma\gamma})$

$\qquad\qquad \mathbf{end}$
$\qquad\qquad \mathbf{in}\ f(\varphi)(\{\})(\{\})$
$\qquad\qquad \mathbf{end}$

A resolved constraint set, written $\overline{\varphi}$, is defined as follows:

$$\overline{\varphi} = \mathbf{let}\ \varphi' = \mathcal{F}(\varphi)\ \mathbf{in}\ \mathbf{let}\ (\varphi_\tau, \varphi_{\sigma\gamma}) = \mathcal{S}(\varphi'),\ \theta = \widehat{\varphi}_{\sigma\gamma}\ \mathbf{in}\ (\widetilde{\theta\varphi_\tau}) \circ \theta\ \mathbf{end}\ \mathbf{end}$$

The function that performs the resolution of effect and call graph constraints is written $\widehat{\varphi}$ and is presented in Table 9.

The semantic function that performs the resolution of type constraints is written $\widetilde{\varphi}$ and is defined as follows:

$\widetilde{\varphi}\ = \mathbf{case}\ \varphi\ \mathbf{of}$
$\qquad\qquad \{\} \Rightarrow \mathrm{Id}$
$\{\tau \preccurlyeq \alpha\} \cup \varphi' \Rightarrow \mathbf{let}\ \theta = \widetilde{\varphi'}$
$\qquad\qquad\qquad \mathbf{in\ if}\ \alpha \mapsto \tau' \in \theta\ \mathbf{then}\ \theta \dagger [\alpha \mapsto \pi_2(\bigsqcup(\theta\tau, \theta\tau'))]\ \mathbf{else}\ \theta \dagger [\alpha \mapsto \theta\tau]\ \mathbf{end}$
$\qquad\qquad\qquad \mathbf{end}$
$\qquad \mathbf{end}$

where $\pi_2(\bigsqcup(\theta\tau, \theta\tau'))$ stands for the type that is the second projection of the couple generated by the least upper bound function $\bigsqcup$. The latter is presented in Table 10 and is used by the resolution function of type constraints. It allows to combine two types that appear in a covariant position. Notice that the least upper bound of two function types is a function type annotated by the union of

Table 9. Resolving Effect and Call Graph Constraints

$\widehat{\varphi} = \mathbf{case}\ \varphi\ \mathbf{of}$
$\qquad\qquad \{\} \Rightarrow Id$
$\{\sigma \preccurlyeq \varsigma\} \cup \varphi' \Rightarrow \mathbf{let}\ \theta = \widehat{\varphi'}$
$\qquad\qquad\qquad \mathbf{in\ if}\ \varsigma \mapsto \sigma' \in \theta\ \mathbf{then}\ \theta \dagger [\varsigma \mapsto \theta(\sigma \cup \sigma')]\ \mathbf{else}\ \theta \dagger [\varsigma \mapsto \theta\sigma]\ \mathbf{end}$
$\qquad\qquad\qquad \mathbf{end}$
$\{\gamma \preccurlyeq \delta\} \cup \varphi' \Rightarrow \mathbf{let}\ \theta = \widehat{\varphi'}\ \mathbf{in}$
$\qquad\qquad\qquad \mathbf{if}\ \delta \mapsto \gamma' \in \theta\ \mathbf{then}$
$\qquad\qquad\qquad\qquad \mathbf{if}\ \delta \in fv(\theta\gamma + \theta\gamma')\ \mathbf{then}\ \theta \dagger [\delta \mapsto rec\ \delta.(\theta\gamma + \theta\gamma')]$
$\qquad\qquad\qquad\qquad\qquad\qquad \mathbf{else}\ \theta \dagger [\delta \mapsto (\theta\gamma + \theta\gamma')]\ \mathbf{end}$
$\qquad\qquad\qquad \mathbf{else}$
$\qquad\qquad\qquad\qquad \mathbf{if}\ \delta \in fv(\theta\gamma)\ \mathbf{then}\ \theta \dagger [\delta \mapsto rec\ \delta.(\theta\gamma)]$
$\qquad\qquad\qquad\qquad\qquad\qquad \mathbf{else}\ \theta \dagger [\delta \mapsto (\theta\gamma)]\ \mathbf{end}$
$\qquad\qquad\qquad \mathbf{end}$
$\qquad\qquad \mathbf{end}$
$\qquad \mathbf{end}$

---

the effect annotations and by the sum of the call graph annotations. The function $\sqcap$ presented in Table 11 is used by the resolution function of type constraints. It allows to combine two types that appear in a contravariant position. An effect (respectively a call graph) that annotates a function type that appears in a contravariant position, is necessarily an effect variable (respectively a call graph variable). The reason is that effects as well as call graphs are completely unknown since the function type is associated with a function that denotes a formal parameter in a higher-order expression. Consequently, the greatest lower bound will combine two function types (appearing in a contravariant position) by renaming annotation variables of one of the two function types into varibales of the other function type.

Since types are decorated by effect annotations, it is possible that an effect makes reference to a type annotated by that effect. As a consequence, some expressions may now have recursively defined types and effects, and shall thus be rejected by the static semantics. This phenomenon motivates the definition hereafter.

Definition 5.2. (Well-Formed Constraint Set) A constraint set φ is well formed, written $wf(\varphi)$, if and only if, for every $\sigma \preccurlyeq \varsigma$ such that $\varphi = \varphi' \cup \{\sigma \preccurlyeq \varsigma\}$ we have $\forall \mu(\rho, \tau) \in \overline{\varphi}'\sigma, \varsigma \notin fv(\tau)$ where $\mu \in \{chan, in, out\}$.

The following lemmas state that well-formed constraint sets are solvable by finite substitutions.

Lemma 5.3. (Model Preservation) *Let φ be a set of type, effect and call graph constraints. If φ is well-formed then $\theta \models \varphi$ if and only if $\theta \models \mathcal{F}(\varphi)$.*

Lemma 5.4. (Constraint Resolution) *Let φ be a set of type, effect and call graph constraints. If φ is well-formed and if $\overline{\varphi}$ does not fail, then $\overline{\varphi} \models \varphi$.*

Table 10. Least Upper Bounds on Types

$\bigsqcup(\tau, \tau') = $ **case** (τ, τ') **of**

$\qquad\qquad (\alpha, \tau'') \mid (\tau'', \alpha) \Rightarrow ([\alpha \mapsto \tau''], \tau'')$

$\qquad\qquad (chan_\varrho(\tau_i), chan_{\varrho'}(\tau_i')) \Rightarrow$ **if** $\bigsqcup(\tau_i, \tau_i') = fail$

$\qquad\qquad\qquad\qquad$ **then** $fail$

$\qquad\qquad\qquad\qquad$ **else let** $\theta = [\varrho \mapsto \varrho']$

$\qquad\qquad\qquad\qquad\qquad\qquad (\theta', \tau_f) = \bigsqcup(\theta\tau_i, \theta\tau_i')$

$\qquad\qquad\qquad\qquad\qquad\qquad$ **in** $(\theta' \circ \theta, chan_{\theta'\varrho}(\tau_f))$ **end**

$\qquad\qquad$ **end**

$\qquad\qquad (\tau_i \xrightarrow{\sigma,\gamma} \tau_f, \tau_i' \xrightarrow{\sigma',\gamma'} \tau_f') \Rightarrow$ **if** $(\prod(\tau_i, \tau_i') = fail)$ **or** $(\bigsqcup(\tau_f, \tau_f') = fail)$

$\qquad\qquad\qquad\qquad$ **then** $fail$

$\qquad\qquad\qquad\qquad$ **else let** $(\theta_1, \tau_1) = \prod(\tau_i, \tau_i')$

$\qquad\qquad\qquad\qquad\qquad\qquad (\theta_2, \tau_2) = \bigsqcup(\theta_1\tau_f, \theta_1\tau_f')$

$\qquad\qquad\qquad\qquad\qquad\qquad \theta = \theta_2 \circ \theta_1$

$\qquad\qquad\qquad\qquad\qquad\qquad$ **in** $(\theta, \tau_1 \xrightarrow{\theta(\sigma \cup \sigma'), \theta(\gamma + \gamma')} \tau_2)$ **end**

$\qquad\qquad$ **end**

$\qquad\qquad$ **else if** $\tau = \tau'$ **then** (Id, τ) **else** $fail$

$\qquad\qquad$ **end**

Table 11. Greatest Lower Bounds on Types

$\prod(\tau, \tau') = $ **case** (τ, τ') **of**

$\qquad\qquad (\alpha, \tau'') \mid (\tau'', \alpha) \Rightarrow ([\alpha \mapsto \tau''], \tau'')$

$\qquad\qquad (chan_\varrho(\tau_i), chan_{\varrho'}(\tau_i')) \Rightarrow$ **if** $\prod(\tau_i, \tau_i') = fail$

$\qquad\qquad\qquad\qquad$ **then** $fail$

$\qquad\qquad\qquad\qquad$ **else let** $\theta = [\varrho \mapsto \varrho']$

$\qquad\qquad\qquad\qquad\qquad\qquad (\theta', \tau_f) = \prod(\theta\tau_i, \theta\tau_i')$

$\qquad\qquad\qquad\qquad\qquad\qquad$ **in** $(\theta' \circ \theta, chan_{\theta'\varrho}(\tau_f))$ **end**

$\qquad\qquad$ **end**

$\qquad\qquad (\tau_i \xrightarrow{\varsigma,\delta} \tau_f, \tau_i' \xrightarrow{\varsigma',\delta'} \tau_f') \Rightarrow$ **if** $(\bigsqcup(\tau_i, \tau_i') = fail)$ **or** $(\prod(\tau_f, \tau_f') = fail)$

$\qquad\qquad\qquad\qquad$ **then** $fail$

$\qquad\qquad\qquad\qquad$ **else let** $\theta = [\varsigma \mapsto \varsigma', \delta \mapsto \delta']$

$\qquad\qquad\qquad\qquad\qquad\qquad (\theta_1, \tau_1) = \bigsqcup(\theta\tau_i, \theta\tau_i')$

$\qquad\qquad\qquad\qquad\qquad\qquad (\theta_2, \tau_2) = \prod((\theta_1 \circ \theta)\tau_f, (\theta_1 \circ \theta)\tau_f')$

$\qquad\qquad\qquad\qquad\qquad\qquad$ **in** $(\theta_2 \circ \theta_1 \circ \theta, \tau_1 \xrightarrow{\varsigma',\delta'} \tau_2)$ **end**

$\qquad\qquad$ **end**

$\qquad\qquad$ **else if** $\tau = \tau'$ **then** (Id, τ) **else** $fail$

$\qquad\qquad$ **end**

In the static semantics, type schemes are of the form $\forall v_1, \ldots, v_n.\tau$ where each v_i can be type, region, effect or call graph variable. In the algorithm, effects and call graphs are represented by variables and are subjected to sets of constraints. Consequently, type schemes will be now of the form $\forall v_1, \ldots, v_n.(\tau, \varphi)$ where φ is a set of type, effect and call graph constraints. The latter will be resolved in such a way to bind each effect and call graph variable to its greatest lower bound.

The notation $wf(\varphi)$ is extended to type schemes by $wf(\forall v_1 \ldots v_n.(\tau, \varphi))$ iff $wf(\varphi)$ and to type environments by $wf(\mathcal{E})$ iff $wf(\mathcal{E}(x))$ for every x in $dom(\mathcal{E})$.

In order to relate the constrained type schemes and environments of the algorithm to the static semantics, we write $\overline{\forall v_1, \ldots, v_n.(\tau, \varphi)}$ to denote $\forall v_1, \ldots, v_n.\overline{\varphi}\tau$ and we define $\overline{\mathcal{E}}$ by extension as $\overline{\mathcal{E}}(x) = \overline{\mathcal{E}(x)}$ for all $x \in dom(\mathcal{E})$.

Our inference algorithm, presented in Table 12, proceeds by case analysis on the structure of expression. It takes as input a 3-tuple made of a static environment, a set of type, effect and call graph constraints and an expression. The algorithm either fails or terminates successfully producing a 5-tuple whose components are: a substitution, a type, an effect, a call graph and a set of constraints. The substitution records those substitutions that take place during the various recursive calls of the inference algorithm. The type produced by the algorithm is the inferred type of the argument expression. The effect produced by the algorithm corresponds to the minimal approximation of communication effects that may be generated when the expression is evaluated. Similarly, the call graph produced by the algorithm corresponds to the minimal approximation of the call graph induced by the execution of the original expression. The constraint set produced by the algorithm corresponds to those constraints gathered during the inference process. The resolution of these constraints yields a substitution whose application to the type produced by the algorithm yields the principal type of the original expression.

In order to type a constant expression, our algorithm simply applies the function $CTypeOf$ (that allows the typing of built-in primitives), described in Table 13, to that constant. Consequently, the original set of constraints is extended with those constraints reported in the basis of the type system. To type an identifier, the algorithm refers simply to a fresh instance of the type scheme reported in the static environment. When the identifier does not belong to the domain of the static environment, the inference procedure fails. The generation of the constraint generated is similar to that of the constant case. In both the constant and identifier cases, it is obvious that neither effect nor call graph are reported. The typing of the function abstraction proceeds as follows: first, a recursive call to the inference algorithm is made so as to type the body of the functional abstraction. The static environment used in this inference is the original one extended by the association that maps the argument of the function to a type variable and an empty constraint set. The type produced by this inference together with the substitution generated and the type variable used in the environment are combined to compute an arrow type for the whole function. The algorithm records the effect and call graph generated by the typing of

Table 12. The Inference Algorithm

$\text{Infer}(\mathcal{E}, \varphi, \mathtt{cte}) =$
    $\mathbf{let}\ \forall v_1, ..., v_n.\ (\tau, \varphi') = CTypeOf(\mathtt{cte})$
    $\mathbf{in\ let}\ v_1', ..., v_n'\ \mathbf{new}, \quad \theta = [v_i \mapsto v_i' | i = 1, ..., n]$
        $\mathbf{in}\ (Id, \theta\tau, \emptyset, nil, \varphi \cup \theta\varphi')$
        $\mathbf{end}$
    $\mathbf{end}$
$\text{Infer}(\mathcal{E}, \varphi, x) =$
    $\mathbf{if}\ x \notin dom(\mathcal{E})\ \mathbf{then}\ fail$
    $\mathbf{else}$
        $\mathbf{let}\ \forall v_1, ..., v_n.\ (\tau, \varphi') = \mathcal{E}(x)$
        $\mathbf{in\ let}\ v_1', ..., v_n'\ \mathbf{new}, \quad \theta = [v_i \mapsto v_i' | i = 1, ..., n]$
            $\mathbf{in}\ (Id, \theta\tau, \emptyset, nil, \varphi \cup \theta\varphi')$
            $\mathbf{end}$
        $\mathbf{end}$
    $\mathbf{end}$
$\text{Infer}(\mathcal{E}, \varphi, f\ \mathbf{where}\ f(x){=}e) =$
    $\mathbf{let}\ \alpha, \varsigma, \delta\ \mathbf{new}$
        $(\theta, \tau, \sigma, \gamma, \varphi') = \text{Infer}(\mathcal{E}_x \dagger [x \mapsto (\alpha, \{\})], \varphi, e)$
    $\mathbf{in}\ (\theta, \theta\alpha \xrightarrow{\varsigma, \delta} \tau, \emptyset, nil, \varphi' \cup \{\sigma \preccurlyeq \varsigma, f.\gamma \preccurlyeq \delta\})$
    $\mathbf{end}$
$\text{Infer}(\mathcal{E}, \varphi, e\ e') =$
    $\mathbf{let}\ (\theta, \tau, \sigma, \gamma, \varphi') = \text{Infer}(\mathcal{E}, \varphi, e)$
        $(\theta', \tau', \sigma', \gamma', \varphi'') = \text{Infer}(\theta\mathcal{E}, \varphi', e')$
        $\alpha, \varsigma, \delta\ \mathbf{new}$
        $\theta'' = \mathcal{U}_{\varphi''}(\theta'\tau, \tau' \xrightarrow{\varsigma, \delta} \alpha)$
    $\mathbf{in}\ (\theta'' \circ \theta' \circ \theta, \theta''\alpha, \theta''(\theta'\sigma \cup \sigma' \cup \varsigma), ((\theta''\theta'\gamma; \theta''\gamma'); \theta''\delta), \theta''\varphi'')$
    $\mathbf{end}$
$\text{Infer}(\mathcal{E}, \varphi, \mathbf{let}\ x{=}e\ \mathbf{in}\ e'\ \mathbf{end}) =$
    $\mathbf{let}\ (\theta, \tau, \sigma, \gamma, \varphi') = \text{Infer}(\mathcal{E}, \varphi, e)$
        $\forall v_1, ..., v_n.(\tau, \varphi'') = Gen_{\varphi'}(\theta\mathcal{E}, \sigma, \gamma)(\tau)$
        $\mathcal{E}' = \theta\mathcal{E}_x \dagger [x \mapsto \forall v_1, ..., v_n.(\tau, \varphi'')]$
        $(\theta', \tau', \sigma', \gamma', \varphi''') = \text{Infer}(\mathcal{E}', \varphi'', e')$
    $\mathbf{in}\ (\theta' \circ \theta, \tau', \theta'\sigma \cup \sigma', (\theta'\gamma; \gamma'), \varphi''')$
    $\mathbf{end}$
$\text{Infer}(\mathcal{E}, \varphi, \mathbf{if}\ e\ \mathbf{then}\ e'\ \mathbf{else}\ e''\ \mathbf{end}) =$
    $\mathbf{let}\ (\theta, \tau, \sigma, \gamma, \varphi') = \text{Infer}(\mathcal{E}, \varphi, e)$
        $\theta' = \mathcal{U}_{\varphi'}(\tau, bool)$
        $(\theta'', \tau', \sigma', \gamma', \varphi'') = \text{Infer}(\theta'\theta\mathcal{E}, \theta'\varphi', e')$
        $(\theta''', \tau'', \sigma'', \gamma'', \varphi''') = \text{Infer}(\theta''\theta'\theta\mathcal{E}, \varphi'', e'')$
        $\alpha, \varsigma, \delta\ \mathbf{new}$
        $\varphi_0 = \varphi''' \cup \{\tau' \preccurlyeq \alpha, \tau'' \preccurlyeq \alpha, (\sigma'' \cup \theta'''(\sigma' \cup \theta''\theta'\sigma)) \preccurlyeq \varsigma, ((\theta'''\theta''\theta'\gamma); (\theta'''\gamma' + \gamma'')) \preccurlyeq \delta\}$
    $\mathbf{in}\ (\theta''' \circ \theta'' \circ \theta' \circ \theta, \alpha, \varsigma, \delta, \varphi_0)$
    $\mathbf{end}$

Table 13. The Constrained Static Initial Basis

$$
\begin{aligned}
&CTypeOf = [\\
&() \mapsto (unit, \{\}),\\
&\textbf{true} \mapsto (bool, \{\}),\\
&\textbf{false} \mapsto (bool\{\}),\\
&\textbf{channel} \mapsto (\forall \alpha, \varrho, \varsigma, \delta.\ unit \xrightarrow{\varsigma,\delta} chan_\varrho(\alpha), \{create(\varrho,\alpha) \preccurlyeq \varsigma, channel.nil \preccurlyeq \delta\}),\\
&\textbf{receive} \mapsto (\forall \alpha, \varrho, \delta.\ chan_\varrho(\alpha) \xrightarrow{\emptyset,\delta} event_{in(\varrho,\alpha),nil}(\alpha), \{receive.nil \preccurlyeq \delta\}),\\
&\textbf{transmit} \mapsto (\forall \alpha, \varrho, \delta.chan_\varrho(\alpha) \times \alpha \xrightarrow{\emptyset,\delta} event_{out(\varrho,\alpha),nil}(unit), \{transmit.nil \preccurlyeq \delta\}),\\
&\textbf{choose} \mapsto \forall \alpha, \varsigma', \varsigma'', \delta', \delta'', \delta.\\
&\qquad event_{\varsigma',\delta'}(\alpha) \times event_{\varsigma'',\delta''}(\alpha) \xrightarrow{\emptyset,\delta} event_{\varsigma' \cup \varsigma'', \delta' + \delta''}(\alpha), \{choose.nil \preccurlyeq \delta\}),\\
&\textbf{spawn} \mapsto (\forall \varsigma, \varsigma', \delta, \delta'.\ (unit \xrightarrow{\varsigma',\delta'} unit) \xrightarrow{\varsigma,\delta} unit, \{fork(\varsigma') \preccurlyeq \varsigma, spawn.fork(\delta').nil \preccurlyeq \delta\}),\\
&\textbf{sync} \mapsto (\forall \alpha, \varsigma, \delta.\ event_{\varsigma,\delta'}(\alpha) \xrightarrow{\varsigma,\delta} \alpha, \{sync.\delta' \preccurlyeq \delta\})\\
&]
\end{aligned}
$$

the body of the function, as subtypes of respectively the latent effect and call graph of the function type. Since a function abstraction refers to a definition (no evaluation), an empty effect and an empty call graph are generated. The typing of an application expression is as follows: first, a recursive call to the inference algorithm is made to type the function expression. Second, a new call to the inference algorithm is made to type the argument expression (taking into account the substitution and the constraint set produced by the first call). Third, a call to the unification procedure is made so as to determine the type of the whole expression. For the conditional expression, the algorithm begins with the static evaluation of the first expression (condition) and then unifying the resulting type with *bool*. Then the algorithm proceeds by statically evaluating the "then" and the "else" branches respectively. Our algorithm should assure that both "then" and "else" branches have similar type structure but potential dissimilar effect and call graph annotations. This is achieved through the use of subtyping. The rest of the cases are straightforward and the corresponding intuitions can be easily reconstructed using the explanations above.

5.2 Generalization

In order to define the generalization function employed by the algorithm, we need the following two auxiliary definitions.

Definition 5.5. A set V of variables is said to *respect* a set φ of constraints if each constraint of φ satisfies that it either involves variables of V or of its complement:

$$
\forall \sigma \preccurlyeq \varsigma, \gamma \preccurlyeq \delta \in \varphi \ : \ fv(\sigma \preccurlyeq \varsigma, \gamma \preccurlyeq \delta) \subseteq V \lor fv(\sigma \preccurlyeq \varsigma, \gamma \preccurlyeq \delta) \cap V = \emptyset
$$

Table 14. Unification Procedure

$$
\begin{aligned}
\mathcal{U}_\varphi(\tau, \tau') = \;& \textbf{case } (\tau, \tau') \textbf{ of} \\
& (\alpha, \alpha') \Rightarrow [\alpha \mapsto \alpha'] \\
& (\alpha, \tau'') \mid (\tau'', \alpha) \Rightarrow \textbf{if } \alpha \in fv(\overline{\varphi}\tau'') \textbf{ then } fail \textbf{ else } [\alpha \mapsto \tau''] \textbf{ end} \\
& (chan_\varrho(\tau''), chan_{\varrho'}(\tau''')) \Rightarrow \textbf{let } \theta = [\varrho \mapsto \varrho'] \textbf{ in } (\mathcal{U}_{\theta\varphi}(\theta\tau'', \theta\tau''')) \circ \theta \textbf{ end} \\
& (\tau_i \xrightarrow{\varsigma,\delta} \tau_f, \tau_i' \xrightarrow{\varsigma',\delta'} \tau_f') \Rightarrow \textbf{let } \theta_i = \mathcal{U}_\varphi(\tau_i, \tau_i') \quad \theta_f = \mathcal{U}_{\theta_i\varphi}(\theta_i\tau_f, \theta_i\tau_f') \\
& \qquad\qquad \theta = [\theta_f(\theta_i\varsigma) \mapsto \theta_f(\theta_i\varsigma'), \theta_f(\theta_i\delta) \mapsto \theta_f(\theta_i\delta')] \circ \theta_f \circ \theta_i \\
& \qquad \textbf{in if } wf(\theta\varphi) \textbf{ then } \theta \textbf{ else } fail \textbf{ end end} \\
& \textbf{else if } t = t' \textbf{ then } Id \textbf{ else } fail \textbf{ end end}
\end{aligned}
$$

Definition 5.6. We define the closure of a set X under φ by the following formula:

$$
V^\varphi = \{v_n \mid v_0 \in V \wedge \forall i < n : (\ldots v_{i+1} \ldots \leq v_i) \in \varphi\}
$$

The generalization function employed by the inference algorithm states that a variable cannot be generalized if it is free in the type environment $\mathcal{E}$ or if it is present in the inferred effect or call graph. The reader should refer to [NN94a] for a detailed explanation of this issue. It is defined as follows:

$$
Gen_\varphi(\mathcal{E}, \sigma, \gamma)(\tau) = \textbf{let } \{v_{1..n}\} = \mathcal{G}(\mathcal{E}, \varphi, \sigma, \gamma)(\tau) \textbf{ in } \forall v_{1..n}.(\tau, \varphi) \textbf{ end}
$$

where $\mathcal{G}(\mathcal{E}, \varphi, \sigma, \gamma)(\tau) = \bigcup \{V \mid V \subseteq fv(\tau)^\varphi \backslash (fv(\sigma) \cup fv(\gamma) \cup fv(\mathcal{E})),$
$$
V \text{ respects } \varphi\}.
$$

5.3 Unification

The inference algorithm uses a unification procedure modulo a set of type, effect and call graph constraints. The procedure takes as input two types and returns, when succeeding, a substitution that stands for the most general unifier of the two given types. The unification procedure also checks the well-formedness of the set of constraints. The procedure is defined in Table 14.

The following lemma establishes the soundness of the unification procedure.

Lemma 5.7. (Soundness of $\mathcal{U}$) If φ is well-formed and $\mathcal{U}_\varphi(\tau, \tau') = \theta$, then $\theta\varphi$ is well-formed and $\theta\tau = \theta\tau'$.

The following lemma establishes the completeness of the unification procedure.

Lemma 5.8. (Completeness of $\mathcal{U}$)) Let φ be well-formed. Whenever $\theta'\tau = \theta'\tau'$ for a substitution θ' satisfying φ, then $\mathcal{U}_\varphi(\tau, \tau') = \theta$, $\theta'\varphi$ is well-formed and there exists a substitution θ'' satisfying $\theta\varphi$ such that $\theta' = \theta'' \circ \theta$.

6   Soundness

In the following, the intention is to prove that our inference algorithm is sound with respect to the typing rules. The soundness theorem states that the inferred type, effect and call graph are provable in the static semantics, assuming any solution of the collected constraints.

We need a special notion of applying a substitution θ (a model of a set of constraints) to a constrained type scheme $\forall v_1, \ldots, v_n.(\tau, \varphi)$ in order to obtain a type scheme [NN94a]:

$$\theta\langle \forall v_1 \ldots v_n.(\tau, \varphi)\rangle = , \forall v_1' \ldots v_m'.\theta\tau \text{ où } v_i' \in \bigcup_{i=1}^{n} fv(\theta v_i)$$

We need also to define a notion of compatibility of a model with respect to the static environment. The latter stipulates that the solutions to a generic scheme is compatible with the solutions to its instantiations [NN94a].

Definition 6.1. Given a type environment $\mathcal{E}$, the substituion θ is said to be compatible with $\mathcal{E}$ and we write $\theta \ddagger \mathcal{E}$ if:

$$\forall x \in Dom(CTypeOf \dagger \mathcal{E}) \; \forall \tau \lhd (CTypeOf \dagger \mathcal{E})(x).$$
$$\textbf{let } \forall v_1 \ldots v_n.(\tau', \varphi) = CTypeOf \dagger \mathcal{E})(x)$$
$$\textbf{in } \exists \theta'. \; \theta\tau = \theta'\theta\tau'$$
$$\textbf{end}$$

Definition 6.2. Given a type environment $\mathcal{E}$, an expression e, a set of constraints φ and $Infer(\mathcal{E}, \varphi, e) = (\theta, \tau, \sigma, \gamma, \varphi')$, we define $B(e)$ to be the set of bound variables of $\mathcal{E}$ and the variables generalized during the evaluation of e. Similarly, we define $F(e)$ to be the set of free variables of $\mathcal{E}$ and the fresh variables that are generated while evaluating e.

Theorem 6.3 (Soundness) *Given a type environment $\mathcal{E}$, an expression e and a set of constraints φ, if $Infer(\mathcal{E}, \varphi, e) = (\theta, \tau, \sigma, \gamma, \varphi')$ and ϕ is such that:*

(i) $\phi \models \varphi'$
(ii) $\forall x \in Dom(\mathcal{E}). \; \phi \models \theta(\mathcal{E}(x))$
(iii) $\phi \ddagger \mathcal{E}$
(iv) $\forall v_1, \ldots, v_n \in B(e)$ and $\forall v_1', \ldots, v_n' \in F(e)$, we have:
$$fv(\phi\{v_1, ..., v_n\}) \cap fv(\phi\{v_1', ..., v_m'\}) = \emptyset$$

then there exists τ', σ' and γ' such that:

$$\tau' \preccurlyeq_\phi \tau, \quad \sigma' \preccurlyeq_\phi \sigma, \quad \gamma' \preccurlyeq_\phi \gamma \quad \text{and} \quad \phi\langle \theta\mathcal{E}\rangle \vdash e : \tau', \sigma', \gamma'$$

7 Conclusion

In this paper, we reported a type-based framework that resolves the problem of control-flow analysis for concurrent and functional languages. We presented an efficient algorithm that propagates automatically types, communication effects and call graphs. The algorithm comes with a logical characterization that consists of a type proof system. The latter operates on a Concurrent ML core-syntax: a strongly typed, polymorphic kernel that supports higher-order functions and concurrency primitives. Effects are represented as algebraic terms that record communication effects resulting from channel creation, sending and receiving. Call graphs record function calls and are captured by a term algebra that is close to usual process algebras. Types are annotated with effects and call graphs. For the sake of flexibility, a subtyping relation is considered on the type algebra. We present the language syntax together with its static semantics that consists of the typing rules and an inference algorithm. The latter is proved to be sound with respect to the typing rules. We have made an implementation of this algorithm using C, Lex and Yacc on a Concurrent ML interpreter. Actually, the program is about 8000 lines of code and shows very good performance.

As a future research, we plan to extend this framework in order to capture a richer and a more precise information. In addition, we project to develop a framework that unifies our control-flow analysis technique with the one based on abstract interpretation.

References

[ASU86] A. V. Aho, R. Sethi, and J. D. Ullman. *Compilers principles, techniques, and tools*. Addison-Wesley, Reading, MA, 1986.

[BD93a] D. Bolignano and M. Debbabi. A coherent type inference system for a concurrent, functional and imperative programming language. In *Proceedings of the AMAST'93 Conference*. Springer Verlag, June 1993.

[BD93b] D. Bolignano and M. Debbabi. A denotational model for the integration of concurrent functional and imperative programming. In *Proceedings of the ICCI'93 Conference*. IEEE, May 1993.

[BD94] D. Bolignano and M. Debbabi. A semantic theory for CML. In *Proceedings of the TACS'94 Conference*. Springer Verlag, April 1994.

[BMT92] D. Berry, A.J.R.G. Milner, and D. Turner. A semantics for ML concurrency primitives. In *Proc. 17th ACM Symposium on Principles of Programming Languages*, 1992.

[CC92] P. Cousot and R. Cousot. Inductive definitions, semantics, and abstract interpretation. In *Conference Record of the 19th Annual ACM Symposium on Principles of Programming Languages*, pages 83–94, Albuquerque, NM, January 1992.

[Deb94] M. Debbabi. *Intégration des paradigmes de programmation parallèle, fonctionnelle et impérative : fondements sémantiques*. Université Paris Sud, Centre d'Orsay, July 1994. Thèse de Doctorat.

[DM82] L. M. M. Damas and R. Milner. Principal type schemes for functional programs. In *Proceedings of the 9th ACM Symposium on Principles of Programming Languages, Albuquerque*, pages 207–212, New York, NY, 1982. ACM.

[GJLS87] D.K. Gifford, P. Jouvelot, J.M. Lucassen, and M.A. Sheldon. Fx-87 reference manual. Technical Report MIT/LCS/TR-407, MIT Laboratory for Computer Science, September 1987.

[Ler92] X. Leroy. *Typage polymorphe d'un langage algorithmique*. PhD thesis, Université de Paris VII, June 1992.

[Mil89] A.J.R.G. Milner. *Communication and Concurrency*. Prentice-Hall, 1989.

[Mil91] A.J.R.G. Milner. A calculus of communicating systems. In *Lecture Notes in Computer Science 92*, pages 281–305. Springer-Verlag, 1991.

[NN94a] F. Nielson and A. R. Nielson. Constraints for polymorphic behaviours of concurrent ML. *Lecture Notes in Computer Science*, 845:73–??, 1994.

[NN94b] Hanne Riis Nielson and Flemming Nielson. Higher-order concurrent programs with finite communication topology. In *Conference Record of the 21st ACM SIGPLAN-SIGACT Symposium on Principles of Programming Languages (POPL'94)*, pages 84–97, Portland, Oregon, January 17–21, 1994. ACM Press. Extended abstract.

[Rep91a] J.H. Reppy. CML: A higher-order concurrent language. In *Proceedings of the ACM SIGPLAN '91 PLDI*, pages 294–305. SIGPLAN Notices 26(6), 1991.

[Rep91b] J.H Reppy. An operational semantics of first-class synchronous operations. Technical Report TR 91-1232, Department of Computer Science, Cornell University, August 1991.

[Shi88] O. Shivers. Control flow analysis in scheme. In *Proceedings of the ACM SIGPLAN '88 Conference on Programming Language Design and Implementation*, volume 23, pages 164–174, Atlanta, GA, June 1988.

[Shi90] O. Shivers. *Control-Flow Analysis of Higher-Order Languages or Taming Lambda*. PhD thesis, School of Computer Science, Carnegie Mellon University, May 1990. also published as CMU Technical Report CMU-CS-91-145.

[Tan94] Y. M. Tang. *Systèmes d'Effet et Interprétation Abstraite pour l'Analyse de Flot de Contrôle*. PhD thesis, Université de Paris VI, March 1994.

[Tho93] B. Thomsen. Polymorphic sorts and types for concurrent functional programs. Technical Report Draft, ECRC, Munich, March 1993.

[TJ92] J. Talpin and P. Jouvelot. The type and effect discipline. In *Proc. Logic in Computer Science*, 1992.

[TJ94] Y. M. Tang and P. Jouvelot. Separate abstract interpretation for control-flow analysis. In *Proceedings of the TACS'94 Conference*. Springer Verlag, April 1994.

Calculating a Functional Module for Binary Search Trees

Walter Dosch[1] and Bernhard Möller[2]

[1] Institut für Softwaretechnik und Programmiersprachen,
Medizinische Universität zu Lübeck, D–23538 Lübeck
[2] Institut für Informatik, Universität Augsburg, D–86135 Augsburg

Abstract. We formally derive a functional module for binary search trees comprising search, insert, delete, minimum and maximum operations. The derivation starts from an extensional specification that refers only to the multiset of elements stored in the tree. The search tree property is systematically derived as an implementation requirement.

1 Introduction

Search trees are a well-known dynamic data structure for storing and retrieving data [AHU83, CLR90, K73, Mh84, S88]. There are various types of search trees used in different applications. The algorithms for binary search trees are not complex; nevertheless none of the standard text books on data structures verifies their correctness rigorously or — more desirably — calculates them from the specification.

In the present paper we systematically derive a functional module for binary search trees comprising search, insertion, deletion, minimum, and maximum operations. The binary tree represents a multiset, since there may be multiple occurrences of the same element. The functions on search trees are specified by referring only to this multiset, but not to the internal structure of trees.

In the derivation we stress algebraic calculation rather than logical deduction. The development is carried out at the level of functional programs; it widely exploits the algebraic properties of the underlying data structures.

The formal derivation of the algorithms gives insight into the algorithmic principles underlying search trees. In particular, we precisely locate the simplifications originating from the *binary search tree property* stating that each node is an upper (lower) bound for the nodes in the left (right) subtree. This constraint is not imposed from the beginning; rather it is derived as an implementation requirement. We present functional techniques for the joint development of the data and the control structure.

Throughout the paper we show how the creative steps in the development, viz. abstracting and generalizing subtasks, naturally arise from simple calculations using induction over the tree structure. We base the derivation on weak assumptions; this avoids overspecification and preserves the freedom for further refinements.

A functional algorithm for inserting elements into 2-3-trees was already given in [HD83]. For the deletion of elements in 2-3 trees, a rigorous correctness proof involving subtypes was provided by [R92]. In contrast to the backward oriented verification of a given algorithm, this paper concentrates on deductive design from the specification in forward direction.

We assume that the reader has a basic knowledge of functional programming (for overviews see [B89, H89]) and of transformational program design (see [BMPP89, Me86, P90]). Throughout the paper we use traditional mathematical notation. Functions are defined using axioms

$$t = \begin{cases} t_1 & \text{if } \alpha \\ t_2 & \text{if } \beta \end{cases}$$

with terms t, t_1, t_2. Such an axiom is by definition equivalent to

$$((\alpha \wedge \neg\beta) \Rightarrow t = t_1) \wedge$$
$$((\neg\alpha \wedge \beta) \Rightarrow t = t_2) \wedge$$
$$((\alpha \wedge \beta) \Rightarrow (t = t_1 \vee t = t_2)).$$

If both conditions α and β hold, the overlapping patterns do not lead to a contradiction; rather they express an underspecification, since then the formula is satisfied by a *set of functions*. It is a matter of later refinement to determine which of these functions actually is taken as the implementation.

2 The Data Structures

Let $(\mathcal{B}; \wedge, \vee, \neg)$ be the Boolean algebra of *truth values* with $\mathcal{B} = \{T, F\}$. Furthermore let $(\mathcal{E}; \leq, min, max, -\infty, +\infty)$ be the set of *elements*; it is equipped with a linear order possessing smallest and greatest elements.

2.1 Multisets

The specification of search trees refers to the multiset of data stored. For simplicity, we take as data just (atomic) elements.

The Multiset Algebra The algebra of multisets with elements from $\mathcal{E}$ comprises the set $\mathcal{M}$ of all *finite multisets* inductively generated by the following constant and operations:

$\emptyset \in \mathcal{M}$	$\{$empty multiset$\}$
$\{.\} : \mathcal{E} \to \mathcal{M}$	$\{$forming singleton multisets$\}$
$.\cup. : \mathcal{M} \times \mathcal{M} \to \mathcal{M}$	$\{$multiset union$\}$

The algebra $(\mathcal{M}, .\cup., \emptyset)$ forms a commutative monoid:

$$(m \cup n) \cup o = m \cup (n \cup o) \tag{1}$$
$$\emptyset \cup m = m = m \cup \emptyset \tag{2}$$
$$m \cup n = n \cup m \tag{3}$$

The containment relation $.\in.: \mathcal{E} \times \mathcal{M} \to \mathcal{B}$ satisfies the equations

$$x \in \emptyset = F \tag{4}$$
$$x \in \{y\} = (x = y) \tag{5}$$
$$x \in (m \cup n) = x \in m \lor x \in n. \tag{6}$$

The deletion $.\backslash.: \mathcal{M} \times \mathcal{E} \to \mathcal{M}$ of an element obeys the laws

$$\emptyset \backslash y = \emptyset \tag{7}$$
$$\{x\} \backslash y = \begin{cases} \emptyset & \text{if } y = x \\ \{x\} & \text{if } y \neq x \end{cases} \tag{8}$$
$$(m \cup n) \backslash y = (m \backslash y) \cup n \qquad \text{if } y \in m \lor y \notin n \tag{9}$$

The premise of equation (9) can always be established using the commutativity of multiset union (3), for example

$$(\{y\} \cup \{x\}) \backslash x = (\{x\} \cup \{y\}) \backslash x = (\{x\} \backslash x) \cup \{y\} = \emptyset \cup \{y\} = \{y\}.$$

The smallest element $minel: \mathcal{M} \to \mathcal{E}$ of a multiset is defined by the equations

$$minel(\emptyset) = +\infty \tag{10}$$
$$minel(\{x\}) = x \tag{11}$$
$$minel(m \cup n) = min(minel(m), minel(n)); \tag{12}$$

the greatest element $maxel: \mathcal{M} \to \mathcal{E}$ is defined symmetrically. This completes the definition of the multiset algebra $\mathcal{M}$.

Lower and Upper Bounds The linear order $\leq$ on the set $\mathcal{E}$ of elements induces a lower bound relation between elements and multisets:

$$x \sqsubseteq \emptyset = T \tag{13}$$
$$x \sqsubseteq \{y\} = x \leq y \tag{14}$$
$$x \sqsubseteq m \cup n = x \sqsubseteq m \land x \sqsubseteq n \tag{15}$$

The upper bound relation is defined symmetrically:

$$\emptyset \sqsubseteq y = T \tag{16}$$
$$\{x\} \sqsubseteq y = x \leq y \tag{17}$$
$$m \cup n \sqsubseteq y = m \sqsubseteq y \land n \sqsubseteq y \tag{18}$$

The corresponding strict lower and strict upper bound relations are defined analogously. The bound relations are transitive in the following sense:

$$y < x \land x \sqsubseteq m \Rightarrow y \sqsubset m \tag{19}$$
$$m \sqsubseteq x \land x < y \Rightarrow m \sqsubset y \tag{20}$$

Strict bound relations allow concluding non-membership:

$$x \sqsubset m \;\Rightarrow\; x \notin m \tag{21}$$
$$m \sqsubset x \;\Rightarrow\; x \notin m \tag{22}$$

Moreover, bound relations are monotonic wrt. the deletion of elements:

$$m \sqsubseteq x \;\Rightarrow\; m \backslash y \sqsubseteq x \tag{23}$$
$$x \sqsubseteq m \;\Rightarrow\; x \sqsubseteq m \backslash y \tag{24}$$

The computation of the smallest and greatest elements of a multiset union can be simplified if one of the multisets is a singleton $\{x\}$ and the other is bounded by x:

$$x \sqsubseteq m \Rightarrow minel(\{x\} \cup m) = x \tag{25}$$
$$x \sqsubseteq m \Rightarrow maxel(\{x\} \cup m) = \begin{cases} x & \text{if } m = \emptyset \\ maxel(m) & \text{if } m \neq \emptyset \end{cases} \tag{26}$$

Symmetrically we have:

$$m \sqsubseteq x \Rightarrow maxel(m \cup \{x\}) = x \tag{27}$$
$$m \sqsubseteq x \Rightarrow minel(m \cup \{x\}) = \begin{cases} x & \text{if } m = \emptyset \\ minel(m) & \text{if } m \neq \emptyset \end{cases} \tag{28}$$

Finally, the extremal elements of non-empty multisets are related to bounds. For $m \neq \emptyset$ we have:

$$x = minel(m) \;\Leftrightarrow\; x \in m \wedge x \sqsubseteq m \tag{29}$$
$$x = maxel(m) \;\Leftrightarrow\; x \in m \wedge m \sqsubseteq x \tag{30}$$

Relations (19)–(30) can all be shown by simple structural induction on multisets.

2.2 Binary Trees

The set $\mathcal{T}$ of *binary trees* with elements $\mathcal{E}$ as nodes is defined inductively as the least set with

$$(i)\ \ \varepsilon \in \mathcal{T} \tag{31}$$
$$(ii)\ \ \mathcal{T} \times \mathcal{E} \times \mathcal{T} \subseteq \mathcal{T}, \tag{32}$$

where $\times$ is the ternary, non-associative cartesian product. In the sequel, ε denotes the empty binary tree while the triple $\langle l, x, r \rangle$ denotes a non-empty binary tree with left subtree $l \in \mathcal{T}$, node $x \in \mathcal{E}$, and right subtree $r \in \mathcal{T}$.

2.3 Representation

The multiset of elements a binary tree represents is obtained by forgetting the tree structure. The corresponding abstraction function $multi\colon \mathcal{T} \to \mathcal{M}$ reads:

$$multi(\varepsilon) = \emptyset \tag{33}$$

$$multi(\langle l, x, r \rangle) = multi(l) \cup \{x\} \cup multi(r) \tag{34}$$

It is the unique homomorphism from the algebra $(\mathcal{T}; \varepsilon, \langle ., ., . \rangle)$ of binary trees to the algebra $(\mathcal{M}; \emptyset, . \cup \{.\} \cup .)$ of multisets. The empty and all singleton multisets are uniquely represented by trees:

$$multi(t) = \emptyset \ \text{ iff } \ t = \varepsilon \tag{35}$$

$$multi(t) = \{x\} \ \text{ iff } \ t = \langle \varepsilon, x, \varepsilon \rangle \tag{36}$$

The converse of the abstraction function $multi$ yields a one-to-many representation relation.

2.4 Derivation Techniques

Many of our functions f on search trees are specified implicitly in the form $multi(f(t)) = E$, where E is some expression in t not involving f. Our strategy then is to find some tree t' with $multi(t') = E$ as well. Then $f(t) = t'$ is a correct implementation. To avoid excessive tree rearrangements, it is advantageous to choose t' as similar to t as possible.

3 Search

The search function for an element in a binary tree is specified by referring to the associated multiset:

$$search\colon \mathcal{T} \times \mathcal{E} \to \mathcal{B}$$

$$search(t, y) = y \in multi(t) \tag{37}$$

3.1 Direct Recursion

We derive a direct recursion for the function $search$ (37) by induction on the tree structure (31)–(32) exploiting the laws of the containment relation. The comments on the right-hand side justify the deduction step between the formulas in the current and the subsequent line.

Induction basis

$$\begin{aligned}
& search(\varepsilon, y) && \{\text{unfold } search \ (37)\} \\
&= y \in multi(\varepsilon) && \{\text{unfold } multi \ (33)\} \\
&= y \in \emptyset && \{\text{by } (4)\} \\
&= F
\end{aligned}$$

Induction step

$$
\begin{array}{lll}
& search(\langle l, x, r\rangle, y) & \{\text{unfold } search \ (37)\} \\
= & y \in multi(\langle l, x, r\rangle) & \{\text{unfold } multi \ (34)\} \\
= & y \in multi(l) \cup \{x\} \cup multi(r) & \{\text{by } (6)\} \\
= & y \in multi(l) \vee y \in \{x\} \vee y \in multi(r) & \{\text{by } (5)\} \\
= & y \in multi(l) \vee (y = x) \vee y \in multi(r) & \{\text{fold } search \ (37)\} \\
= & search(l, y) \vee (y = x) \vee search(r, y) & \{\text{sequentialize disjunction}\} \\
= & \begin{cases} T & \text{if } y = x \\ search(l, y) \vee search(r, y) & \text{if } y \neq x \end{cases}
\end{array}
$$

With the last transformation step, we achieve early termination when finding an occurrence of the search element in the tree. In summary, the search can be implemented by the cascading recursion

$$search(\varepsilon, y) = F \tag{38}$$

$$search(\langle l, x, r\rangle, y) = \begin{cases} T & \text{if } y = x \\ search(l, y) \vee search(r, y) & \text{if } y \neq x \end{cases} \tag{39}$$

where both the left and the right subtrees of a composite tree are inspected.

3.2 Search Trees

The cascading recursion (39) of the function *search* simplifies to a linear recursion if one of the disjuncts reduces to the neutral element F of the disjunction. Hence we calculate a sufficient condition for the left disjunct:

$$
\begin{array}{lll}
& search(l, y) = F & \{\text{unfold } search \ (37)\} \\
= & y \notin multi(l) & \{\text{by } (21) \text{ and } (22)\} \\
\stackrel{(\star)}{\Leftarrow} & y \sqsubset multi(l) \vee y \sqsupset multi(l) & \{\text{by } (19) \text{ and } (20)\} \\
\stackrel{(\star\star)}{\Leftarrow} & y < x \sqsubseteq multi(l) \vee y > x \sqsupseteq multi(l)
\end{array}
$$

With the first design decision $(\star)$ we implement the test for non-membership by the strict bound relations. In the next step $(\star\star)$ we introduce a cut element to localize the test for the bound relations to the comparison of two elements. Symmetrically, we derive for the right disjunct

$$search(r, y) = F \ \Leftarrow \ y < x \sqsubseteq multi(r) \vee y > x \sqsupseteq multi(r) \, .$$

This allows refining the search function (39) as follows:

$$
search(\langle l, x, r\rangle, y) = \begin{cases}
T & \text{if } y = x \\
search(l, y) & \text{if } y < x \sqsubseteq multi(r) \vee y > x \sqsupseteq multi(r) \\
search(r, y) & \text{if } y < x \sqsubseteq multi(l) \vee y > x \sqsupseteq multi(l) \\
search(l, y) \vee search(r, y) & \text{otherwise} \, .
\end{cases} \tag{40}
$$

The disjuncts in condition (40) are mutually exclusive, since for a linear order $x \neq y$ implies either $y < x$ or $y > x$. Hence equation (40) allows two solutions, either

$$
search(\langle l, x, r\rangle, y) = \begin{cases} T & \text{if } y = x \\ search(l, y) & \text{if } y < x \sqsubseteq multi(r) \\ search(r, y) & \text{if } y > x \sqsupseteq multi(l) \\ search(l, y) \vee search(r, y) & \text{otherwise} \end{cases} \quad (41)
$$

or the symmetrical version

$$
search(\langle l, x, r\rangle, y) = \begin{cases} T & \text{if } y = x \\ search(l, y) & \text{if } y > x \sqsupseteq multi(r) \\ search(r, y) & \text{if } y < x \sqsubseteq multi(l) \\ search(l, y) \vee search(r, y) & \text{otherwise}. \end{cases} \quad (42)
$$

Equation (41) simplifies to a linear recursion only if the bottom case "otherwise" never holds. To achieve this, we have to satisfy both conjuncts $x \sqsubseteq multi(r)$ and $x \sqsupseteq multi(l)$ as assertions in the data structure.

As the decisive design decision, we therefore confine the representation to binary trees where uniformly each node is an upper (lower) bound for the elements occurring in the left (right) subtree. This subset $\mathcal{S}$ of binary *search trees* is defined inductively by

(i) $\varepsilon \in \mathcal{S}$ (43)

(ii) If $l, r \in \mathcal{S}$ and $x \in \mathcal{E}$ with $multi(l) \sqsubseteq x \sqsubseteq multi(r)$, then $\langle l, x, r\rangle \in \mathcal{S}$.   (44)

The set $\mathcal{S}$ of search trees is closed when forming subtrees, but not closed under the ternary tree constructor. The search function restricted to search trees

$$
find: \mathcal{S} \times \mathcal{E} \to \mathcal{B}
$$
$$
find = search \mid (\mathcal{S} \times \mathcal{E}) \quad (45)
$$

then allows the intended simplification of (41) to

$$
find(\varepsilon, y) = F \quad (46)
$$

$$
find(\langle l, x, r\rangle, y) = \begin{cases} find(l, y) & \text{if } y < x \\ T & \text{if } y = x \\ find(r, y) & \text{if } y > x. \end{cases} \quad (47)
$$

The resulting search function *find* is tail-recursive and can be implemented by a simple loop.

In summary, the transformation to linear recursion exhibited the search tree property as an assertion on the data structure that allows replacing the blind (cascading) search by a strategic search based on the local comparison of elements.

4   Smallest and Greatest Elements

The smallest element of a search tree is specified by referring to the multiset representation:

$$minkey: \mathcal{S} \to \mathcal{E}$$

$$minkey(t) = minel(multi(t)) \tag{48}$$

We derive a direct recursion by induction on the tree structure (43)–(44) exploiting the algebraic properties of least elements of multisets.

Induction basis

$$
\begin{aligned}
& minkey(\varepsilon) && \{\text{unfold } minkey \ (48)\} \\
& = minel(multi(\varepsilon)) && \{\text{unfold } multi \ (33)\} \\
& = minel(\emptyset) && \{\text{unfold } minel \ (10)\} \\
& = +\infty
\end{aligned}
$$

Induction step, assuming $multi(l) \sqsubseteq x \sqsubseteq multi(r)$.

$$
\begin{aligned}
& minkey(\langle l, x, r \rangle) && \{\text{unfold } minkey \ (48)\} \\
& = minel(multi(\langle l, x, r \rangle)) && \{\text{unfold } multi \ (34)\} \\
& = minel(multi(l) \cup \{x\} \cup multi(r)) && \{\text{by } (25)\} \\
& = minel(multi(l) \cup \{x\}) && \{\text{by } (28)\} \\
& = \begin{cases} x & \text{if } multi(l) = \emptyset \\ minel(multi(l)) & \text{if } multi(l) \neq \emptyset \end{cases} && \begin{aligned} & \{\text{by } (35)\} \\ & \{\text{fold } minkey \ (48)\} \end{aligned} \\
& = \begin{cases} x & \text{if } l = \varepsilon \\ minkey(l) & \text{if } l \neq \varepsilon \end{cases}
\end{aligned}
$$

Again, the search tree property allows directing the search for the smallest element. In the resulting tail recursion

$$minkey(\varepsilon) = +\infty \tag{49}$$

$$minkey(\langle l, x, r \rangle) = \begin{cases} x & \text{if } l = \varepsilon \\ minkey(l) & \text{if } l \neq \varepsilon \end{cases} \tag{50}$$

the least element is found by successively visiting the left subtrees. The search function *maxkey* for the greatest element

$$maxkey: \mathcal{S} \to \mathcal{E}$$

$$maxkey(t) = maxel(multi(t)) \tag{51}$$

can be derived symmetrically:

$$maxkey(\varepsilon) = -\infty \tag{52}$$

$$maxkey(\langle l, x, r \rangle) = \begin{cases} x & \text{if } r = \varepsilon \\ maxkey(r) & \text{if } r \neq \varepsilon \end{cases} \tag{53}$$

The functions *find*, *minkey* and *maxkey* derived so far only inspect the search tree, but do not modify it.

5 Insertion

The insertion of an element into a search tree is defined by the implicit specification

$$insert:\ \mathcal{S} \times \mathcal{E} \rightarrow \mathcal{S}$$

$$multi(insert(t, x)) = multi(t) \cup \{x\}. \tag{54}$$

This specification leaves complete freedom how to restructure the search tree after the insertion of an element. We aim at deriving a direct recursion for the function *insert*. Since (54) makes sense for general trees in $\mathcal{T}$ as well, we first derive some necessary conditions by induction on the tree structure (31)–(32), exploiting properties of the multiset union.

Induction basis

$$\begin{aligned}
& multi(insert(\varepsilon, y)) && \{\text{unfold } insert\ (54)\} \\
& = multi(\varepsilon) \cup \{y\} && \{\text{unfold } multi\ (33)\} \\
& = \emptyset \cup \{y\} && \{\text{by } (2)\} \\
& = \{y\}
\end{aligned}$$

With (36) we conclude $insert(\varepsilon, y) = \langle \varepsilon, y, \varepsilon \rangle$.

Induction step, assuming $\langle l, x, r \rangle \in \mathcal{T}$.

$$\begin{aligned}
& multi(insert(\langle l, x, r \rangle, y)) && \{\text{unfold } insert\ (54)\} \\
& = multi(\langle l, x, r \rangle) \cup \{y\} && \{\text{unfold } multi\ (34)\} \\
& = (multi(l) \cup \{x\} \cup multi(r)) \cup \{y\} && \{\text{by } (3)\} \\
& = multi(l) \cup \{x\} \cup (multi(r) \cup \{y\}) && \{\text{fold } insert\ (54)\} \\
& = multi(l) \cup \{x\} \cup multi(insert(r, y)) && \{\text{fold } multi\ (34)\} \\
& = multi(\langle l, x, insert(r, y) \rangle)
\end{aligned}$$

Hence we may choose

$$insert(\langle l, x, r \rangle, y) = \langle l, x, insert(r, y) \rangle$$

in this case. Analogously we derive the symmetric equation and may choose

$$insert(\langle l, x, r \rangle, y) = \langle insert(l, y), x, r \rangle$$

as well. So for general trees the element could be inserted arbitrarily into the left or into the right subtree. For search trees we calculate the conditions under which insertion into the left subtree yields a search tree again.

Induction basis

$$\begin{aligned}
& \langle \varepsilon, y, \varepsilon \rangle \in \mathcal{S} && \{\text{by } (44)\} \\
& = \varepsilon \in \mathcal{S} \wedge multi(\varepsilon) \sqsubseteq y \wedge y \sqsubseteq multi(\varepsilon) \wedge \varepsilon \in \mathcal{S} && \{\text{by } (43), \text{unfold } multi\ (33)\} \\
& = T \wedge \emptyset \sqsubseteq y \wedge y \sqsubseteq \emptyset \wedge T && \{\text{by } (13) \text{ and } (16)\} \\
& = T
\end{aligned}$$

Induction step, assuming $\langle l, x, r \rangle \in S$ and $insert(l, y) \in S$.

$$\langle insert(l, y), x, r \rangle \in S \qquad \{\text{by } (44)\}$$
$$= insert(l, y) \in S \land multi(insert(l, y)) \sqsubseteq x \land \ x \sqsubseteq multi(r) \land r \in S$$
$$\qquad \qquad \{\text{by assumption and induction hypothesis}\}$$
$$= multi(insert(l, y)) \sqsubseteq x \qquad \{\text{unfold } insert \ (54)\}$$
$$= multi(l) \cup \{y\} \sqsubseteq x \qquad \{\text{by } (18)\}$$
$$= multi(l) \sqsubseteq x \land \{y\} \sqsubseteq x \qquad \{\text{by assumption}\}$$
$$= \{y\} \sqsubseteq x \qquad \{\text{by } (17)\}$$
$$= y \leq x$$

Symmetrically, if $\langle l, x, r \rangle \in S$ and $insert(r, y) \in S$, then $\langle l, x, insert(r, y) \rangle \in S$ simplifies to $y \geq x$. This establishes the soundness of the final solution

$$insert(\varepsilon, y) = \langle \varepsilon, y, \varepsilon \rangle \tag{55}$$

$$insert(\langle l, x, r \rangle, y) = \begin{cases} \langle insert(l, y), x, r \rangle & \text{if } y \leq x \\ \langle l, x, insert(r, y) \rangle & \text{if } y \geq x. \end{cases} \tag{56}$$

The conditions of equation (56) overlap for $x = y$: an element that occurs multiply can be added either to the left or to the right subtree. The equations (55)–(56) do not specify a single insertion function, rather a set of possible insertion functions; this leaves room for further design decisions. We can also narrow the choice uniformly for all nodes, for example, and strengthen the condition $y \geq x$ in (56) to $y > x$.

6 Deletion

The deletion of an element from a search tree is again specified implicitly by referring to the associated multiset:

$$delete: S \times \mathcal{E} \to S$$
$$multi(delete(t, y)) = multi(t) \backslash y \tag{57}$$

6.1 Direct Recursion

We try to derive a direct recursion by induction on the structure of search trees (43)–(44) using the properties of the deletion operator on multisets.

Induction basis

$$multi(delete(\varepsilon, y)) \qquad \{\text{unfold } delete \ (57)\}$$
$$= multi(\varepsilon) \backslash y \qquad \{\text{unfold } multi \ (33)\}$$
$$= \emptyset \backslash y \qquad \{\text{by } (7)\}$$
$$= \emptyset$$

With (35) we conclude $delete(\varepsilon, y) = \varepsilon$.

Induction step, assuming $multi(l) \sqsubseteq x \sqsubseteq multi(r)$. To increase readability, we separate the cases.

Case $y < x$

$$
\begin{aligned}
& multi(delete(\langle l, x, r\rangle, y)) && \{\text{unfold } delete \ (57)\} \\
={}& multi(\langle l, x, r\rangle)\backslash y && \{\text{unfold } multi \ (34)\} \\
={}& (multi(l) \cup \{x\} \cup multi(r))\backslash y \\
&&& \{\text{by (9) since } y \notin \{x\}\cup multi(r) \text{ by (19) and (21)}\} \\
={}& (multi(l)\backslash y) \cup \{x\} \cup multi(r) && \{\text{fold } delete \ (57)\} \\
={}& multi(delete(l, y)) \cup \{x\} \cup multi(r) && \{\text{fold } multi \ (34)\} \\
={}& multi(\langle delete(l, y), x, r\rangle)
\end{aligned}
$$

Case $y = x$

$$
\begin{aligned}
& multi(delete(\langle l, x, r\rangle, y)) \\
={}& multi(\langle l, x, r\rangle)\backslash y && \{\text{unfold } delete \ (57)\} \\
={}& (multi(l) \cup \{x\} \cup multi(r))\backslash y && \{\text{unfold } multi \ (34)\} \\
={}& multi(l) \cup (\{x\}\backslash y) \cup multi(r) && \{\text{by (9) since by (5) } y \in \{x\}\} \\
={}& multi(l) \cup \emptyset \cup multi(r) && \{\text{by (8) and design decision}\} \\
={}& multi(l) \cup multi(r) && \{\text{by (2)}\}
\end{aligned}
$$

It is easily checked that the resulting partial solution

$$
delete(\varepsilon, y) = \varepsilon \tag{58}
$$

$$
delete(\langle l, x, r\rangle, y) = \begin{cases} \langle delete(l, y), x, r\rangle & \text{if } y < x \\ \langle l, x, delete(r, y)\rangle & \text{if } y > x \end{cases} \tag{59}
$$

fulfills the search tree condition:

Induction basis

$$
\begin{aligned}
& delete(\varepsilon, y) \in S && \{\text{unfold } delete \ (58)\} \\
={}& \varepsilon \in S && \{\text{by (43)}\} \\
={}& T
\end{aligned}
$$

Induction step for $y < x$, assuming $\langle l, x, r\rangle \in S$ and $delete(l, y) \in S$.

$$
\begin{aligned}
& delete(\langle l, x, r\rangle, y) \in S && \{\text{unfold } delete \ (59)\} \\
={}& \langle delete(l, y), x, r\rangle \in S && \{\text{by (44)}\} \\
={}& delete(l, y) \in S \wedge multi(delete(l, y)) \sqsubseteq x \wedge x \sqsubseteq multi(r) \wedge r \in S \\
&&& \{\text{by assumption and induction hypothesis}\} \\
={}& multi(delete(l, y)) \sqsubseteq x && \{\text{unfold } delete \ (57)\} \\
={}& multi(l)\backslash y \sqsubseteq x && \{\text{by (23)}\} \\
\Leftarrow{}& multi(l) \sqsubseteq x && \{\text{by assumption}\} \\
={}& T
\end{aligned}
$$

The case $y > x$ is treated symmetrically. If the element to be deleted is found at the root of the search tree, we arrive at a new task, viz. deleting that root.

6.2 Root Deletion

The deletion of the root of a nonempty search tree is specified by

$$
\begin{aligned}
& delroot: S\backslash\{\varepsilon\} \to S \\
& multi(delroot(\langle l, x, r\rangle)) = multi(l) \cup multi(r). \tag{60}
\end{aligned}
$$

We aim at deriving a direct recursion, for example by induction on the structure (43)–(44) of the search tree l.

Induction basis

$$multi(delroot(\langle \varepsilon, x, r \rangle))$$ {unfold *delroot* (60)}
$$= multi(\varepsilon) \cup multi(r)$$ {unfold *multi* (33)}
$$= \emptyset \cup multi(r)$$ {by (2)}
$$= multi(r)$$

Induction step, assuming $l \neq \varepsilon$.

$$multi(delroot(\langle l, x, r \rangle))$$ {unfold *delroot* (60)}
$$= multi(l) \cup multi(r)$$ {split $multi(l) \neq \emptyset$ by introducing *some*}
$$= (multi(l) \backslash some(l)) \cup \{some(l)\} \cup multi(r)$$ {fold *delete* (57)}
$$= multi(delete(l, some(l))) \cup \{some(l)\} \cup multi(r)$$ {fold *multi* (34)}
$$= multi(\langle delete(l, some(l)), some(l), r \rangle)$$

The choice function yields an arbitrary element of a non-empty search tree:

$$some: \mathcal{S} \backslash \{\varepsilon\} \to \mathcal{E}$$
$$some(t) \in multi(t) = T \tag{61}$$

The choice is only restricted by the search tree property ($l \neq \varepsilon$):

$$\langle delete(l, some(l)), some(l), r \rangle \in \mathcal{S}$$ {by (44) and weaken conjunction}
$$\Rightarrow multi(delete(l, some(l))) \sqsubseteq some(l)$$ {unfold *delete* (57)}
$$= multi(l) \backslash some(l) \sqsubseteq some(l)$$ {by (61)}
$$= multi(l) \sqsubseteq some(l)$$

Using the characterization (30) of the maximal element, this uniquely determines the choice: $some = maxkey$. It is easily derived that this equation is also sufficient for establishing the search tree property. Of course, symmetrically we could also delete an occurrence of the smallest element in the right subtree. In summary, the root deletion

$$delroot(\langle l, x, r \rangle) = \begin{cases} r & \text{if } l = \varepsilon \\ \langle delmax(l), maxkey(l), r \rangle & \text{if } l \neq \varepsilon \\ l & \text{if } r = \varepsilon \\ \langle l, minkey(r), delmin(r) \rangle & \text{if } r \neq \varepsilon \end{cases} \tag{62}$$

leads to two new subtasks. The function *delmax* deletes a maximal node from a non-empty search tree

$$delmax: \mathcal{S} \backslash \{\varepsilon\} \to \mathcal{S}$$
$$delmax(t) = delete(t, maxkey(t)) \; ; \tag{63}$$

symmetrically *delmin*: $\mathcal{S} \backslash \{\varepsilon\} \to \mathcal{S}$ deletes a minimal one. Equation (62) again specifies a set of possible deletion functions. The remaining freedom can be exploited to meet further implementation constraints, for example to keep the tree balanced.

6.3 Deleting a Maximal/Minimal Element

We calculate a direct recursion for *delmax* (63), assuming $\langle l, x, r \rangle \in \mathcal{S}$.

$$
\begin{aligned}
& multi(delmax(\langle l, x, r \rangle)) && \{\text{unfold } delmax \ (63)\} \\
={}& multi(delete(\langle l, x, r \rangle, maxkey(\langle l, x, r \rangle)) && \{\text{unfold } delete \ (57), maxkey \ (51)\} \\
={}& multi(\langle l, x, r \rangle) \backslash maxel(multi(\langle l, x, r \rangle)) && \{\text{unfold } multi \ (34)\} \\
={}& multi(\langle l, x, r \rangle) \backslash maxel(multi(l) \cup \{x\} \cup multi(r)) && \{\text{by } (27)\} \\
={}& multi(\langle l, x, r \rangle) \backslash maxel(\{x\} \cup multi(r)) = \ldots
\end{aligned}
$$

Equation (26) now suggests the following case distinction:

Case $multi(r) = \emptyset$, that is $r = \varepsilon$.

$$
\begin{aligned}
={}& multi(\langle l, x, \varepsilon \rangle) \backslash x && \{\text{unfold } multi \ (34)\} \\
={}& (multi(l) \cup \{x\} \cup multi(\varepsilon)) \backslash x && \{\text{by } (33), (2), (9)\} \\
={}& multi(l) \cup (\{x\} \backslash x) && \{\text{by } (8)\} \\
={}& multi(l) \cup \emptyset && \{\text{by } (2)\} \\
={}& multi(l)
\end{aligned}
$$

Case $multi(r) \neq \emptyset$, that is $r \neq \varepsilon$.

$$
\begin{aligned}
={}& multi(\langle l, x, r \rangle) \backslash maxel(multi(r)) && \{\text{fold } maxkey \ (48)\} \\
={}& multi(\langle l, x, r \rangle) \backslash maxkey(r) && \{\text{unfold } multi \ (34)\} \\
={}& (multi(l) \cup \{x\} \cup multi(r)) \backslash maxkey(r) && \{\text{by } (9)\} \\
={}& multi(l) \cup \{x\} \cup (multi(r) \backslash maxkey(r)) && \{\text{fold } delete \ (57), delmax \ (63)\} \\
={}& multi(l) \cup \{x\} \cup multi(delmax(r)) && \{\text{fold } multi \ (34)\} \\
={}& multi(\langle l, x, delmax(r) \rangle)
\end{aligned}
$$

In summary, a maximal node is deleted by successively visiting the right subtrees:

$$
delmax(\langle l, x, r \rangle) = \begin{cases} l & \text{if } r = \varepsilon \\ \langle l, x, delmax(r) \rangle & \text{if } r \neq \varepsilon \end{cases} \tag{64}
$$

Symmetrically, the deletion of a minimal node leads to

$$
delmin(\langle l, x, r \rangle) = \begin{cases} r & \text{if } l = \varepsilon \\ \langle delmin(l), x, r \rangle & \text{if } l \neq \varepsilon. \end{cases} \tag{65}
$$

It is straightforward to show that *delmax* (64) and *delmin* (65) maintain the binary search tree property.

6.4 Combining the Subdevelopments

When combining the subdevelopments from Sections 6.1 to 6.3, we expand the auxiliary routine *delroot* (62) and obtain from (58)–(59)

$$
delete(\varepsilon, y) = \varepsilon \tag{66}
$$

$$
delete(\langle l, x, r \rangle, y) = \begin{cases} \langle delete(l, y), x, r \rangle & \text{if } y < x \\ r & \text{if } y = x \wedge l = \varepsilon \\ l & \text{if } y = x \wedge r = \varepsilon \\ \langle delmax(l), maxkey(l), r \rangle & \text{if } y = x \wedge l \neq \varepsilon \\ \langle l, minkey(r), delmin(r) \rangle & \text{if } y = x \wedge r \neq \varepsilon \\ \langle l, x, delete(r, y) \rangle & \text{if } y > x. \end{cases} \tag{67}
$$

Again, the remaining choice in equation (67) can be exploited to meet further implementation constraints. A uniform choice taking at every node for example the left subtree, yields

$$delete(\varepsilon, y) = \varepsilon \tag{68}$$

$$delete(\langle l, x, r \rangle, y) = \begin{cases} \langle delete(l, y), x, r \rangle & \text{if } y < x \\ r & \text{if } y = x \wedge l = \varepsilon \\ \langle delmax(l), maxkey(l), r \rangle & \text{if } y = x \wedge l \neq \varepsilon \\ \langle l, x, delete(r, y) \rangle & \text{if } y > x. \end{cases} \tag{69}$$

6.5 Merging Multiple Tree Traversals

The function *delete* (68)–(69) traverses the successive left subtrees twice: once for calculating the greatest element and once more for deleting it. Hence we merge the two subtasks *delmax* and *maxkey* into a single function *delmaxkey* using function tupling:

$$delmaxkey \colon \mathcal{S}\backslash\{\varepsilon\} \to \mathcal{S} \times \mathcal{E}$$

$$delmaxkey = [delmax, maxkey] \tag{70}$$

It is now straightforward to derive a direct recursion:

Induction basis

$$\begin{aligned} & delmaxkey(\langle l, x, \varepsilon \rangle) & & \{\text{unfold } delmaxkey \text{ (70)}\} \\ = & (delmax(\langle l, x, \varepsilon \rangle), maxkey(\langle l, x, \varepsilon \rangle)) & & \{\text{unfold } delmax \text{ (64)}, maxkey \text{ (53)}\} \\ = & (l, x) \end{aligned}$$

Induction step, assuming $r \neq \varepsilon$.

$$\begin{aligned} & delmaxkey(\langle l, x, r \rangle) & & \{\text{unfold } delmaxkey \text{ (70)}\} \\ = & (delmax(\langle l, x, r \rangle), maxkey(\langle l, x, r \rangle)) & & \{\text{unfold } delmax \text{ (64)}, maxkey \text{ (53)}\} \\ = & (\langle l, x, delmax(r) \rangle, maxkey(r)) & & \{\text{introduce constants } s \in \mathcal{S}, k \in \mathcal{E}\} \\ = & \lceil (s, k) = (delmax(r), maxkey(r)); (\langle l, x, s \rangle, k) \rfloor & & \{\text{fold } delmaxkey \text{ (70)}\} \\ = & \lceil (s, k) = delmaxkey(r); (\langle l, x, s \rangle, k) \rfloor \end{aligned}$$

This yields the final version

$$delete(\varepsilon, y) = \varepsilon \tag{71}$$

$$delete(\langle l, x, r \rangle, y) = \begin{cases} \langle delete(l, y), x, r \rangle & \text{if } y < x \\ r & \text{if } y = x \wedge l = \varepsilon \\ \langle delmaxkey(l), r \rangle & \text{if } y = x \wedge l \neq \varepsilon \\ \langle l, x, delete(r, y) \rangle & \text{if } y > x \end{cases} \tag{72}$$

where

$$delmaxkey(\langle l, x, r \rangle) = \begin{cases} (l, x) & \text{if } r = \varepsilon \\ \lceil (s, k) = delmaxkey(r); (\langle l, x, s \rangle, k) \rfloor & \text{if } r \neq \varepsilon. \end{cases} \tag{73}$$

Both functions *delete* and *delmaxkey* show a linear, but non-tail recursion.

6.6 Realization

This completes the calculation of the functional module

$$(S; \varepsilon, \textit{find}, \textit{minkey}, \textit{maxkey}, \textit{insert}, \textit{delete})$$

for binary search trees. The binary search tree property is guaranteed only for those trees that are generated from the empty tree ε using the functions *insert* and *delete* . Hence the representation of the search trees has to be encapsulated and the ternary tree constructor $\langle .,.,. \rangle$ must not be provided to the user of the functional module.

The algorithms derived can directly be transcribed into a functional programming language. Heading towards an implementation on the VON NEUMANN machine, in the next step a pointer structure for binary search trees can safely be introduced using pointer algebra [Mö97].

7 Reusing the Development

In the formal development of the search tree module we have jointly derived from the specification an efficient algorithmic solution together with an implementation of the data structure. In this section we show how *redesign* techniques are well supported by transformational programming.

There is an increasing demand for reusing software and adapting it to changing requirements. However, it is difficult to modify existing code to meet a changing specification. If the design of an algorithm is documented by a program derivation, then the development can often be "replayed" starting with a slightly modified specification. As an example, we "recalculate" the algorithm for a different basic data type with a similar set of laws.

7.1 Redesign

We consider the related problem of implementing binary search trees with pairwise different elements which can be used as keys. Then the search tree represents a *set* (and not a multiset) of elements.

For the algebra $(S; \emptyset, \{.\}, .\cup., .\backslash., . \in .)$ of finite sets, equations (1)–(8) from Section 2.1 hold. The set union satisfies the additional law

$$m \cup m = m, \tag{74}$$

and equation (9) simplifies to

$$(m \cup n)\backslash y = (m\backslash y) \cup (n\backslash y). \tag{75}$$

Moreover, one can show relations analogous to (19)–(30) using the abstraction function *set*: $\mathcal{T} \to S$ defined by

$$set(\varepsilon) = \emptyset \tag{76}$$
$$set(\langle l, x, r \rangle) = set(l) \cup \{x\} \cup set(r), \tag{77}$$

compare (33)–(34). The derivation of the search function then leads to *repetition-free search trees* $\mathcal{R} \subseteq \mathcal{T}$ inductively generated by

(i) $\varepsilon \in \mathcal{R}$ (78)

(ii) If $l, r \in \mathcal{R}$ and $x \in \mathcal{E}$ with $set(l) \sqsubset x \sqsubset set(r)$, then $\langle l, x, r \rangle \in \mathcal{R}$, (79)

compare (43)–(44). The remaining derivations of the functions *find*, *minkey* and *maxkey* do not change, since they are only based on the containment and order relation. The replayed derivation of the function *insert* yields

$$insert(\varepsilon, y) = \langle \varepsilon, y, \varepsilon \rangle \qquad (80)$$

$$insert(\langle l, x, r \rangle, y) = \begin{cases} \langle insert(l, y), x, r \rangle & \text{if } y < x \\ \langle l, x, r \rangle & \text{if } y = x \\ \langle l, x, insert(r, y) \rangle & \text{if } y > x, \end{cases} \qquad (81)$$

compare (55)–(56). Here the additional case distinction arises from using equation (74) in the induction step. Similarly, the derivation of the function *delete* can be replayed for repetition-free search trees; it leads with slightly different reasoning to the same result (71)–(73) as for search trees.

In this way the expense of a formal program development pays, since it provides a wide spectrum of related algorithms as a by-product. This allows replacing the textual modification of existing programs — which is current practice — by a semantics-based redevelopment.

7.2 Refinement

If a program is derived under weak assumptions, then the development refines the specification in each step only gradually and no more than necessary. The remaining algorithmic freedom can be exploited to impose further implementation constraints in order to improve efficiency. As an example we revisit the search function (38)–(39)

$$search(\varepsilon, y) = F$$

$$search(\langle l, x, r \rangle, y) = \begin{cases} T & \text{if } y = x \\ search(l, y) \vee search(r, y) & \text{if } y \neq x \end{cases}$$

from Section 3.1. The simplification of the cascading recursion to a linear recursion gave rise to search trees. A different efficiency improvement consists in limiting the maximal recursion depth of the search function. However, the recursion depth of the function *search* (38)–(39) corresponds to the height of the tree:

$$height: \mathcal{T} \rightarrow \mathcal{N}$$

$$height(\varepsilon) = 0 \qquad (82)$$

$$height(\langle l, x, r \rangle) = 1 + max(height(l), height(r)). \qquad (83)$$

The design decision to limit the recursion depth by constraining the data structure leads to the set $\mathcal{H}$ of *(height-)balanced trees* inductively generated by

$$(i) \quad \varepsilon \in \mathcal{H} \tag{84}$$

$$(ii) \quad \text{If } l, r \in \mathcal{H} \text{ and } x \in \mathcal{E} \text{ with } |height(l) - height(r)| \leq 1,$$
$$\text{then } \langle l, x, r \rangle \in \mathcal{H}, \tag{85}$$

compare [AL62]. On the subset of height-balanced search trees the corresponding algorithms (see, for example, [AHU83, CLR90, K73, Mh84, S88]) can be derived in a similar, yet more involved manner as for simple search trees.

8 Conclusion

There is a large conceptual gap between an abstract problem-oriented specification and a fully detailed, efficiently executable machine-oriented program. Transformational programming replaces the traditional "programming in one blow" by a series of small, formally controllable, semantics-preserving steps, each adding details through design decisions. In this way transformational programming guarantees the correctness of the final program with respect to the initial specification.

The development gives insight into the algorithmic principles underlying a program: a particular implementation is not understood through its code but by the design decisions that lead to it. When developing a family tree of different algorithms from the same specification, the derivation relates the different implementations which cannot be compared at the code level. The transformation rules as well as the development strategies formalize programming knowledge. The calculational nature of program manipulation also supports building program development systems (for an overview see [F87]).

Functional programming lends itself particularly well to this purpose: its expressions are manipulated with the same ease as conventional, mathematical expressions. Moreover, frequently the data and control structures involved obey a rich set of algebraic laws. This eliminates much of the burden of manipulating quantifiers explicitly and leads to concise and perspicuous derivations.

So there is hope that in the long run formal program development techniques will play the same rôle for software engineering as mathematics plays in traditional engineering disciplines.

Acknowledgements We thank F. Nickl and M. Russling for valuable discussions, C. Runciman for a pointer to the literature, and the anonymous referees for helpful comments.

References

[AL62] G.M. Adelson-Velskii, Y.M. Landis: *An Algorithm For the Organisation of Information.* Doklady Akademia Nauk SSR *146*, 263–266 (1962). English translation: Soviet Math. *3*, 1259–1263

[AHU83] A.V. Aho, J.E. Hopcroft, J.D. Ullman: *Data Structures and Algorithms*. Reading, Mass.: Addison-Wesley 1983

[BMPP89] F.L. Bauer, B. Möller, H. Partsch, P. Pepper: *Formal Program Construction by Transformations — Computer-aided, Intuition-guided Programming*. IEEE Transactions on Software Engineering *15*, 165–180 (1989)

[B89] R. Bird: *Lectures on Constructive Functional Programming*. In: M. Broy (ed.): Constructive Methods in Computer Science. NATO ASI Series F: Computer and Systems Sciences *55*. Berlin: Springer 1989, 151–216

[CLR90] T.H. Cormen, C.E. Leiserson, R.L. Rivest: *Introduction to Algorithms*. The MIT Electrical Engineering and Computer Science Series. Cambridge, Mass.: M.I.T. Press/New York: McGraw-Hill 1990

[F87] M. Feather: *A Survey and Classification of Some Program Transformation Approaches and Techniques*. In: L.G.L.T. Meertens (ed.): Proceeding of the IFIP TC2/WG2.1 Working Conference on Program Sepcification and Transformation. Amsterdam: North-Holland 1987, 165–196

[HD83] C.M. Hoffman, M.J. O'Donnell: *Programming with Equations*. ACM Transaction on Programming Languages and Systems *4*:6, 83–112 (1983)

[H89] P. Hudak: *Conception, Evolution, and Application of Functional Programming Languages*. ACM Computing Surveys *21*:3, 359–411 (1989)

[K73] D.E. Knuth: *The Art of Computer Programming*. Vol. *3*: Sorting and Searching. Reading, Mass.: Addison-Wesley 1973

[Me86] L.G.L.T. Meertens: *Algorithmics — Towards Programming as a Mathematical Activity*. Proceedings CWI Symposium on Mathematics and Computer Science. CWI Monographs Vol. *1*. Amsterdam: North–Holland 1986, 289–334

[Mh84] K. Mehlhorn: *Data Structures and Algorithms 1: Sorting and Searching*. EATCS Monographs in Theoretical Computer Science. Berlin: Springer 1984

[Mö97] B. Möller: *Calculating with pointer structures*. In: R. Bird, L. Meertens (eds.): Algorithmic Languages and Calculi. Proc. IFIP TC2/WG2.1 Working Conference, Le Bischenberg, Feb. 1997. Chapman&Hall 1997 (to appear)

[P90] H.A. Partsch: *Specification and Transformation of Programs — A Formal Approach To Software Development*. Berlin: Springer 1990

[R92] C.M.P. Reade: *Balanced Trees with Removals: An Exercise in Rewriting and Proof*. Science of Computer Programming *18*, 181–204 (1992)

[S88] R. Sedgewick: *Algorithms*. Reading, Mass.: Addison-Wesley 1988

Springer
and the
environment

At Springer we firmly believe that an
international science publisher has a
special obligation to the environment,
and our corporate policies consistently
reflect this conviction.
We also expect our business partners –
paper mills, printers, packaging
manufacturers, etc. – to commit
themselves to using materials and
production processes that do not harm
the environment. The paper in this
book is made from low- or no-chlorine
pulp and is acid free, in conformance
with international standards for paper
permanency.

Springer

Lecture Notes in Computer Science

For information about Vols. 1–1191

please contact your bookseller or Springer-Verlag

Vol. 1192: M. Dam (Ed.), Analysis and Verification of Multiple-Agent Languages. Proceedings, 1996. VIII, 435 pages. 1997.

Vol. 1193: J.P. Müller, M.J. Wooldridge, N.R. Jennings (Eds.), Intelligent Agents III. XV, 401 pages. 1997. (Subseries LNAI).

Vol. 1194: M. Sipper, Evolution of Parallel Cellular Machines. XIII, 199 pages. 1997.

Vol. 1195: R. Trappl, P. Petta (Eds.), Creating Personalities for Synthetic Actors. VII, 251 pages. 1997. (Subseries LNAI).

Vol. 1196: L. Vulkov, J. Waśniewski, P. Yalamov (Eds.), Numerical Analysis and Its Applications. Proceedings, 1996. XIII, 608 pages. 1997.

Vol. 1197: F. d'Amore, P.G. Franciosa, A. Marchetti-Spaccamela (Eds.), Graph-Theoretic Concepts in Computer Science. Proceedings, 1996. XI, 410 pages. 1997.

Vol. 1198: H.S. Nwana, N. Azarmi (Eds.), Software Agents and Soft Computing: Towards Enhancing Machine Intelligence. XIV, 298 pages. 1997. (Subseries LNAI).

Vol. 1199: D.K. Panda, C.B. Stunkel (Eds.), Communication and Architectural Support for Network-Based Parallel Computing. Proceedings, 1997. X, 269 pages. 1997.

Vol. 1200: R. Reischuk, M. Morvan (Eds.), STACS 97. Proceedings, 1997. XIII, 614 pages. 1997.

Vol. 1201: O. Maler (Ed.), Hybrid and Real-Time Systems. Proceedings, 1997. IX, 417 pages. 1997.

Vol. 1203: G. Bongiovanni, D.P. Bovet, G. Di Battista (Eds.), Algorithms and Complexity. Proceedings, 1997. VIII, 311 pages. 1997.

Vol. 1204: H. Mössenböck (Ed.), Modular Programming Languages. Proceedings, 1997. X, 379 pages. 1997.

Vol. 1205: J. Troccaz, E. Grimson, R. Mösges (Eds.), CVRMed-MRCAS'97. Proceedings, 1997. XIX, 834 pages. 1997.

Vol. 1206: J. Bigün, G. Chollet, G. Borgefors (Eds.), Audio- and Video-based Biometric Person Authentication. Proceedings, 1997. XII, 450 pages. 1997.

Vol. 1207: J. Gallagher (Ed.), Logic Program Synthesis and Transformation. Proceedings, 1996. VII, 325 pages. 1997.

Vol. 1208: S. Ben-David (Ed.), Computational Learning Theory. Proceedings, 1997. VIII, 331 pages. 1997. (Subseries LNAI).

Vol. 1209: L. Cavedon, A. Rao, W. Wobcke (Eds.), Intelligent Agent Systems. Proceedings, 1996. IX, 188 pages. 1997. (Subseries LNAI).

Vol. 1210: P. de Groote, J.R. Hindley (Eds.), Typed Lambda Calculi and Applications. Proceedings, 1997. VIII, 405 pages. 1997.

Vol. 1211: E. Keravnou, C. Garbay, R. Baud, J. Wyatt (Eds.), Artificial Intelligence in Medicine. Proceedings, 1997. XIII, 526 pages. 1997. (Subseries LNAI).

Vol. 1212: J. P. Bowen, M.G. Hinchey, D. Till (Eds.), ZUM '97: The Z Formal Specification Notation. Proceedings, 1997. X, 435 pages. 1997.

Vol. 1213: P. J. Angeline, R. G. Reynolds, J. R. McDonnell, R. Eberhart (Eds.), Evolutionary Programming VI. Proceedings, 1997. X, 457 pages. 1997.

Vol. 1214: M. Bidoit, M. Dauchet (Eds.), TAPSOFT '97: Theory and Practice of Software Development. Proceedings, 1997. XV, 884 pages. 1997.

Vol. 1215: J. M. L. M. Palma, J. Dongarra (Eds.), Vector and Parallel Processing – VECPAR'96. Proceedings, 1996. XI, 471 pages. 1997.

Vol. 1216: J. Dix, L. Moniz Pereira, T.C. Przymusinski (Eds.), Non-Monotonic Extensions of Logic Programming. Proceedings, 1996. XI, 224 pages. 1997. (Subseries LNAI).

Vol. 1217: E. Brinksma (Ed.), Tools and Algorithms for the Construction and Analysis of Systems. Proceedings, 1997. X, 433 pages. 1997.

Vol. 1218: G. Păun, A. Salomaa (Eds.), New Trends in Formal Languages. IX, 465 pages. 1997.

Vol. 1219: K. Rothermel, R. Popescu-Zeletin (Eds.), Mobile Agents. Proceedings, 1997. VIII, 223 pages. 1997.

Vol. 1220: P. Brezany, Input/Output Intensive Massively Parallel Computing. XIV, 288 pages. 1997.

Vol. 1221: G. Weiß (Ed.), Distributed Artificial Intelligence Meets Machine Learning. Proceedings, 1996. X, 294 pages. 1997. (Subseries LNAI).

Vol. 1222: J. Vitek, C. Tschudin (Eds.), Mobile Object Systems. Proceedings, 1996. X, 319 pages. 1997.

Vol. 1223: M. Pelillo, E.R. Hancock (Eds.), Energy Minimization Methods in Computer Vision and Pattern Recognition. Proceedings, 1997. XII, 549 pages. 1997.

Vol. 1224: M. van Someren, G. Widmer (Eds.), Machine Learning: ECML-97. Proceedings, 1997. XI, 361 pages. 1997. (Subseries LNAI).

Vol. 1225: B. Hertzberger, P. Sloot (Eds.), High-Performance Computing and Networking. Proceedings, 1997. XXI, 1066 pages. 1997.

Vol. 1226: B. Reusch (Ed.), Computational Intelligence. Proceedings, 1997. XIII, 609 pages. 1997.

Vol. 1227: D. Galmiche (Ed.), Automated Reasoning with Analytic Tableaux and Related Methods. Proceedings, 1997. XI, 373 pages. 1997. (Subseries LNAI).

Vol. 1228: S.-H. Nienhuys-Cheng, R. de Wolf, Foundations of Inductive Logic Programming. XVII, 404 pages. 1997. (Subseries LNAI).

Vol. 1230: J. Duncan, G. Gindi (Eds.), Information Processing in Medical Imaging. Proceedings, 1997. XVI, 557 pages. 1997.

Vol. 1231: M. Bertran, T. Rus (Eds.), Transformation-Based Reactive Systems Development. Proceedings, 1997. XI, 431 pages. 1997.

Vol. 1232: H. Comon (Ed.), Rewriting Techniques and Applications. Proceedings, 1997. XI, 339 pages. 1997.

Vol. 1233: W. Fumy (Ed.), Advances in Cryptology — EUROCRYPT '97. Proceedings, 1997. XI, 509 pages. 1997.

Vol 1234: S. Adian, A. Nerode (Eds.), Logical Foundations of Computer Science. Proceedings, 1997. IX, 431 pages. 1997.

Vol. 1235: R. Conradi (Ed.), Software Configuration Management. Proceedings, 1997. VIII, 234 pages. 1997.

Vol. 1236: E. Maier, M. Mast, S. LuperFoy (Eds.), Dialogue Processing in Spoken Language Systems. Proceedings, 1996. VIII, 220 pages. 1997. (Subseries LNAI).

Vol. 1238: A. Mullery, M. Besson, M. Campolargo, R. Gobbi, R. Reed (Eds.), Intelligence in Services and Networks: Technology for Cooperative Competition. Proceedings, 1997. XII, 480 pages. 1997.

Vol. 1239: D. Sehr, U. Banerjee, D. Gelernter, A. Nicolau, D. Padua (Eds.), Languages and Compilers for Parallel Computing. Proceedings, 1996. XIII, 612 pages. 1997.

Vol. 1240: J. Mira, R. Moreno-Díaz, J. Cabestany (Eds.), Biological and Artificial Computation: From Neuroscience to Technology. Proceedings, 1997. XXI, 1401 pages. 1997.

Vol. 1241: M. Akşit, S. Matsuoka (Eds.), ECOOP'97 – Object-Oriented Programming. Proceedings, 1997. XI, 531 pages. 1997.

Vol. 1242: S. Fdida, M. Morganti (Eds.), Multimedia Applications, Services and Techniques – ECMAST '97. Proceedings, 1997. XIV, 772 pages. 1997.

Vol. 1243: A. Mazurkiewicz, J. Winkowski (Eds.), CONCUR'97: Concurrency Theory. Proceedings, 1997. VIII, 421 pages. 1997.

Vol. 1244: D. M. Gabbay, R. Kruse, A. Nonnengart, H.J. Ohlbach (Eds.), Qualitative and Quantitative Practical Reasoning. Proceedings, 1997. X, 621 pages. 1997. (Subseries LNAI).

Vol. 1245: M. Calzarossa, R. Marie, B. Plateau, G. Rubino (Eds.), Computer Performance Evaluation. Proceedings, 1997. VIII, 231 pages. 1997.

Vol. 1246: S. Tucker Taft, R. A. Duff (Eds.), Ada 95 Reference Manual. XXII, 526 pages. 1997.

Vol. 1247: J. Barnes (Ed.), Ada 95 Rationale. XVI, 458 pages. 1997.

Vol. 1248: P. Azéma, G. Balbo (Eds.), Application and Theory of Petri Nets 1997. Proceedings, 1997. VIII, 467 pages. 1997.

Vol. 1249: W. McCune (Ed.), Automated Deduction – CADE-14. Proceedings, 1997. XIV, 462 pages. 1997. (Subseries LNAI).

Vol. 1250: A. Olivé, J.A. Pastor (Eds.), Advanced Information Systems Engineering. Proceedings, 1997. XI, 451 pages. 1997.

Vol. 1251: K. Hardy, J. Briggs (Eds.), Reliable Software Technologies – Ada-Europe '97. Proceedings, 1997. VIII, 293 pages. 1997.

Vol. 1252: B. ter Haar Romeny, L. Florack, J. Koenderink, M. Viergever (Eds.), Scale-Space Theory in Computer Vision. Proceedings, 1997. IX, 365 pages. 1997.

Vol. 1253: G. Bilardi, A. Ferreira, R. Lüling, J. Rolim (Eds.), Solving Irregularly Structured Problems in Parallel. Proceedings, 1997. X, 287 pages. 1997.

Vol. 1254: O. Grumberg (Ed.), Computer Aided Verification. Proceedings, 1997. XI, 486 pages. 1997.

Vol. 1255: T. Mora, H. Mattson (Eds.), Applied Algebra, Algebraic Algorithms and Error-Correcting Codes. Proceedings, 1997. X, 353 pages. 1997.

Vol. 1256: P. Degano, R. Gorrieri, A. Marchetti-Spaccamela (Eds.), Automata, Languages and Programming. Proceedings, 1997. XVI, 862 pages. 1997.

Vol. 1258: D. van Dalen, M. Bezem (Eds.), Computer Science Logic. Proceedings, 1996. VIII, 473 pages. 1997.

Vol. 1259: T. Higuchi, M. Iwata, W. Liu (Eds.), Evolvable Systems: From Biology to Hardware. Proceedings, 1996. XI, 484 pages. 1997.

Vol. 1260: D. Raymond, D. Wood, S. Yu (Eds.), Automata Implementation. Proceedings, 1996. VIII, 189 pages. 1997.

Vol. 1261: J. Mycielski, G. Rozenberg, A. Salomaa (Eds.), Structures in Logic and Computer Science. X, 371 pages. 1997.

Vol. 1262: M. Scholl, A. Voisard (Eds.), Advances in Spatial Databases. Proceedings, 1997. XI, 379 pages. 1997.

Vol. 1263: J. Komorowski, J. Zytkow (Eds.), Principles of Data Mining and Knowledge Discovery. Proceedings, 1997. IX, 397 pages. 1997. (Subseries LNAI).

Vol. 1264: A. Apostolico, J. Hein (Eds.), Combinatorial Pattern Matching. Proceedings, 1997. VIII, 277 pages. 1997.

Vol. 1265: J. Dix, U. Fuhrbach, A. Nerode (Eds.), Logic Programming and Nonmonotonic Reasoning. Proceedings, 1997. X, 453 pages. 1997. (Subseries LNAI).

Vol. 1266: D.B. Leake, E. Plaza (Eds.), Case-Based Reasoning Research and Development. Proceedings, 1997. XIII, 648 pages. 1997 (Subseries LNAI).

Vol. 1267: E. Biham (Ed.), Fast Software Encryption. Proceedings, 1997. VIII, 289 pages. 1997.

Vol. 1268: W. Kluge (Ed.), Implementation of Functional Languages. Proceedings, 1996. XI, 284 pages. 1997.

Vol. 1269: J. Rolim (Ed.), Randomization and Approximation Techniques in Computer Science. Proceedings, 1997. VIII, 227 pages. 1997.

Vol. 1270: V. Varadharajan, J. Pieprzyk, Y. Mu (Eds.), Information Security and Privacy. Proceedings, 1997. XI, 337 pages. 1997.

Vol. 1271: C. Small, P. Douglas, R. Johnson, P. King, N. Martin (Eds.), Advances in Databases. Proceedings, 1997. XI, 233 pages. 1997.